MEDITERRANEAN CONNECTIONS

MEDITERRANEAN CONNECTIONS

How the sea links people and transforms identities

Edited by:

LAURA C. SCHMIDT, ANJA RUTTER, LUTZ KÄPPEL, OLIVER NAKOINZ

SCALES OF TRANSFORMATION I 18

Published by Sidestone Press, Leiden
www.sidestone.com

Imprint: Sidestone Press Academics

Layout & cover design: CRC 1266/Esther Thelen and Sidestone Press
Cover image: Anja Rutter

ISBN 978-946-427-069-3 (softcover)
ISBN 978-946-427-070-9 (hardcover)
ISBN 978-94-6427-071-6 (PDF e-book)

ISSN (print) 2590-1222 | (e-book) 2950-2438

DOI 10.59641/i8m573bk

The STPAS publications originate from or are involved with the Collaborative Research
Centre 1266, which is funded by the Deutsche Forschungsgemeinschaft (DFG, German
Research Foundation; Projektnummer 290391021 – SFB 1266).

Foreword of the series editors

With this book series, the Collaborative Research Centre *Scales of Transformation: Human-Environmental Interaction in Prehistoric and Archaic Societies* (CRC 1266) at Kiel University enables the bundled presentation of current research outcomes of the multiple aspects of socio-environmental transformations in ancient societies. As editors of this publication platform, we are pleased to be able to publish monographs with detailed basic data and comprehensive interpretations from different case studies and landscapes as well as the extensive output from numerous scientific meetings and international workshops.

The book series is dedicated to the fundamental research questions of CRC 1266, dealing with transformations on different temporal, spatial and social scales, here defined as processes leading to a substantial and enduring reorganization of socio-environmental interaction patterns. What are the substantial transformations that describe human development from 15,000 years ago to the beginning of the Common Era? How did interactions between the natural environment and human populations change over time? What role did humans play as cognitive actors trying to deal with changing social and environmental conditions? Which factors triggered the transformations that led to substantial societal and economic inequality?

The understanding of human practices within often intertwined social and environmental contexts is one of the most fundamental aspects of archaeological research. Moreover, in current debates, the dynamics and feedback involved in human-environmental relationships have become a major issue, particularly when looking at the detectable and sometimes devastating consequences of human interference with nature. Archaeology, with its long-term perspective on human societies and landscapes, is in the unique position to trace and link comparable phenomena in the past, to study human involvement with the natural environment, to investigate the impact of humans on nature, and to outline the consequences of environmental change on human societies. Modern interdisciplinary research enables us to reach beyond simplistic monocausal lines of explanation and overcome evolutionary perspectives. Looking at the period from 15,000 to 1 BCE, CRC 1266 takes a diachronic view in order to investigate transformations involved in the development of Late Pleistocene hunter-gatherers, horticulturalists, early agriculturalists, early metallurgists as well as early state societies, thus covering a wide array of societal formations and environmental conditions.

The volume *Mediterranean Connections. How the sea links people and transforms identities* integrates papers of an extraordinarily wide interdisciplinary range, rooted in multiple disciplines (Classics, Classical Archaeology, Near Eastern Archaeology, Maritime Archaeology, Greek Literature, Greek Philology, Latin Philology, Ancient history, and Theoretical Physics) and integrates a wide range of topics and methodology (poetry, history, material culture, geography, networks, and GIS techniques). The integration of such different traditions succeeds in an elegant way; to cite one of the editors, here the literary interpretations of the classical tradition are "set in conversation" with landscape archaeology. The volume is framed by an excellent synthesis by two of the editors, discussing how, in the past, the Mediterranean Sea served to bring people together, rather than separating people. At a time when the Mediterranean has become a death trap for refugees from the South, this volume takes a counter perspective from ancient history. It describes the Mediterranean as transforming the identities of people from different backgrounds and assigns value to the Mediterranean as a unifying, connecting medium.

Wiebke Kirleis and Johannes Müller

Contents

Foreword of the series editors   **5**

List of contributors   **9**

Foreword of the editors   **13**

Introduction   **15**
     Anja Rutter, Laura C. Schmidt

Part 1: Identity of centres and peripheries

Seafaring and the reception of (some) archaic Greek lyric poetry   **21**
     Maria Noussia-Fantuzzi

Chalcidic connectivity between Sithonia and Pallene: Transmutations of epichoric identity and resilience in the long 5th and 4th *c.* BCE   **35**
     Maria G. Xanthou

The importance of geography to the networked Late Bronze Age Aegean   **47**
     Paula Gheorghiade, Henry Price, Ray Rivers

To be Greek or not to be: About the "Greekness" of Epirus and Southern Illyria. An overview through urbanism and theatrical architecture from a Mediterranean perspective   **63**
     Ludovica Xavier de Silva

Frozen wine and the frozen Black Sea. Ovid as an exiled poet faced with climatic extremes (trist. 3.10; Pont. 4.7; 4.9; 4.10)   **83**
     Stefan Feddern

A sea of wine and honey: Networks of narratives as resources for the negotiation of identities. A heuristic approach in the Hellenistic western Mediterranean   **109**
     Raffaella Da Vela

Part 2: Connectivity by sea and networking of seafarers

Seafaring songs in Pindar's *Epinikia* and *Enkomia*   **129**
     Thomas Kuhn-Treichel

Maritime cultural landscapes of fishing communities in Roman Cyprus   141

Maria M. Michael, Carmen Obied

Sea storms and aristocratic identity in Alcaeus   161

Ippokratis Kantzios

The ideology of seafaring in the *Odyssey* and Telemachos' hanging of the slave girls (*Od.* 22,461-474)   171

Hauke Schneider

Malta's connections and cultural identity: Remarks on the architectural language in the western Mediterranean in the 4ᵗʰ and 3ʳᵈ centuries BCE   187

Francesca Bonzano

Becoming a man ashore: The role of the sea in Sappho's Brothers Song   211

Laura C. Schmidt

List of contributors

Editors

Prof. Dr. Lutz Käppel

Studies of Classics in Tübingen and Oxford, PhD 1990, Habilitation 1997, Professor of Classics, especially Greek Literature at Kiel University 1999-present, Ordinary Member of the German Archaeological Institute 2000-present, Dean of the Faculty of Humanities 2006-2008, Co-Coordinator of the Kiel Graduate School 'Human Development in Landscapes' 2007-2016; Speaker of the University's Research Focus 'Social, Environmental, Cultural Change' 2007-present.

Prof. Dr. Oliver Nakoinz

Oliver Nakoinz is a lecturer at Kiel University. He obtained his PhD in 2004 with "Studien zur räumlichen Abgrenzung und Strukturierung der älteren Hunsrück-Eifel-Kultur" and his habilitation in 2010 with "Archäologische Kulturgeographie der ältereisenzeitlichen Zentralorte Südwestdeutschlands". His work is focused on quantitative archaeology, landscape archaeology and interaction and connectivity, in particular in the Iron Age. Furthermore, he is dedicated to the idea of interdisciplinary integration and integrating theory and method.

Anja Rutter

Holding an MA in medieval history (Universität Bielefeld) and another in maritime archaeology (University of Southampton), Anja Rutter has been an interdisciplinary researcher from the outset. After gaining experience as a research diver and a field archaeologist, she is now writing her PhD on Bronze Age networks in the Levant at Kiel University. Her main research focuses on networked identities, mental maps and the question of continuitiy in societies during and after upheaval and forced change.

As Anja Rutter also has long-time experience in museum didactics and citizen science, she has a special interest in making research accessible and understandable to the public and in the role the humanities can play in shaping our ideas of the future.

Laura Schmidt

Laura Schmidt has studied Classics at Kiel University and the Aristotle University of Thessaloniki. She defended her PhD thesis under the title "From Lesbos to Athens: Sappho's Place in the Symposium and Greek Learning" in 2020. She has been member of the Graduate School 'Human Development in Landscapes' (2016-2020). She worked on Plato's concept of optics at the CRC 1266 "Scales of Transformation" at Kiel (2020) and participated in the interdisciplinary project "Gardens, Human Senses and Eudaimonia" of the Cluster of Excellence ROOTS at Kiel (2021). She is currently researching the "thin Anthropocene" in classical antiquity as a member of the ROOTS Cluster of Excellence.

Contributors

Francesca Bonzano

Francesca Bonzano is Associate Professor in Classical Archaeology at Università Cattolica del Sacro Cuore of Milan, Department of History, Archaeology and Art History.

Since 2003, she has been a member of the Italian Archaeological Mission in Hierapolis of Frigia (Turkey) and since 2002 a member of the Italian Archaeological Mission in Malta. Since 2013, Francesca has been head of the Università Cattolica of Milan research unit in the Italian Archaeological Mission in Malta (Director: prof. G. Recchia, Università La Sapienza, Rome).

In 2017, she published the monograph "Fanum Iunonis melitense. L'area centrale del santuario di Tas-Silġ a Malta in età tardo-repubblicana", based on her doctoral and post-doctoral research. Her research interests focus on Hellenistic and Roman Architecture, archaeology of cult places, archaeology of Northern Italy.

Raffaella Da Vela

Raffaella Da Vela studied Classics at the University of Florence (Italy) and wrote her PhD in Classical Archaeology at the University of Florence and Bonn. She is currently a post-doc researcher at the DFG-Collaborative Research Center 1070 ResourceCultures of the University of Tübingen and co-speaker of the Interest Group AG Etrusker & Italiker of the DArV e.V.

Ludovica Xavier de Silva

PhD in classical archaeology (Sapienza University of Rome and Université Lumière Lyon 2). Currently Eureka PhD student at the University of Macerata. Member of the Archaeological Missions of the University of Macerata at Hadrianopolis and Drino Valley (Albania), Gortyn (Crete, Greece) and Urbs Salvia and Villa Magna (Italy), with the main task of cataloguing and studying pottery finds.

Main research interests: Common ware and cooking ware pottery, especially from the Roman to Byzantine era; theatres and urbanisation in Epirus and Southern Illyria; Adriatic archaeological parks and their enhancement.

Stefan Feddern

Stefan Feddern is an Assistant in Classics (Latin Philology) at the University of Kiel (Germany). He is currently pursuing a research project on fiction theories in early modern times at the University of Cologne. In his German habilitation, he analysed ancient theories of literary fiction (publication in 2018). He has recently published a book about ancient narratology and is preparing a book about Ovid's exile poems.

Paula Gheorghiade

Paula Gheorghiade (PhD, University of Toronto), is a postdoctoral researcher at the Centre of Excellence in Ancient Near Eastern Empires (ANEE) at the University of Helsinki.

Ippokratis Kantzios

Ippokratis Kantzios is the Peter and Sophia Kourmolis Associate Professor of Greek Language and Literature at the University of South Florida. In addition to his monograph "The Trajectory of Archaic Greek Trimeters" (Brill 2005), he has published on archaic and Hellenistic poetry, Greek tragedy and comedy, and the reception of Classics. He has presented numerous papers at professional conferences in the United States and abroad. In recent years, he has been concentrating on the archaic poet Alcaeus.

Thomas Kuhn-Treichel

Thomas Kuhn-Treichel, PhD in Latin Philology (University of Göttingen, 2016), habilitation in Classical Philology (University of Heidelberg, 2020), currently Wissenschaftlicher Mitarbeiter (research assistant) at the University of Heidelberg. His research interests range from early Greek lyric, including a monograph on Pindar, to late antique Christianity, including monographs on Gregory of Nazianzus and Latin biblical epic.

Maria Michael

Maria Michael holds an undergraduate degree in archaeology and history from the University of Cyprus in Cyprus, and a MA in Maritime Archaeology from the University of Southampton in the UK. Her MA thesis was entitled "Ship Graffiti: Context as Indicators of Social, Ritual, Practical and Economic Activities in the past". Her doctoral research at the University of Southampton, *To fish or not to fish? The case study of fishing activity in Cyprus*, attempts for the first time to gather all the available evidence for fishing in Cyprus in a single body of evidence. It is an attempt to acquire a better general understanding of the formative phases of fishery on the island through time, from Neolithic to Early Christian periods. Her research for this project was supported by the Honor Frost Foundation (HFF). Since 2006, Maria has participated in many terrestrial and underwater projects in Cyprus, Greece, Egypt and the UK, and she has presented her work in various conferences (*e.g.* POCA, IKUWA, HFF conference, MAGS). She has also participated in many outreach projects and training courses about remote sensing techniques, GIS and conservation. Since 2012, Maria has been working as a field archaeologist at the Committee on Missing Persons in Cyprus (Bi-communal programme), where she has directed and conducted excavations and exhumations on both sides of the island.

Maria Noussia-Fantuzzi

Maria Noussia-Fantuzzi is Senior Lecturer of Ancient Greek Philology at the Aristotle University of Thessaloniki.

She is the author of the book "Solon of Athens: The Poetic Fragments" published by Brill Academic Publishers in 2010, and many articles in international journals and conference proceedings. She has co-edited – with Marco Fantuzzi – the volume "Solone: frammenti dell' opera poetica" by Biblioteca Universale in 2001, with Gregory Nagy the volume "Solon in the Making: The Early Reception in the Fifth and Fourth Centuries" by De Gruyter in 2014, and with Flora Manakidou "ΑΡΧΟΜ' ΑΕΙΔΕΙΝ. Thirteen Essays on Greek Hymns", Dardanos Publishers in 2018.

Carmen Obied

Dr. Carmen Obied is a Maritime Archaeologist and Photogrammetrist. Carmen's doctoral thesis at the University of Southampton UK – "Rethinking Roman Perceptions of Coastal Landscapes: A Case-Study of the Levant" – focused on understanding ancient maritime space, sea routes, navigation, and ancient geographers/mariners in the eastern Mediterranean using a multi-disciplinary approach that combined archaeological evidence, ancient sources, sensory navigation, and geographic information systems (GIS/QGIS). She has over a decade of experience conducting international maritime and terrestrial archaeological excavations, geoarchaeological and geophysical surveys, and managing photogrammetry, GIS, and outreach projects (notably in the eastern Mediterranean, India, UK, USA, and the Balkans). Carmen has collaborated with research institutions, governmental agencies, outreach organisations, and museums (Natural History Museum of L.A. County, British Museum, Mary Rose Museum, Western Australian Museum) and has presented/published research for conferences such as IKUWA, HFF, SCRIPPS-SCMA. She currently leads a project developing 3D photogrammetric models and training workshops for the Natural History Museum of LA County, works on scientific-commercial archaeological fieldwork, and acts as an expert archaeologist and presenter for the Past Preservers media agency for scientifically-informed documentaries in educational outreach.

Henry Price
Henry Price is a Doctoral Candidate in the Theoretical Physics Group, and a member of the Centre for Complexity Science at Imperial College London.

Ray Rivers
Ray Rivers is Professor Emeritus in Theoretical Physics and Distinguished Research Fellow in The Blackett Laboratory and Centre for Complexity Science at Imperial College London.

Hauke Schneider
Hauke Schneider studied Classics and History at Kiel University, where he works as a Research Associate, completing his PhD on Aristophanes.

Maria G. Xanthou
Dr. Maria G. Xanthou, FHEA, is a Senior Research Associate in Resilient Communities (University of Bristol) and a Research Associate in Pindaric Studies (CHS Washington DC, Harvard University). She has worked as a researcher in 'The Social and Cultural Construction of Emotions: The Greek Paradigm' project at the University of Oxford (ERC Grant 2009-2013; PI: Prof. Angelos Chaniotis). She taught Classics and Ancient History at Aristotle University of Thessaloniki, Hellenic Open University, Open University of Cyprus, University of Bristol, and University of Leeds. She was Visiting Fellow 2020 at Seeger CHS (Princeton University), and CHS Residential Fellow 2015 (Harvard University). She is a recipient of academic scholarships from Aristotle University of Thessaloniki Academic Excellence Scheme, Hellenic State Scholarships Foundation, and Nicos and Lydia Trichas Foundation for Education and European Culture. Her interests lie within the intersection of ancient history, material culture, and classical philology, and include resilience in ancient communities and urban clusters, epichoric identities in the coastline of northern Greece, Greek lyric poetry, both monodic and choral (Stesichorus, Pindar, and Bacchylides), Aristophanic and Attic comedy (5th c. BCE), Attic rhetoric (Isocrates), history of classical scholarship (German classical scholarship of the 19th c.), textual criticism, literary theory, ancient theory of rhetoric (definition and use of asyndeton), and e-learning.

Foreword of the editors

In March 2019, the contributors and editors of this volume together with various other scholars had the opportunity to engage in scholarly exchange about the connectivity of the Mediterranean. The discussions took place during Session 7 of the workshop entitled 'Socio-Environmental Dynamics over the Last 15,000 Years: The Creation of Landscapes VI', generously funded and organised by the 'Human Development in Landscapes' graduate school and the Collaborative Research Center 1266 'Scales of Transformation' of the CAU Kiel.

As in previous years, what was unassumingly called a "workshop" was actually an international, extremely well-attended conference, and as usual it brought together a great range of researchers from very different fields for academic exchange, intellectual challenge and the interpersonal networking that used to be considered a pleasant but rather trivial side effect of such events.

Session 7 – the presentations of which for some part form this volume – focused on ancient networks, asking about their emergence role and conscious use in the contact area of the Mediterranean, and what new interpretations and theories might result from this approach. On the session premises and during the accompanying "social programme", the workshop proved to be a networking event in itself, with the academic spirit of exchanging ideas and learning from each other at its best.

Since then, the world has fundamentally changed, teaching us the significance of personal interaction and chance meetings. In the turmoil of pandemic-induced lockdown with closed libraries, children in home-schooling and cases of serious illness, many of our contributors were unable to follow up on their commitment.

While we are very sorry to have lost many fascinating contributions, we are relieved and proud that our fledgling network of one workshop has held, and that with a lot of support and under extremely difficult circumstances, it has been possible to bring the present volume to publication.

We hope that it may contribute to an appreciation of network research as a method of understanding the past and the strengthening of academic networks in a divided world. We are particularly grateful to Prof. Lutz Käppel and Senior Lecturer Dr. Oliver Nakoinz for first conceiving the idea for Session 7 and their continued and unfailing support, and to Dr. Francesca Fulminante, with whom we spent fruitful hours deciding on and arranging the papers for the conference.

Our thanks go to all of the participants who originally enriched the workshop with their expertise and interest, to those who have stayed in touch with us since then and who were able – despite the difficult circumstances – to contribute their paper to this volume, to the sponsors and organisers of the workshop at Kiel and, finally, to the editorial office of the CRC 1266, especially Dr. Nicole Taylor: without their help, this volume would never have become real.

Kiel, 9 November 2021
Anja Rutter
Laura Schmidt

Introduction

Anja Rutter, Laura C. Schmidt

The present publication constitutes the proceedings of Session 7 of the 'Creation of landscapes VI' workshop hosted by the CAU Kiel in 2019. The session was entitled 'Mediterranean connections: How the sea links people and transforms identities'.

With our focus on the linkage of people, this volume can be understood as a contribution to recent network research. However, network research – especially when employed in the humanities – is often looked at with scepticism, not to say mistrust: Isn't this just a game with numbers? Does it really relate to the type of data that we are used to in our research, to poems, sherds or seal impressions? Can it say anything at all about... life?

In fact, the various articles of this volume are not restricted to the strict technical approach of classical network research. Our session on Mediterranean networks started from the idea that for the inhabitants of this relatively integrated region, the sea evidently influenced their lives and thinking in a significant way. In fact, it was the sea that provided the medium for such integration at various levels. The substantial body of data produced by long-standing research in diverse disciplines makes it possible to chart the emergence of ancient perceptions of distance and movement, connectivity and identities. This approach allows us to observe ancient awareness of the role of the sea in these processes. It also allows us to connect across academic boundaries and build a network of disciplines to gain a much more cohesive picture of past life.

In this book, contributions from archaeology, literature and history attempt to ascertain the way in which identities – whether individual or communal – relate to physical space and how movement across the sea might assert or alter self-perception. This movement might relate to individuals travelling or translocating, whole groups finding new places of residence or maintaining contacts over long distances, but also object movement. On the one hand, access or exposure to "moved" objects as well as ideas and – even more so – displacement of people or peoples challenges and alters identity and might even be resisted as such.

On the other hand, the ability to cross the sea to distant places and the way of living engendered by long-distance contacts might also be integral to an identity. It would thus not be tied to a place but to a maritime and highly connective "skillset" and the people who shared it.

This research context exposes the severe limitations of the traditional tendency to define political or cultural entities spatially. Instead, the perception of collective identities as networked spheres of interest allows us to progress towards an understanding of processes within the Mediterranean as a dynamic area of common cultures and conflicts. Shared mental maps and networks thus help to understand the collapse of powers, systems, and identities, the emergence of new ones, and the role of possibly persisting parts of a network in such processes.

These aspects in particular highlight the potential of the disciplines collaborating here for an in-depth understanding of identity formation at the level of individuals, groups and societies, including today. The concept of networked identities might show a way to handle or even overcome the divisive and restrictive spatial boundaries of political geography and find aspects of identity across such borders.

The volume is organised in two thematic parts. The first six papers focus on questions of centrality and periphery in looking at various places and their societies and asking how they situate themselves in the world. Looking at places as the nodes of networks highlights the wide variety of connections, their possible roles and their (sometimes truly material) benefits.

The journey starts with Maria Noussia-Fantuzzi, who leads us into the poetical world of Hellenistic Egypt, although the journey does not stop there; rather, she highlights the web drawn by the poets across chronological and spatial boundaries, from Homer over Sappho and Pindar to the Hellenistic poets, and from various points on the Greek mainland across several Mediterranean islands to Egypt. Similar to ourselves, the Hellenistic poets searched for ways to approach the diverse poetical traditions that had come to them from times of old and places far away, and they creatively included them in their own networked poetical world. Maria Noussia-Fantuzzi's focus lies especially on the image of the sea as used by the poets to depict these networks.

Next, our journey takes us to the Greek peninsula Chalkidiki during the 5th and 4th centuries. Maria G. Xanthou introduces to us the two cities of Olynthus and Potidaea. They are connected at many levels, and it is their networks that ultimately allow them to regenerate after disasters and keep renewing their identities. This paper also exemplifies the methodological strengths of combining historical, geographical and archaeological sources and viewpoints.

In the most technical contribution, the research by Paula Gheorghiade together with Henry Price and Ray Rivers considers proper archaeological data – namely sherds from Crete in the Late Bronze Age – sets them in relation to geographical information and uses a mathematical model to test the relevance of the results. These show the relation of distance and geography, and how accessibility bears on the role of communities in a maritime network.

Reaching out over the sea, the question of a common identity beyond clearly-defined regions became pertinent for the inhabitants of *poleis* in Epirus and Southern Illyria during Hellenistic times. While earlier research described the history and identity of these places in form of a Greek/non-Greek dichotomy, Ludovica Xavier de Silva uses the architectural language of theatrical buildings to uncover the bases of the specific Adriatic-Ionian identity shared by these two cities.

For one unhappy individual, the answer to the same question is vital at least for his intellectual survival: Ovid – in exile on the shores of the Black Sea – must not only adapt to the idea of being a Roman on the fringes of the Empire but perhaps also to a very different climate, as Stefan Feddern undertakes to ascertain. The use of similar vocabulary and references to similar phenomena as in other ancient authors have often been understood as indicators of "fictionality", and thus against the authenticity of Ovid's account. By contrast, Stefan Feddern shows how they rather prove Ovid's participation in an ancient discourse. Especially the phenomenon of the freezing of wine helps Ovid to shape his identity in the web of both his literary and geographical world.

Almost at opposite shores – at least geographically – Raffaella Da Vela looks at Hellenistic sites on the north-western coast of the Mediterranean and asks how local communities interact with international goods, as well as how these in turn might reflect common social narratives. A semantic two-mode network proves to be a useful methodology to visualise and analyse consumptionscapes and their role in local social hierarchies.

The second set of contributions adopts as its topic connectivity by sea, the networking of seafarers and how identity is shaped by a skillset and lifestyle. In following their paths across the eastern Mediterranean through space and time, we find this identity expressed in a wide variety of sources and at very different levels.

We start with quite a peculiar case: rather than presenting himself as crossing the sea and connecting to people far away, the Greek poet Pindar sends his poetry in seafaring songs "like merchandise" from Greek Thebes to Syracuse, Aigina or Akragas. In fact, he imagines them to reach the whole world. Thomas Kuhn-Treichel shows how the poet – although not stirring from home – establishes connections between himself and the Mediterranean in and by his poetry. The songs combine a local perspective with Thebes as the poet's hometown and a pan-Hellenic one in which the whole Mediterranean functions as the space of his poetic-commercial outreach. Both perspectives are relevant for the identity of the poet, his work and the addressee.

In an environment that differs from the previous one at almost all levels, the self-perception of Roman-era fishermen in Cyprus can only be approached indirectly. Maria Michael and Carmen Obied illustrate how a combination of data from a wide array of applicable disciplines is necessary when we want to arrive at the factors that determine identity in context. Their research conclusively refutes a perceived absence of fishing activities in Roman Cyprus and goes some way to investigate perceptions of the local seascape, which also constitute the basis for long-distance travel.

The political journeys described by Alcaeus are of a purely metaphorical nature. Despite being centred on the motif of sea storms as political turbulences, they exert an exceptional influence on the union of Alcaeus' "crew", his *hetairoi*. Ippokratis Kantzios shows us how the decisive lack of realism in Alcaeus' narrations of nautical journeys leads his aristocratic audience to recognise their own situation and close their ranks and become a resilient crew against their shared enemy.

In common understanding, the *Odyssey* is perceived so much as the archetypical seafaring narrative that it appears almost trivial to include it here. However, Hauke Schneider combines philological and historical methods to make an intriguing point about the role of seafaring identity and its bearing upon status in Homeric Society. Its relevance for the society of Ithaca becomes most evident in the Telemachy and especially in the changes of behaviour in and respect for Telemachus after his own seafaring exploits.

Linking back to the first part and the use of architecture as a means of uncovering identity, Francesca Bonzano's paper on Malta in the 4th and 3rd centuries BCE allows us to understand how a small place in a large network comes to be defined by exchange while retaining a specific and original identity. The architectural semantics – although untranslatable today – clearly exhibit an inclination for adopting and adapting stylistic models from a common cultural basis that reaches far across the sea.

Finally, we return ashore with Laura Schmidt. On the Greek island of Lesbos, the archaic poet Sappho prefers to set her hopes on young Larichus who remains ashore and has to struggle for his recognition as an adult rather than on young Charaxus who follows the recognised way of establishing his position by seafaring. Nevertheless, in her considerations about Larichus, Sappho remains in the maritime mindset, so that young Larichus has to cope with the sea, despite remaining ashore.

Part 1: Identity of centres and peripheries

Seafaring and the reception of (some) archaic Greek lyric poetry[1]

Maria Noussia-Fantuzzi

Abstract

This paper discusses the relationship between seafaring and the Hellenistic reception of some archaic Greek lyric poetry. Although most of the texts in question have recently been discussed, the role of the sea has been underplayed or overlooked. The paper argues that the idea of seafaring is an aspect of the poems on the Hellenistic reception of archaic lyric poetry that deserves more attention as it seems to often support/help the continuity between archaic and classical Greece and thriving Egyptian literature and scholarship. The sea unites more than it divides, and it seems to ensure the contact at the end of the journey, instead of emphasising its risks.

Hellenistic poetry, Archaic lyric poetry, reception, seafaring

Introduction

A concern with travel over the open seas recurs throughout some Hellenistic poems regarding the reception of archaic Greek lyric poetry. Seafaring across the Mediterranean Sea can be argued to have a natural role in the chrono-topic definition of Hellenised Egypt, and in particular with the Ptolemaic program of maritime expansion and conquest. Unsurprisingly, then – and most appropriately in a Ptolemaic perspective – our poems can be said to describe the frequent and solid networks of communications in the Aegean and the Mediterranean Seas and the underlying reality of increased maritime mobility, combined with shorter distances between places in the Mediterranean, and interaction in these areas.

---

1   I wish to thank the organisers of the Section on Mediterranean Connections – How the sea links people and transforms identities of the Conference at Kiel for their kind invitation, and Lutz Käppel for valuable discussion on that occasion. Particular thanks are owed to Marco Fantuzzi, who read and commented on an earlier version of this paper. I am also indebted to Kathryn Gutzwiller for advice and criticism in preparing the published version.

However, I would like to argue that the perception of the sea is an aspect of these poems that deserves more attention.[2] In fact, seafaring around the Mediterranean seems to contribute to a continuum between Archaic and Classical Greece and thriving Ptolemaic/Egyptian literature and scholarship. In investing geographic movement through the open sea with poetological significance,[3] the poems also create a framework for talking about genre and the Hellenistic poets' flexible reception and transformation of previous lyric material to new ends,[4] given that a culture in transition mobility and "mapping" provide a useful context for a cultural fashioning. Thus, the seafaring references reflect something about the ways in which the Hellenistic Greeks consumed the texts, conceptualised and articulated the nature of poetic composition and re-evaluated the identity of lyric genre. The sea apparently unites more than it divides, destructs or ends, and it seems to ensure the contact at the end of the journey, instead of emphasising its risks. This recognition of the sea – which opposes its most usual perception as "a place of no return" – as well as the significance of this new attitude cannot be overlooked.[5]

Travel over water in Phanocles and Posidippus

A long fragment from Phanocles (fr. 1.11-28 Powell) – a poet of whom we know nothing, but we consider to belong to the early third century – offers a version of the story of Orpheus' death. Orpheus was torn to pieces by the women of Thrace as he wandered through the countryside thinking of his beloved Calais, then his dismembered body was thrown into the Hebrus river, which carried it out to sea where the waves brought his head and lyre to the shores of Lesbos:

Τοῦ δ᾽ ἀπὸ μὲν κεφαλὴν χαλκῷ τάμον, αὐτίκα δ᾽ αὐτὴν

εἰς ἅλα Θρηϊκίῃ ῥῖψαν ὁμοῦ χέλυϊ

ἥλῳ καρτύνασαι, ἵν᾽ ἐμφορέοιντο θαλάσσῃ

ἄμφω ἅμα, γλαυκοῖς τεγγόμεναι ῥοθίοις.

Τὰς δ᾽ ἱερῇ Λέσβῳ πολιὴ ἐπέκελσε θάλασσα.

....

....

ἠχὴ δ᾽ ὣς λιγυρῆς πόντον ἐπέσχε λύρης,

νήσους τ᾽ αἰγιαλούς θ᾽ ἁλιμυρέας. Ἔνθα λίγειαν

ἀνέρες Ὀρφείην ἐκτέρισαν κεφαλήν,

ἐν δὲ χέλυν τύμβῳ λιγυρὴν θέσαν, ἣ καὶ ἀναύδους

---

2   In this treatment of the poems, I confine myself strictly to the role of the sea, which has been underplayed or overlooked in discussions of the poems. This will necessarily preclude any attempt at a complete reading of the poems.

3   On the ways in which the language of ships (and sailing) is used metaphorically to represent the art of poetry, and specifically the representation of the poetic process in ship construction and their ability to sail already in Homer, see Dougherty 2001. Other relevant passages for such a connection can also be found in Hesiod (with Rosen 1990), Ibycus (with Steiner 2005) and Pindar (*e.g.* Péron 1974). See Nünlist 1998 for the pre-Hellenistic references.

4   See Acosta-Hughes 2010 for the response of the Alexandrians to several Lyric poets, especially Sappho.

5   For the use and perception of the sea in the ancient Greek world based on literary evidence, see Lesky 1974; Vryonis 1993. For the perception of the sea as 'a place of no return' and an 'away-place', see Lindenlauf 2004 with previous bibliography.

πέτρας καὶ Φόρκου στυγνὸν ἔπειθεν ὕδωρ.
Ἐκ κείνου μολπαί τε καὶ ἱμερτὴ κιθαριστὺς
νῆσον ἔχει, πασέων δ' ἐστὶν ἀοιδοτάτη.
Θρῆκες δ' ὡς ἐδάησαν ἀρήϊοι ἔργα γυναικῶν
ἄγρια, καὶ πάντας δεινὸν ἐσῆλθεν ἄχος,
ἃς ἀλόχους ἔστιζον, ἵν' ἐν χροῖ σήματ' ἔχουσαι
κυάνεα στυγεροῦ μὴ λελάθοιντο φόνου·
ποινὰς δ' Ὀρφῆϊ κταμένῳ τίνουσι γυναῖκες
εἰσέτι νῦν κείνης εἵνεκεν ἀμπλακίης.

They cut off his head with a sword of bronze, and threw it at once

in the sea along with the Thracian lyre.

binding them strongly with a nail, so they would both be carried

on the sea together, soaked by the billowing surf.

And the foaming sea drove them to sacred Lesbos.

....

....

And likewise the clear echo of the lyre spread across the sea

and over the islands and sea-beaten shores, thereupon men

interred the clear-sounding Orphic head

and set in the tomb of the bright-ringing lyre, which used to persuade

even mute stones and the hateful water of Phorkos.

From that time forth, songs and lovely cithara music

have occupied the island, the most musical of them all.

As for the warlike Thracian men, when they had

learned the women's savage deeds and

dire grief had sunk into them all, they

began the custom of tattooing their wives,

so that having on their flesh signs of dark

blue, they would not forget their hateful

murder. And even now, the women pay

reparations to the dead Orpheus because of that sin.

The αἴτιον theme is clearly prominent in this fragment of Phanocles' poem Ἔρωτες ἢ Καλοί, an apparent survey of *paidika*: we learn why the Thracians tattoo their women (the main *aition*), who first introduced homosexuality among them and why Lesbos is famous for song. Ll. 15-20 contain the ending of the first of the two aetiologies and present a double miracle, a double *adynaton*: the cut-off head of the singer keeps singing and his lyre keeps accompanying him. It is to express exactly the quality of this miraculous mobile and ever-accompanying music that Phanocles uses an insistent repetition of keywords for sweetness of sound in four successive lines (cf. λίγειαν … κεφαλήν, sandwiched[6] between λιγυρῆς … λύρης and χέλυν … λιγυρήν). Hopkinson in his *Hellenistic anthology* adopts Rawe's suggestion of two lines' lacuna and a strong punctuation before ἔνθα (17 since the text as transmitted has no mention of the famous detail of the singing head (except indirectly in 17 λίγειαν)).

The story is told again by Lucian in his *adversus indoctum* (11-12):

Οὐκ ἄκαιρον δ' ἂν γένοιτο καὶ Λέσβιον μῦθόν τινα διηγήσασθαί σοι πάλαι γενόμενον. ὅτε τὸν Ὀρφέα διεσπάσαντο αἱ Θρᾷτται, φασὶ τὴν κεφαλὴν αὐτοῦ σὺν τῇ λύρᾳ εἰς τὸν Ἕβρον ἐμπεσοῦσαν ἐκβληθῆναι εἰς τὸν μέλανα κόλπον, καὶ ἐπιπλεῖν γε τὴν κεφαλὴν τῇ λύρᾳ, τὴν μὲν ᾄδουσαν θρῆνόν τινα ἐπὶ τῷ Ὀρφεῖ, ὡς λόγος, τὴν λύραν δὲ αὐτὴν ὑπηχεῖν τῶν ἀνέμων ἐμπιπτόντων ταῖς χορδαῖς, καὶ οὕτω μετ' ᾠδῆς προσενεχθῆναι τῇ Λέσβῳ, κἀκείνους ἀνελομένους τὴν μὲν κεφαλὴν καταθάψαι ἵναπερ νῦν τὸ Βακχεῖον αὐτοῖς ἐστι, τὴν λύραν δὲ ἀναθεῖναι εἰς τοῦ Ἀπόλλωνος τὸ ἱερόν, καὶ ἐπὶ πολύ γε σώζεσθαι αὐτήν,

It would not be out of place to tell you another story about something that happened in Lesbos long ago. They say that when the women of Thrace tore Orpheus to pieces, his head and his lyre fell into the Hebrus, and were carried out into the Aegean Sea; and that the head floated along on the lyre, singing a dirge (so the story goes) over Orpheus, while the lyre itself gave out sweet sounds as the winds struck the strings. In that manner they came ashore in Lesbos to the sound of music, and the people there took them up, burying the head where their temple of Dionysus now stands and hanging up the lyre in the temple of Apollo, where it was long preserved. (tr. Harmon).

Lucian retains the level of wonder regarding the singer's head while he blends it with a logical explanation as to the lyre's singing ("the lyre itself gave out sweet sounds as the winds struck the strings," τὴν λύραν δὲ αὐτὴν ὑπηχεῖν τῶν ἀνέμων ἐμπιπτόντων ταῖς χορδαῖς).

Phanocles' lines clearly overturn the most widespread motif of the sea as the ideal place for persons and things to be disposed of irretrievably,[7] since by floating upon the sea the head and the lyre of Orpheus are driven to Lesbos. Greek literature testifies to a long association between poetry and water and the fact that the water keeps Orpheus' poetic voice alive may be related to the symbolism that the water carries as a life-giver.[8] However, as both Orpheus and the lyre (and thus Greek musical culture) are the centre of attention (indeed Phanocles painstakingly notes that the two are bound together with a nail), their travel to Lesbos (which is aetiological for Lesbos' fame for song and music) despite the uncertainties of the sea and the stormy passage displays the fluid dynamics of movement and travel rather than the power of water to give life. The clear song that emanates from the head and lyre of Orpheus might also contain meta-poetic resonances that connect him to the figure of Phanocles himself, whereby he might indirectly represent some aspects of the poet. A poet with Orpheus' charisma, charm of voice and sweetness of song – "which used to persuade even mute stones and the hateful water of Phorkos" – the sea and rocks being proverbially unhearing and unsympathetic in Greek literature – may be considered sufficiently versatile to encompass Phanocles' voice of aetiological elegy and its catalogic character, not only poetry writ large. Similarly, the reference to Lesbos is not impossible to also work

---

6   Thus Marcovich 1979, 364 for Phanocles' intended stylistic repetition.
7   We can think of the episode of the Samian tyrant Polycrates' ring (Herodotus 3.40-43) that Polycrates throws into the sea to be conspicuously destroyed. According to Hooker 1989, 142, the anecdote works out the theme of 'what will be, will be.' However, the sea only serves as a temporary away-place and the ring is unusually retrieved. Bacchylides 17 offers another instance where the belief in the sea as a place of no return fails again. See Buxton 1994 for a list of anecdotes on retrieved goods.
8   See for instance the story of Aphrodite's birth with Simon 1959.

at another level: it might also be significant that Theocritus – a contemporary of Phanocles – clearly associates the homoerotic content of the *paidika* form with Lesbos, since his *Idylls* 29-31 are in Aeolic dialect.[9] If this can be accepted, the geographic choice would carry an additional nuance to the connectives established.

It further shows how Greek musical and poetic traditions of the archetypal and Archaic Greek past were reimagined by Hellenistic poets in their individual poetic choices. The story is clearly part of the Hellenistic poetic trend to insistently engage with the history of the literary forms in which the poet operates, with sources and founder poets. Nonetheless, it emphasises the element of geographic displacement through travel *over the sea whose turbulence is no longer corrupting*: the constant movement of the sea does not make Orpheus' head disappear. In reality, the choices of the foaming sea (described in a variety of terms to show its many different properties, including ἅλς, θάλασσα twice and πόντος) and its seemingly thoughtless waves on the shores and surfs (αἰγιαλός, ῥόθιον) are summoned to confirm literary history (the musicality of Lesbos).

However, it is with Posidippus (from the third century BCE) that the full potentiality of this conception of the sea is explored. In the epigram (AB 37)[10] – discovered in 2001 as part of the Milan Papyrus – another object, a symbol of a world of earlier poetry, voyages to Ptolemaic land and Arsinoe's Philadelphus temple brought ashore by Arion's dolphin/or a dolphin like Arion's.[11]

Ἀρσινόη, σοὶ τή[ν]δε λύρην ὑπὸ χειρ[......]ῦ

φθεγξαμ[ένην] δελφὶς ἤγαγ᾽ Ἀριόνιο[c

ου..ελου[....]αc ἐκ κύματος αλλοτ[

κεῖνος αν[....]c λευκὰ περᾶι πελά[γη

πολλαπο[....].τητι καὶ αἰόλα τῆι .[

φωνῆι π[....]ακον κανον ἀηδον[

ἄνθεμα δ᾽, [ὦ Φιλ]άδελφε, τὸν ἤλασεν [......]ίων,

   τόνδε δέ[χου, .]υcου μ‹ε›ίλια ναοπόλο[υ.

To you, Arsinoe, this lyre from the hand? (. . .) made to resound,

a dolphin like Arion's brought. (. . .) from the wave (. . .), that one crossed the white sea – and many varied things (. . .)-with voice (. . .). As an offering,

Brother(-loving one), receive this (which brought? . . .) gift from the temple guard.

Our epigram is revealing in a number of ways. First of all, it both provides a modern counterpart to the well-known Lesbian tale of Orpheus' lyre recounted by Phanocles and an imagery of another extended sea journey (a violent one with a safe ending). Second, the epigram also alludes to the legend of Arion's rescue as told by Herodotus 1.24 and his subsequent dedication of a statue of a man riding a dolphin, likewise made at a shrine on a cape. Finally, as Bing 2005[12] notes, the poem would represent an example of how an object may be made to embody the cultural/historical heritage, and become the vehicle of its relocation to a new place. By describing how this lyre – together with the tradition it evokes – came to Egypt,

---

9   On the combination of geography and literary tradition in Theocritus, see Krevans 1983.

10   AB = Austin and Bastianini 2002.

11   Greek sources on Arion are collected by Sutton 1989, 13-15. On Arion as inventor of tragedy, see Noussia-Fantuzzi 2010, 519-520. For the reading Ἀριόνιο[c, see Puelma 2006, 63-64.

12   Bing 2005, 127-131. There are also other implicit encomiastic purposes in the epigram, as has been shown by recent work: see Fantuzzi 2004 on the equation of Arsinoe with Poseidon and Stephens 2004 for Arsinoe's equation with previous artistic patrons such as Periander of Corinth.

the poet links the third-century-BCE shrine of Arsinoe-Aphrodite and the Ptolemies' cultural politics[13] to one of the great figures of archaic poetry, and with him to the rich tradition of the erotic contents of Lesbian lyric and the tradition of the short poem.

Bing is correct in seeing the tale in Posidippus' epigram as "emblematic of the Ptolemies' claim to be the true inheritors and guardians of the literary legacy of Hellas, in particular here the great tradition of Lesbian song".[14] The Arion story may have been very appropriate to the Ptolemies (since Arion's native Methymna on Lesbos came to serve as an important strategic base for Ptolemaic interests overseas), and especially Queen Arsinoe, who as a maritime goddess – Arsinoe-Aphrodite Zephyritis – presided over the seaways and networks of the Ptolemaic maritime empire.[15] Furthermore, Posidippus himself relied on the solid networks of communications in the Aegean for his travel(s) from native Pella (in epigram 22 the speaker presents himself as a traveller heading towards Egypt).

Posidippus' poem serves a function comparable to that of Callimachus' epigram about the conch shell, which in a memorable *prosopopeia* speaks of its route to Egypt before its dedication at the shrine of Arsinoe-Aphrodite Nephritis by a certain Σεληναίη from Aeolian Smyrna (v. 12), who found it on the beach at Iulis on Ceos on her way from Smyrna to Alexandria. The element of journey is emphasised through the shell's characterisation of itself as "old", παλαίτερος (v. 1), showing that it – like the lyre in AB 37 – has also travelled extensively.

Arsinoe's shrine draws objects "as if by a magnetic force"[16] but also marks the intersection of several disparate itineraries and origins,[17] with the sea functioning as a transitive agent. Ceos and Smyrna were suggestive place names as the birthplaces of great lyric poets: both Simonides and Bacchylides came from Ceos, and Smyrna is connected with Mimnermus' origins in some ancient sources (Pausanias 9.29.4). This collection of sites with culturally loaded symbolism is intertwined with increasing Ptolemaic economic activities and contemporary politics. As has been observed,[18] the Cean town of Coresia (the harbor at Iulis) became an important port in the mid-3rd century BCE, which (significantly) was renamed Arsinoe after the queen's death.

I would like to emphasise how the poetic stories of these objects' sea migrations can reveal themselves not as special one-off or fortuitous situations but rather as parts of a much broader consciousness of a circulation of culture around a heavily interconnected Mediterranean and its relocation to the shores of Alexandria. In the texts of Posidippus, and Phanocles above, the connections established are specifically carried out by the sea and its creatures. In other words, in both texts the sea constitutes an *agent of transmission* of the lyric archetypal past to the lyric present/future, a guarantee of continuity and identity.

The image of (some kind of) seaborne travel to places that have literary significance should not be dismissed as merely a standard conceit in Hellenistic poetry for signalling evocation of an Archaic poet, but rather deserves a more complex exposition, as further more or less obvious poetic ambitions and aspirations may be floating just below the surface.

---

13 See Curtis 2017, who connects the Ptolemaic dynasty's cultural project with Augustus' regime in Rome.

14 Bing 2005, 130.

15 See Posidippus AB 39 "She'll grant good sailing or make the sea, for those / who call upon her in the storm, smooth as oil", and AB 119 "Whether you're to brave the sea or grapple your ship / to shore, shout 'Hail!' to Arsinoe of Good Sailing, / calling our lady goddess from her temple – the son of Boiscus, / admiral at the time, Samian Callicrates, put her here, / sailor, especially for you. And not only for you – often / have others, in need of good sailing, looked to her."

16 Curtis 2017, 288.

17 See Selden 1998, 309-314 on the notion of displacement. Curtis 2017, n. 14 reminds us that like Posidippus, Arsinoe also underwent her journey of "displacement" as she spent much of her life in Macedonia, despite being born in Egypt.

18 Cf. Robert 1960, reported by Bing 2005, 131 n. 26.

Travel across temporal seas

The theme of sea travel can also articulate the nature of relationships with the poets of the past without necessarily reinforcing the emphasis on Archaic poetry. An epigram by Nossis (*AP* 7.718) – a native of Epizephyrian Locri in Southern Italy and a poetess working a generation earlier than Posidippus – highlights her own poetic portrait by cleverly playing with the *propemptikon* mode in the following mock epitaph:[19]

ὦ ξεῖν', εἰ τύ γε πλεῖς ποτὶ καλλίχορον Μιτυλήναν

τᾶν Σαπφοῦς χαρίτων ἄνθος ἐναυσόμενος,

εἰπεῖν ὡς Μούσαισι φίλαν τήνᾳ τε Λόκρισσα

τίκτεν· ἴσαις δ' ὅτι μοι τοὔνομα Νοσσίς, ἴθι.

> Stranger, if you sail to Mytilene of the lovely dances to be inspired by the flower of Sappho's graces, say that a woman of Locris bore one dear to the Muses and to her; you may know that my name is Nossis. Go (tr. Fantuzzi, Hunter).

The idea that one should visit the birthplace of the author whose model one intends to imitate is implicitly rejected, since Nossis herself is unwilling (or unable) to sail from Locris to Mytilene, Sappho's homeland. She assumes that anyone sailing to Mytilene would be going there to breathe in the flowers of Sappho's graces, *i.e.* to seek poetic inspiration by Sappho's poems. This would seem to imply that Sapphic poetry had a well-defined original performative context (in the epigram this is conceptualised as songs performed with dances, καλλίχορον Μιτυλήναν, v. 1) and inspiration by her poetry would demand a reproduction of such a context. Although Nossis must herself have been inspired by Sappho's poetry, otherwise her gesture would not make sense,[20] the point of her text – properly understood – must be that she did so without having had to travel to that place (Mytilene). The reason is most probably that – in an emulative rather than imitative connection with Sappho – Nossis pays a homage to the great lyric poetess of the past, but states her independence from her. Sappho is the great Sappho and Nossis does not deny that if one wishes to compose Sapphic poetry one must travel to Lesbos. Although not without locating herself squarely in the Sapphic tradition,[21] Nossis has set off in new directions. Nossis wants to compose post-Sapphic poetry in her own mode, adapting it to epigram, and will not go to Mytilene.

Within a generation of Nossis, in *iamb* 13, vv. 11-19[22] Callimachus defends his composition of iambics in the manner of Hipponax, without – among other accusations[23] – going to Ephesus in Ionia, Hipponax's hometown (even if he admits that Ephesus is the place from which anyone who intends to produce limping verses not unwisely draws the flame of his inspiration):

---

19   See Gutzwiller 1998, 253-255 on Nossis' modification of the epitaphic form so as to serve the proclamation of her poetic lineage in the epigram. Skinner 1989, 11-12.

20   On the motif of "conveying the message," in the context of funerary epigrams see Tarán 1979, 132-149.

21   As Acosta-Hughes 2010, 86 notes: "The poem evolves into a celebration not of Sappho but rather of Nossis in relation to her." Bowman 1998.

22   Again in the last extant lines, where he repeats the critics' language of vv. 11-14 and ironically appropriates their first charge: "I do sing, neither having visited Ephesus nor mixed with the Ionians," (vv. 63-66): see Steiner 2007.

23   The indiscriminate mixture of dialects is another accusation, vv. 16-18.

[οὔτ'] Ἴωσι συμμείξας

οὔτ' Ἔφεσον ἐλθών, ἥτις ἐστι, αμ.[

Ἔφεσον, ὅθεν περ οἱ τά μέτρα μέλλοντες

τὰ χωλὰ τίκτειν μὴ ἀμαθῶς ἐναύονται·

ἀλλ' εἴ τι θυμὸν ἢ 'πι γαστέρα πνευσ[

εἴτ' οὖν ἐπ ἀρχαῖον εἴτ' ἀπαι[

τοῦτ' ἐμπέπλεκται καὶ λαλευσ[

Ἰαστὶ καὶ Δωριστὶ καὶ τὸ σύμμικ[τον

τεῦ μέχρι τολμᾶις; οἱ φίλοι σε δήσουσι'.

neither having mixed with Ionians nor gone to Ephesus, which is ... Ephesus, from where those who wish skillfully to give birth to limping verses draw the fire of inspiration. But if something [? fires] spirit or stomach, whether archaic or .... this is woven in and [?] they speak ... Ionic and Doric and a mixture. What is the limit of your recklessness? Your friends will bring you up...'.

The critics of Callimachus claim that anyone who wants to produce limping verses – faithfully imitating the model of Hipponax of Ephesus – must immediately travel to Ephesus in "search of a historical authenticity".[24] Travel to the geographic space of a poet-model of the past is the condition under which a concept of poetic genre conceived in terms of context-dependent conventions can come into existence. The idea of inspiration (rendered by ἐναύεσθαι, also found in Nossis – as Fantuzzi and Hunter note[25] – "suggests *enthousiasmos* and external possession") is complemented side by side in Callimachus with the idea of learned recreation of a performative content.[26]

To recreate the conditions of the utterance of *iambi* (the social and linguistic environment of Hipponax), Callimachus clearly does not need to travel to Ephesus: in *Iamb* 13, it is the learned literary recreation of a performative context – vv. 14, and also 66 – and not the imitation of the conventions that traditionally tied an Archaic poem to its performative occasion or the combination of strictly formal elements that allows Callimachus to confute his denigrators and declare in the last extant lines of the poem that he is "singing" (ἀείδω) *iambi*. This is something distinct from what his critics believe the genre to be: iambi are not a sung verse, first of all, but Callimachus wants to produce quasi-lyric iambs, in the tradition of the short poem in lyric verse of the archaic age.

Poems as cargo shipped across the sea

In another epigram – AB 122 – in which songs are travelling as cargo (of praise) on ships, Posidippus reworks an image from the world of Homer where the practices of commercial trade with suggestions of profit link good poetry and overseas trade, and enrich the metaphorical connection between songs and ships at work in the poetics of the *Odyssey*.[27]

---

24   Hunter 1997, 43.
25   Fantuzzi and Hunter 2004, 16.
26   As Depew 1992, 327 notes, "the challenge to the contemporary poet who cannot possess the culture-specific authority to compose in traditional genres, is to possess sufficient *techne* to recreate, self-consciously and fictionally, the conditions of their utterance."
27   See Dougherty 2001, 38-50.

Δωρίχα, ὀστέα μὲν σὰ πάλαι κόνις ἦν ὅ τε δεσμὸς

χαίτης ἥ τε μύρων ἔκπνοος ἀμπεχόνη,

ἦ ποτε τὸν χαρίεντα περιστέλλουσα Χάραξον

σύγχρους ὀρθρινῶν ἥψαο κισσυβίων·

Σαπφῷαι δὲ μένουσι φίλης ἔτι καὶ μενέουσιν

ᾠδῆς αἱ λευκαὶ φθεγγόμεναι σελίδες.

οὔνομα σὸν μακαριστόν, ὃ Ναύκρατις ὧδε φυλάξει

ἔστ᾽ ἂν ἴῃ Νείλου ναῦς ἐφ᾽ ἁλὸς πελάγη.

Doricha, your bones were dust long ago and the band of your hair, and the perfume-breathing shawl in which you once wrapped the handsome Charaxos, and, joining him to your flesh, grasped the wine cup in the small hours. But the bright ringing pages of Sappho's dear song abide and will still abide. Happy your name, which Naucratis will preserve thus as long as a ship from the Nile goes upon the wide salt sea (tr. Campbell modified).

The poet promises Doricha[28] – a hetaera of Naucratis in Egypt, famous as the mistress of Sappho's brother, Charaxos – that her name will be preserved as long as the fame of Sappho's poetry abides and as long as a ship sails out from the Nile across the sea (vv. 5-8). It is significant that Posidippus foregrounds the issue of circulation of texts after the theme of fame (thanks to written preservation), as if to suggest that he saw circulation as a key element to this quality for poetry.

I follow Campbell and print a strong punctuation after σελίδες. I understand the Naucratite ship to be conveying Posidippus' *own* song texts and not merely that it is laden with poetic scrolls (Sappho's). This in turn would show Posidippus' conscious awareness that poetic preservation for posterity is assured through the well-developed book trade,[29] rather than the notion that preservation is ensured more generally by the literary heritage of Greek poetry. Rosenmeyer[30] takes the final distich to refer to Sappho's poetry (and no strong punctuation after σελίδες). However, this would be a reiteration of the topic of preservation already stated for Sappho, whose enduring power of verse Posidippus significantly linked with its written medium ("the bright ringing pages of Sappho's clear song", vv. 5-6), and it would destroy the parallelism in the last two distichs between the already-mentioned immortality of Sapphic poetry and Posidippus' own. In any case, it is more relevant to my point that the journey of the ship carrying the poems of Posidippus (or of Sappho) is seen as a token of comparison for the duration of text-songs, and a guarantor of survival of Doricha's name almost at the same level as the eternalising power of poetry.

A brief look at the association between sailing images and songs in elegiac poetry and archaic lyric reveals a similar metaphorical system already at work in early poetry: Theognis – who first within the poetic tradition introduces the explicit claim to perpetuate the fame of a *laudandus* – invokes the image of overseas travel in the elegy promising fame and renown to Cyrnus (237-254). Travel and movement can be associated with all of the flexibility and mobility of oral poetry, but in particular

---

28   On the courtesan named Doricha or Rhodopis, see the ancient references collected by Voigt, tests. 252-254 and also Lidov 2002; Yatromanolakis 2007, 312-37; Kivilo 2010, 175-77; Lefkowitz 2012, 41-44; Gribble 2016, 31-41. Martin 2016, 119 suggests that Doricha is a negative nickname invented by Sappho, punning on δῶρον, to counter the positive nickname, Rhodopis ("rosy"), that the courtesan normally used for her work.

29   Despite the reference to a well-organised trade, Posidippus does not seem to consider the idea that poetry must be a profitable enterprise as well. On songs sold overseas, see Pindar, *Isthmian* 2 with Bernadette 1993, 63-64.

30   Rosenmeyer 2014, 330.

with the fluency and expansiveness of this elegiac composition: as Adkins remarks, all but the last of the nine hexameters (253) are enjambed in West's edition, and three of the nine pentameters (238, 242, 246):[31]

Σοὶ μὲν ἐγὼ πτέρ' ἔδωκα, σὺν οἷσ' ἐπ' ἀπείρονα πόντον

πωτήσηι, κατὰ γῆν πᾶσαν ἀειρόμενος

ῥηϊδίως· θοίνηις δὲ καὶ εἰλαπίνηισι παρέσσηι

ἐν πάσαις πολλῶν κείμενος ἐν στόμασιν,

καί σε σὺν αὐλίσκοισι λιγυφθόγγοις νέοι ἄνδρες

εὐκόσμως ἐρατοὶ καλά τε καὶ λιγέα

ἄισονται. καὶ ὅταν δνοφερῆς ὑπὸ κεύθεσι γαίης

βῆις πολυκωκύτους εἰς Ἀίδαο δόμους,

οὐδέποτ' οὐδὲ θανὼν ἀπολεῖς κλέος, ἀλλὰ μελήσεις

ἄφθιτον ἀνθρώποισ' αἰὲν ἔχων ὄνομα,

Κύρνε, καθ' Ἑλλάδα γῆν στρωφώμενος, ἠδ' ἀνὰ νήσους

ἰχθυόεντα περῶν πόντον ἐπ' ἀτρύγετον,

οὐχ ἵππων νώτοισιν ἐφήμενος· ἀλλά σε πέμψει

ἀγλαὰ Μουσάων δῶρα ἰοστεφάνων.

πᾶσι δ', ὅσοισι μέμηλε, καὶ ἐσσομένοισιν ἀοιδή

ἔσσηι ὁμῶς, ὄφρ' ἂν γῆ τε καὶ ἠέλιος.

αὐτὰρ ἐγὼν ὀλίγης παρὰ σεῦ οὐ τυγχάνω αἰδοῦς,

ἀλλ' ὥσπερ μικρὸν παῖδα λόγοις μ' ἀπατᾶις.

I have given you wings with which you will fly, soaring easily, over the boundless sea and all the land. You will be present at every dinner and feast, lying on the lips of many, and lovely youths accompanied by the clear sounds of pipes will sing of you in orderly fashion with beautiful, clear voices. And whenever you go to Hades' house of wailing, down in the dark earth's depths, never even in death will you lose your fame, but you will be in men's thoughts, your name ever immortal. Cyrnus, as you roam throughout the land of Greece, and among the islands, crossing over the fish-filled, undraining sea, not riding on the back of horses, but it is the splendid gifts of the violet-wreathed Muses that will escort you. For all who care about their gifts, even for future generations, you will be alike the subject of song, as long as earth and sun exist. And yet I do not meet with a slight respect from you, but you deceive me with your words, as if I were a small child (tr. Gerber).

Theognis' poetry gives Cyrnus wings to fly with ease about over the sea, to range across the mainland of Greece and the islands. Theognis does not fail to mention the role that audiences also play in spreading (vv. 240-243) and preserving the oral poetic message (vv. 245-246). Cyrnus' name will be forever known because the gifts of the Muses will accompany it everywhere. As Dougherty[32] remarks, "in this respect, the familiar trope of the immortality of poetic fame takes on a geographical cast." This association of poetry and travel (although Theognis' image is not strictly one of

_____

31   Adkins 1985, 143.
32   Dougherty 2001, 62.

sailing) situates Cyrnus' fame in a perspective that is both pan-Hellenic and timeless while reflecting on some key issues of an oral poem's production, preservation and broader dissemination.

The theme of poetry travelling[33] (as ship's cargo) is elaborated by Pindar twice in the *Nemean Odes* (5.1-3 and 6.33-35) and *Pythian* 2.[34] Thus, in *Nemean* 5 the poet states:

Οὐκ ἀνδριαντοποιός εἰμ᾽, ὥστ᾽ ἐλινύσοντα ἐργά-

ζεσθαι ἀγάλματ᾽ ἐπ᾽ αὐτᾶς βαθμίδος

ἑσταότ᾽· ἀλλ᾽ ἐπὶ πάσας

ὁλκάδος ἔν τ᾽ ἀκάτῳ, γλυκεῖ᾽ ἀοιδά,

στεῖχ᾽ ἀπ᾽ Αἰγίνας διαγγέλλοισ᾽,

I am no sculptor whose statues stand

idle on their base!

But go forth, sweet song, with every

vessel and merchant bark,

setting sail from Aegina, bearing the news…

In his allusion to merchant ships, Pindar compares his victory ode to their cargo, thus situating his own poetry (and the victor celebrated by the ode[35]) within a larger network of profit and value. Just as the Muse of Theognis reached many audiences, unbounded by constrains of space and even time, and in stark contrast to other celebratory possibilities for Pytheas' victory (such as a statue fixed on its base), the mobility of these cargo ships will put poetry into foreign harbours, spreading the fame of both athlete/client and poet well beyond a merely local audience and the original site of the athletic victory. In creating a product that can be exchanged all over the world for other valuable goods/profit (since it is being treated like a commodity), the poet of the aristocratic families comes close to occupying the role of the archaic merchant trader who is ever attentive to his cargo and its potential for swift economic gain.

Posidippus takes up the image of (merchant) ships and song when he refers to Naucratis' role in circulating the poem worldwide through maritime networks. Posidippus does not say (as Pindar does in *Ol.* 9.21-27) that he will spread Doricha's fame "faster than any ship or horse can travel," nor does he emphasise the unconditional longevity of his praise as Theognis has done. In realistically connecting dissemination with the papyrus trade from Naucratis – "the city whose power is in ships" – Posidippus shows awareness about seafaring as a mechanism of safe preservation and circulation of texts. It will be precisely by transporting the poem of Posidippus to faraway places that the name of Doricha will be preserved.

Moreover, Pindar's aforementioned *Nemean* 6.51-59 – from another poem for a wealthy trading family of Aegina – characterises epinician songs as cargo shipped across the sea at the family's initiative:

---

33 Gentili 1988, 163 discusses both Theognis' passage and Pindar's *Nemean* 5. See also Goldhill 1991, 109-11, von Reden 1995, 43-44.

34 *Pyth.* 2.58-68, composed for Hieron's chariot victory, refers to poetry as a ship's merchandise and places emphasis on the poet's own participation and presence in the process of shipment. In Calame's words (2012, 316-317), we observe a "metamorphosis from poem object into commercial product dispatched across the sea."

35 See Hubbard 2004 on epinician's function as 'public relations' statement.

ἀοιδαὶ καὶ λόγοι τὰ καλά σφιν ἔργ' ἐκόμισαν·

Βασσίδαισιν ἅ τ' οὐ σπανίζει, παλαίφατος γενεά,

ἴδια ναυστολέοντες ἐπι-

κώμια, Πιερίδων ἀρόταις

δυνατοὶ παρέχειν πολὺν ὕμνον ἀγερώχων ἐργμάτων

ἕνεκεν.

Song and stories transport/preserve (ἐκόμισαν) the fair deeds of the Bassidae,

Which are not few in number. A race famous of old,

Shipping out their own encomia,

They are able to provide the Pierides' plowmen with much source of song

Thanks to their proud accomplishment (tr. Hubbard).

As Hubbard notes, the ambiguity of the verb ἐκόμισαν in the first line of this passage – equally attested in Pindar with the meaning transport and preserve (Slater *s.v.*) – must be meant to have both implications in the present context, "since it is precisely by transporting the encomia of the Bassidae on the open seas to faraway places that their fair deeds are preserved".[36]

Again, the association between poetry and travel so explicitly articulated in the works of the late archaic poet Pindar – and in particular its role in representing the broad scope and range of his poetic skill – helps to guide our thinking about how the Hellenistic poet envisioned his poems' preservation and broader dissemination. The ship's potential for organised trade locates the consumption and circulation of Pindar's era poetry – like Posidippus' – within the framework of seafaring, exchange and value. The image of the ship in both Pindar and Posidippus underscores now the connections between travel and song and the notion of travelling song texts. Likewise, Posidippus' promise to Doricha that Naucratis will preserve her name as long *as ship sails from Nile across the salt sea* (implying forever) updates Theognis' promise of immortality to Cyrnus that "for all who care about [the gifts of the Muses], even for future generations, you will be alike the subject of song, *as long as earth and sun exist*". Posidippus' promise articulates a notion of preservation that is exclusively associated with the perspective of book-conscious Hellenistic Egypt at every level.

To conclude, while our poems are realistically and literally linked to the international world to which they belong and the reality of sea communication and long-range movement in their emphasis on sea travel, they also set sea journey as a framework for locating the Hellenistic poets' own accomplishments. Objects easily survive the sea to articulate a movement from "over there" to "over here," which links home with literary models abroad signalling the lyric genre and specific authors. A mental map of the literary past is thus superimposed, albeit without exhibiting 'path dependence' across the successful transitions.

---

36   Hubbard 2004, 89.

References

Acosta-Hughes, B., 2010. *Arion's Lyre. Archaic Lyric into Hellenistic Poetry*. Princeton and Oxford: Princeton University Press.

Adkins, A.W.H., 1985. *Poetic Craft in the Early Greek Elegists*. Chicago and London: The University of Chicago Press.

Austin, C. and Bastianini, G., 2002. *Posidippi Pellaei quae supersunt omnia*. Milan: LED Edizioni Universitarie.

Bernadette, S., 1993. The Poet-Merchant and the Stranger From the Sea. *In*: S. Vryonis, ed. *The Greeks and the Sea*. New York: Aristide D. Caratzas, 59-65.

Bing, P., 2005. The Politics and Poetics of Geography in the Milan Posidippus, Section One: On Stones (AB 1-20). *In*: K. Gutzwiller, ed. *The New Posidippus. A Hellenistic Poetry Book*. Oxford: Oxford University Press, 119-140.

Bowman, L., 1998. Nossis, Sappho and Hellenistic Poetry. *Ramus*, 27, 39-59.

Buxton, R., 1994. *Imaginary Greece: The Contexts of Mythology*. Cambridge: Cambridge University Press.

Calame, C., 2012. Metaphorical Travel and Ritual Performance in Epinician Poetry. *In*: P. Agócs, C. Carey and R. Rawles, eds. *Reading the Victory Ode*. Cambridge: Cambridge University Press, 303-320.

Curtis, L., 2017. Becoming the Lyre: Arion and Roman Elegy. *Arethusa*, 50, 283-310.

Depew, M., 1992. ἰαμβεῖον καλεῖται νῦν: Genre, Occasion, and Imitation in Callimachus, frr. 191 and 203Pf. *TAPA*, 122, 313-330.

Dougherty, C., 2001. *The Raft of Odysseus*. New York: Oxford University Press.

Fantuzzi, M., 2004. Sugli epp. 37 e 74 Austin-Bastianini del "P. Mil. Vogl." VIII 309. *ZPE*, 146, 31-35.

Fantuzzi, M. and Hunter, R., 2004. *Tradition and Innovation in Hellenistic Poetry*. Cambridge: Cambridge University Press.

Gentili, B., 1988. *Poetry and Its Public in Ancient Greece*. Trans. Th. Cole. Baltimore: The Johns Hopkins University Press.

Goldhill, S., 1991. *The Poet's Voice*. Cambridge: Cambridge University Press.

Gribble, D., 2016. Getting Ready to Pray: Sappho's New 'Brothers' Song. *G&R*, 63, 29-68.

Gutzwiller, K., 1998. *Poetic Garlands. Hellenistic Epigrams in Context*. Berkeley and Los Angeles: University of California Press.

Hooker, J.T., 1989. Arion and the Dolphin. *G&R*, 36, 141-146.

Hopkinson, N., 1988. *A Hellenistic Anthology*. Cambridge: Cambridge University Press.

Hubbard, T.K., 2004. The Dissemination of Epinician Lyric: Pan-Hellenism, Reperformance, Written Texts. *In*: C.J. Mackie, ed. *Oral Performance and Its Context*. Leiden: Brill, 71-94.

Hunter, R.L., 1997. Callimachus' Iambic Program. *PCPhS*, 43, 41-52.

Kivilo, M., 2010. *Early Greek Poets' Lives: The Shaping of the Tradition*. Leiden: Brill.

Krevans, N., 1983. Geography and the Literary Tradition in Theocritus 7. *TAPA*, 113, 201-220.

Lefkowitz, M.R., 2012. *The Lives of the Greek Poets*. London: Bristol Classical Press.

Lesky, A., 1974. *Thalatta: Der Weg der Griechen zum Meer*. Wien: Rudolf M. Rohrer Verlag.

Lidov, J.B., 2002. Sappho, Herodotus, and the Hetaira. *CP*, 97, 203-37.

Lindenlauf, A., 2004. The Sea as a Place of No Return in Ancient Greece. *World Archaeology*, 35, 416-433.

Marcovich, M., 1979. Phanocles AP. Stob. 4.20.47. *AJP*, 100, 360-366.

Martin, R.P., 2016. Sappho, Iambist: Abusing the Brother. *In*: A. Bierl and A. Lardinois, eds. *The Newest Sappho: P. Sapph Obbink and P. GC inv. 105, frs. 1-4*. Leiden: Brill, 110-126.

Noussia-Fantuzzi, M., 2010. *Solon the Athenian. The Poetic Fragments.* Leiden and Boston: Brill.

Nünlist, R., 1998. *Poetologische Bildersprache in der frühgriechischen Dichtung.* Stuttgart: B.G. Teubner Verlag.

Péron, J., 1974. *Les images maritimes de Pindare.* Paris: Éditions Klincksieck.

Puelma, M., 2006. Arions Delphin und die Nachtigall: Kommentar zu Poseidippos ep. 37 A.-B. (= P. Mil. Vogl. VII 309, Kol. VI 18-25). *ZPE*, 156, 60-74.

Reden, S. von, 1995. *Exchange in Ancient Greece.* London: Duckworth.

Robert, L., 1960. Sur un decret des Koresiens au musee de Smyrne. *Hellenica*, 11-12, 132-76.

Rosen, R.M., 1990. Poetry and Sailing in Hesiod's Works and Days. *CA*, 9, 99-113.

Rosenmeyer, P., 2014. Poetic Cargo: Intertextuality in Meleager's Message to Phanion (*AP* 12.53). *Arethusa*, 47, 321-338.

Selden, D.L., 1998. Alibis. *CA*, 17, 289-412.

Simon, E., 1959. *Die Geburt der Aphrodite.* Berlin: De Gruyter.

Skinner, M.B., 1989. Sapphic Nossis. *Arethusa*, 22, 5-18.

Slater, W.J., 1969. *Lexicon to Pindar.* Berlin: De Gruyter.

Steiner, D.S., 2005. Nautical matters: Hesiod's 'Nautilia' and Ibycus fragment 282 PMG. *CP*, 100, 347-355.

Steiner, D.S., 2007. Galloping (or Lame) Consumption: Callimachus' Iamb 13.58-66 and Traditional Representations of the Practice of Abuse. *MD*, 58, 13-42.

Stevens, S., 2004. "For you, Arsinoe…" *In*: B. Acosta-Hughes, E. Kosmetatou and M. Baumbach, eds. *Labored in Papyrus Leaves: Perspectives on an Epigram Collection attributed to Posidippus (P. Mil. Vogl. VIII309).* Cambridge, MA: Center for Hellenic Studies, 161-176.

Sutton, D.F., 1989. *Dithyrambographi Graeci.* Hildesheim: Weidmann.

Tarán, S.L., 1979. *The Art of Variation in the Hellenistic Epigram.* Leiden: Brill.

Voigt, E.M., 1971. *Sappho et Alcaeus fragmenta.* Amsterdam: Polak & van Gennep.

Vryonis, S., ed., 1993. *The Greeks and the Sea.* New York: Aristide D. Caratzas.

West, M.L., 1972. *Iambi et Elegi Graeci ante Alexandrum Cantati. 2. Vol.* Oxford: Clarendon Press.

Yatromanolakis, D., 2007. *Sappho in the Making: The Early Reception.* Washington, D.C.: Center for Hellenic Studies.

Chalcidic connectivity between Sithonia and Pallene: Transmutations of epichoric identity and resilience in the long 5th and 4th *c.* BCE

Maria G. Xanthou

Abstract

The paper examines the potential link between two ancient Graeco-Roman resilient cities, Olynthus and Potidaea. The study focuses on the impact of natural catastrophes and violence on their societies. Both cities suffered great losses or disappeared as a result of destruction but also gained the advantage of revival. My purpose is to investigate the capacity of Olynthus and Potidaea in exhibiting diverse patterns of resilience while enduring war, hunger, and seaquake. Since their foundation, the urban clusters of Olynthus and Potidaea had occupied significant geographical locations with Potidaea being located on the Isthmus of Pallene and Olynthus in the hinterland of the Chalcidica peninsula with access to the gulf of Torone. My critical analysis focuses on the symbiotic relation enjoyed by the two cities since the Peloponnesian War. We will examine Olynthus's manifold capacity to endure the elimination of its original population (Hdt. 8.127) and become the epicentre of the Chalcidic League (Thuc. 1.58.2). Olynthus benefitted from resettlement by inhabitants from the coastal cities, resulting in its enlargement and a federation transcending ethnic and epichoric barriers. Despite the dissolution of the league (Xen. Hell. 5.2.1ff.), the city of Olynthus managed to re-emerge. It allied with Philip II, eventually gaining Potidaea. The latter – although founded as a Corinthian colony – became a member of the Athenian League after a two-year siege and its capitulation in 430/429 BCE. The town was resettled, serving as a major focal point for the Athenians during the Peloponnesian War (Thuc. 1.56-65; 2.31.2; 2.31.58; 2.31.67; 2.31.70; 2.31.79; 4.7; 4.120f.; 129.3; 135.1; Syll.374f.). In the post-war era, Potidaea was returned to its former inhabitants, became a member of the Chalcidic League, and a base for Spartans in their war with Olynthus. Later, the non-Athenian inhabitants were enslaved by Philip and the city rendered to the Olynthians. After its utter destruction, Olynthus and the region formed the polis territory of the new foundation of Cassandra. The paper concludes with a critical analysis offering at least a partial understanding of the dynamics of the city-citizen interaction especially in the 4th and 3rd *c.* BCE.

Chalcidica peninsula, dialectic resilience, resources management, regional interaction, natural vs. man-made catastrophes

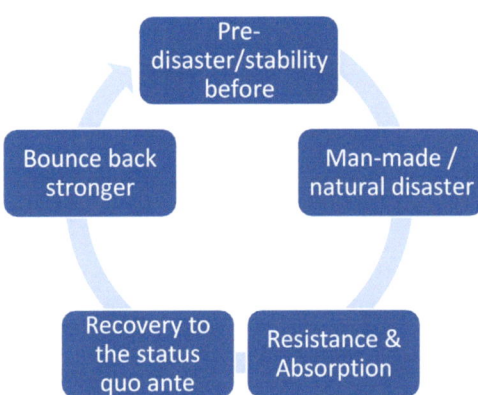

Olynthus and Potidaea: two resilient cities (?)

- Proximity to the sea
- Resources (mines)
- Governance
- Fortification
- Interactions / Regional alliances

Figure 1. Stages of Resilience Cycle.

Introduction: a holistic approach to resilience

Resilience is nowadays considered a key concept to human well-being and safety. It is multifaceted and includes every aspect of human culture. In order to be deemed effective, resilience should be underpinned by the synergy of society, infrastructure, and environment of a specific area.[1] Moreover, resilience results from an embedded feeling of safety built across society during times of stability and, in general, it is based on a cycle including the following stages: stability before, absorption and resistance that follow during disasters, and recovery as the final stage after disasters.[2]

This pattern may not fully apply to ancient societies. However, the need for securing sustainability and stability created the need for forecast, foreknowledge, and reflection. In this sense, ancient societies would learn from disasters and move the location of their urban development to safer areas allowing societies to exist symbiotically with the environment.[3]

My choice to discuss Olynthus and Potidaea was prompted by the challenge to investigate the resilient, symbiotic relation of these cities. The relation was forged by a number of factors such as subsistence and sustainability, patterns of population policies such as *anoikismos* or *synoikismos*, and the creation of a common but distinct epichoric identity.

Location of Olynthus and Potidaea

The ancient city of Olynthus[4] lies on two elongated hills situated in a valley at the neck of Toronaeus Gulf between Pallene and Sithonia, the western and central prongs of the Chalcidic peninsula in northern Greece, about 2.5 kilometres inland from the sea. To the north, the Polygyros mountain range rises to some 1,000 m.

---

1   Pitrėnaitė-Žilėnienė and Torresi 2014, 1.
2   Pitrėnaitė-Žilėnienė and Torresi, 2014, 10.
3   Shondell Miller and Rivera 2011, xxxv-li.
4   For an updated appreciation of Olynthus as an urban cluster see Nevet *et al.* 2017, 155-206.

Figure 2. Sinus Toronaeus (Τορωναῖος κόλπος) aka Toronaeus Gulf, Chalcidica Peninsula, Greece (west to east: left to right side; south to north: upper to lower side of the image. © Image data: SIO, NOAA, U.S. Navy, NGA, GEBCO, Landsat/Copernicus, Google, TerraMetrics, Maxar Technologies, CNES/Airbus; © Map data: TerraMetrics).

Figure 3. Sinus Toronaeus (Τορωναῖος κόλπος) aka Toronaeus Gulf, Chalcidica Peninsula, Greece (north-west to south-east: left to right side; south-east to north-west: upper to lower side of the image. © Image data: SIO, NOAA, U.S. Navy, NGA, GEBCO, Landsat/Copernicus, Google, TerraMetrics, Maxar Technologies, CNES/Airbus; © Map data: TerraMetrics).

Figure 4. The archaeological site of Ancient Olynthus facing south-south-east; photo © Dr Maria G. Xanthou, 2018.

Figure 5. Aerial view of modern city of Potidaea. © Image data: SIO, NOAA, U.S. Navy, NGA, GEBCO, Google, TerraMetrics; © Map data: CNES/Airbus, European Space Imaging, Landsat/Copernicus, Maxar Technologies.

Mēkybērna – its harbour – is located eastwards on the northern shoreline of Toronaeus Gulf, in the coastal area near the modern village of Kalyves Polygyrou. It was first mentioned in Hecataeus (*FGrHist* 1 F 120) and in the context of Xerxes' campaign (Hdt. 7.122). Strabo's (7 fr. 29) characterisation of Mēkybērna as *epineion Olynthou* was further validated by an underwater survey, which attested Strabo's view that the settlement functioned as the harbour town of Olynthus.[5]

The city of Potidaea is located about seven miles (60 stadia = 11.2 km) away from Olynthus. Its location was picked up by the Corinthians as too inviting and probably reminiscent of their *mētropolis*. Potidaea holds a key geographical position as it is situated at the very entrance to the peninsula and may be used as a transitional point between the Thermaic Gulf and the Toronaeus Gulf. Its key position between two gulfs and its proximity to the Chalcidic interior prompted much of the trade of the mainland of Greece with the Chalcidic region to pass through Potidaea. The low shore suitable for beaching ships was Potidaea's unique advantage among other cities of Pallene, and shared only with Mēkybērna, Olynthus' *epineion*, thus forging a resilient coexistence. Potidaea most probably possessed an actual harbour, on the east side of the isthmus since it appears more suitable.[6] Finally, there are three important factors, which contributed largely to Potidaea's soon achieved wealth and prominence among other important cities of Chalcidica, and eventually its resilience: a) its friendly relations with Corinth, its mētropolis, b) her favourable location for commerce and trade, and c) the fertility of the surrounding territory.

Sustainability and subsistence in Sithonia and Chalcidic coastline

At this point I would like to comment on sustainability and subsistence in Sithonia and Chalcidic coastline as regards the formation of settlements and urban clusters in the area. Xenophon's (*Hell.* 5.2.16) comment on Olynthian sustainability points towards the factors which supported the choice of the settlement sites:

τί γὰρ δὴ καὶ ἐμποδών, ὅπου ξύλα μὲν ναυπηγήσιμα ἐν αὐτῇ τῇ χώρᾳ ἐστί, χρημάτων δὲ πρόσοδοι ἐκ πολλῶν μὲν λιμένων, ἐκ πολλῶν δ᾽ ἐμπορίων, πολυανθρωπία γε μὴν διὰ τὴν πολυσιτίαν ὑπάρχει;

The country itself possesses ship-timber and has revenues from many ports and many trading-places, and likewise an abundant population on account of the abundance of food?

(a) proximity to the sea for trade facilitation and communication, (b) natural fortification against inland attacks and pirates' raids from the sea, (c) the existence of fertile arable land, and (d) in certain cases, proximity to the mines.[7]

---

5   Papazoglou 1988, 427; Flensted-Jensen 2004, 831; Tiverios 2008, 48-49; Zahrnt, M. 2006a; Zahrnt 2015, 343.

6   Diodorus (12.46.3-4) in relating the Athenian siege of Potidaea in 432-429 BCE, notes that the besieged city successfully resisted the Athenian general Hagnon's attacks from the harbour. This point could be affirmed with certainty if one could accurately date the remains of an ancient embankment discovered at the east end of the canal; Alexander 1963, 18-19.

7   Tsigarida and Xydopoulos 2015, 44; cf. the modern debate on goldmining in Skouries by Eldorado Gold Corporation.

First challenge: A man-made disaster in Olynthus and a natural phenomenon in Potidaea

Artabazus' siege of Olynthus and Potidaea in 479 BCE marked a milestone in the recorded history of the two cities and gave a new momentum towards two diverse patterns of resilience enhancement.

> Hdt. 8.126.3 When the king had marched away past the town and the Persian fleet had taken flight from Salamis, Potidaea had openly revolted from the barbarians and so too had the rest of the people of Pallene.

> Hdt. 8.127 Thereupon Artabazus laid siege to Potidaea, and suspecting that Olynthus too was plotting revolt from the king, he laid siege to it also. This town was held by Bottiaeans who had been driven from the Thermaic gulf by the Macedonians. Having besieged and taken Olynthus, he brought these men to a lake and there cut their throats and delivered their city over to the charge of Critobulus of Torone and the Chalcidian people. It was in this way that the Chalcidians gained possession of Olynthus.

In the case of Olynthus, Artabazus' decision to put to death a large part of its population set in motion a pattern of population substitution, which had a long-term effect on its identity, its cohesion, and ultimately its history. The majority of the population initially comprised Bottiaeans, a local tribe, who – according to Herodotus (8.127 and 7.122) – had been exiled from the Thermaic Gulf by the Macedonians.[8] It is safe to assume that Artabazus did not annihilate the Bottiaean population of Olynthus, as they formed an important element of the citizen body later on, minting their own coinage in parallel with the Chalcidic.[9] After 479 BCE, Artabazus' handing over the settlement to Critobolus of Torone and the Chalcidian people led to an immigration into Olynthus of new settlers from nearby Chalcidic communities, somewhat akin to the influx at the beginning of the Peloponnesian War. This man-made disaster caused the city, already ethnically mixed, to become even more diverse, including Chalcidians, Bottiaeans, and probably remnants of the original, pre-Bottiaean population. The Persian siege of Potidaea had a different outcome, and this in turn led to a different resilience scenario. During the siege of Potidaea, a tsunami occurred, which worked in favour of the besieged population and doomed the Persian infantry, as Herodotus (8.129.1-2) informs us.The disastrous outcome of this unforeseen tsunami contributed to Artabazus' decision to raise the siege and lead the remnants of his troops to Thessaly.[10] Its destructive force had an immediate positive impact on the Potidaeans, who – after a three-month siege – were unexpectedly saved. It was definitely a gain for contemporary Greeks in general in many ways: this event strengthened their self-esteem and their belief in the gods, since they interpreted it as a «miracle of divine vengeance» in response to the sacrilege of the Persians (Herod. 8.129.1). From a political perspective, this was also a further blow against the already-damaged power of the Persians in Greece.[11]

---

8   Sprawski 2010, 139.
9   Gude 1934, 9; Cahill 2002, 34. As Cahill (2002, 29) suggested, Artabazus' siege of Olynthus in 479 BCE points towards an existing fortification of the South Hill of Olynthus at least that early.
10   Alexander 1963, 33.
11   Stefanakis 2006, 8.

Olynthus reloaded: Population diversity and reorganisation of national domain into political power through strategic alliances, adaptability, and agility

Until 432 BCE Olynthus was a relatively small city, entirely negligible for the most part of what may be called Bottiaean period due to its population consistence. After 479 BCE, it gained momentum when the Chalcidians took hold of it, and it rose to prominence after two or three generations of Chalcidians having grown up in it.[12] The uninterrupted payment of the tribute to the First Delian Confederacy points towards a rather uneventful stability in her relations with Athens.[13] It may also suggest that this stability over the *pentēkontaetia* probably contributed towards an amalgamation of the Bottiaean and the Chalcidian element in its population, since many of the Bottiaean country folk may have been left undisturbed in their holdings, and kept up their connections with the new city that grew up on the site of the old.[14] Despite its modest significance due to its small size before the 432 BCE *anoikismos*, Olynthus was chosen as the stronghold of the region during the Peloponnesian War and the centre of the newly-established Chalcidic League due to undoubtedly geographical factors: its central location, distance from the sea, and the availability of a naturally defensible area on which to build.[15] Athens' rude command to the Potidaeans – whose city was only seven miles away from Olynthus – to cut off relations with Corinth, give hostages, and raze her walls towards Pallene, gave the momentum to Potidaeans, the Chalcidians, and the Bottiaeans to form a strategic alliance with Perdiccas II, adapt their defence against the Athenian demands, and exhibit an unprecedented agility towards uniting the resources of the majority of the Chalcidians and turning their national domain into political power.[16]

Potidaea in 429 BCE: A change of population and a *nostos*

A significant consequence of Potidaea's capitulation in 429 BCE after the two-year Athenian siege was the change of its population. The inhabitants who were descendants of the Corinthian settlers took refuge to other places across Chalcidica. The Athenians resettled the city by sending a number of their own citizens known as *epoikoi* to colonise it.[17] However, the Athenian occupation of Potidaea lasted until the end of the Peloponnesian War. Soon after the Spartan victory at Aegospotami in 405 BCE another switch of population took place: the old inhabitants or their survivors were repatriated, while the Athenian *epoikoi* in Potidaea left for Athens in the aftermath of the humiliating defeat of their *metropolis*.[18] Although the Potidaeans joined the Chalcidic League shortly before 382 BCE, they switched their affiliation

---

12   Gude 1934, 6; Cahill 2002, 35.
13   Gude 1934, 9.
14   Doubtless many of those who were driven out of the city proper drifted back in time. Those members of the "Chalcidic tribe" who came to cultivate their new holdings must have had to reckon with an appreciable Bottiaean element; Gude 1934, 10.
15   Cahill 2002, 35.
16   Gude 1934, 10-11; Tiverios 2008, 49-50.
17   Alexander 1963, 75. According to Diodorus Siculus, the number of settlers was 1000 and both the city and the land were divided into lots; Alexander 1963, 77. This new type of Athenian settlement bore some special characteristics of its own, resulting from unusual political or military circumstances relative to its establishment, and it was eventually used as a strong base of operations against the Chalcidic cities.
18   Alexander 1963, 81.

and voluntarily went over to the Spartan side as soon as the Spartan general Eudamidas reached Pallene. Henceforth, their city was used by Spartans as a base in their war with Olynthus.[19] Their goal was to check the growing power of Olynthus and the Chalcidic League.[20] After several battles and a close siege of Olynthus, the Spartans and the Olynthians concluded peace and an alliance was forged between Sparta and the Chalcidians in 379 BCE. It is notable that during this time Potidaea's status as ally of Sparta was retained as long as Spartan supremacy in Chalcidica was recognised. After the revival of Athenian sea-power, Spartans lost control of the Chalcidic peninsula, and Olynthus began to act independently of Sparta by trying to regain many of the former members and allies of the Chalcidic League. At the time of Timotheus' campaigns in Chalcidica (364-362 BCE), Potidaea was already an ally of the league.[21]

In the spring of 362 BCE, after Timotheus' capture of Potidaea with the assistance of Perdiccas III of Macedon (364/3 BCE), the Potidaeans requested from Athens to have cleruchs sent to their city. It is notable that Potidaea was the only city of the area which came under the influence of Athens to receive willingly cleruchs in 362/1 BCE. The reason for this open acknowledgement of affiliation may be found in the desire on the part of the Potidaeans to establish better relations with Athens and thus receive certain concessions. In addition, the presence of Athenian cleruchs would strengthen their position against attacks of the Chalcidic League into their territory.[22] Their cordial relations with the Athenian cleruchs prompted the Athenians at home to pass a decree (361/0 BCE) honouring the Potidaeans for their friendly attitude. In 356 BCE Philip II marched against Potidaea with the help of the Chalcidians and he captured the city after siege. Before the siege, an alliance between Philip and the Olynthians was concluded, which gave Anthemus to the Olynthians, its old claimants. Unfortunately, Athenian aid arrived too late to save Potidaea, and the Athenian cleruchs were deprived of their possessions and sent to Athens. Demosthenes mentions that the land of the Potidaeans was given to the Olynthians. Thus far, Philip kept his promise to the Olynthians and at the same time succeeded in depriving Athens of her last stronghold in Chalcidica.[23] A possible explanation for the non-destruction of Potidaea may lie in Diodorus' account of the siege of the city, where we learn that after capturing the city, Philip sent the Athenian garrison to Athens and delivered the enslaved city and its outlying possessions to the Olynthians as a gift. In this sense, he might have been able to use the *epoikoi* and the city as a leverage for his foreign policy towards Athens and Chalcidians. However, in the case of Olynthus, Philip's destruction of the city indicates his commitment towards curbing decisively the Athenian influence on Chalcidica peninsula after the conclusion of peace between Olynthus and Athens in contravention of their agreement with Philip (Dem. *Or.* 3.7; 23.10f.).[24] Those Olynthians who survived the destruction of their city became part of Cassandreia, the outcome of a peculiar *synoecism* founded by the Macedonian king Cassander, who united the cities of the peninsula, Potidaea, and many neighbouring towns and settled there "those of the Olynthians who survived, not few in number."[25]

19 Xen. *Hell.* 5.2.24; 39; 3.6; Zahrnt, M. 2006b.
20 Alexander 1963, 84.
21 Alexander 1963, 85.
22 Alexander 1963, 87.
23 Alexander 1963, 88-89; Zahrnt 2015, 352-354.
24 Zahrnt 2015, 357.
25 Alexander 1963, 90; for Cassandreia as a city under Macedon and then as a Roman colony see Samsaris 1987, 353-437.

Conclusions

The cities of Potidaea and Olynthus provide different but complementary patterns of resilience. They had unique characteristics in terms of geographical location, proximity, surroundings, and resources. Potidaea was a city situated in a key position between two gulfs of Thermaic and Toronaeus, and in a fertile land to secure its subsistence. Based on two hills, Olynthus provides an excellent example of a city situated remotely from the sea, thus being secured from pirates. Potidaea grew out as a Corinthian *apoikia*, which eventually integrated Athenians and inhabitants from different cities. It experienced a change of population and a homecoming (*nostos*) of its old inhabitants. Olynthus acted as a Chalcidic melting pot. Initially a small Bottiaean city, Olynthus headed the attempt for a union of Bottiaeans and local Chalcidic inhabitants. Its population was eventually enriched by Potidaeans who took refuge there after the peace treaty with Athens in 429 BCE.

Although resilience is often associated with continuity, the case of Potidaea and Olynthus challenge this in quite different ways. If there is one feature that Potidaea's resilience is to be associated with, it is adaptability. The close relation between Potidaea and Corinth that entailed the parent city's support of the *apoikia* possibly contributed – at an initial stage – to its enhanced resilience. In this sense, Potidaea's political resilience relied on its adaptive affiliation to Corinth, Athens, or Sparta. Although they tried to be consistent with their affiliation to their parent city, this did not deter the Potidaeans from inviting Athens to send them Athenian *epoikoi*, who were later used by Philip II in his foreign policy towards Athens. Other factors that enhanced the safety factor included its strong fortification, its government, religious

Figure 6. The archaeological site of Ancient Olynthus with New Olynthus village in the background; photo © Dr. Maria G. Xanthou, 2018.

institutions, and financial sustainability. However, the Potidaeans did not rely exclusively on natural resources and geographical assets to secure the sustainability of their city. Their sense of flexibility in foreign policy and the mixed population of their city probably helped them to survive Athens' attack. After Philip's II conquest in 356 BCE, the city emerged anew through Cassander's foundation of an enlarged and extended *synoecism* including inhabitants of the former cities of Potidaea, Olynthus, the towns of Pallene and the region to the north of the isthmus.

Olynthus as a city gained its significance and its new identity through the *anoikismos* of 432 BCE. Its population gave the city a unique epichoric identity as it comprised Thracian Chalcidians (Sithōnes), Bottiaeans, who were expelled by Macedonians, or Potidaeans who took refuge to the city after the peace treaty with Athens in 429 BCE. The relocations instigated by Perdikkas II and the fear of imminent Athenian attacks across the Chalcidic coastline almost tripled the population of Olynthus. However, one significant impact of the Peace of Nicias (421 BCE) was the cancellation of the 432 BCE *anoikismos*: not only did the Athenians not acknowledge the Chalcidic state, but they also broke it down into its original parts.[26] In the 4th *c.* BCE the Chalcidic League was founded and dissolved twice. The second dissolution was fatal as it was marked by the destruction of Olynthus, which remained uninhabited after its destruction. Despite being "shortlived, violently destroyed, and extensively excavated," Olynthus offers a record of household assemblages and activities unique in the Greek world.[27] Despite being violently discontinued through historical times, Olynthus' resilience is to be reappreciated. Although the city ceased to exist as such, the quality of its archaeological remains are among the best preserved of any Greek *polis*.[28] Rephrasing Nicholas Cahill,[29] we would add that our interpretation of Olynthus' resilience should go beyond the *anoikismos* and the destruction and be reframed within the overall resilience of these remains and the surrounding environment, the arable land, and their interaction with the new inhabitants of Myriophyto village, who were refugees from the Ottoman Empire in 1922 and were recruited by David Moore Robinson for the Olynthus excavations.

References

Alexander, J., 1963. *Potidaea: Its History and Remains.* Athens, GA: University of Georgia Press.

Cahill, N., 2000. Olynthus and Greek Town Planning. *CW*, 93 (5), 497-515.

Cahill, N., 2002. *Household and City Organization at Olynthus.* New Haven and London: Yale University Press.

Flensted-Jensen, P., 2004. Thrace from Axios to Strymon. *In*: M.H. Hansen and T.H. Nielsen, eds. *An Inventory of Archaic and Classical Poleis.* Oxford: Oxford University Press, 810-53.

Gude, M., 1934. *A History of Olynthus, with Prosopographia and Testimonia.* Oxford University Press.

Larsen, J.A.O., 1968. *Greek Federal States: Their Institutions and History.* Oxford: Clarendon Press.

Mylonas, G.E. 1943. Excavations at Mecyberna 1934, 1938. *AJA*, 47 (1), 78-87.

Nevett, L.C., Tsigarida, E.B., Archibald, Z.H., Stone, D.L., Horsley, T.J., Ault, B.A., Panti, A., Lynch, K.M., Pethen, H., Stallibrass, S.M., Salminen, E., Gaffney, C., Sparrow, T.J., Taylor, S., Manousakis, J. and Zekkos, D., 2017. Towards a Multi-scalar,

---

26 Larsen 1968, 70-71; Zahrnt 1971, 66-72; Zahrnt 2006c, 602-604; Zahrnt 2015, 348.
27 Cahill 2000, 498.
28 Cahill 2000, 499.
29 Cahill 2002, 25.

Multidisciplinary Approach to the Classical Greek City: The Olynthos Project. *ABSA*, 112, 155-206.

Papazoglou, F., 1988. *Les villes de Macedoine à l'époque romaine.* Athènes: Ecole française d'Athènes; Paris: Diffusion de Boccard.

Pitrėnaitė-Žilėnienė, B. and Torresi, F., 2014. Integrated Approach to a Resilient City: Associating Social, Environmental and Infrastructure Resilience in its Whole. *European Journal of Interdisciplinary Studies*, 6 (2), 1-13.

Samsaris D.C., 1987. La Colonie Romaine de Cassandréa en Macédoine (Colonia Iulia Augusta Cassandrensis). *Dodona ["Δωδώνη"]*, 16, 353-437.

Shondell Miller, D., and Rivera, J.D., 2011. Introduction: The Unique Opportunities and Challenges from a Social and Scientific Perspective. *In*: D. Shondell Miller and J.D. Rivera, eds. *Community disaster recovery and resiliency: exploring global challenges*. Boca Raton: CRC Press, 35-51.

Sprawski, S., 2010. The Early Temenid kings to Alexander I. *In*: J. Roisman and I. Worthington, eds. *A Companion to Ancient Macedonia*, Chichester: Wiley-Blackwell, 127-44.

Stefanakis, M.I., 2006. Natural Catastrophes in the Greek and Roman World: Loss or Gain? Four Cases of Seaquake-Generated Tsunamis. *Mediterranean Archaeology and Archaeometry*, 6 (2), 5-22.

Tiverios, M., 2008. Greek Colonisation of the Northern Aegean. *In*: G.R. Tsetskhladze, ed. *Greek Colonisation: An Account of Greek Colonies and Other Settlements Overseas. Vol. 2*. Leiden: Brill, 1-154.

Tsigarida. E. and Xydopoulos, I., 2015. Halkidiki: Landscape, Archaeology, and Ethnicity. *In*: B.C. Gounaris, ed. *Mines, Olives and Monasteries: Aspects of Halkidiki's Environmental History*. Thessaloniki: Epikentro Publishers S.A., 35-69.

Zahrnt, M., 1971. *Olynth und die Chalkidier: Untersuchungen zur Stadtbildung auf der Chalkidischen Halbinsel im 5. und 4. Jahrhundert v. Chr.* München: Beck'sche Verlagbuchhandlung.

Zahrnt, M., 2006a. Mecyberna. *In*: H. Cancik, H. Schneider and M. Landfester, eds.) *Brill's New Pauly*. [online] Available from: doi:10.1163/1574-9347_bnp_e729880

Zahrnt, M., 2006b. Potidaea. *In:* H. Cancik, H. Schneider and M. Landfester, eds. *Brill's New Pauly.* [online] *Available from:* doi:10.1163/1574-9347_bnp_e1006720

Zahrnt M., 2006c. Macedonia and Thrace in Thucydides. *In*: A. Rengakos and A. Tsakmakis, eds. *Brill's Companion to Thucydides*. Boston: Brill, 589-614.

Zahrnt, M., 2015. The Chalkidike and the Chalkidians. *In:* H. Beck and P. Funke, eds. *Federalism in Greek Antiquity*. Cambridge: Cambridge University Press, 341-357.

The importance of geography to the networked Late Bronze Age Aegean

Paula Gheorghiade, Henry Price, Ray Rivers

Abstract

Maritime trade and interaction in the Late Bronze Age Mediterranean have been studied from a range of perspectives primarily focusing on reconstructing sailing itineraries from recovered shipwrecks or rediscovering harbours that may have served as the origin or destination for these voyages. This visual presentation of routes provides little interpretive value for assessing how and why certain settlements interacted, and how this interaction accords with the archaeological data. In this paper we consider one method for approaching interaction at this macro Mediterranean scale to ask the question: do coastal communities arise or flourish as a result of their geographical positioning, advantageous with respect to sea paths? In answering this question, we rely on two types of data: 1) material ceramic evidence from five sites on Crete; and 2) spatial data points of known sites or regions occupied during this period. With this two-pronged approach, we consider how the 'geography' or maritime space of the eastern Mediterranean – as seen from Crete – has expedited exchange within it. Our analysis combines a distance-limiting null model with centrality measures in discussing how select sites on Crete benefit from their geographical positions on the island when direct travel or cabotage are considered.

Late Bronze Age, Crete, network modelling, mobility, prehistoric trade

Introduction

During the Late Bronze Age (LBA), the Mediterranean Sea was central for communication, trade, and the mobility of people and things, to the extent that it could be considered "a peninsula in reverse" (Horden and Purcell 2000, 11). Maritime interaction served to link island communities to the larger surrounding landmasses. In the LBA, the extent of this long-distance connectivity has been strikingly displayed by the Uluburun and Cape Gelidonya shipwrecks (Bass 1991; Pulak 1998). The rapid expansion of connectivity in this period is also exemplified

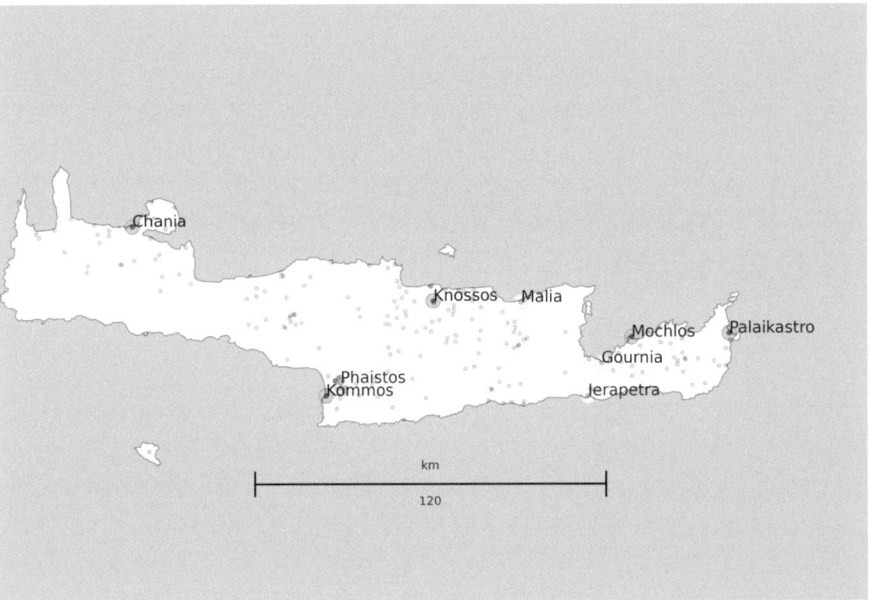

Figure 1. Map of the locations of the nine Cretan sites discussed in this paper. The five deposition sites are marked with black circles, the remaining four with open circles. The unlabelled sites are archaeologically identified settlements dated to the LM II-IIIB2 period, the source of inland Cretan-regional imports to our deposition sites. Map by Henry Price.

by finds recovered archaeologically, particularly high value goods catalogued from sites across the Mediterranean basin over the last 30 years (*e.g.* Cline 1994; Lambrou-Phillipson 1990; Phillips 2008) which indicate widespread connections between Crete, the Levantine coast, Egypt and even Italy and Sardinia.

Interaction in this period has been studied with a focus on identifying harbours, reconstructing maritime trade routes and – in the case of shipwrecks – attempting to ascertain the origin and possible destination of the intended cargo. However, the visual presentation of ship routes alone provides little interpretive power for assessing how and why certain settlements might have interacted, and how this interaction accords (if at all) with the recovered archaeological data.

In this paper, we consider one method for approaching interaction at this macro, Mediterranean scale. We focus on LBA interaction and exchange particularly on Crete during the Late Minoan (LM) II-IIIB2 ceramic phases (equivalent to Late Helladic (LH) IIA-IIIB on mainland Greece). We rely on two types of data: 1) excavated ceramic imports collected from the Cretan sites of Mochlos, Chania, Knossos, Palaikastro, and Kommos (see Fig. 1); and 2) an additional collection of 91 spatial data points for sites or regions occupied during this period across the Mediterranean at which import evidence has been recorded. Four additional sites for Crete round out the spatial data for the island and are also included in this count: Gournia, Ierapetra[1], Malia, and Phaistos.

With this two-pronged approach we are interested in exploring how the 'geography' or maritime space of the eastern Mediterranean, as seen from Crete, has expedited exchange within it, by also taking into account the state of maritime technology and seafaring skills at this time. Can we identify broad patterns within the data which enable us to embed it in an East Mediterranean social and cultural context? How does this accord with a changing regional 'identity'? Although our goals are less ambitious, our work is very much in the spirit of the questions posed by Tartaron in his influential book on the Mycenaean world:

"Did environmental forces play a determining role in coastal settlement patterns, and even in maritime social relations? That is, did coastal communities arise or flourish because they were positioned advantageously with respect to sea paths

---

1   The location of this site is hypothetical and has yet to be confirmed archaeologically. See Chalikias 2009.

favoured by environmental forces such as winds and currents? Further, were their external relations patterned, or even determined, by movement along these favourable routes? If so, it should be possible to create a simple predictive model for the existence of significant Bronze Age coastal settlements at well-placed nodes along these routes."

T. E. Tartaron (2013, 114)

Historical background

Our paper focuses on a 250-year period (1450-1200 BCE) during which the island of Crete underwent cultural and political changes. In the aftermath of the earlier LM IB disruptions that swept the island destroying all other palatial centres, only the palace at Knossos was rebuilt. It remained the only palatial centre until its final destruction at the end of LM IIIA2. It has been argued that the new elites in power at Knossos during this period were 'Mycenaean' in origin (Tartaron 2013, 20-21), in part due to the introduction and dissemination of a mainland Greek cultural package that included new kinds of drinking vessels, burial customs, and architectural elements (*cf.* Preston 2004; 2008).

Despite this novelty, much of the Cretan material retains a 'Minoan' character, highlighting a continuity with earlier traditions, especially in ceramic production. Driessen and Langohr (2007) have suggested that Knossian elites used the local 'Minoan' past as a strategy to consolidate and legitimise power during the LM II-IIIA2 period, even if this cultural package was invariably incorporated by sites across the island. An in-depth examination of the local ceramic assemblage highlights these various connections and mobilities that are missed when only long-distance imports are considered (Gheorghiade 2020). The incorporation of new mainland Greek ceramic shapes and styles with otherwise local 'Minoan' traditions suggests the emergence of a new Cretan identity in this period (Gheorghiade 2021). Our ceramic dataset, therefore, includes both local Minoan-style ceramics and mainland Greek or Mycenaean-style pottery, seen both in imports and locally made examples.

Imports from the wider Mediterranean, such as those from the Near East and Egypt, remain heavily biased towards Crete, where they are primarily found at Kommos in LM IIIA1 (Gheorghiade 2020, 151-152; Cline 1994, 92; 2007). Tartaron (2003, 21) has noted that mainland Greek polities were not particularly active in the Aegean or eastern Mediterranean in the earlier LH I – II period, most likely due to the Minoan control of sea routes (Mee 2008, 381). By LH IIIA/LM IIIA1 the broadening of Mycenaean overseas contact into the Aegean has been argued to have resulted from an incorporation of previously Minoan maritime trade routes to the east (*e.g.* Hägg and Marinatos 1984; Niemeier 2009; Wiener 2013). The continuation of long-distance connections in this period demonstrates the robustness of economic relations between cultures in the larger Mediterranean basin despite political changes and social disruptions (Horden and Purcell 2000, 343-44). Mainland Greek ceramics begin to be exported in larger quantities across the Aegean, the larger eastern Mediterranean and to Crete, and we contend that the long-distance networks through which these travelled owe much to earlier, Neopalatial foundations.

Interestingly, towards the end of our study period (LM/LH IIIB – IIIC) the nature of long-distance Cretan contact changes, with the island increasingly connected to the west; Kommos, for example, shows strong links with Sardinia. Sardinian imports are especially prominent in LM IIIB and quite well represented in House X at Kommos (Rutter 2017). Shapes include both open and closed handmade vessels in medium coarse and coarse fabrics (Gheorghiade 2020). In contrast to Italian examples found in other parts of the island, such as at Chania, the Sardinian ceramics at Kommos are represented by shapes that differ from mainland Italian examples (Rutter and Van de Moortel 2006, 677).

In this paper we are primarily concerned with the relatively rare extra-Cretan imports which reflect this shifting pattern. There is the inevitable problem that our data also exclude information on the movement and exchange of perishable extra-Cretan goods such as textiles, foodstuffs, and people, which may have been more common and important than our surviving ceramic evidence suggests. If this archaeological record is only the remaining trace of what was once a significant volume of exchange, it would suggest a degree of independent trade. On the other extreme, limited exchange for which the visible record is a good proxy is best explained in large part in terms of elite gift exchange unconnected to markets or private traders (see Tartaron 2013, 21-27 for a discussion of these extremes). A well-organised and regulated mercantile exchange network over substantial distances that included middlemen and a sophisticated framework for contracts had already been established in Assyria and elsewhere by the Middle Bronze Age (MBA), persisting in the Near East until the 12th century (*e.g.* Barjamovic *et al.* 2017). Consequently, we assume a large mercantile component to our extra-Cretan ceramic exchange. Although no written records describing mercantile activity exists from this period on Crete, the presence of such behaviour is suggested by the nature of some of the imports, particularly closed vessels such as stirrup jars for transporting foodstuffs such as oil, wine, or perfume (Pratt 2016).

The material and spatial data

The ceramic data were collected into a relational database by one of us (PG) from published excavation catalogues. In a familiar pattern for large archaeological data sets our Cretan data are not 'big data', but 'lots of data.' By this we mean that the data includes too much detail to codify simply, but on the other hand there is too little detail for reliable statistics. As such, unless we are careful it falls between permitting inductive (data) modelling and deductive (theory) modelling. The spatial data were collected for two different regions. In addition to the five main Cretan sites from which published ceramic data were included in the database, an additional 91 sites were collected from published excavations and survey reports that also identified ceramics from this period (Kanta 1985; Langohr 2009; Murray 2017). We have no information in our dataset on exports *from* Crete or information on exchange relationships between all other sites that do not involve our five Cretan deposition sites. The underlying assumption behind the collection and inclusion of these sites is that even though we cannot discern *how* certain imports moved, their presence can be taken as a proxy for interaction. These 96 sites, in total (Fig. 2), are for the present paper considered adequate for exploring long-distance interaction in the East Mediterranean using spatial modelling[2]. In this paper, we can do no more than provide an overview of some of the key characteristics of the data and their interpretation. A more extended analysis will be given in a forthcoming paper. As

---

2   These data points, excluding those on Crete itself, are: Akanthou Moulos, Akko, Alalakh, Alexandria, Amman, Anevolema Kalochoraphitis, Apolakkia, Aradippou, Argos, Ashdod, Ashkelon, Athens, Beirut, Beqaa Valley, Bir el-Abd, Cyprus, Dendra, Dhenia Kefalla, El Arish, Emar, Enkomi, Episkopi Bamboula, Gavdos, Gezer, Hattusa, Hazor, Heliopolis, Ialysos, Kamid el-Loz, Karpathos, Kastri, Khalkis, Kilise Tepe, Kition, Kos, Kouklia Matissa, Kythera, Lachish, Lapithos, Larnaka Salt Lake, Liman Tepe, Lipari, Maa Palaeokastro, Malia, Maroni, Marsa Matruh, Masat Huyuk Tapikka, Megiddo, Memphis, Miletus, Minet el-Beida, Muskebi, Mycenae, Myrtou Pighades, Naxos, Nitovikla Korovia, Olympia, Pyla, Pylos, Ras Ibn Hani, Ras Shamra, Rhodes, Riqqeh, Saqqara, Sardinia, Sarepta, Scoglio Del Tonno, Sedment, Serraglio, Sidon, Tarsus, Tell Abu Hawam, Tell Dan, Tell Abu al-Kharaz, Tell Deir Alla, Tell el-Ajjul, Tell es-Saidiyeh, Tell Sukas, Thapsos, Thebes, Tille Huyuk, Tiryns, Toumba tou Skourou, Troy, Tyre, Vourvatsi, Dhekelia, and Tel Kazel.

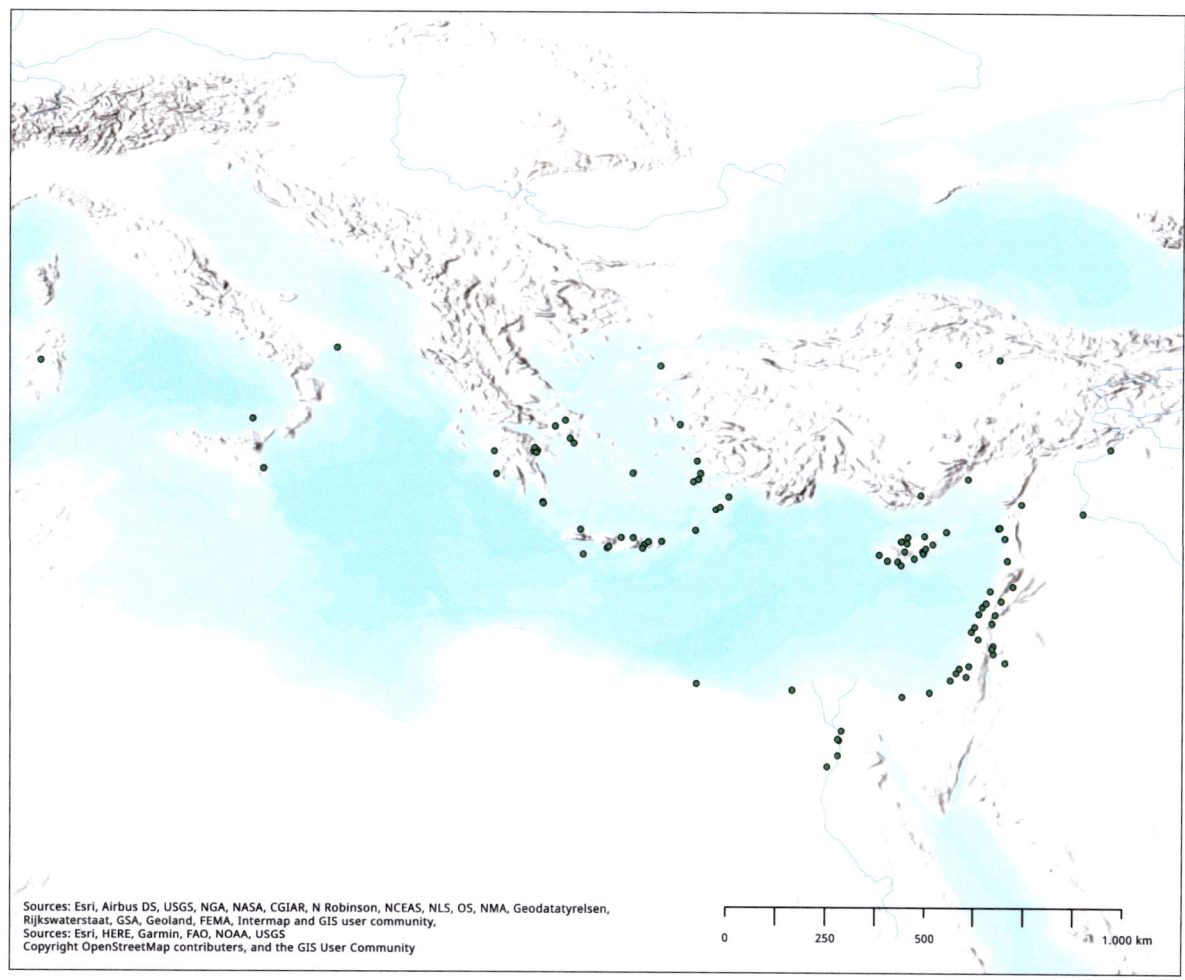

Sources: Esri, Airbus DS, USGS, NGA, NASA, CGIAR, N Robinson, NCEAS, NLS, OS, NMA, Geodatatyrelsen,
Rijkswaterstaat, GSA, Geoland, FEMA, Intermap and GIS user community,
Sources: Esri, HERE, Garmin, FAO, NOAA, USGS
Copyright OpenStreetMap contributers, and the GIS User Community

0   250   500   1.000 km

a first step, we put emphasis on the effective *distance* of artefact origin from our deposition sites in Crete as a filter, both geographical and in terms of ease of access. We define the (effective) distance scales as:

Figure 2. Location of the 96 data points mentioned in this paper. Map by Paula Gheorghiade.

- Cretan-local, with artefacts originating no more than 10 kilometres from their deposition.
- Cretan-regional, with artefacts originating within Crete, between settlements located more than 10 kilometres from deposition, but not exceeding 250 kilometres (the length of the island itself). This includes all nine sites on Crete.
- Extra-Cretan, with artefacts imported to Crete from other East Mediterranean sites. At this scale we consider maritime mobility to be most common, with long-distance interaction exceeding 250 kilometres from deposition.
- These distance scales are reflected in the fractions of artefact import origins of the larger dataset, in which we find (with some time and site dependence):

    - Cretan-local (~ 90%),
    - Cretan-regional (~ 8%),
    - Extra-Cretan (~ 2-4%).

A coarse overview of the ceramic data seems to support Tobler's First Law of geography, that interaction falls off with distance, where the difficulty of physical exchange *e.g.* transit time, is more important than map distance. Here *local* and intra-Cretan *regional* interactions are largely overland whereas *extra-Cretan* (East Mediterranean) imports are, of necessity, obtained through long-distance sea voyages. These definitions provide a simple way to separate the data, although at some level these various scales intersect. In this paper we restrict ourselves to an analysis of extra-Cretan imports. These data are too few to permit realistic statistics given the diversity of their origins. It is for this reason that we combine our ceramic data with spatial modelling.

Methodology

In the absence of reliable quantitative data, we assume exchange networks in which – at the very least – *the ability of sites to connect is a sufficient proxy for exchange to have occurred*. Accordingly, if Mediterranean coastal trading sites can access Crete, they will. This enables us to address generic questions concerning regional influence in the Mediterranean littoral[3] as provided by exemplary artefacts, without the need for quantitative analysis. Our goal is to provide a simple, distance-sensitive, null network model for identifying regional exchange. This model links site importance not only based on access to trading partners, but as a consequence of assumed networking. As with all null models, we have isolated the simplest attributes of the data (*i.e.* whether exchange is present or not) and ignored the rest. This parsimonious approach means that nothing more than the provenance of the artefacts (*i.e.* our spatial data) will be required in the first instance.

We were motivated to adopt this approach by an even simpler *distance-limiting* null model proposed by Bakker *et al.* (2018) on maritime Mediterranean trade, also defined in terms of *accessibility* as a proxy for exchange. In the framework of later Phoenician trading, the basic idea of this earlier paper is that for a Mediterranean coastal trading site, the more extensive the coastline and its littoral accessible to this site, the more significant the site will be. This naturally depends on the distance scales over which exchange can occur which are seen most sensibly to be of the order of a few hundred kilometres, permitting North-South crossing of the Mediterranean with relative ease. For the Mediterranean as a whole, the authors adopt a northerly/southerly differential as well as an east-west differential.[4] However, in the first instance identifying trading partners was not even necessary, on the assumption that more coastline means more trading. The output was checked (successfully) against the Pleiades data set (Bagnell *et al.* 2014).

The situation for our present data is somewhat different in that generally we have some information on the origins of our extra-Cretan imports. For the present paper, this information is reflected as the spatial data points used in our analysis. Insofar as the determining features are geographical, there is very little in their model that is specific to the Phoenician Iron Age that is not equally applicable to our Mycenaean LBA. The questions that we are asking are different, and our emphasis is on particular Cretan sites. This enables us to make a natural extension of their approach by introducing the (unweighted) networks that arise from these assumed linkages, both to Crete and between other Mediterranean sites where Aegean imports have been identified. This allows us to estimate the effective 'line-of-sight' importance of Cretan sites as sources of trade and exchange (*i.e.* what Bakker *et al.* term the 'urbanisation' of the site). We can also estimate the importance of sites as stopping-off points in trade routes incorporating Crete and assess the importance of cabotage. This is something that Bakker *et al.* are unable to address.

---

3   Here we define 'littoral' more in the military sense than in an ecological sense. For example, the UK Ministry of Defence defines the littoral as *those land areas (and their adjacent areas and associated air space) that are susceptible to engagement and influence from the sea,* a definition which therefore includes a significant portion of land as well as water area. This roughly corresponds to Tartaron's definition of 'coastscapes'.

4   Hence the presence of 'mice' in the paper's title since the house mouse is assumed to have travelled from the east to the west Mediterranean as a result of trade.

Modelling

Our approach is two-fold:

- We first identify the distance scales for a functioning maritime exchange network in the eastern Mediterranean that naturally incorporate Crete. In particular, we wish to see how our analysis fits into the multiscale analysis of seascape/small-world/regional maritime interaction spheres as defined by Tartaron (2013) and also explored by Broodbank (2000; 2013).
- Secondly, we assess how select sites on Crete benefit from their geographical positions on the island by considering both direct travel and cabotage. With this we return to the earlier question, to consider whether coastal communities arise or flourish as a result of their geographical positioning, advantageous with respect to sea paths.

In considering long-distance scales for imports to Crete some care is needed. Superficially, we cannot make a simple translation from Iron Age to LBA exchange, because Iron Age trade benefitted from superior maritime technology and navigation. For the LBA period, sailing vessels had rectangular sails stretched between a yard and a boom fixed to the mast (see Tartaron 2013, 53). This gave the crew limited ability to sail into the wind, forcing the ship to be at anchor (or rowed) when the wind was unfavourable. It was only later towards the end of the Bronze Age and early Iron Age (LM IIIC) that this yard-boom system had been replaced by the more flexible brailed rig, making the ship more capable of tacking against the wind (see Tartaron 2013, 53-54; Wachsmann 1988, 251). With this rigging, Phoenician ships could make open-sea voyages across the entire Mediterranean without needing to rely on land visibility for navigation.

For the more limited East Mediterranean journeys envisaged here, open-water long-distance sailing is less of a problem. The most common journeys from Crete, for example north into the Aegean Sea, and west towards the Ionian and Adriatic Seas maintain land visibility and are possible as both open-sea journeys and cabotage. Travelling south to the North African coast and Egypt requires much longer open-sea travel, out of sight of land especially if attempted directly. If the assumed voyage for the vessel of the Uluburun shipwreck is correct, this is but the first leg of an anticlockwise cabotage around the most eastern part of the Mediterranean before returning to the Greek mainland (see Wachsmann 1988, Fig. 13.1, 296; Tartaron 2013, 113).

A key ingredient in the analysis of Bakker *et al.* was the effect of latitude across the Mediterranean. Climatic variation gives a North-South gradient, favouring northern coastal sites. This is counterpoised against the problem that the prevailing winds in the South Aegean are northerly in the sailing season (Fig. 4 in Papageorgiou 2009, 210; Leidwanger 2013) which, although expediting travel to Crete from the Greek mainland, makes travelling back to the mainland relatively difficult with a yard-boom. This has been demonstrated with the vessel *Minoa* (2004) a 'recreation' of an MBA Minoan galley which sailed up the western coasts from Crete to Athens for the 2004 Olympics, with such rigging (Simandiraki 2005). Against even low winds it took many days, often requiring supplementation by oar.

For our null model, we assume a rough cancellation between climatic variation and wind. Our null model is a distance-limited network model in which we link all sites that are not further apart than a maximum geographical distance *S* (attachment scale) when taking headlands into account. Within this mode, special circumstances can be accommodated, as is the case for Kommos located on the south coast of Crete. On the one hand, the mountains of Crete shield the south coast against northern winds. The effect of east-west sea current circulation along the southern coast strongly suggests clockwise motion for ships following the Cretan coast (Papageorgiou 2008). We return to this later in the paper.

Analysis and discussion of distance scales

The threshold *S* is the distance beyond which it becomes more difficult to establish communication. A value in the range of 100-150 kilometres is sufficient to permit Crete to link to the southern Aegean and for the southern Aegean to connect with itself and the Peloponnese and Dodecanese coastlines, albeit with island hopping. The same distance scale enables Cretan sites to connect to each other. As was suggested elsewhere (Knappett *et al.* 2011) it was the coincidence of this 100+ kilometres distance scale for South Aegean connectivity – a distance that sail permitted ships to travel in about a day, in good conditions – that enabled the spread of Minoan culture throughout the South Aegean in the MBA. This is in contrast with Early Bronze Age largely oar-powered exchange networks at much smaller distances (~ 50 kilometres) in the Cyclades (Broodbank 2000, 2005). Nonetheless, each of these, in their own way, can be considered a maritime small world as defined by Tartaron (2013, 186). Although maritime technology did not undergo a similar transformation between the early MBA and our LBA periods of interest, changes in the nature of the exchange, its organisation, and the increasing use of the anchor led to an increase in cabotage for which larger distance scales are appropriate. It is tempting to see an increase in distance scales as reflecting improved technology and seamanship going hand in hand with an expansion of cultural interaction and exchange.

In our first iteration (Fig. 3a) we consider distances up to 300 kilometres. The resulting East Mediterranean network is here split between three distinct zones: the west with connections between Adriatic Sea points such as Sardinia and Italy; the east which sees a web of connections between Cyprus and the Levantine coast; and the southern Aegean with ties between Cretan sites and other nodes in the Aegean Sea. Interestingly, already at this distance scale the ease with which the southern Aegean becomes multi-connected is commensurate with Tartaron's 'Mycenaean maritime cultural region,' encompassing parts of central Greece, the Peloponnese, Attica, the Cyclades, the Dodecanese, and Crete (cf. Fig. 6.1 in Tartaron 2013, 201).

At this scale, the network is disconnected from the East Mediterranean regional sphere centred on Cyprus and the Levant. For these two to connect, we need to increase our distance scale to 500 kilometres (Fig. 3b). This increase allows the Aegean 'small-world' network to connect to the Cypro-Levantine 'small-world' network, essentially creating a bridge between these previously separate regions. As we have already noted, winds undoubtedly played a significant role in the frequency and directionality of maritime journeys. Based on this modelling when we consider the journey of the Uluburun ship, we could argue for a preferred directionality in voyaging, especially along the Levantine coast.[5] This 500-kilometre distance also sets the scale for the Phoenician network as discussed by Bakker *et al.*, although the straight lines that connect nodes in Figures 3a and 3b imply possible linkages between these datapoints, rather than straight-line travel, which would require a consideration of winds and currents and remains beyond the scope of this paper (cf. Leidwanger 2013).

Analysis and discussion of individual sites

Figures 3a and 3b implicitly highlight the importance of the inputted nine Cretan sites. Here, we only briefly discuss the implications that these internal and external connections have on our five Cretan depositories. Figures 3a and 3b lack the

---

5   It should be noted, however, that our datapoints do not reflect harbours, nor do they assume to represent a complete picture of sites that were actively occupied during this period. Consequently, the present modelling reflects only possibilities for interaction on the basis of the inputted datapoints and distance parameters.

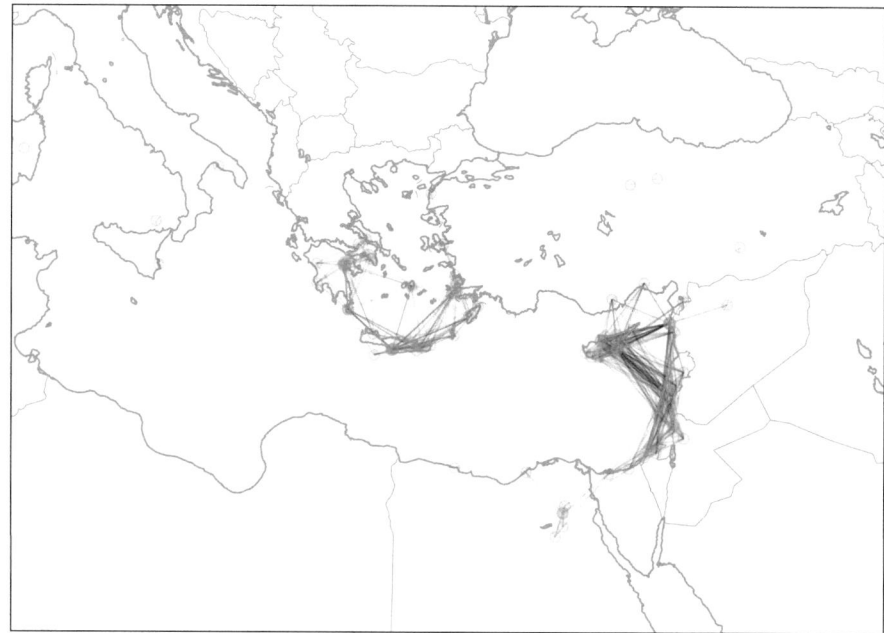

Figure 3a. Mediterranean network showing attachment scales at 300 kilometres. Figure by Henry Price.

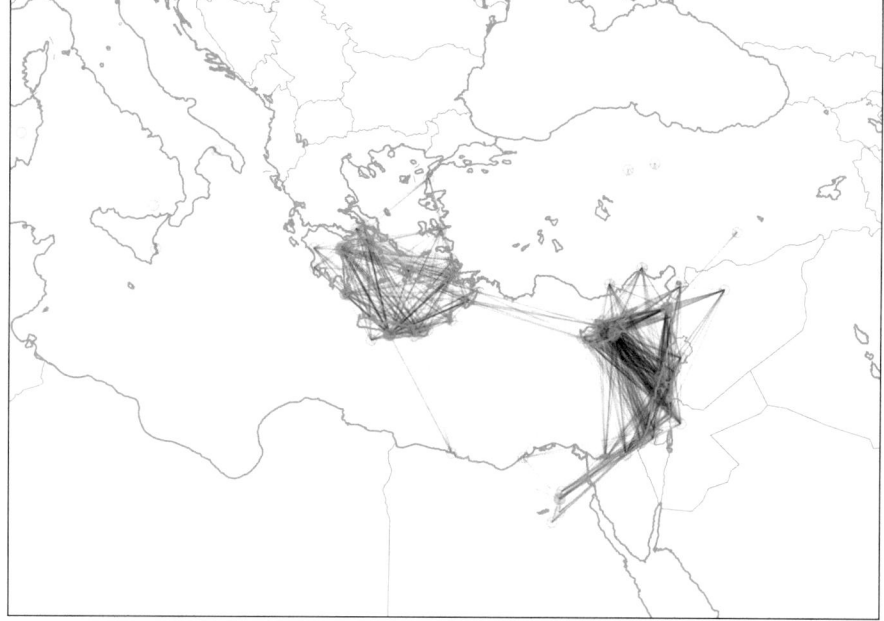

Figure 3b. Mediterranean network showing attachment scales at 500 kilometres. Figure by Henry Price.

resolution to explicitly highlight the intra-regional ties between these nine sites, but we can use other measures to ascertain and count the number of direct links between them using the tools of network centrality (Newman 2010). One such measure – degree centrality – allows us to assign importance to a site based on direct links: the more trade or exchange partners that a site has, the more significant the site is assumed to be.

A more informative measure of site importance is given by betweenness centrality (see Newman 2010; Brandes *et al.* 2008), which considers the shortest route to a site when all sites within a network are considered. This measure evaluates the extent to which the site can be considered a 'bridge' for communication within the network. Sites with high betweenness centralities may have considerable influence within a network, and their removal would result in the disruption of ties across the larger network. This can reflect site importance as a consequence of cabotage. As befits our null model, this is an optimised and over-prescribed form of exchange[6] (Goh *et al.* 2001; Butts 2014), although it captures something that degree centrality with its emphasis on direct forms of travel cannot. We stress again that in our null model we are looking for tendencies that point to one type of behaviour over another.

Our results show that when we consider distances up to $S \leq 200$ kilometres, Knossos and Kommos have a higher centrality when compared to our other Cretan sites. This distance scale – with its high but not overwhelming South Aegean connectivity – recreates a 'small-world' that is disconnected from the Levant. When longer journeys beyond the confines of the Cretan landscape are considered, especially with increased connectivity in the southern Aegean, the centrality of Kommos and Knossos decreases. It is only at scales approaching $S = 500$ kilometres that Crete's connection to North Africa and Egypt tends to optimise the degree centralities. In these upper distance ranges, the site of Palaikastro on the east coast of the island becomes somewhat more prominent as a connecting node to the eastern Mediterranean, linking to Karpathos and the larger Dodecanese. In general, these results are unsurprising as an increase in distance thresholds opens up more avenues for connecting beyond the confines of the island. Nonetheless, we find these significant to consider in discussions of LBA interaction, especially for trying to understand diachronic changes in maritime connectivity between the MBA and LBA period.

Figure 4 outlines betweenness centrality measures against a distance scale up to 500 kilometres for the sites of Chania, Knossos, Kommos, Mochlos, and Palaikastro. Here we are interested in the smaller distance scales that shed light on intra-Cretan site relations. At an attachment radius of 50-100 kilometres (low range), we notice that Knossos dominates. At this short range, Knossos is the most ideally positioned site for both terrestrial and maritime travel north towards the Cyclades and towards mainland Greece. Our key result is the observed sensitivity of Knossos, Mochlos, and Chania (but also Palaikastro to a lesser extent) to distance changes at a range of 120+ kilometres. This suggests that this distance threshold is critical when considering pan-Cretan interaction.

Chania remains dominant as a stop-off point up to 350 kilometres, indicating its stability as an important bridging site for interaction spanning 120-350 kilometres. The balances of centrality are in flux from around 120+ kilometres which could be inferred as a primary threshold range of activity, necessitating settlement development or founding. This increased range of travel could theoretically lead to a shift in settlement importance in the central Mediterranean. Other centrality measures could also be considered to get a more complete picture of importance in the resultant theoretical trade networks, and they are discussed in a forthcoming paper.

At approximately 300 kilometres, Knossos and Chania act as way stations along shortest paths in the network. Knossos appears to be the only settlement exhibiting this kind of behaviour across all distance ranges up to approximately 300 kilometres. When considering the fully connected network (~400+ kilometres), Palaikastro becomes more prominent in these upper ranges. As with degree centrality measures, Palaikastro becomes a connecting point or bridge on the east Cretan coast towards the Dodecanese and, beyond it, the East Mediterranean. It is at this threshold that Kommos becomes significant for the first time, making it possible to connect to the North African coast and Egypt. This could be sensitive to currents and wind which a direct line-of-sight connectivity does not take into account.

---

6   The relation to cabotage is seen through a slight variant of betweenness defined through flows of goods between sites. Specifically, assume that each site sends a unit of some commodity to each other site to which it is connected according to the following priority: given an input of goods *g* arriving at a given site with a given destination, the site divides *g* equally among all neighbours of minimum geodesic distance to the destination. The total flow passing through a given site via this process is defined as its *load*, but is its simplest betweenness centrality in all but name.

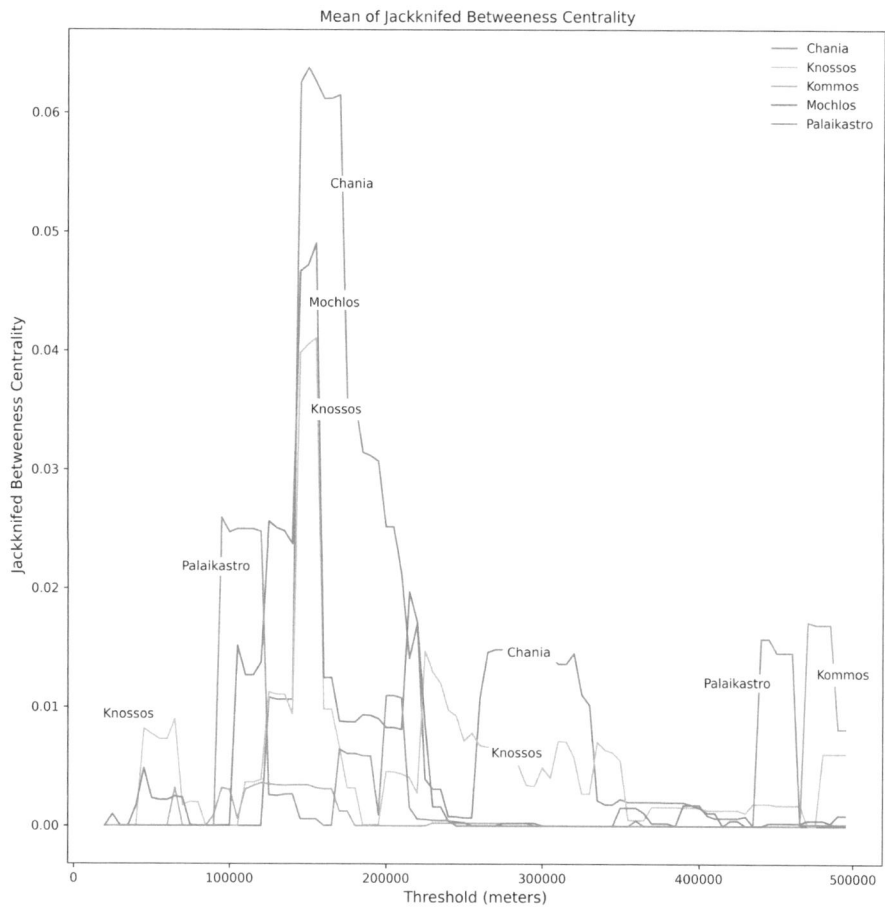

Figure 4. Betweenness centrality transitions for the five Cretan sites discussed in this paper as a function of the attachment scale S. The greater the betweenness, the more the site is a bridge within the E Mediterranean exchange network. This figure highlights the robustness of Chania, and the sensitivity of Knossos to changes in S. Figure by Henry Price.

However, it should be noted that directionality is very important in this instance, as our measures fail to consider currents and winds beyond the simple balancing act mentioned earlier. For example, travelling south from Kommos to North Africa is much easier than sailing north from the coast of Africa towards the Aegean Basin and Crete. A Palaikastro based cabotage around the eastern Mediterranean may be more effective or necessary when sailing conditions are taken into account, especially when sailing in a counter-clockwise direction.

We have two comments. First, we could have performed a similar analysis for the other five listed sites on Crete. Although they are of less interest to us since we have no import statistics for them, this is irrelevant as far as the modelling is concerned, since our modelling did not rely on the imported ceramic data. We have done so and the results are similar. Malia shows similar behaviour to Knossos and Mochlos, peaking at just above 150 kilometres; Gournia is overshadowed by Mochlos, as is Phaistos by Kommos. Ierapetra comes into its own in step with Palaikastro and Kommos at 400+ kilometres, matching Kommos, but with twice the betweenness of Palaikastro. Again, this reflects the ability of southern Crete to connect to North Africa at this scale.

Second, some of the places that we have listed are somewhat hypothetical as sites for these periods (*e.g.* Ierapetra), while others are representative of larger regions when specific sites could not be pinpointed (*e.g.* Gavdos, Beqaa Valley). Our modelling of betweenness centrality takes this into account, in part, by a jack-knifing procedure in which sites are removed in turn from the listing and betweenness is calculated in their absence. The centralities of Figure 4 represent the statistical averages of these results that remain unaffected by changes in presence or absence of any one site.

Conclusions

We can now provide partial answers to some of the questions that Tartaron posed in our introduction: "*... did coastal communities arise or flourish because they were positioned advantageously with respect to sea paths favoured by environmental forces such as winds and currents? Further, were their external relations patterned, or even determined, by movement along these favourable routes?*" Our results show that *accessibility* plays a big role in determining how site relations are patterned by movement in a maritime space. By *accessibility* we mean the way in which the maritime infrastructure (*i.e.* natural or man-made harbours) and sailing technology overcome the impedance of geographical separation. For our present analysis, landmarks do not affect accessibility directly although it could be said that they would have a practical impact on how easily places can be located. Accessibility is, of course, also conditioned by winds and currents although for the present paper and Cretan dataset, this was not taken into consideration. At our null level of modelling we further ignore the more complex localised variables such as institutional and political decisions and infrastructures that undoubtedly shaped how and why people connected. Despite this, when only distance and geography are considered, we demonstrate that 'geography matters' (*cf.* Tartaron 2018) in setting the accessible distance scales that allow for a transition from localised MBA Minoan connectivity centred around the Aegean Sea to an increasingly expanded LBA Mycenaean maritime interaction sphere across the larger Mediterranean basin. This LBA maritime world connected mainland Greece, the Cyclades, and Crete to the East Mediterranean through Cyprus, which acted as a bridging node to the larger Levantine coast.

We would further argue that, to a limited extent, these results help address Tartaron's question as to whether coastal communities arise or flourish because they are positioned advantageously with respect to sea paths favoured by winds and currents. Figures 3a and 3b optimised degree centrality directly as a measure of a region's influence, which includes political power. Simply by looking at the networks of Figures 3a and 3b, it is not difficult to see those sites that have a large degree centrality (a large number of links terminating on them). This is not the case for betweenness centrality, which does not have an immediate visual impact as it counts the paths that pass through a site in question across all scales. Based on these values and the presence of peaks in our betweenness measures at around 120 kilometres, we can draw some conclusions. These peaks are particularly interesting as their distance range matches the approximate hypothetical distance that a Mycenaean or an earlier Minoan vessel could traverse in a day. This hypothetical distance parameter suggests that at this threshold certain sites were significant as hubs for contact and interaction that could be carried out relatively quickly within a day. Above this distance, a vessel would naturally consider a break in travel. Not only does this distance set the scale of interaction between Cretan sites, but this distance scale connects northern Crete to sites in the southern Aegean.

We might have expected key sites on Crete to have been distributed to benefit from the transport technologies of the day, but we had not expected such a clear signal in the data. Such tuning would be unsurprising if settlement locations were globally optimised for influence or dominance subject to technology of exchange. This is the underlying assumption of Bakker's initial programme, which allocates sites according to their effective degree centrality. To confirm this, we would need to compare our results with a sensitivity analysis which would consider, for example, if changes in betweenness importance can be observed when sites are displaced from their original locations. Our results could be expanded through the integration of ceramic data allowing us to draw further connections from the recovered archaeological evidence. This is a necessary step for future diachronic analysis which we have avoided here, but which we will explore in a future paper.

Acknowledgements

The authors would like to thank Anya Rutter and Laura Schmidt, the organisers of the International Open Workshop: *Socio-Environmental Dynamics over the Last 15,000 Years: The Creation of Landscapes VI* at Kiel University, March 2019, for a stimulating and thought-provoking session. The ideas in this paper were originally presented by Henry Price during this workshop and we thank the organisers for allowing us to expand on them by contributing to this volume. Finally, we also extend our thanks to Tim Evans and Carl Knappett for the many helpful comments on earlier drafts of this paper.

References

Bagnell, R. *et al.*, eds., 2014. *Pleiades: A Gazetteer of Past Places.* Available from: http://pleiades.stoa.org

Bakker, J.D., Maurer, S., Pischke, J.-S. and Rauch, F., 2018. Of Mice and Merchants: Trade and Growth in the Iron Age. *Centre for Economic Performance, CEP (LSE) Discussion Paper No. 1558.*

Barjamovic, G., Chaney, T., Cosar, K.A.and Hortasu, A., 2017. Trade, merchants, and the lost cities of the Bronze Age. *The Quarterly Journal of Economics*, 134, 1455-1503.

Bass, G.F., 1991. Evidence of Trade from Bronze Age Shipwrecks. *In*: N.H. Gale, ed. *Bronze Age Trade in the Mediterranean* (SIMA 90). Göteborg: P. Åströms Förlag, 69-82.

Brandes, U., 2008. On variants of shortest-path betweenness centrality and their generic computation. *Social Networks*, 30, 136-145.

Broodbank, C., 2000. *An island archaeology of the Early Cyclades.* Cambridge: Cambridge University Press.

Broodbank, C., 2005. Minoanisation. *Proceedings of the Cambridge Philological Society*, 50, 46-91.

Broodbank, C., 2013. *The Making of the Middle Sea.* Cambridge: Cambridge University Press.

Butts, C.T., 2014. sna: Tools for Social Network Analysis. *R package version 2.3-2.* Available from: http://CRAN.R-project.org/package=sna

Chalikias, K., 2009. Searching for the Missing "Palace": Proto- and Neopalatial Settlement Dynamics in the Southern Ierapetra Isthmus. *Aegean Archaeology*, 10, 33-46.

Cline, E.H., 1994. *Sailing the Wine-Dark Sea: International Trade and the Late Bronze Age Aegean.* British Archaeological Reports International Series 591. Oxford: Tempus Reparatum.

Cline, E.H., 2007. Rethinking Mycenaean International Trade with Egypt and the Near East. *In*: M. Galaty and W. Parkinson, eds. *Rethinking Mycenaean Palaces II: Revised and Expanded Edition.* Los Angeles: Cotsen Institute of Archaeology, 190-200.

Gheorghiade, P., 2020. *A Network Approach to Interaction and Maritime Connectivity on Crete during the Late Bronze Age – Late Minoan II-IIIB2.* Doctoral Thesis, University of Toronto.

Gheorghiade, P., 2021. Beyond Maritime Connectivity: Assessing Regional Interaction and Mobility in Late Bronze Age Crete. *In*: J. Driessen and A. Vanzetti, eds. *Communication Uneven. Acceptance of and Resistance to Foreign Influences in the connected Ancient Mediterranean* (*Aegis* 20). Louvain-la-Neuve: Presses Universitaires de Louvain, 85-97.

Goh, K.-I., Kahng, B. and Kim, D., 2001. Universal behavior of load distribution in scale-free networks. *Physical Review Letters*, 87 (27), 87-91.

Hägg, R., and Marinatos, N., eds., 1984. *The Minoan Thalassocracy: Myth and Reality.* Stockholm: Svenska institutet i Athen.

Horden, P., and Purcell, N., 2000. *The Corrupting Sea: A Study of Mediterranean History.* Oxford and Malden: Blackwell.

Kanta, A., 1980. *The Late Minoan III period in Crete: a survey of sites, pottery and their distribution.* Göteborg: P. Åströms Förlag.

Knappett, C., Evans, T. and Rivers, R., 2008. Modelling maritime interaction in the Aegean Bronze Age. *Antiquity*, 82, 1009-24.

Knappett, C., Evans, T. and Rivers, R., 2011. Modelling maritime interaction in the Aegean Bronze Age, II: The eruption of Thera and the burning of the palaces. *Antiquity*, 85, 1008-23.

Langohr, C., 2009. *Périphéreia: Etude régionale de la Créte aux Minoen Récent II-IIIB (1450-1200 av. J.-C.). Vol. 1: La Créte centrale et occidentale, AEGIS 3.* Louvain-la-Neuve: Presses Universitaires de Louvain.

Lambrou-Phillipson, C., 1990. *'Hellenorientalia': The Near Eastern presence in the Bronze Age Aegean, ca. 3000-1100 BC: interconnections based on the material record and the written evidence; plus Orientalia: a catalogue of Egyptian, Mesopotamian, Mitannian, Syro-Palestinian, Cypriot, and Asia Minor objects from the Bronze Age Aegean.* Göteborg: P. Åströms Förlag.

Leidwanger, J., 2013. Modeling distance with time in ancient Mediterranean seafaring: a GIS application for the interpretation of maritime connectivity. *Journal of Archaeological Science*, 40, 3302-08.

Mee, C., 2008. Mycenaean Greece, the Aegean, and Beyond. *In*: C.W. Shelmerdine, ed. *The Cambridge Companion to the Aegean Bronze Age.* Cambridge: Cambridge University Press, 362-86.

Murray, S., 2017. *The Collapse of the Mycenaean Economy. Imports, Trade and Institutions 1300-1700 BCE.* Cambridge: Cambridge University Press.

Newman, M., 2010. *Networks: An Introduction.* Oxford: Oxford University Press.

Niemeier, W.-D., 2009. 'Minoanisation' *versus* 'Minoan Thalassocracy'- an Introduction. *In*: C.F. Macdonald, E. Hallager and W.-D. Niemeier, eds. *The Minoans in the Central, Eastern and Northern Aegean – New Evidence.* Monographs of the Danish Institute at Athens 8. Athens: Monographs of the Danish Institute at Athens, 11-29.

Papageorgiou, D., 2008. The Marine Environment and its Influence on Seafaring and Maritime Routes in the Prehistoric Aegean. *European Journal of Archaeology*, 11, 199-222.

Phillips, J., 2008. *Aegyptiaca on the island of Crete in their chronological context: a critical review.* Wien: Verlag der Österreichischen Akademie der Wissenschaften.

Pratt, C., 2016. The Rise and Fall of the Transport Stirrup Jar in the Late Bronze Age Aegean. *American Journal of Archaeology*, 120 (1), 27-66.

Preston, L., 2004. A Mortuary Perspective on Political Changes in Late Minoan II-IIIB Crete. *American Journal of Archaeology*, 108, 321-348.

Preston, L., 2008. Late Minoan II to IIIB Crete. *In*: C.W. Shelmerdine, ed. *The Cambridge Companion to the Aegean Bronze Age.* Cambridge: Cambridge University Press, 362-86.

Pulak, C., 1998. The Uluburun Shipwreck: An Overview. *International Journal of Nautical Archaeology*, 27, 188-224.

Rutter, J., 2017. *House X at Kommos. A Minoan mansion near the sea, part 2. The Pottery.* Philadelphia: INSTAP Academic Press.

Rutter, J. and Van de Moortel, A., 2006. Minoan Pottery from the Southern Area. *In*: J. Shaw and M. Shaw, eds. *Kommos V. The Monumental Minoan Buildings at Kommos.* Princeton: Princeton University Press, 261-716.

Simandiraki, A., 2005. "Minoan Archaeology in the Athens 2004 Olympic Games," *European Journal of Archaeology*, 8 (2), 157-181.

Tartaron, T., 2013. *Maritime Networks in the Mycenaean World.* Cambridge: Cambridge University Press.

Tartaron, T., 2018. Geography Matters; Defining Maritime Small Worlds in the Aegean Bronze Age. *In*: J. Leidwanger and C. Knappett, eds. *Maritime Networks in the Ancient Mediterranean World.* Cambridge: Cambridge University Press, 61-92.

Wachsmann, S., 1988. *Seagoing Ships and Seamanship in the Bronze Age Levant.* College Station: Texas A&M University Press.

Wiener, M.H., 2013. Realities of Power: The Minoan Thalassocracy in Historical Perspective. *In*: R.B. Koehl, ed. *AMILLA: The Quest for Excellence. Studies Presented to Guenter Kopcke in Celebration of His 75th Birthday.* Philadelphia: INSTAP Academic Press, 149-73.

To be Greek or not to be: About the "Greekness" of Epirus and Southern Illyria. An overview through urbanism and theatrical architecture from a Mediterranean perspective

Ludovica Xavier de Silva

Abstract

The analysis presented here is born out of a doctoral research project concerning the study and the cataloguing of the architectural buildings of Epirus and Southern Illyria, through which it was possible to approach and reconsider some debated issues and subjects related to urbanistic and architectural development of these regions.

However, it is not the aim of this paper to present a detailed overview of the research on theatrical building or the overall interpretation of the urbanisation process related to it. The objective is rather to draw some lines which will be helpful in framing a "Mediterranean" context, definitely cutting across those that link the study of these territories to the dichotomy 'Greek-not Greek', which has for too long shaped the debate about their history and identity.

In order to contextualise Epirus and Southern Illyria in the Mediterranean and – more specifically – in the Adriatic-Ionian space, we will approach key themes such as the definition of the *polis-ethnos* dichotomy, the understanding of the urbanisation process in these regions, and the shaping of a Hellenistic urbanistic and architectural syntax. Ultimately, we will come to an analysis of the place the theatre had in the realisation of these concepts.

Epirus, Southern Illyria, Hellenism, theatre, identity

Introduction

*J'ai tenté de mieux faire connaître l'histoire d'une région bien souvent négligée
[...]. Sa position même rend, pourtant, cette étude pleine d'intérêt, car l'Epire est
la mieux placée pour refléter les influences différentes venues de Grèce et d'Illyrie.*
(Cabanes 1976, *Avant Propose*)

What is definitely clear about this phrase – written by the historian Pierre Cabanes
at the beginning of his volume *L'Épire de la mort de Pyrrhos à la conquête romaine* –
is that in order to understand the history and therefore the identity of a community,
it is crucial to know and acknowledge the importance of its position, mostly in terms
of connections with other communities.

Starting from this perspective, the aim of this paper is to provide an overview
of Hellenistic Epirus and Southern Illyria, taking into account the role their position
in the wider network of cultures may have had in shaping and building the identity
of the communities who inhabited these territories. More specifically, and in
accordance with the general aim of the Kiel International Workshop Session to
which this paper belongs, the analysis will focus on the relation the communities
had within the Mediterranean context they were part of, trying to highlight in which
way the network existing in this area determined how they perceived others as well
as themselves and, ultimately, attempting to clarify whether they acknowledge this
very process or not.

In order to sustain the perspective that this paper suggests, it will be necessary to
approach some debated and complex questions such as the *polis-ethnos* definition,
the role of urban planning in the Hellenistic kingdoms, and the existence of an
Adriatic-Ionian *koinè* Eventually and in relation to the above subjects, the analysis
of the theatrical buildings of Epirus and Southern Illyria will be used as an
hermeneutical tool to frame these regions in the Mediterranean context and read
their history through this specific lens.

To be Greek or not to be: From the *polis-ethnos* dichotomy to the urbanisation process of Epirus and Southern Illyria

Studies that take into account the building and shaping of identities and, consequently,
alterities, are deeply involved with the understanding of connectivity and networks,
a path that still has an enormous potential in the Mediterranean area.

Assuming this perspective in the study of the Mediterranean communities and
their interactions is not only fruitful but – in specific cases – can also enlighten some
interesting yet sometimes neglected aspects of long-ranging debates.

The study of Epirus and Southern Illyria still raises some questions about the
understanding and interpretation of their urbanisation process, especially if seen
from the perspective of a *polis*-centred system such as the Greek one has usually
been considered to be.

More specifically, the borders and the interactions between different communities
are quite difficult to read in the territory which appears as a constellation of
numerous ethnic and tribal groups tied to transhumance. As we will later discuss,
this system leads to a substantial delay in the proper establishment of a *polis*-based
settlement model in the region. Here is not the place to breach the wide and complex
subject related to the administrative and political history of the territory but we
can briefly – although certainly not exhaustively – say that the administrative
organisation of Epirus proceeds through a hierarchical grouping of small tribes into

wider administrative units, the so-called *koina*, united themselves in larger *ethne* such as *Molossians, Chaonians* and *Thesprotians*. These larger *koina* also tend to associate in more complex administrative and political systems and for this very reason, in the 3rd century BCE, they gave birth both to the Aeacid monarchy (about the nature of the Molossian reign and its fall see: Fantasia 2017, 136-148) and, after its fall (232 BCE), to the *Koinon of the Epirotes* (about the history of Epirus after Pyrrhus see: Cabanes 1976. For a good summary of the administrative and political evolution of the region see: Melfi and Piccinini 2012a).

At this point, it is crucial to introduce the most recent developments concerning the definition of the well-known dichotomy *polis-ethnos* which so far has tended to shape the debate about the inclusion or exclusion of Mediterranean communities in a Greek-like system of territorial and administrative organisation. Recent studies on the subject tend to reassess the aforementioned dichotomy with the aim to overcome a sharp opposition between the two concepts of *polis* and *ethnos* and rather underline the political and cultural similarities between the two (Vlassopoulos 2007). This new research trend can be linked to the work of the *Copenhagen Polis Centre*, which has the merit of having clarified – through extensive work – the actually complex and multifaceted meaning of what we call *polis*, introducing the essential concept of *dependent polis*, which actually resize the importance of the autonomy as a breaking point between what can be considered a *polis* and what not (Hansen, Nielsen 2004, 12ff.).

Among the most recent studies, a very useful contribution to better understand the territories of Epirus and Southern Illyria has been published by Chiara Lasagni, who specifically focused on those realities that were difficult to frame in the classic dichotomy *polis-ethnos* (Lasagni 2011; also see it for an overview of the debate related to the concept of *polis*). In her analysis, she defined the new concept of *tribal poleis*, which can provide a very useful perspective in the study of the administrative and urbanistic organisation of territory in the regions chosen for this paper. The concept specifically applies to the administrative entities in Epirus and Aetoloakarnania, and in a way redefines the classic relationship *polis-chora* and *polis*-ethnic identity, taking into account a peculiar system that has so far been forced into the main parameters of the usual dichotomy. Simplifying the complex analysis to meet the issue we are trying to raise in this paper, we could say that Lasagni's *tribal poleis* are specifically characterised by being topographically linked to transhumance, thus partially subverting the *polis* settlement model and adjusting it to the *ethnos* one, resulting also in a more complex relationship between the ethnic identity and the administrative unit (Lasagni 2018).

Moreover, Lasagni's work enlightens us on how *polis* and *ethnos* actually answered to two distinct concepts of self-identification essentially based on a different way of territorial interaction. Nonetheless, especially during the Hellenistic era, the *ethnos* begins to be more structured around an administrative perspective, following models that resemble the *polis* administration, while – on the other hand – the *poleis* start to aggregate in federal systems (Lasagni 2011, 180). This process tends to downsize the difference between the two systems and defines a more complex scenario in which the definition of *tribal poleis* better finds its place.

What we need to remember about the characterising dynamic of an *ethnos*-based system is the nature of constant negotiation of the central power with the local administrations which ultimately makes the central power the result of an agreement between local communities: this peculiar aspect was apparently borrowed by the *tribal poleis* and will therefore be useful for understanding some dynamics in the regional history of Epirus and Southern Illyria.

The named difficulty of framing Epirus and Southern Illyria in the usual *polis-ethnos* dichotomy goes hand in hand with the debate concerning the so-called *polis*-birth in the territory. The question whether or not Epirus should have been included in the *polis*-kind world has actually ancient roots as the literary and epigraphic sources give us a complex set of information about the subject. In fact, Thucydides still defined the *Chaonians*, one of the most prominent Epirote communities, as barbarians (Thuc. I, 47; Thuc. II, 80) while, starting from the IV century BCE, we have sources that seem to testify a different perception of Epirus from mainland Greece (for an exhaustive overview of the subject see: Melfi, Piccinini 2012b). A very interesting debate, related both to the presence of an urban entity possibly definable as *polis* in Epirus during the IV century and the interpretation of the term *polis* itself, has born around an inscription from Dodona mentioning ἁ πόλις ἁ τῶν Χαόνων (*SEG* XV, 397): this *polis* has been normally identified with *Phoinike* but concerning the value and the meaning of the phrase, scholars are quite divided between who refers it to the whole so-called *koinon* as a political unit – thus called *polis* – and who tends to think that the phrase may refer to *Phoinike* as the administrative entity of the Chaonian ethnos (or a discussion of all of the different positions taken by the scholars about the matter: Lasagni 2018, 173. On the importance the definition of such an entity must have had for the territory: Cabanes 2007, 233 and Melfi, Piccinini 2012a, 40). This phrase may be read through the lens of Lasagni's *tribal polis* concept, trying to understand the mentioned subversion of the equation *polis-polis* identity-ethnic identity: the territorial organisation typical of Epirus and similar other regions probably led to a complex system of administrative networks and ethnic identities, resulting in a tribal organisation that, even having a leading administrative centre, still identified itself in the wider concept of the *ethnos* (Lasagni 2018).

If we focus precisely on the actual urbanisation issue, whatever the identity concept Epirotes had in relation to the *polis* and – more in general – to the rest of Greece, the most recent field research and studies are definitely progressing towards a clearer yet more complex view of the urbanisation dynamics of Epirus and Southern Illyria. Specifically, in order to have an overview of at least part of the territory, we can look at the latest studies conducted on the Drino and Bistriça Valleys from the Universities of Macerata and Bologna which, while focusing on the Chaonian territory, can also enlighten the change of perspective ongoing in most of the studies on the region which now tend to look to the urbanisation phenomenon rather than searching for a precise chronology for the *polis*-birth (Giorgi, Bogdani 2012; Marziali, Perna, Qirjaqi, Tadolti 2012; Perna 2014).

The result of the mentioned studies has been, in the first place, a general re-examination of the settlement system chronology, further confirming the necessity to definitely overcome those historiographical and archaeological statements that aim to prove the birth of a urban civilisation in Epirus and Southern Illyria before the IV-III century BCE, supposing an acting influence on the region from the Corinthian and Elean colonies already founded on the coasts.

This being told, it is possible to describe the Hellenistic settlement system of the region as a network of defensive small fortresses placed with the aim of dominating the valleys, also seen as means to foster exchanges and openings. This defensive military system denounce the activity of a central power which could guarantee its functionality putting on force a hierarchisation of the settlements, which it is possible to identify in all of the Aeacid Kingdom, from Southern Illyria to Thesprotia, although with the due local differences (for a general overview of the matter see: Caliò 2017, while, for a focus on the differences between the Drino and Bistriça Valleys in Chaonia see: Perna 2014, 197-209). This characteristic of the settlement system brings together the territory we are focusing on with Macedonia and Thessaly where, for the same period, similar fortified settlements and territorial hierarchies can be identified (Soueref 2015).

Thus, as already mentioned, the establishment of a proper *polis*-based settlement system in Epirus is not proper of the Hellenistic period, and can actually be identified during the Roman era, between the I century BCE and the I century CE, as it shown by the case of Sofratikë, later *Hadrianopolis*, through which it is possible to appreciate a solid shifting of the settlements system from the hilltops towards the valleys as the Romans started to be more influent on the territory (Precisely, Sofratikë seems to progressively assume the role Pyrrhus' Antigonea previously had in the Drino region, after the establishment of the *Koinon* of the *Prasaiboi*. On the subject see: Perna 2012; Perna 2014; Perna 2017). In few words, Epirus and Southern Illyria show a substantial heterogeneity in the developing and declination of the urbanisation process which tends to be highly dependent on both the conformation and exploitation of the territory and the importance of the ethnic-tribal units with their transhumant activities.

The maintenance throughout the centuries of a structured system of *koina* as well as the aforementioned negotiation of power that has to be identified in the way in which both the Aeacid monarchy and the later *Koinon* of the Epirotes worked ultimately explain why some processes and activities – also related to the identity building and perception – did not cease to exist or being promoted after the fall of a central strong power such the one of Pyrrhus, as we will later discuss.

The Hellenistic kingdoms and the building of a common language: The powerful syntax of the urbanistic and architectural planning

In order to understand the urbanistic and architectural context of Epirus and Southern Illyria, trying as well to relate it to the identity question, it is crucial to frame it in the wider debate about the Hellenistic urban planning and architecture.

The subject is certainly too complex to be discussed here but a brief overview of some essential issues and research paths can help putting into perspective some of the data related to the region we are focusing on. In fact, it is well known that the Hellenistic architecture has only recently been the focus of more centred studies, while previously being more marginal compared to the Classical and Imperial studies on urbanism and architecture (for this reason the work of Lauter, *Die Architektur des Hellenismus* continues to be an obliged starting point for the studies on the subject: Lauter 1986).

In the most recent studies about the Hellenistic architecture, the necessity of understanding and declining the different regional expressions of this era has often been highlighted (the latest works on the Greek architecture having also sections on the Hellenistic one: Hellmann 2002, 2006 e 2010. A dedicated monography on the subject: Winter 2006). Closely connected to our analysis, is one of the latest overviews Enzo Lippolis gave on the subject: he specifically focused on the urge of considering the Hellenism and its urbanistic and architectural declinations as a Mediterranean phenomenon in which it is crucial to identify both the peculiar regional declinations and the circulations of ideas and models, ultimately trying to establish which were the propulsor centres of the cultural spread and, mostly, what shape must have had the network connecting them. The Mediterranean Sea has to be studied as a unitarian, yet complex, reality in which it is possible to observe a set of entangled phenomena, processes and changes (Lippolis 2017, 15). Compared to the Classical era the real distinctive mark of the Hellenism can be identified in the creation of an urban-architectural syntax visible in the public projects through all of the period. In fact, the experimentation of new forms and languages seems no longer concentrated on the single buildings but rather on their interaction, namely the image that one could appreciate looking at their relationships with each other as well as with the surrounding landscape. In this context the *stoa* becomes an essential structure of the formal Hellenistic elaboration, often used at the service of a monumental syntax with a clear scenographic intent.

Concerning the regional elaborations of the Hellenistic urbanistic and architecture, an important role must have been played by some capitals of the Hellenistic Kingdoms, such as Alexandria in Egypt or Pergamon, although we luck a lot of information about many of those. Some important *poleis*, such as Rhodes, Athens and Corinth, but also some cities in Southern Italy and Sicily, must have given their contributions to the spread of some models in the Mediterranean Sea, and it is not to be forgotten the importance of some interventions in regional and pan-Hellenic sanctuaries, promoted by monarchs (for an overview of the regional declinations of the Hellenistic architecture and an updated bibliography on the subject see: Lippolis 2017).

Another crucial aspect of the urbanistic and architectural development during the Hellenistic period seems to be the peculiar relationship that this had with the political power, especially during the III century BCE and in relation to Hellenistic kings and prominent military figures. The growth of the Hellenistic monarchies and the union between the individualism and the personal enrichment provided the basis for an explicit propagandistic and political use of the architecture and the urban planning. In fact, Hellenistic sovereigns are often famous for having founded cities, named after them or their family members, as well as for promoting the monumentalisation of important centres and sanctuaries, actually being able, through these very actions, to communicate their power not only on a local but – more importantly – on a Mediterranean scale (for a complete discussion on the subject and for the related bibliography see: de Courtils 2015).

In the frame of the context discussed above, the analysis and study of the theatrical architectures has provided a valid hermeneutical tool to investigate the urbanisation dynamics from a peculiar angle, offering the opportunity to analyse the architectural culture and its relation to the topography within the communities object of this study. Theatres are indeed part of a complex and articulated system which links together the city and the territory, using the viability as a qualifying instrument and giving to the urban panoply a determinant representative meaning.

Concerning the Greek theatre, this building has always been considered as a typical monument of the *polis*, but this statement finds some exceptions such as the cases of the sanctuaries or the documented theatres in the Attic demes (Frederiksen 2002, 79). This simple, yet determinant, observation forces us to reconsider the usually accepted relationship between the *polis* and the theatre both from a conceptual and an urbanistic perspective: the equation *polis*-theatre is indeed dominant but not exclusive, not only because theatres could be built by different political or administrative entities but also taking into account the fact that not all *poleis* had a theatre. On this account it is also important to note that the building of a theatre was a costly activity and its presence in a given place is therefore dependant on a large numbers of factors, among which we can name the economic capacity of the city/sanctuary (or the donor) and the supposed importance of the building for the community, both as a gathering place and as an ideological feature (Frederiksen 2002, 80. The relation between the presence of a theatre or its capacity and the demographic analysis of a city or territory tends to be a lot downsized in the most recent studies on the subject: Di Napoli 2013, 123-124, with related bibliography).

The building of a theatre presents nonetheless some other significant challenges related to the necessity of the Greek building to use a hillside or a slope to sustain the structure of the *koilon*. The Greek theatre was indeed far more demanding on an urban planning perspective if compared to the later Roman free-standing cavea, an issue that is even more important if we consider that most of the theatrical buildings were founded in Greece after the IV century BCE, when most of the cities already had a long urban history and, consequently, were already furnished with many other buildings (Moretti 2014). Nonetheless, and especially taking into account the studies on the Hellenistic architecture, the planning challenges related to the Greek theatre building did not stop the realisation of complex and sophisticated urban syntaxes that played with the relationships of these buildings with the surrounding landscape and monuments (on the subject a very recent contribution highlights not only the importance of the ideological meaning of the relationship between the theatre and the urban planning but also the necessity of proceeding with caution in interpreting these spatial relations only based on planimetric documents: Kreeb 2019). Thus, the usual opposition that wanted the Roman theatre to be more and better integrated in the city planning than the Greek one, whose possibilities on this account were almost totally affected by the morphology of the territory, is nowadays resized and reconsidered in the light of the Hellenistic urbanistic and architecture, actually emphasising a bond between the Hellenism and the Roman era (Winter 2006, 207).

Concerning the role of the theatre in the Hellenistic urban planning, it is worth considering the debate related to the association between theatres and *agorai*, especially in those cities whose planning is dated to the late IV century BCE. Specifically, even if it cannot be defined as a rule, during the Hellenistic period a proximity or a intended connection between the theatres and the citys' *agorai*, often underlined by a peculiar use of other buildings such as the *stoai*, can be identified and, once again, makes clear the often ideological intention that is possible to read in the Hellenistic planning syntax (on the subject see the latest works of Dickenson, who discuss the issue taking into account the different positions of other scholars and giving a thorough overview of the *status quaestionis*: Dickenson 1013 and 2017, especially 109-113). Moreover, it has been recently underlined how the public spaces and their designing had assumed a determinant role in the process of that already-mentioned negotiation of power between the Hellenistic kings and the cities included in their kingdoms. In fact, the Hellenistic sovereigns had a strong interest in founding new cities and monumentalising the existing ones, namely they often concentrated their efforts in the *agora* space, choosing it as the privileged place for their relationship with the communities (Dickenson 2013).

The aforementioned association theatre-*agora* leads us to the related problem of the function of the theatrical buildings, which is still highly debated in the dedicated literature. Again, this is not the right place to offer a thorough overview of such a complex subject, but it is nonetheless essential for our analysis to underline some aspects related to it. To summarise, we can say that some scholars tend to stress the unbreakable link with the dramatic and religious function, often addressing as proof the existence of theatre-like building dedicated to assemblies and political activities, such as *ekklesiasteria* and *bouleutheria*, while others prefer to look at the strategic position of the theatre in the city and call for a political function for it, highlighting the rarity of buildings dedicated to assemblies in most cities and underlining the diffuse connection between theatrical buildings and *agorai* (this last thesis is particularly sustained by Kolb but discussed and opposed especially by Hansen and Fisher-Hansen. For the all discussion see: Kolb 1981; Hansen, Fisher-Hansen 1994).

Overcoming the dedicated debate about the original function, it nonetheless seems to be generally accepted that the theatre was a highly polyfunctional building which served many purposes for the communities which had one. Moreover, it is clear that not only their presence is subject to different needs and challenges but also their diffusion is far from being homogeneous in the Mediterranean context or, at least, it does not seem to respond to the same criteria. In fact, whatever the original function of the theatre may have been, most of the buildings were founded at the time of the Hellenistic kingdoms, thus escaping from the ratio and dynamics related only to the *polis*. The building of many theatres, as well as the monumentalisation of many existing ones, must be framed, then, in the Hellenistic Mediterranean scenario and, therefore, read in that already discussed language based on an urban syntax proper of this period. This consideration forces us to take into account the ideological and propagandistic role these buildings may had and not only their practical function. Precisely on this account it has been highlighted how theatres have been, during the Hellenistic period, one of the places the kings loved choosing for their public appearances: in fact, they were functional to gather a lot of people as well as 'theatralising' their entrance, stressing their power (however, other places, such the *agorai*, were also used for these purposes: Dickenson 2013, 54-56). This use is apparently linked to what Angelo Chaniotis has efficiently called a *theatrical mentality*, proper of the Hellenistic period and functional to the maintenance of the monarchic order: the monarchs had indeed the necessity of showing themselves in front of their subjects and be able to give them a clear image of authority, seeking consensus to legitimise their power (Chaniotis 1997).

Mediterranean networks: The Adriatic-Ionian *koinè*

In order to understand the dynamics characterising the Mediterranean context, it is worth mentioning the debate about the existence of a cultural, but also architectural and urbanistic, *koinè* in the Adriatic and Ionian space. The terms of the question had been set already in the last decade of the XX century: the problem concerning the relationship between Magna Graecia and Epirus have been largely shaped during the XXIV Congress on Magna Graecia (on the subject see: D'Andria 1990; Lepore 1990) but the existence of an artistic and architectonic *koinè* in the Adriatic Sea, having as the central point the strait of Otranto, had already been discussed by Jean-Luc Lamboley on the occasion of the first international congress on Epirus and Southern Illyria at Clermont-Ferrand (Lamboley 1987; for an updated overview of the subject see: Lamboley1993; D'Andria 1995; for an accurate bibliography of the exchanges involving the strait of Otranto, see: Castiglioni, Lamboley 2015). These fist contributions started to shape a concept that focuses on the diffusion of cultural models and schemes which the communities were able to re-elaborate through their own taste, a context in which Taranto and the Macedonian territory seem to have played a crucial role. Although the first framing of the issue remains valid, the progresses of the research in both Italy and the Balkans as well as Greece keep providing new interesting data that can help to shape the subject more accurately. Thus, over the years, the question has been enriched taking into account the complexity of the different realities converging into the greater context of the Adriatic Sea, also pushing towards a deeper reflection on the role of the Greek colonisation in this space and the relationship between the Adriatic and the Ionian seas. In this respect, recent studies all highlight the necessity of considering the Adriatic Sea as a unitarian – even if not homogeneous – context, enlighten the impossibility of truly understanding the communities which are part of this network without considering its role on their histories and identities but also keeping in mind the constellation of ethnic entities that composes this very context (Castiglioni, Lamboley 2015. In this contribution it is also highlighted the lack of a work of synthesis on the Adriatic Sea, if we exclude Cabanes' *Histoire de l'Adriatique*: Cabanes 2001, especially 43-106).

The relations acting in the Adriatic and Ionian space seem to have been at least influenced by the role of the Corinthian-Corcyrean colonisation which was determinant in defining the importance of the strait of Otranto. On these first contacts would later be built a communication axis that – from the Macedonian area, through Epirus – would contribute to what has been called the 'Hellenisation' of *Apulia*, as it is confirmed by archaeological and documentary evidence on both an urbanistic and an administrative profile (some first remarks on the subject in: Lepore 1990). Alexander the Molossian and Pyrrhus' Adriatic interests and policies will be followed by Roman activities and interventions: the sources, as well as the archaeological data confirm indeed the intensification of the relationship between the two coasts from the late Hellenistic period to the Roman era (Coviello 2003).

To conclude this brief overview, it is worth mentioning that some recent studies have been focusing their interest in the urbanistic aspects of this *koinè*, tracing the development of the urban assets both in Magna Graecia and Sicily and in Epirus and Southern Illyria, not forgetting also the close relationship these territories had with the communities of northern Greece, Macedonia, the Peloponnesian area and, later, with the growing dominant power of Rome (about the way models and ideas were transmitted and re-elaborated through this network of contacts and relation, and with a focus on the Epirote territory, see: Podini 2014, specifically 121-124).

On this account, it is possible to notice, already from the time of Alexander the Molossian, some parallelisms in the development of the settlement settings typologies in Epirus and Magna Graecia, namely a new interpretation has recently been proposed around the sources concerning the death of Alexander, which should enlighten the development of a precise typology of settlement system influenced by the Epirote presence in the territories inhabited by the Bruttians and Lucanians (Caliò 2017, 323-327).

A further analysis of some aspects precisely linked to architectural features and developments in the region we chose for this paper could certainly contribute to a clearer contextualisation of Epirus and Southern Illyria concerning the circulation of ideas and models and the elaboration or re-elaboration of some urbanistic and architectural solutions. Unfortunately, the evidence on this subject is scarce in the territory due to an often-poor preservation of buildings and structures as well as to a massive reuse of materials and architectonical elements in late antique and Byzantine times and an often highly hypothetical anastylosis of some monuments.

Nonetheless, Marco Podini's recent work on the architectural culture of the Chaonian region offers some ideas and paths to follow in order to draw some interpretative lines to understand the urbanistic and architectural development of Epirus and Southern Illyria. Specifically, the scholar underlines the intense connection between the region and the Peloponnesian area, a relation which starts taking its shape in the late Classical period and reaches its acme during the Hellenistic times, initially defining a sort of north-western *koinè* with religious and architectonic characteristics (Mancini 2013, p. 86). Peloponnesian models seem indeed to condition, between the IV and the III century BCE, not only the Greek continent but also the Macedonian raising power, whose connection with Epirus is continuous. The most interesting aspect of this connection Epirus had with both the Peloponnesian and the Macedonian areas seems to be related to the use of the so-called polygonal-octagonal order, an architectural feature that was highly used in public buildings especially during the Aeacid monarchy, being re-elaborated from a Peloponnesian model and used, as it seems, to define a peculiar regional style (Podini 2014, 91-94 and 120).

Returning to the connection identifiable in the Adriatic context, it seems that throughout the III century BCE, the Chaonians remained more tied to the north-western Greek and the Peloponnesian world while southern Illyria cultivated its relation on an axis that from the Macedonian territories went to southern Italy and Sicily. In this context, a first vehiculation of north-western and Peloponnesian models must have taken the routes from these regions through Epirus and then, from Southern Illyria to *Apulia* and Sicily, where they seem to have been re-elaborated and later travelled back in their new form (Podini 2014, 123).

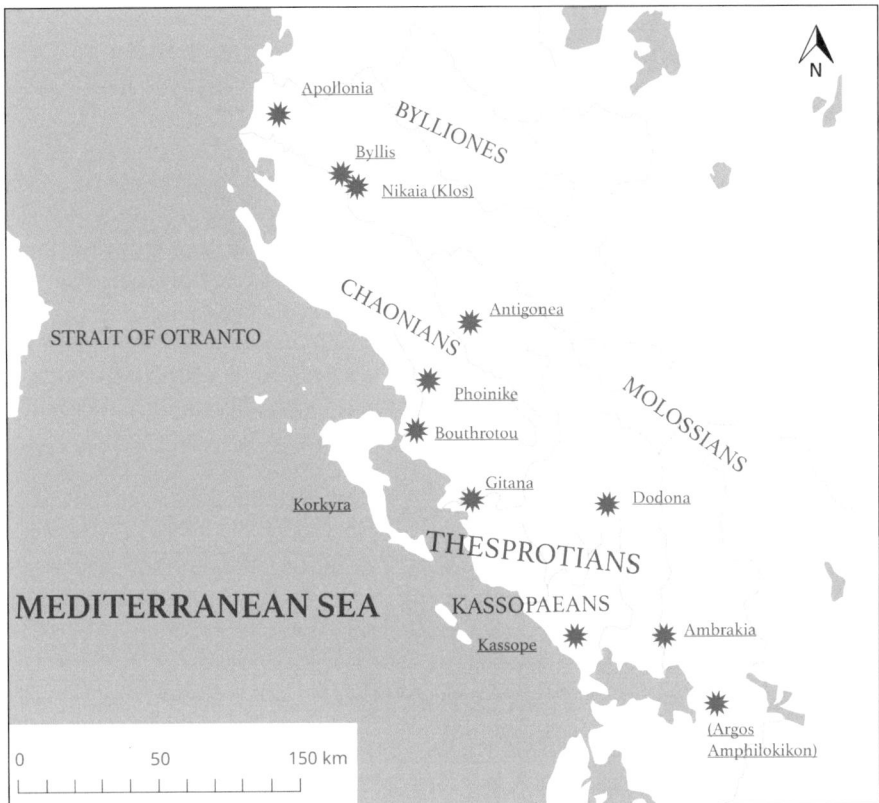

Figure 1. Map showing the cities of Epirus and Southern Illyria in which Hellenistic theatres have been detected (Author's elaboration). In light grey: the area corresponding to Pyrrhus' Great Epirus according to Cabanes (Cabanes 2016, pl. 3).

Theatres and cities in Epirus and Southern Illyria: From the Illyrian-Epirote to the Adriatic-Ionian *koinè*

As we have already been able to discuss, theatres represent an interesting perspective to see and understand some dynamics concerning the urbanistic and architectural development of territories.

Concerning precisely Epirus and Southern Illyria, before the Roman era, we can certainly find theatres in the cities of Apollonia, Byllis, Nikaia (Klos), *Phoinike*, *Buthroton*, Dodona, Gitana, *Kassope* and *Ambrakia*, while is still debated whether or not there was a theatre in *Argos Amphilokikon* (the first mention of the theatre can be found in: Rhomaios 1916; after that no excavation has been done on the site which is now part of a private property) and Antigonea (on the subject: Schettino, Çondi, Perna, Pierantoni, Ghezzi 2016), the city founded by Pyrrhus himself (Fig. 1).

Of course, this is not the proper place to give a detailed description of the characteristic and history of the Epirote and Illyrian theatres, also taking into account the complex issue about their chronology, their actual shape and functions (for a general overview of the theatres of the territory: Baçe 2002/2003, Soueref 2012, Jaupaj 2018, Xavier de Silva 2019). Nonetheless, some brief overviews on crucial aspects concerning the Epirote and Southern Illyrian theatres need to be introduced to proceed with the present analysis. First, it is necessary to say that with the exception of the theatres at Apollonia and *Ambrakia*, which are dated to the IV century BCE, all of the other buildings are no older than the III century BCE, thus being connected with the rise of the Aeacid monarchy and, later, to the activity still ongoing during at the time of the *Koinon* of the Epirotes, which actually needs to be re-evaluated in terms of propulsor and original urbanistic and architectural activity (an example of the shifting in chronology of some theatres' foundations or interventions can be seen in the interpretation Milena Melfi proposed for the Hellenistic theatre at Butrint: Melfi 2012).[1] Another important aspect to be underlined is that, with the exception of the colonies of Apollonia and *Ambrakia*, almost all of the other settlements in which the presence of a theatre is confirmed have been, at least for a part of their history, chosen as the administrative or representative centres of a *koinon*: namely, Byllis was the centre of the *Koinon* of the *Byllliones* (the question about the theatre at the nearby Nikaia is complex and yet to be resolved; see on the subject: Papajani 1979, 55; Cabanes 1986, 128), Dodona, other than being a sanctuary, was also the representative seat of the Molossians and the prominent centre of the *Koinon* of the Epirotes, *Phoinike* was the administrative centre of the *Chaonians*, Gitana was the seat of the *Thesprotians*, *Kassope* of the *Kassopaeans* and, ultimately, *Buthroton* was the main city of the *Prasaiboi*. These considerations, although not being directly connected with the architectural nor the topographic characteristics of these theatres, will be crucial to contextualise the analysis we are developing in this paper.

Concerning the theatres of this region, many are the theories and interpretations that aim to use or include these buildings in the definition of a regional architectural and urbanistic style, especially framed in the Hellenistic period and, sometimes even more precisely during Pyrrhus' monarchy.

One of the first interpretations on this subject was the one that identified a so-called Illyrian-Epirote *koinè* in the territory, a path recognisable in the urbanistic and architectonic characteristics of both regions, also often used to meet an ideological interpretation of the Epirote urbanisation that ties it with the Illyrian context and tends to anticipate the chronology of the monumentalisation of its centres compared to what is now generally accepted (for the theorisation of the Illyrian-Epirote *koinè* see: Ceka 1993). Between the main characteristics of this regional style we can name the shape of most of the settlements of the two regions, having impressive walls enclosing a vast area, which is largely not occupied by buildings, and the definition of broad monumental spaces in which is noted the connection between theatres and *agorai* as well as the proximity of this complex with the city walls. This last characteristic has often been used as one of the main arguments to underline the different function of the theatre in the cities of the *koina* compared to the *poleis*, interpreting the position of the theatre as the result of a preeminent political and administrative function, proper and characterising of the 'world of the *koina*' in opposition to the one of the *poleis*. Concerning specifically the architectural features of the buildings in Illyria and Epirus, it has been noted the tendency theatres have to present straight *analemmata* as well as a *proskenion* very close to the *koilon* (Fig. 2), and the widespread use of the polygonal order in many buildings of the III century BCE, mostly in the *stoai*.

Even if those elements cannot be neglected, and certainly contribute to define a regional Hellenistic style, more recent studies tend to focus on a wider contextualisation, namely an Adriatic-Ionian or even Mediterranean one.

Precisely concerning the association between theatres and *agorai*, as we have already briefly discussed, this is not peculiar only in the Illyrian and Epirote territories (for an extensive study on the *agorai* of Epirus in the Hellenistic period

---

1   The research done for my doctoral thesis, recently discussed and under review for the future publication, focuses exactly on the analysis, updating and contextualisation of all the data concerning Epirote and Southern Illyrian theatres. A dedicated analysis also compared data related to the buildings to the ones concerning the administrative status and history of the cities from their foundation to the Imperial times. The study, taking into account the most recent research on the territory and the related sources, but also considering the Mediterranean context, has led to a redefinition and reinterpretation of the whole corpus of theatres from the Hellenistic to the Roman period. Specifically, the study gave an updated overview of the chronology related to the theatres' foundation and monumentalisation, re-evaluating the later period of the *Koinon of the Epirotes* previously often neglected, at least in general studies, in favour of Pyrrhus' Kingdom.

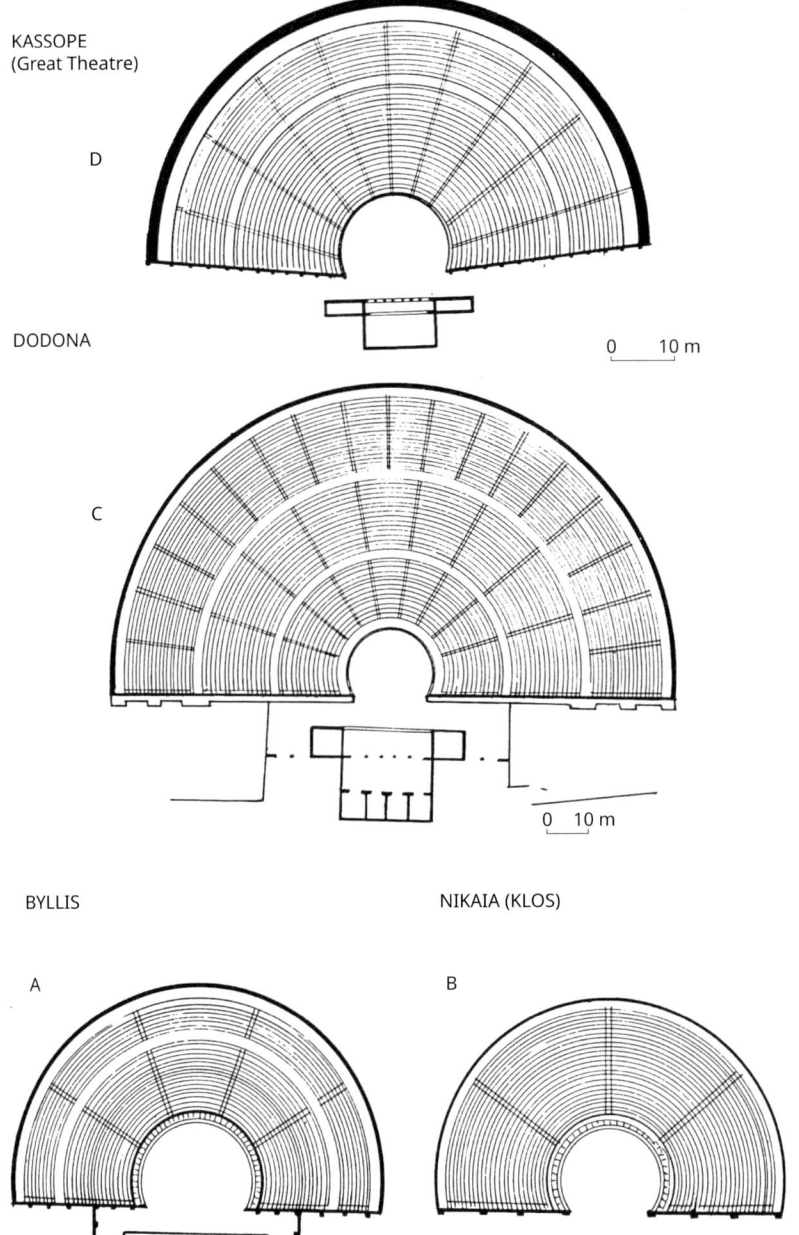

KASSOPE
(Great Theatre)

D

DODONA

0   10 m

C

0   10 m

BYLLIS

NIKAIA (KLOS)

A

B

0   10 m

0   10 m

*Figure 2. Ceka's Illyrian-Epirote
Koiné: a comparison of similar
theatre buildings in Epirus and
Southern Illyria (from Ceka 1993,
Tav. IV).*

see: Rinaldi 2020). On this account, the recent study of Dickenson has underlined how a close connection between theatres and *agorai* can start to be noticed, during the III century BCE, both in the Peloponnesian and the Macedonian areas, sometimes producing settings with similar characteristics compared to the Illyrian-Epirote ones (Dickenson names the cases of Argo, Messene, Megalopolis and Elis but also Mieza and Aigai in Macedonia: Dickenson 2018, 109-113). This picture clearly frames Epirus and Southern Illyria in the well-known network we discussed in the previous chapter and that actually characterised all of the history of this region.

It is also appropriate to notice that the theatre-*agora*-city walls scheme is clearly readable in the Illyrian-Epirote territory only in Byllis (and the nearby Nikaia, taking

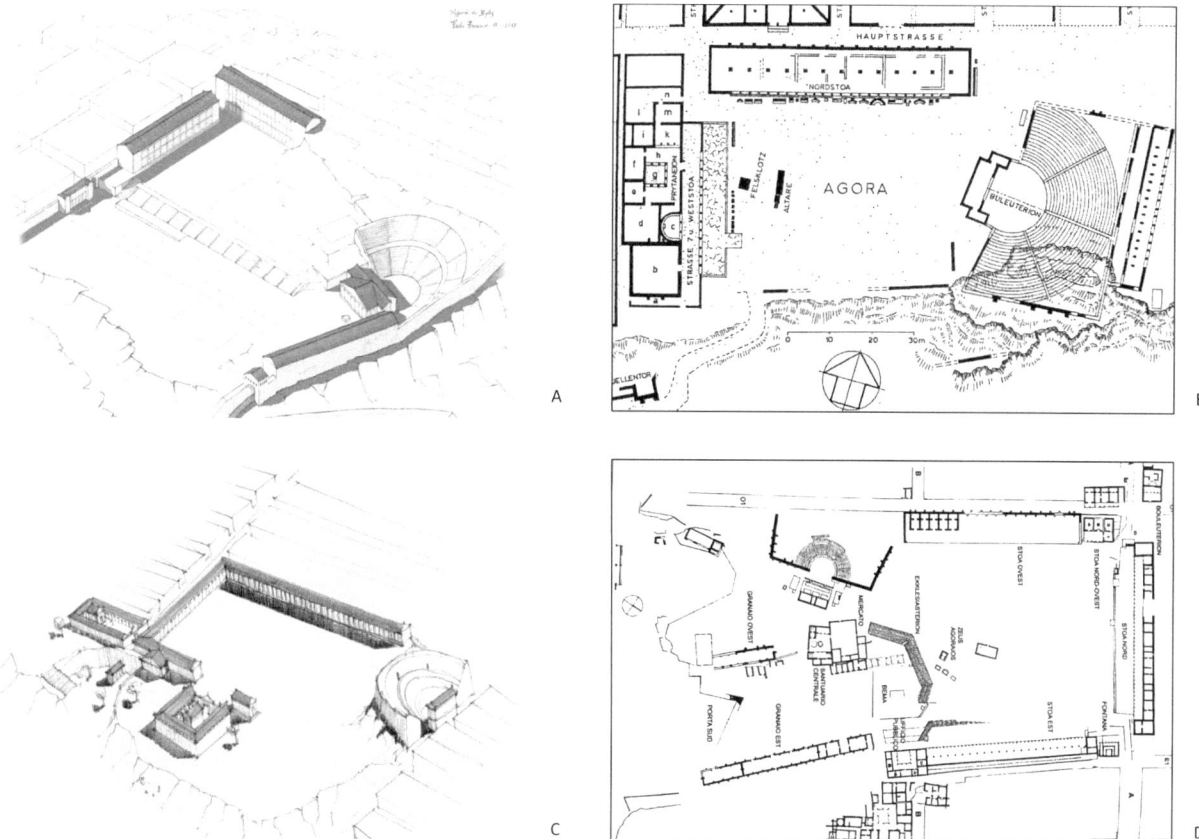

Figure 3. The theatre-agora
relationship in Illyrian-Epirote
and Sicilian cities: A. Byllis
(drawing by P. Baronio, from Belli
Pasqua, Përzhita 2017, Fig. 4),
B. Kassope (from Hoepfner,
Schwandner 1994), C. Agrigentum (drawing by A. Fino, from
Caliò 2019b), D. Morgantina
(from Ampolo 2012).

into account all of the problems concerning the relationship between these two cities and the lack of information on the planimetry of the site) and *Kassope*, where the building of the so-called *bouleuterion* seems actually to be dated in connection with the independence of the *koinon*, while at Byllis the theatre should be dated during the Aeacid monarchy. Intended connections with the *agorai* were also structured through different topographical and architectural means both at *Buthroton* and *Phoinike* (for the planimetry of Butrint see: Hodges, Hansen 2007, Fig. 2.8; for the theatre at Phoinike and the realisation of a monumental *periphatos* on top of the bulding see the analysis in Villichic 2018).

Moreover, it is possible to compare these *agorai* syntaxes also with examples related to *Magna Graecia* and Sicily (Fig. 3), underlining, once again, the connections existing in the Adriatic-Ionian space. Specifically, the *agorai* of Byllis and Kassope have been often compared to the Italian examples of Morgantina and Castiglione di Paludi (Caliò 2017, 364-367 and 2019a, 31-32) in which is possible to appreciate the same ratio behind the use of volumes and spaces, as testified by the use of the *theatron* at Morgantina and the stadium at Byllis. To these examples, after the most recent research, it is now possible to add the one of Agrigentum, whose disposition of the buildings and spaces in the *agora*, as well as the position of the theatre – also presenting straight *analemmata* – is very similar to Byllis and dated at the beginning of the III century BCE (Fino 2019; Caminneci, Lionetti, Parello 2019; Caliò 2019b).

Focusing now on the architectonic characteristics of the theatrical buildings, another interesting issue has been brought to light by Luigi Caliò who, in his recent articles, has underlined the presence, in some theatres on both sides of the Adriatic and Ionian seas, of a corridor proceeding from behind the scene building to the centre of the orchestra (Caliò 2019b, 213-225). This peculiar characteristic is common to the theatres of Byllis, Syracusa, Morgantina and, although in relation to different types of scene buildings, to Dodona, Gitana and Monte Iato, denouncing the need of an external access to the centre of the theatre, a spectacular entrance that Caliò suggests must be related to the conception of the theatre as an instrument for the royal propaganda. These theatres – as also shown in some urban settings, such as the ones at Byllis and Agrigentum – are part of a 'processional' path that has to be read in the light of that 'theatricality' typical of the Hellenism (Santagati 2019, 57-70). Thus, proceeding from the analysis of the association between the theatre and the palace in centres as Verghina or Pella to arrive at the formal elaboration of the *agora*-theatre scheme in Byllis and *Kassope*, we can trace the spread of an ideological use of the theatre, tied with the role of the king, which has its roots in the self-representation of the monarch already promoted by Philip II and Alexander the Great (Diod. 16, 93 and Diod. 17, 106, 3-7; Plut. *Alex.* 29) and identify itself, then, not as a regional peculiar characteristic, but as the outcome of a Hellenistic, therefor Mediterranean, idea.

A similar use of the theatre has been suggested for the theatrical buildings of Sicily, in a view of the architectural development of the island mainly attributed at the activity of Agathocles and Hiero II of Syracuse (the latest consideration on the subject in: Santagati 2019). However, on this account, it is essential to mention that the chronology of the monumentalisation of some settlements as well as the building of many theatres in Sicily is highly debated and often tends – in these last years – to be shifted to the late III and the beginning of the II century BCE (on the subject, among others: Campagna 2011, La Torre 2019, Marconi 2012, Vassallo 2019).

A contribution to the definition of the directions and extension of the Mediterranean networks could definitely come from a better understanding of the urbanistic and architectural development of the Ptolemaic Kingdom[2]. It is well known and diffusely debated the intervention that the Ptolemaic monarchs made in the foreign policies of both Epirus and Sicily and how they were often tied to other monarchs in these regions through weddings (on the subject: Fantasia 2017, 141, Lepore 2019). Unfortunately, evidence on Ptolemaic theatres as well as some urban-architectural assets is scarce. Nonetheless, it is possible to trace and understand possible influences on the Epirote and Italian architecture through the analysis of some 'bridge-cases' such as the one of Mytilene, whose theatre has been recently object of new studies (Triantafyllidis 2019 and Rocco, Livadiotti 2019). Recent research tends to date back the Ptolemaic influence on the north-eastern Aegean to the activity of Ptolemy Philadelphus, during the first years of the III century BCE: the presence of the Ptolemaic kings where the absence of Lysimachus had left a power void and – more specifically – in Samothrace seems to have had consequences also on Lesbos, where the Ptolemaic influence is later even more clear under Philopator (Meadows 2013a, 28-29 and 2013b, 5626). This been said, it is possible to identify in the theatrical building at Mytilene, whose foundation is placed at the beginning of the Hellenist period but the visible remains of the scene building are dated to the half of the II century BCE, many characteristics common to the Illyrian-Epirote and Southern-Italian and Sicilian theatres: the theatre has indeed Γ-shaped *parodoi* as the ones visible in the scene buildings of Dodona, Byllis, Morgantina and Iaitas, it presents the characteristic *pylones* used as monumental features of the same lateral entrances as known in Dodona and Epidaurus, while the *analemmata* are only slightly inclined, thus being very close to the typical Adriatic-Ionian straight ones (Rocco, Livadiotti 2019, 120).

It is clear, at this point, that, although tempting, trying to trace the directions of some shared models and ideas in the so-called Adriatic-Ionian *koinè* can be hasty, given the state of the current debate on the Sicilian theatres and the constant updating of the information on both sides of the Adriatic but also the numerous possibilities opened by recent studies which cannot be ignored but have still a highly embryonal shape.

---

2   I need to thank Professor Luigi Caliò for having suggested to take into account this path during my doctoral research. The theme needs of course a more thorough analysis, which is now being conducted for the future publication of the thesis.

Conclusions

We have started this analysis from a question: can the communities of Epirus and Southern Illyria be considered part of the Greek historical and archaeological environment or is their identity rather defined by opposition from it?

We have then briefly discussed many of the subjects and themes that, in a way or another, can be related to the definition of the historical and urbanistic dynamics of these territories and, therefore, to their identity concept, or at least the way they represented themselves to others.

Going through the definition of the *polis-ethnos* dichotomy, the study of the urbanisation process in Illyria and Epirus, the definition of a regional urbanistic and architectural style for the territories and, ultimately, the analysis of the place the theatre had in its realisation, it became clear that a better understanding of the dynamics proper of these regions always happens outside of that usual path of inclusion-exclusion with respect to the Greek world of the *polis*. Thus, the definition of a regional urbanistic and architectural history for Epirus and Southern Illyria is better accomplished in a wider context, namely the Mediterranean one and, more specifically, the Adriatic-Ionian space.

As we have seen, the growing number of data, concerning both the Balkan regions and the Italian ones, allows a more thorough analysis of the Hellenistic period in these territories. The realisation of a militarised and, at the same time, hierarchised landscape through the diffusion of fortified systems and the elaboration of a new syntax for the public spaces have been put in relation to the rise of a monarchic power both in Epirus and in Sicily.

The royal propaganda expresses itself through the urbanistic planning and the fortified landscape, as well as through the monumental syntax of spaces and volumes that serve the dynastic rituality. As we have already stated, the well-known dynastic relations between Epirus and Sicily – often sealed through weddings – suggest reading the archaeological evidence through the lens of the intense cultural exchange of models, ideas, possibly workforce, in the definition of a similar urbanistic-architectural syntax, ultimately respondent to a Mediterranean Hellenistic language that sets its roots in the Macedonian world and in the well-known experiences in Caria and at Pella under Cassander (on the subject see: Caliò 2017, specifically 356-367).

Surely, the constitution of the Aeacid Kingdom gave a determinant impulse to the urbanistic and architectural development of Epirus and Southern Illyria and must be seen as responsible for having spread and adapted a typically Hellenistic culture on the territory, especially concerning the concept of spaces and volumes, also re-enforcing relations with the principal actors on the Mediterranean scene. Anyway, it is also clear how the dynamics and the way this culture was assimilated depended on the peculiar organisation of the territory itself: as we could see, Pyrrhus' reign was not the only period in which Illyrian and Epirote cities had seen a flourishing building activity. The building and monumentalising activities during the later period of the *Koinon* of the Epirotes can lead us to two main statements: first, the aforementioned negotiation of power between the *koina* and the leading dynasty never ceased to operate, always showing some kind of autonomy in the local sub-administration which was clearly at the bottom of the future administrative re-organisation; and second, even after the fall of the Aeacid monarchy, the territory shows how deep the assimilation of the Hellenistic culture and language was, still acting on the same self-representation dynamics as before.

To conclude, given the history of the region, we can attempt to affirm that the communities of the Southern Illyrian and Epirote territories must have had a quite clear perception of the Mediterranean context of which they were part, this resulting in a visible effort of representing themselves to this very context through an acquired but also originally elaborated common language, as we have seen in the elaboration of the urbanistic-architectural syntax of the public spaces.

In contrast with a view that wants Epirus and Southern Illyria having shaped their identity concept and self-representation looking back at their own history, it is rather clear that they mostly expressed it through a path that underlines their connections from the Corinthian colonisation to the Roman era, with these connections being centred in the Mediterranean and more specifically in the Adriatic-Ionian context.

All of the elements analysed above ultimately suggest the idea that the Epirote communities actually acknowledged the role of the sea and namely the Mediterranean in shaping and defining their identities. Thus, it seems quite crucial to frame these regions in the Hellenistic Mediterranean context to read their history and understand their identity perception as well as the dynamics that defined their urban and architectural culture.

References

Ampolo, C., ed., 2012. *Agora greca e agorai di Sicilia*. Firenze: Edizioni della Normale.

Baçe, A., 2002/2003. Griechische Theater des 5. bis 3. Jahrhunderts in Illyrien und Epirus. *Bonner Jahrbücher*, 365-411.

Belli Pasqua, R., and Përzhita, L., 2017. Dalla tradizione alle nuove tecnologie: metodi di analisi integrati per lo studio della città di Byllis. *In*: L. Përzhita, ed. *New Archaeological Discoveries in the Albanian Regions. Proceedings of the International Conference, 30-31 January Tirana 2017*. Tirana: Botimet Albanologjike, 665-683.

Cabanes, P., 1976. *L'Epire, de la mort de Pyrrhos à la conquête romaine, 272-167 av. J.C.* Besançon: Université de Franche-Comté.

Cabanes, P., 1986. Recherches archéologiques en Albanie 1945-1985. *RA*, 1, 107-142.

Cabanes, P., 2001. *Histoire de l'Adriatique*. Paris: Éditions du Seuil.

Cabanes, P., 2007. Les Chaones et l'Épire, de l'independance a l'association (Ve-IIe siecles avant J.-C.). *In:* S. De Maria and S. Gjongecaj, eds. *Phoinike IV*. Bologna: Ante Quem Editoria, 227-238.

Cabanes, P., ed., 2016. *Corpus des inscriptions grecques d'Illyrie méridionale et d'Épire 3*. Études Épigraphiques 2. Athens: École française d'Athènes.

Caliò, L.M., 2017. L'architettura fortificata in occidente tra la Sicilia e l'Epiro. *In*: L.M. Caliò and J. des Courtils, eds. *L'architettura greca in Occidente nel III secolo a.C. Atti del convegno di studi, Pompei-Napoli, 20-22 maggio 2015*. Rome: Edizioni Quasar, 323-368.

Caliò, L.M., 2019a. Dalla polis immaginata all'asty delle immagini. Percorsi di analisi dell'immagine di città nel mondo antico. *In*: R. Belli Pasqua, L.M. Caliò, L.M. Liviadotti and G. Martines, eds. *Theatroeideis 1. L'immagine della città greca ed ellenistica. L'immagine della città, la città delle immagini. Atti del Convegno Internazionale, Bari, 15-19 giugno 2016*. Bari: Edizioni Quasar, 15-46.

Caliò, L.M., 2019b. Il teatro di Agrigento e lo sviluppo della città monumentale. Appunti di storia urbana. *In*: V. Caminneci, M.C. Parello and M.S. Rizzo, eds. *Theaomai. Teatro e società in età ellenistica. Atti delle XI Giornate Gregoriane (Agrigento, 2-3 dicembre 2017)*. Firenze: All'Insegna del Giglio, 201-228.

Caminneci, V., Lionetti, A.L. and Parello, M.C., 2019. Il teatro di Agrigento. Rapporto delle ricerche sul campo. *In*: V. Caminneci, M.C. Parello and M.S. Rizzo, eds. *Theaomai. Teatro e società in età ellenistica. Atti delle XI Giornate Gregoriane (Agrigento, 2-3 dicembre 2017)*, Firenze: All'Insegna del Giglio, 181-192.

Campagna, L., 2011. L'archeologia dei teatri nella Sicilia ellenistica tra tradizione e nuove prospettive di ricerca. *In*: D. Tomasello, ed. *La scena dell'isola. Turismo, cultura e spettacolo in Sicilia. Atti del convegno nazionale della CUT (Consulta universitaria del Teatro). Messina-Noto, 9-11 ottobre 2008*. Rome: Aracne, 41-57.

Castiglioni, M.P. and Lamboley, J.-L., 2015. Les Grecs en Adriatique, bilan et perspectives. *In*: Y. Marion and F. Tassaux, eds. *AdriAtlas et l'histoire de l'espace adriatique du VIe s. a.C. au VIIIe s. p.C. Actes du colloque international de Rome (4-6 novembre 2013)*. Ausonius Scripta Antiqua 79. Bordeaux: Ausonius Éditions, 149-160.

Ceka, N., 1993. La koinè illyro-épirote dans le domaine de l'architecture. *IMEA II*, 123-133.

Chaniotis, A., 1997. Theatricality Beyond the Theater. Staging Public Life in the Hellenistic World. *In*: B. Le Guen, ed. *De la scène aux gradins*. PALLAS 47. Toulouse: Presses universitaires du Mirail, 219-259.

Coviello, G., 2003. Roma, gli Italici, l'Adriatico e il mondo ellenistico. *Hesperia*, 17, 89-113.

D'Andria, F., 1990. Documenti del commercio arcaico tra Ionio ed Adriatico. *In*: G. Pugliese Carratelli, ed. *Magna Grecia, Epiro e Macedonia, Atti del Ventiquattresimo convegno di studi sulla Magna Grecia. Taranto 5-10 ottobre 1984*. Taranto: Istituto per la storia e l'archeologia della Magna Grecia, 321-377.

D'Andria, F., 1995. Corinto e l'Occidente: la costa adriatica. *In*: A. Stazio and S. Ceccoli, eds. *Corinto e l'occidente. Atti del trentaquattresimo convegno di studi sulla Magna Grecia. Taranto, 7-11 ottobre 1994*. Taranto: Istituto per la storia e l'archeologia della Magna Grecia, 457-508.

De Courtils, J., 2015. *Introduction. In*: J. de Courtils, ed. *L'architecture Monumentale Grecque ai IIIe siècle a.C.* Mémoires 40. Bordeaux: Ausonius Éditions, 11-19.

Di Napoli, V., 2013. *Teatri della Grecia romana: forma, decorazione, funzioni. La provincia d'Acaia. MEΛΕΤΗΜΑΤΑ 67. At*hens and Paris: Fondazione nazionale delle ricerche, Istituto di studi storici per l'Antichità greche e romane (Diff. de Boccard).

Dickenson, C.P., 2013. Kings, cities and marketplaces – negotiating power through public space in the Hellenistic world. *In*: C.P. Dickenson and O.M. van Nijf, eds. *Public space in the post-classical city*. Caeculus: Papers on Mediterranean Archaeology and Greek and Roman Studies. Leuven: Peeters Publishers, 37-75.

Dickenson, C.P., 2017. *On the Agorà. The Evolution of a Public Space in Hellenistic and Roman Greece (c. 323 BC – 267 AD)*. Mnemosyne Supplements 398. London and Boston: Brill.

Fantasia, U., 2017. *Ambracia dai Cipselidi ad Augusto. Contributo alla storia della Grecia nord-occidentale fino alla prima età imperial*. Diabaseis 7. Pisa: Edizioni ETS.

Fino, A., 2019. Il teatro di Agrigento: per uno studio dell'architettura. *In*: V. Caminneci, M.C. Parello and M.S. Rizzo, eds. *Theaomai. Teatro e società in età ellenistica. Atti delle XI Giornate Gregoriane (Agrigento, 2-3 dicembre 2017)*. Firenze: All'Insegna del Giglio, 163-180.

Frederiksen, R., 2002. The Greek Theatre. A typical building in the urban centre of the *polis? In*: T.H. Nielsen, ed. *Even more studies in the ancient Greek polis*. Papers of the Copenaghen Polis Centre 6 (HISTORIA Einzelschriften 162). Stuttgart: Steiner, 65-124.

Giorgi, E. and Bogdani, J. 2012. *Il territorio di Phoinike in Caonia. Archeologia del paesaggio in Albania meridionale*. Bologna: Ante Quem Editora.

Hansen, M.H. and Nielsen, T.H., 2004. *An inventory of archaic and classical poleis*. Oxford: Oxford University Press.

Hansen, M.H. and Fischer-Hansen, T., 1994. Monumental Political Architecture in Archaic and Classical Greek *Poleis*. Evidence and Historical Significance. *In*: D. Whitehead, ed. *From Political Architecture to Stephanus Byzantintius. Sources for the Ancient Greek Polis*. Papers of the Copenhagen Polis Centre 1 (HISTORIA Einzelschriften 87). Stuttgart: Steiner, 23-90.

Hellman, M.C., 2002. *L'architecture grecque 1, Les principes de la construction.* Paris: Picard.

Hellman, M.C., 2006. *L'architecture grecque 2, Architecture religieuse et funéraire.* Paris: Picard.

Hellman, M.C., 2010. *L'architecture grecque III. Habitat, urbanisme et fortification.* Paris: Picard.

Hodges, R. and Hansen, I.L., eds., 2007. *Roman Butrint: an assessment.* Oxford: Oxbow Books.

Hoepfner, W, Schwandner, E.L., Dakaris, S., Gravani, K. and Tsingas, A., 1994. Kassope. Bericht über die Ausgrabungen einer spätklassischen Streifenstadt in Nordwestgriechenland. *In*: W. Hoepfner and E.L. Schwandner, eds. *Haus und Stadt im klassichen Griechenland, Wohnen in der klassichen Polis I.* München: Deutscher Kunstverlag, 114-161.

Jaupaj, L., 2018. Les théâtres dans les villes d'Illyrie méridionale et d'Épire. *In*: J.-L. Lamboley, L. Përzhita and A. Skënderaj, eds. *L'Illyrie Méridionale et l'Épire dans l'Antiquité. Actes du VIe Colloque International de Tirana (20-23 mai 2015). Vol. III.* Paris: Diffusion de Boccard, 1029-1044.

Kolb, F., 1981. *Agorà und Theater, Volks- und Festversammlung.* Archäologische Forschungen 9. Berlin: Mann Verlag.

Kreeb, M., 2019. La posizione dell'edificio teatrale greco in età ellenistica e la sua relazione con la città. *In*: V. Caminneci, M.C. Parello and M.S. Rizzo, eds. *Theaomai. Teatro e società in età ellenistica. Atti delle XI Giornate Gregoriane (Agrigento, 2-3 dicembre 2017).* Firenze: All'Insegna del Giglio, 11-17.

La Torre, G.F., 2019. Il teatro nelle *poleis* della Sicilia ellenistica: ubicazione e funzioni. *In*: V. Caminneci, M.C. Parello and M.S. Rizzo, eds. *Theaomai. Teatro e società in età ellenistica. Atti delle XI Giornate Gregoriane (Agrigento, 2-3 dicembre 2017).* Firenze: All'Insegna del Giglio, 19-32.

Lamboley, J.-L., 1987. Le canal d'Otrante et les relations entre les deux rives de l'Adriatique. *In*: P. Cabanes, ed. *L'Illyrie Méridionale et l'Épire dans l'Antiquité. Actes du Colloque International de Clermond-Ferrand (22-25 octobre 1984).* Clermond-Ferrand: Editions Adosa, 195-202.

Lamboley, J.-L., 1993. État de la recherche sur les relations sud-adriatiques. Bilan et perspectives. *In*: P. Cabanes, ed. *L'Illyrie Méridionale et l'Épire dans l'Antiquité. Actes du Colloque International de Clermond-Ferrand (25-27 octobre 1990).* Paris: De Boccard, 231-237.

Lasagni, C., 2011. *Il concetto di realtà locale nel mondo greco. Uno studio introduttivo nel confronto tra* poleis *e stati federali.* Rome: Aracne Editrice.

Lasagni, C., 2018. "Tribal *poleis*" in Northwestern Greece. *In:* S. Montel and A. Pollini, eds. *La question de l'espace au IVe siècle avant J.-C. dans les mondes grec et étrusco-italique: continuités, ruptures, reprises.* Besançon: Institut des Sciences et Techniques de l'Antiquité, 159-188.

Lauter, H., 1986. *Die Architektur des Hellenismus.* Darmstadt: Wissenschaftliche Buchgesellschaft.

Lepore, E., 1990. Il problema storico dei rapporti tra Epiro e Magna Grecia. *In*: G. Pugliese Carratelli, ed. *Magna Grecia, Epiro e Macedonia, Atti del Ventiquattresimo convegno di studi sulla Magna Grecia. Taranto 5-10 ottobre 1984.* Taranto: Istituto per la storia e l'archeologia della Magna Grecia, 7-16.

Lippolis, E., 2017. L'architettura di III sec. a.C. *In*: L.M. Caliò, and J. des Courtils, eds. *L'architettura greca in Occidente nel III secolo a.C. Atti del convegno di studi, Pompei-Napoli, 20-22 maggio 2015.* Rome: Edizioni Quasar, 13-43.

Mancini, L., 2013. Templi, *thesauroi*, 'temples-trésors'. Note sull'edilizia templare non periptera nei santuari dell'Epiro ellenistico. *Ocnus*, 21, 77-101.

Marconi, C., 2012. Between performance and identity. The social context of stone theatres in late Classical and Hellenistic Sicily. *In*: K. Boscher, ed. *Theater outside*

Athens. Drama in Greek Sicily and South Italy. Cambridge: Cambridge University Press, 175-207.

Marziali, A., Perna, R., Qirjaqi, V. and Tadolti, M., 2012. La Valle del Drino in età ellenistica. *In*: R. Perna and D. Çondi, eds. *Hadrianopolis II. Risultati delle indagini archeologiche 2005-2010.* Bari: Edipuglia, 67-102.

Meadows, A., 2013a. The Ptolemaic League of Islanders. In: K. Buraselis, M. Stefanou and D.J. Thompson, eds. *The Ptolemies, the Sea and the Nile: Studies in Waterborne Power.* Cambridge: Cambridge University Press, 19-38.

Meadows, A., 2013b. Ptolemaic Possessions outside Egypt. *In*: R.S. Bagnall, K. Brodersen, C.B. Champion, A. Erskine and S.R. Huebner, eds. *The Encyclopedia of Ancient History, First Edition.* New Jersey: Wiley, 5625-5629.

Melfi, M., 2012. Butrinto: da Santuario di Asclepio a centro federale. *In*: G. de Marinis, G.M. Fabrini, G. Paci, R. Perna and M. Silvestrini, eds. *I processi formativi ed evolutivi della città in area adriatica.* BAR International Series 2419. Oxford: Archaeopress, 23-30.

Melfi, M. and Piccinini, J., 2012a. Geografia storica del territorio di *Hadrianopolis* nella valle del Drino (V sec. a.C. – 44 a.C.). *In*: R. Perna and D. Çondi, eds. *Hadrianopolis II. Risultati delle indagini archeologiche 2005-2010.* Bari: Edipuglia, 37-50.

Melfi, M. and Piccinini, J., 2012b. Le Fonti. *In:* R. Perna and D. Çondi, eds. *Hadrianopolis II. Risultati delle indagini archeologiche 2005-2010.* Bari: Edipuglia, 51-65.

Moretti, J.-C., 2014. The Evolution of the Theatre Architecture Outside Athens in the Fourth Century. *In*: E. Csapo, H.R. Goette, J.R. Green and P. Wilson, eds. *Greek Theatre in the Fourth Century B.C.* Berlin and Boston: De Gruyter, 107-137.

Papajani, L., 1979. Le théâtre de la ville illyrienne à Klos de Malakster et les travaux de restauration qui y ont été effectués. *Monumentet*, 18, 43-55.

Perna, R., 2012. Conclusioni. *In*: R. Perna and D. Çondi, eds. *Hadrianopolis II. Risultati delle indagini archeologiche 2005-2010.* Bari: Edipuglia, 235-256.

Perna, R., 2014. *Hadrianopolis e la valle del Drino (Albania). Considerazioni sulle trasformazioni dell'insediamento e del territorio dall'età ellenistica a quella bizantina (campagne di scavo e surveys 2011-2015).* ASAA XCII (Serie III, 14). Padova: Aldo Ausilio Editore, 195-260.

Perna, R., 2017. I centri minori nella valle del Drino (Albania) tra V e II sec. a.C. *QuadFriulA XXVII*, 99-110.

Podini, M., 2014. *La decorazione architettonica di età ellenistica e romana nell'Epiro del nord.* Bologna: Bononia University Press.

Rhomaios, K., 1916. Paraptema tou arxaiologikou deltiou tou 1916, *ΑΔ* 2. *Chronika*, 51.

Rinaldi, E., 2020. *Agorai ed edilizia pubblica e civile nell'Epiro di età ellenistica.* Bologna: Bononia University Press.

Rocco, G. and Livadiotti, M., 2019. Il teatro ellenistico di Mytilene: note preliminari per la sua ricostruzione. *In*: V. Caminneci, M.C. Parello and M.S. Rizzo, eds. *Theaomai. Teatro e società in età ellenistica. Atti delle XI Giornate Gregoriane (Agrigento, 2-3 dicembre 2017).* Firenze: All'Insegna del Giglio, 113-123.

Santagati, E. 2019, Teatro e *basileus* in età ellenistica: quale rapporto? *In*: V. Caminneci, M.C. Parello and M.S. Rizzo, eds. *Theaomai. Teatro e società in età ellenistica. Atti delle XI Giornate Gregoriane (Agrigento, 2-3 dicembre 2017).* Firenze: All'Insegna del Giglio, 55-62.

Schettino, A., Çondi, D., Perna, R., Pierantoni, P.P., Ghezzi, A., 2016. Searching for the Antigonea Theatre: A Magnetic Survey in an Ancient Epirus City". *Archaeological Prospection* 24 (1), 1-13. Available from: doi:10.1002/arp.1549

Soueref, K., ed., 2012. Αρχαία θέατρα της Ηπείρου. Athens: C.G. Lazos.

Soueref, K., 2015. Macedonia ed Epiro tra Filippo e Pirro. *In*: A. Siciliano, K. Mannino and M.M. Manco, eds. *La Magna Grecia da Pirro ad Annibale: atti del cinquantaduesimo convegno di studi sulla Magna Grecia, Taranto,*

27-30 settembre 2012. Taranto: Istituto per la Storia e l'Archeologia della Magna Grecia, 15-23.

Triantafyllidis, P., 2019. The Theatre at Mytilene: preliminary report, historical and topographical framework. *In*: V. Caminneci, M.C. Parello and M.S. Rizzo, eds. *Theaomai. Teatro e società in età ellenistica. Atti delle XI Giornate Gregoriane (Agrigento, 2-3 dicembre 2017)*. Firenze: All'Insegna del Giglio, 105-111.

Vassallo, S., 2019. Il Teatro di Montagna dei Cavalli: la cronologia. *In*: V. Caminneci, M.C. Parello and M.S. Rizzo, eds. *Theaomai. Teatro e società in età ellenistica. Atti delle XI Giornate Gregoriane (Agrigento, 2-3 dicembre 2017)*. Firenze: All'Insegna del Giglio, 33-40.

Villicich, R., 2018. *Il teatro di Phoinike*. Bologna: Bononia University Press.

Vlassopoulos, K., 2007. *Unthinking the Greek polis: ancient Greek history beyond Eurocentrism*. Cambridge: Cambridge University Press.

Winter, F.E., 2006. *Studies in Hellenistic Architecture*. Toronto, Buffalo and London: University of Toronto Press.

Xavier de Silva, L., 2019. Theatrical architecture as evidence of cultural change. Theatre and society in Epirus and Southern Illyria between 'hellenization' and 'romanization'. *In*: V. Caminneci, M.C. Parello and M.S. Rizzo, eds. *Theaomai. Teatro e società in età ellenistica. Atti delle XI Giornate Gregoriane (Agrigento, 2-3 dicembre 2017)*. Firenze: All'Insegna del Giglio, 71-76.

Frozen wine and the frozen Black Sea. Ovid as an exiled poet faced with climatic extremes (trist. 3.10; Pont. 4.7; 4.9; 4.10)

Stefan Feddern

Abstract

In this paper, we will analyse especially Ovid's exile elegy trist. 3.10, but also three *Epistulae ex Ponto* (Pont. 4.7; 4.9; 4.10) in which Ovid talks about the climatic extremes he is faced with at Tomis. After an introductory and a methodological section, two questions are addressed: does Ovid imitate Virgil's description of the Scythian tribes (georg. 3.249-383)? How reliable is Ovid in telling us the climatic extremes? In our analysis, we try to take into account not only the modern but also the ancient perspective, especially regarding the questions of whether wine and the Black Sea can freeze.

Intertextuality, fictionality, climatic extremes, authority

Introduction

As is generally accepted, Ovid was banished from Rome by Augustus (8 AD) at the age of 50 and relegated to Tomis, situated at the Pontus Euxinus (Black Sea), at the north-eastern frontier of the Roman Empire, where he arrived almost one year later and where he died about ten years later (17 or 18 AD). During his exile, Ovid wrote *inter alia* nine books of elegiac poems, the *Tristia* ("Sadnesses, Lamentations", five books) and the *Epistulae ex Ponto* ("Letters from the Black Sea", four books).

The question how the Mediterranean links people and transforms identities can be applied to Ovid's exile poetry insofar as these poems contain Ovid's complaints about his exile among barbarians in totally different and depressing cultural sorroundings, and – explicitly or implicitly – show the contrast between his former life in the political-religious atmosphere of Rome and his present situation at Tomis.[1] Therefore, these poems seem to be especially useful to shed light on a Roman-Mediterranean identity on one side, and on the changes of identity caused by the absence from the Roman-Mediterranean area on the other side.[2]

However, as I cannot examine all of the relevant Ovidian statements about his change of identity before the background of his former life in Rome and his exile at Tomis, I will limit myself to one important aspect of Ovid's individual identity as exiled poet: how the climatic extremes of the Pontic winter affected Ovid. As it is debated how seriously we must or must not take Ovid's account of the Tomitan winter and his exile poems in general, the focus of this investigation must lie on Ovid's reliability. Nonetheless, this is an important aspect of Ovid's identity also insofar as his poems deal with the different ethnographic and geographical knowledge between the average Roman citizen and himself as an eyewitness of the narrated events who has more precise insights.

Though the climate change that is taking place nowadays in its possible contrast to the ancient climate is not the topic of this paper (we could just speak subjectively of Ovid's individual climate change due to his relegation to Tomis), it is highly relevant to Ovid's description of the extreme Tomitan winter especially in trist. 3.10 because the answer to the question how we have to understand Ovid's complaints about the Black Sea climate, seems to depend significantly on our knowledge and imagination of how hard a winter could and can be (see point 3.2).

Some methodological remarks about fiction, fiction signals, intertextuality and the possible fictionality of Ovid's exile poetry

As to the relation to reality, every text has to be seen on a scale with two extreme points which, in my view, are never achieved totally: no text is a copy of reality, and no text does not have anything at all to do with reality (*i.e.* every text – in some degree – is related to reality). Consequently, every text poses the question on the readers to determine, if possible, the exact (or the approximate) degree of its relation to reality. However, in many cases the readers are unable to judge the exact degree of the factuality or fictionality of the respective text, especially – as in this case – if the poems were written about 2,000 years ago and we do not have other sources to verify the poet's statements. The modern readers can possibly get some help from the knowledge of the literary genres, contexts and conventions that are valid for groups of texts so that – with some probability – the individual text might be expected to follow these generic rules and be (more) factual or (more) fictional. However, there are literary genres whose factuality or fictionality is debated, and this is especially true for Ovid's exile elegies, the majority of researchers – almost without any exception – favouring the view that they have to be regarded as fictional poetry.

When we talk about (the) fictionality (of Ovid's exile poems), this term as well as "fiction" and "fictivity" could be understood in many ways. When I use these terms, I understand them in the traditional and even ancient sense that the narrated events, actors and/or places are invented, that their invention is intentional, but does not involve an accusation of lying or something similar, but is legitimated by a social

---

1   For Ovid's description of Rome (and Tomis) in his exile poetry, cf. Reitz 2013; Dan 2011; Grebe 2004. For the culture of the Black Sea region, cf. Dana 2011.

2   Ovid calls himself a barbarian is his exile poems; cf. trist. 5.10.37: *barbarus hic ego sum* ("here I am a barbarian").

practice that in modern times is often called "fiction pact".[3] With reference to Ovid's exile poetry, these terms can mean that the whole exile is a fiction. This view was hold 30 years ago by Fitton Brown and other scholars,[4] but is almost completely rejected nowadays.[5] Or their meaning can be that the exile itself is historical, but that Ovid's account of his exile is a fictionalisation, *i.e.* a combination of historical facts and fictional elements. This is the current *communis opinio*. If scholars adduce evidence for the view that Ovid's exile poetry is fictional in this sense, they refer especially to two scholars' investigations: to Podossinov, who deals with climatological and ethnographic material in particular;[6] and Chwalek, who presents a list of nine fiction signals, partly relying on Podossinov.[7]

In my view, the fictionality of Ovid's exile poetry is not proven. An analysis of the supposed fiction signals shows that there are perhaps some cases of doubt, but that there is no clear fiction signal. In order to make this view plausible, I cannot discuss Chwalek's whole list of supposed fiction signals, but will limit myself to the most prominent one in the research about Ovid's exile poetry and at the same time to the subject of this paper, namely the similarities between Ovid's description of the winter at Tomis (trist. 3.10) and Virgil's description of the Scythian tribes in his *Georgics* (georg. 3.249-383). If you follow Besslich[8] (and almost all researchers, not only those who discuss trist. 3.10 in particular,[9] but also those who are dealing with Ovid's exile poetry in general, quote Besslich with approval),[10] Ovid is drawing on Virgil to describe his own situation at Tomis.[11] Those researchers who deal with the question of fictionality (as Podossinov and Chwalek) go even a step further and regard this case of (supposed) intertextuality as a fiction signal.[12]

However, it seems doubtful if this conclusion is justified, and the doubt begins with the fact that Besslich holds the view that Ovid is imitating Virgil, but that the main difference between the two poets is that Virgil gives a fictional account of the Scythian tribes, while Ovid gives a factual account of his own personal situation.[13] Therefore, the following questions have to be answered, if possible: First, does Ovid really imitate Virgil? Second, is intertextuality a fiction signal in general? Third, even if Ovid imitates Virgil, is this special case of intertextuality a fiction signal? In this paper, I will argue that it is possible that Ovid imitates Virgil, that intertextuality itself is no (clear) fiction signal, and that even if Ovid would be imitating Virgil, there would be no reason to regard his description of the Tomitan winter as fictional, as long as no invented events or descriptions can be detected.

Before we address the first and the third question in the context of our analysis of trist. 3.10, we should conclude this introductory section with some reflections about

---

3   For the ancient discourse about fictionality cf. Feddern 2018. For the modern discourse cf. Zipfel 2001; Lamarque/Olsen 1994. I use the terms "fictivity" and "fictive" with regard to the narrated events, *i.e.* to the *histoire*, while the terms "fictionality" and "fictional" are related to statements, texts and media that are allowed to utter untrue things. "Fiction" is the generic term of these phenomena. Cf. Klauk/Köppe 2014, 5–7; Kablitz 2008, 14–18.

4   Cf. Fitton Brown 1985; Holleman 1985; Hofmann 1987 and 2001. This view is at least as old as 1923, when Hartman judged *Ovidium omnino non esse relegatum* ("that Ovid was not banished at all"); cf. Florian 2007, 22.

5   For this judgement and for an overview over the debate, cf. Bérchez Castaño 2015, 25-43; Seibert 2014, 48-54; Wulfram 2008, 219-220; Florian 2007, 22-49; Martin 2004, 11-30.

6   Cf. Podossinov 1987.

7   Cf. Chwalek 1996, 32-64. For the fictionality of Ovid's exile poems cf. also Maisuradze/Schollmeyer 2017; Schmitt 2013; Schmitzer 2011, 179-208; Helzle 2006; Gärtner 2005, 16-24; Williams 1994, 8-25; Claassen 1990; Lozovan 1959.

8   Cf. Besslich 1972.

9   Cf. Trevizam/Avellar 2016; Lenz 1993; Gahan 1978; Evans 1975.

10   Cf. Amann 2006, 174; Holzberg 1998, 36; Claassen 1990, 77-80.

11   For Virgil's influence on Ovid's *Tristia* in general, cf. Bews 1984.

12   Cf. Podossinov 1987, 124-126; Chwalek 1996, 44-45.

13   Cf. Besslich 1972, 182-183. The same view is hold by Evans 1975, 1.

the fiction signals in general and intertextuality (as a possible fiction signal). The authors of fictional texts offer the fictional pact to the readers, and this means that with fiction signals they make clear that the text should be perceived in the make-believe mode.[14] However, most of the fiction signals that are discussed in modern narratology and fiction theory hint to the fictionality of the narratives without proving it.[15] The fictionality of a literary text is obvious if some clear signals point in the same direction, *e.g.* if a narrative is called "novel" in the paratext and contains an impossible story in which the heterodiegetic author-narrator uses focalisation, *i.e.* can see through walls and inside brains.[16]

As to intertextuality, I understand this term not just in the meaning of parallel passages, but as an intentional adaptation (imitation) of another author's thoughts and/or words.[17] This concept of intertextuality is more or less equivalent to the ancient notion of imitation (*imitatio*), as is especially shown by a passage in one of the elder Seneca's *suasoriae*, in which – highly relevant to our topic – an Ovidian imitation of a Virgilian expression is discussed and two forms of imitation are distinguished. In this passage the declaimers and literary critics debate about the Virgilian expression *plena deo* ("(she) full of the god") that is not found in the Virgilian works as they are transmitted to us. Seneca the elder reports that the declaimer Arellius Fuscus imitated Virgil, when he said about the seer Calchas who is inspired by divine knowledge:[18]

> *cur hoc sortitur potissimum pectus, quod tanto numine impleat? aiebat se imitatum esse Vergilium: 'plena deo'.*

> Why does he light on *this* heart in particular to fill with such vast power? He said that he had imitated the Virgilian *plena deo*.

In an anecdote, Seneca the elder tells us that *plena deo*, always in its feminine form, became a popular expression inside and outside the declamation schools and that Gallio, in the presence of Messala and Tiberius, used it with reference to hot tempered declaimers. Ovid, too, used this expression, probably in his tragedy *Medea* and perhaps with his friend Gallio as the mediating link between himself and Virgil:[19]

> *hoc autem dicebat Gallio Nasoni suo valde placuisse; itaque fecisse illum, quod in multis aliis versibus Vergilii fecerat, non subripiendi causa sed palam mutuandi, hoc animo ut vellet agnosci. esse autem in tragoedia eius: "feror huc illuc, vae, plena deo".*

---

14   For the fiction signals, cf. Zipfel 2001, 232-243 and Zipfel 2014.

15   Cf. Zipfel 2014, 102-103; Zipfel 2001, 243-247.

16   From an ancient point of view, cf. Augustine's (c. mend. 28) statement that no one ever was so stupid that he regarded the Aesopic fables as lies and not as allegorical fictional narratives.

17   For the concept of imitation in opposition to parallels and similarities and for the difficulty to detect (direct) imitation, cf. West/Woodman 1979, 195 (quoted in Hinds' 1998, 19 fundamental monograph on this topic): "[...] imitation also poses problems. In the first place [...] cases where one author imitates another are difficult to establish. Similarities of word or thought or phrase can occur because writers are indebted to a common source, or because they are describing similar or conventional situations, or because their works belong to the same generic type of poem. [...] Only patient scholarship and a thorough familiarity with the relevant material can reveal whether the similarities cannot be explained by any of these three reasons. In such cases we may be fairly certain that direct imitation of one author by another is taking place." For the concept of imitation in Latin poetry, cf. also Conte 2017.

18   Sen. suas. 3.5. Translation adapted from Winterbottom 1974, 543 who reads *Vergilianum* instead of *Vergilium*. Fuscus' declamation must have been held before 8 BCE because Seneca the elder comments that Fuscus, in this and in other *suasoriae*, imitated Virgil in many points in order to please Maecenas who died in 8 BCE.

19   Sen. suas. 3.7. Translation adapted from Winterbottom 1974, 545.

Gallio said that his friend Ovid had very much liked the phrase: and that as a result the poet did something he had done with many other lines of Virgil – with no thought of plagiarism, but meaning that his piece of open borrowing should be noticed. And in his tragedy you may read: "I am carried hither and thither, alas, full of the god."

If we follow Gallio, Ovid imitated Virgil in many passages. While "imitation" means that he borrowed the thoughts and/or words intentionally from Virgil, here the concept of imitation is further subdivided by the question with which intention one author imitates another: if the imitating author wants the imitation to be recognised, the imitation is accepted and maybe even praised; if he does not want it to be recognised, it is a case of plagiarism.[20]

However, as the discussion reported by the elder Seneca shows, it is often very difficult to decide if one author is imitating another. Who would have recognised that Arellius Fuscus imitated the – at least supposed – Virgilian expression *plena deo* with the paraphrase that a god filled the heart of a person with vast (divine) power (*numine implere*)? Probably, even his contemporaries would have had difficulties to see this intertextuality, if Arellius Fuscus had not explicitly explained it.[21] On the other hand, Ovid's imitation of the Virgilian expression *plena deo* is quite easy to realise, because he is citing verbatim a thought that is in no way an everyday thought. However, this is just one kind of intertextuality and probably not so typical for the Augustan poets as another, more hidden and creative kind of imitation in which the imitator appropriates another author's thoughts or words, as Horace explains regarding common material:[22]

publica materies privati iuris erit, si

non [...]

[...] verbo verbum curabis reddere fidus

interpres nec desilies imitator in artum,

unde pedem proferre pudor vetet aut operis lex.

The common material will become your private property if you do not [...] anxiously render word for word, a (too-)faithful translator, or, in the process of imitation, put yourself in a tight corner from which timidity, or the rule of the craft, forbids you to move.

Intertextuality is not a (clear) fiction signal, because not every case of intertextuality is evidence for fictionality. It can be evidence for the fictionality of the narrative – for example, in the story of Leopold Bloom in Joyce's *Ulysses* – insofar as his life is modelled on that of the Homeric hero Odysseus. On the other side, it is possible to tell a real story with the words of other authors or even in the form of a cento.[23]

Therefore, the intertextual relations between two texts have to exhibit a certain quality, if they are to be seen as a quite clear fiction signal: the events that are told in both texts have to be unusual so that it is improbable that they happened to two different persons in different times and places (impossibility, of course, would

---

20   Cf. Feddern's 2013, 307-311 and 335-337 commentary and discussion.

21   In the same context (suas. 3.4-5), Seneca the elder reports how Arellius Fuscus imitated another Virgilian passage (georg. 1.427-429 and 432-433), and in this case, too, it would be difficult for us to see the intertextuality, if Seneca the elder would not have explained it, maybe referring to Fuscus' own statement.

22   Hor. ars 131-135 with Hinds' 1998, 24 translation.

23   Cf. Zipfel 2001, 237-238.

be a clear fiction signal).[24] An instructive example is given to us in Servius' late antique commentary on Virgil's *Aeneid*. If Turnus kills Alcander, Halius, Noemon, and Prytanis, this is a fiction signal for two reasons: first, due to the intertextuality with Homer's *Iliad*, in which the same characters are presented as being killed by Odysseus; and second (and more important), because it is impossible that the same persons are first killed by Odysseus and then by Turnus, and it is improbable that all of the killed warriors have the same names.[25]

Finally, as we are dealing with the relation between literary texts and reality and we have focused on the concepts of fictionality and intertextuality, we should mention the hyperbole, too, because it is a typical feature of Ovid's exile poems in general.[26] An hyperbole is, as Quintilian defines it, an "elegant straining of the truth" (*decens veri superiectio*).[27] Hyperbole and stylistic figures in general are not identical with fiction and cannot be regarded as fiction signals, unless they express invented events or things. The difference between the hyperbole and fiction lies in the fact that the hyperbole is essentially true, but the true core is embellished by exaggeration and can be recognised at least approximately, while fiction means that an event or thing is not just exaggerated, but invented. Hyperboles are not characteristic for fictional stories in particular, but are a common feature of every type of narrative, as ancient authors explain.[28]

The similarities between Ovid (trist. 3.10) and Virgil (georg. 3.249-383)

When Ovid wrote the elegies of the third book of the *Tristia*, he had experienced his first winter in Tomis (9/10 AD). As is clear from the beginning of the elegy 3.10, he describes the Tomitan winter before the background of the climate change that he had to face due to his relegation from Rome to the Black Sea: he is living now in the midst of the barbarian world (1-4). Ovid explains that during the summer month, the Danube wards off the tribes of Sauromatae, Bessi, and Getae, but in the winter they have easy access to Tomis across the frozen river (5-12).

Next Ovid turns to his long description of winter (13-50), which we shall discuss in detail below, before he describes the warfare which terrorises the region during the winter months (51-66): after the Danube has frozen, the tribes quickly cross it and devastate the countryside. Some of the inhabitants flee, losing all their property. Some are led off into captivity, and others are killed by poisoned arrows. The barbarians destroy everything they cannot carry away. Even in time of peace, Ovid concludes (67-78), men at Tomis live in constant fear of attack. They cannot cultivate their land, and they cannot grow vines or fruit trees. The countryside is bare, without leaves or trees – no place for a happy man![29]

According to Besslich, five parallel passages between Ovid's description of the winter at Tomis and Virgil's description of the Scythian tribes in the *Georgics* prove

---

24 Cf. Zipfel 2014, 109 who discusses improbability as fiction signal and stresses the fact that impro-bability is a problematic fiction signal because also factual stories are partly characterised by unusual and improbable events; otherwise they would not conform to the general criterion of the so-called 'tellability' of the story.

25 Cf. Serv. Aen. 9.764; Verg. Aen. 9.767 [sic]; Hom. Il. 5.678.

26 Cf. Philbrick 2016; Chwalek 1996, 57-62. For the hyperbole in general, cf. Naschert 1998.

27 Cf. Quint. inst. 8.6.67-76, especially 67.

28 Cf. Arist. Poet. 1460a17-18; Quint. inst. 8.6.75; Strabo 1.2.36.

29 For this summary of the elegy trist. 3.10, cf. Evans 1975, 1-2.

definitely that Ovid depends on Virgil.[30] In the first passage, Ovid is speaking about the bare countryside in similar terms as Virgil (I always quote first Ovid and then Virgil):[31]

aspiceres nudos sine fronde, sine arbore, campos.

one may see naked fields, leafless, treeless.

[...] neque ullae

aut herbae campo apparent aut arbore frondes.

[...] and no blade is seen upon the plain, or leaf upon the tree.

This first point, and only the first point, even presents the use of the same vocabulary for the same thoughts, when Ovid (and in a similar way Virgil) says that you can see leafless and treeless fields.[32] Due to the similar wording, this is the strongest evidence that can support the view that Ovid depends on Virgil. However, both poets use the normal words that you have to use when you want to express the thought that you can see leafless and treeless fields. If both poets were using extraordinary vocabulary or if Ovid was using exactly the same words in the same order and the same forms as Virgil, the intertextuality would be clearer.

In the second passage, Ovid and Virgil are talking about the (beginning of the) perpetual winter:[33]

dum tamen aura tepet, medio defendimur Histro:

 ille suis liquidis bella repellit aquis.

at cum tristis hiems squalentia protulit ora [...].

Yet while the warm breezes blow we are defended by the interposing Hister; with the flood of his waters he repels wars. But when grim winter has thrust forth his squalid face [...].

semper hiems, semper spirantes frigora Cauri.

'Tis ever winter; ever Northwest blasts, with icy breath.

According to Besslich, here and in the following points, the intertextuality between Ovid and Virgil presents some variation that nonetheless proves that Ovid depends on Virgil because he does not just copy him, but tries to give his account his own form. While Virgil describes a landscape with a perpetual winter, Ovid speaks of the beginning of the winter.[34] Regarding the third passage, Besslich goes on to stress the different aspects of the depiction of the Tomitan and the Scythian winters:[35]

nix iacet, et iactam ne sol pluviaeque resolvant,

 indurat Boreas perpetuamque facit.

ergo ubi delicuit nondum prior, altera venit,

 et solet in multis bima manere locis.

---

30 Cf. Besslich 1972, 179-184. For the judgement that no serious doubt is possible, cf. ib. 179.

31 Trist. 3.10.75; Verg. georg. 3.352-353. This and all the following translations of Ovid's *Tristia* and *Epistulae ex Ponto* in this paper are adapted from Wheeler's 1965 Loeb edition. All the translations of Virgil's *Georgics* in this paper are adapted from the Loeb edition (Goold/Fairclough 1999, 195-203).

32 According to Besslich 1972, 179-180, Ovid's allusion to Virgil is found in a quite different context. Evans 1975, 5, note 12 contradicted this view with good reason because the idea is the same.

33 Trist. 3.10.7-9; Verg. georg. 3.356.

34 Cf. Besslich 1972, 180.

35 Trist. 3.10.13-16; Verg. georg. 3.354-355. 360. 367.

The snow lies continuously, and once fallen, neither sun nor rains may melt it, for Boreas hardens and renders it eternal. So when an earlier fall is not yet melted another has come, and in many places 'tis wont to remain for two years.

[...] sed iacet aggeribus niveis informis et alto

terra gelu late septemque adsurgit in ulnas.

[...]

concrescunt subitae currenti in flumine crustae.

[...]

interea toto non setius aere ningit.

[...] but far and wide earth lies shapeless under mounds of snow and piles of ice, rising seven cubits high. [...] Sudden ice crusts form on the running stream. [...] No less, meanwhile, does the snow fill the sky.

Besslich states that from the beginning of Virgil's description, the landscape is covered with mounds of snow as a given situation. However, without any explanation of the interrelation, Besslich argues, in a later line (367) Virgil talks about the fact that it snows. In contrast, Ovid gives an exact explanation for the huge masses of snow because he describes a process in its chronological order. In the word *bima* ("for two years", 16), Besslich sees the attempt to reduce the imagination of a perpetual winter to a dimension that is realistic and comprehensible. Although Virgil speaks of the everlasting winter at the beginning of his description, he then describes a process as well, when he says that the sea freezes (360).[36]

In the fourth passage, Besslich claims that Ovid gives a plastic image of the Scythian winter and treats the single phenomena in strict order, while Virgil's description presents a confusing mixture of elements:[37]

tantaque commoti vis est Aquilonis, ut altas

  aequet humo turres tectaque rapta ferat.

pellibus et sutis arcent mala frigora bracis,

  oraque de toto corpore sola patent.   20

saepe sonant moti glacie pendente capilli,

  et nitet inducto candida barba gelu;

nudaque consistunt, formam servantia testae,

  vina, nec hausta meri, sed data frusta bibunt.

quid loquar, ut vincti concrescant frigore rivi,   25

  deque lacu fragiles effodiantur aquae?

So mighty is the power of Aquilo, when once he is aroused, that he levels high towers to the ground and sweeps away buildings. With skins and stitched breeches they keep out the evils of the cold; of the whole body only the face is exposed. Often their hair tinkles with banging ice and their beards glisten white with the mantle of frost. Exposed wine stands upright, retaining the shape of the jar, and they drink, not draughts of wine, but fragments served them. Why tell of brooks frozen fast with the cold and how brittle water is dug out of the pool?

---

36   Cf. Besslich 1972, 180.
37   Trist. 3.10.17-26; Verg. georg. 3.363-366 and 381-383.

aeraque dissiliunt vulgo, vestesque rigescunt

indutae, caeduntque securibus umida vina,

et totae solidam in glaciem vertere lacunae,

stiriaque impexis induruit horrida barbis.

[...]

talis Hyperboreo Septem subiecta trioni

gens effrena virum Riphaeo tunditur Euro

et pecudum fulvis velatur corpora saetis.

Everywhere brass splits, clothes freeze on the back, and with axes they cleave the liquid wine; whole lakes turn into a solid mass, and the rough icicle hardens on the unkempt beard. [...] Such is the race of men lying under the Wain's seven stars in the far north, a wild race, buffeted by the Riphaean East Wind, their bodies clothed in the tawny furs of beasts.

According to Besslich, Ovid first informs us about the inhabitants' clothes (19-20) but omits the fact that they freeze as they are worn, as told by Virgil (363-364). Instead, Ovid repeats the last line of Virgil's description (383), where he says that the Scythians' bodies are covered in the pelts of beasts. The aforementioned power of the winds (17-18), Ovid takes over from Virgil, who likewise mentions it just before (382). Second, he describes the ice in the hair and beard (21-22) with more detail, but less grotesque than Virgil (366). Third, Ovid mentions the frozen wine (23-24), but does not use a paradox, as Virgil does, when he says *caedunt securibus umida vina* ("with axes they cleave the liquid wine", 364), using the adjective *umidus* ("liquid") with reference to the normal nature of wine. Ovid instead avoids the hyperbole *caedunt securibus* ("with axes they cleave") and transfers this element to the water dug out brittle from the pools (26).[38]

In Besslich's view, Ovid describes in the fifth passage the freezing of lakes and rivers (25-34) (and even the Black Sea, 35-40) – in difference to Virgil – in strict order and in the form of a climax:[39]

quaque rates ierant, pedibus nunc itur, et undas

    frigore concretas ungula pulsat equi;

perque novos pontes, subter labentibus undis,

    ducunt Sarmatici barbara plaustra boves.

Where ships had gone before now men go on foot and the waters congealed with cold feel the hoof-beat of the horse. Across the new bridge, above the gliding current, are drawn by Sarmatian oxen the carts of the barbarians.

undaque iam tergo ferratos sustinet orbis,

puppibus illa prius, patulis nunc hospita plaustris.

and anon the water bears on its surface iron-bound wheels – giving welcome once to ships, but now to broad wains!

After mentioning the frozen pools and rivers (25-26), Ovid describes at length how the Danube freezes (27-34), and this passage ends with the depiction of the frozen

---

38   Cf. Besslich 1972, 180-181.

39   Trist. 3.10.31-34; Verg. georg. 3.361-362.

Black Sea (35-40). In Virgil's account, in contrast, there is no connection between the single phenomena, because he speaks about the frozen Danube in lines 360-362 and then, in line 365, about whole lakes that turn to solid ice. Further, he does not describe a process, but the result, as can be seen in lines 361-362. Ovid's description of the frozen Danube, instead, is more dynamic, detailed, and exact, as can be seen in lines 31-34. In this passage, Ovid gives three examples of the new possibilities of transport: you can walk over the river by feet, go by horse or sit on a wagon.[40] With these parallels, Besslich takes it for granted that the intertextuality between Ovid and Virgil is proven, though Ovid's adaptation presents some variation: it is more detailed, more dynamic, better structured, more analytic, more realistic, and less phantastic. In this way, Ovid not only copies Virgil, but adds elements to his description, corrects it, and even omits parts of it.[41] The last operation can be seen in the fact that Ovid does not imitate the burlesque hunting scene described in Virgil's *Georgics*:[42]

hos non immissis canibus, non cassibus ullis

puniceaeve agitant pavidos formidine pennae,

sed frustra oppositum trudentis pectore montem

comminus obtruncant ferro graviterque rudentis

caedunt et magno laeti clamore reportant.

These [sc. oxen and deer] they hunt not by unloosing hounds, or laying nets, or alarming with a scare of the crimson feather, but as their breasts vainly strain against that mountain rampart men slay them, steel in hand, cut them down bellowing piteously, and bear them home with loud shouts of joy.

Besslich's conclusion that these parallels between Ovid's statements about the Tomitan winter and Virgil's description of the Scythian tribes in the *Georgics* prove definitely that Ovid depends on Virgil, does not seem to be a result that dispels all doubts. It would be necessary to discuss the parallels point by point regarding their similarities and their differences, because, in my view, not every variation detected by Besslich can be explained as he does. Especially the second and the third passage do not have much in common with the respective Virgilian statements, because in the second passage Ovid speaks about the beginning of the winter, while Virgil mentions the everlasting cold, and in the third passage Ovid talks about the snow that remains for a long time (two years), while Virgil describes the masses of snow that rise seven cubits high. Therefore, it is possible, but not obvious that Ovid imitates Virgil's description of the Scythian tribes.

Further, other scholars have claimed that Ovid is not just imitating Virgil in trist. 3.10, but that he also alludes to other authors, or that his statements about the Black Sea have to be seen before the background of a larger literary tradition about the Scythian climate and other inhospitable regions at the north-eastern end of the known world.[43] Such a passage can be found in Herodotus:[44]

---

40   Cf. Besslich 1972, 181-182.
41   Cf. Besslich 1972, 182-183. In the second part of his paper (p. 185-191), Besslich discusses Ovid's allusion to Leander (41-42), with parallels between Ovid's situation and Leander's description of his plight in epist. 18.
42   Verg. georg. 3.371-375.
43   For Tomis as inhospitable place (*locus horribilis*), cf. Kettemann 1999; for the winter in Latin poetry, cf. Dehon 1993.
44   Herodotus 4.28. Translation adapted from Godley's 2006, 227 Loeb edition.

δυσχείμερος δὲ αὕτη ἡ καταλεχθεῖσα πᾶσα χώρη οὕτω δή τι ἐστί, ἔνθα τοὺς μὲν ὀκτὼ τῶν μηνῶν ἀφόρητος οἷος γίνεται κρυμός, ἐν τοῖσι ὕδωρ ἐκχέας πηλὸν οὐ ποιήσεις, πῦρ δὲ ἀνακαίων ποιήσεις πηλόν· ἡ δὲ θάλασσα πήγνυται καὶ ὁ Βόσπορος πᾶς ὁ Κιμμέριος, καὶ ἐπὶ τοῦ κρυστάλλου οἱ ἐντὸς τάφρου Σκύθαι κατοικημένοι στρατεύονται καὶ τὰς ἁμάξας ἐπελαύνουσι πέρην ἐς τοὺς Σίνδους.

All this aforementioned country is exceeding cold; for eight months of every year there is frost unbearable, and in these you shall not make mud by pouring out water but by lighting a fire; the sea freezes, and all the Cimmerian Bosporus; and the Scythians dwelling this side of the fosse lead armies over the ice, and drive their wains across to the land of the Sindi.

Indeed, not only Herodotus but also Strabo offers a description of the northern Black Sea that in some points resembles Ovid's account:[45]

ῥήττονται δὲ χαλκαῖ ὑδρίαι, τὰ δ' ἐνόντα συμπήττεται. τῶν δὲ πάγων ἡ σφοδρότης μάλιστα ἐκ τῶν συμβαινόντων περὶ τὸ στόμα τῆς Μαιώτιδος δῆλός ἐστιν. ἁμαξεύεται γὰρ ὁ διάπλους ὁ εἰς Φαναγόρειαν ἐκ τοῦ Παντικαπαίου, ὥστε καὶ πλοῦν εἶναι καὶ ὁδόν· ὀρυκτοί τέ εἰσιν ἰχθύες οἱ ἀποληφθέντες ἐν τῷ κρυστάλλῳ τῇ προσαγορευομένῃ γαγγάμῃ, καὶ μάλιστα οἱ ἀντακαῖοι, δελφῖσι πάρισοι τὸ μέγεθος. Νεοπτόλεμον δέ φασι τὸν τοῦ Μιθριδάτου στρατηγὸν ἐν τῷ αὐτῷ πόρῳ θέρους μὲν ναυμαχίᾳ περιγενέσθαι τῶν βαρβάρων, χειμῶνος δ' ἱππομαχίᾳ.

[...] bronze water-jars burst and their contents freeze solid. But the severity of the frosts is most clearly evidenced by what takes place in the region of the mouth of Lake Maeotis: the waterway from Panticapaeum across to Phanagoria is traversed by wagons, so that it is both ice and roadway. And fish that become caught in the ice are obtained by digging with an implement called the "gangame", and particularly the antacaei, which are about the size of dolphins. It is said of Neoptolemus, the general of Mithridates, that in the same strait he overcame the barbarians in a naval engagement in summer and in a cavalry engagement in winter.

Other authors and passages mentioned by researchers are the Hippocratic work *De aeribus, locis, aquis* (19), the underworld as described in the sixth book of the *Aeneid*, Ovid's account of the home of the personified hunger (*Fames*; met. 8.788-791), and *ex negativo* accounts of the Golden Age.[46]

However, Ovid claims in his exile poetry that he had almost no books at hand.[47] Therefore, it is difficult to imagine that he imitated Virgil and other authors in the complex way, that Besslich and other researchers suggest. An allusion to Virgil is more plausible than an imitation of the other authors,[48] but the assumption of intertextuality would be more evident if there were more similar or identical formulations than simply in the first passage. In any case, Ovid's possible imitation of Virgil concerns the *discours* (discourse) and not the *histoire* (the narrated events), *i.e.* Ovid possibly imitates Virgil in using similar words for similar phenomena, but as long as it is not shown or made plausible that these events are invented, the imitation is limited to the *discours*. However, it is not a correct deductive reasoning that the possible imitation on the level of the *discours* allows us to regard the narrated events as fictive.

45　Strabo 7.3.18; cf. ib. 2.1.16. Translation adapted from Jones' 1983, 225-227 Loeb edition.
46　Cf. Trevizam/Avellar 2016, 114-115; Claassen 2008, 185; Williams 1994, 8-16; Claassen 1990, 77-80.
47　Cf. trist. 3.14.37-38; 5.12.53-54.
48　This can be no surprise because Virgil talks about the Scythian tribes, and Ovid lives in Tomis among them, as he tells us in his poems; cf. trist. 1.3.61; 3.2.1.

The truthfulness of Ovid's description of the Tomitan winter (trist. 3.10; Pont. 4.7; 4.9; 4.10)

The previous section leads us to the question if – even if Ovid does imitate Virgil – this special case of intertextuality is or would be a fiction signal. In my view, there is insufficient reason to see a fiction signal in the similar passages (or somewhere else in trist. 3.10).[49] We have to admit that Ovid expresses thoughts about his place of banishment which correspond to the cultural knowledge or Roman prejudice of Scythia and that Ovid was familiar with it from his education and former life in Rome. This fact surely influences his perception of his new environment, but is not a question of fiction. In order to show that Ovid's account is fictional, as Chwalek believes, it is necessary to exclude (or, at least, to have strong arguments against the view) that Ovid is talking about the real Tomitan winter.

However, Chwalek does not adduce one single argument why it should be impossible or unlikely that the Tomitan winter is as hard as Ovid depicts it.[50] Ovid's account contains some extraordinary elements and might be hyperbolic, but does not seem to be untrue, at least there is no evidence that it is untrue. Therefore, the view that Ovid's depiction of the Pontic climate is fictional, is just a speculation. Moreover, in the context of those passages where Ovid describes the Tomitan winter, you can see statements in which he deals with the Roman reader's possible doubts and affirms that his account is true.[51] In general, such a strategy might arouse suspicions. However, these passages, to which we will turn below (see point 3.3), can hardly be explained if Ovid's account is taken to be fictional.[52]

Due to a lack of contemporary sources, we cannot decide definitely if the winter at Tomis in 9/10 AD was exactly as Ovid describes it. However, we can examine if it is probable or not that Ovid's information is accurate and how the Roman reader might have responded to such accounts. There seem to be three methodologically accurate ways to deal with the question of the truthfulness of Ovid's statements about the Pontic climate: first, to analyse the ancient (scientific) discourse about frigid weather in foreign regions in which the wine and the (Black) Sea possibly freeze; second, to use our modern world knowledge and consider whether Ovid might say the truth or not, trying to take into account the distance of about 2,000 years (*i.e.* the fact that things might change) and the background of the text production in general; and third, to look for inconsistencies or contradictions within Ovid's poems, not just trist. 3.10, but also the other exile elegies in which he speaks about the Tomitan climate (esp. Pont. 4.7; 4.9; 4.10). As there are no inconsistencies or contradictions, but Ovid repeats and affirms his statements about the Pontic climate in other elegies,

---

49 Besslich 1972, 185, Evans 1975,4-5, and Chwalek 1996, 44-45 share the opinion that already Virgil's account of the Scythian tribes is fictional. This premise is by no means obvious, and the critics adduce no argument to make this premise plausible. So, even this premise is doubtful.

50 Cf. Chwalek 1996, 44-45.

51 For an analysis of the passages in which Ovid deals with the spectacular elements that cause doubts in his readers, cf. Galfré 2017.

52 Many of Ovid's statements might be regarded as conventional descriptions of inhospitable regions (at the north-eastern end of the known world), and the ancient idea of the Scythian cold corresponds more or less to the modern proverbial idea of the Sibirian cold. Williams 1994, 10 makes us aware that Plutarch offers a telling insight into the proverbiality of the Scythian climate: in the preface to his life of Theseus (Thes. 1.1), he notes the free licence which geographers allow themselves in plotting on their maps parts of the earth of which they have no first-hand knowledge and to which they append such vague explanatory comments as "Scythian cold". However, this is not an exact parallel because the fictionality of these geographic accounts is clear, given that they have (and nobody has) first-hand knowledge. Ovid, on the other side, as most scholars believe, was relegated to Tomis and has first-hand knowledge of the region. Why should we not allow the possibility that Ovid tells us the truth and that the Pontic region is characterised by many features that are traditionally attributed to the Scythian landscape and climate?

this might be an argument for the factuality of his account, though the repetitions themselves are no definite proof, as we will discuss below (see point 3.3).

With regard to the second and the third approach, we can rely on previous publications, although the results gained through these methods are conflicting. The first approach instead seems to be innovative insofar, as the respective passages are mentioned by critics,[53] but not analysed in their context. In my view, all three of these methods will provide arguments for the assumption that Ovid's description of the Tomitan winter is not invented.

The ancient (scientific) discourse about frigid weather

Albeit not in relation to Ovid's exile poetry, we have ancient discussions about the questions of whether wine and the Black Sea can freeze (according to some scholars, a temperature of about -20°C makes wine congeal,[54] although this seems to be an exaggeration because wine already freezes in less frigid weather). These discussions (in which Herodotus and Strabo take part, but there are other, more telling passages) make clear that the ancients were faced with the same problem as we are: they were sceptical and/or wondered about these extraordinary stories or occurrences, but did not regard them as impossible under certain climatic conditions.

Regarding the first question, the elder Pliny reports that in the Alps the wine is stored in wooden barrels and heated by fire to prevent it from freezing:[55]

magna et collecto iam vino differentia in caelo. circa Alpes ligneis vasis condunt tegulisque cingunt atque etiam hieme gelida ignibus rigorem arcent. rarum dictu, sed aliquando visum, ruptis vasis stetere glaciatae moles, prodigii modo, quoniam vini natura non gelascit; alias ad frigus stupet tantum.

Even in regard to wine already vintaged there is a great difference in point of climate. In the neighbourhood of the Alps they put it in wooden casks and close these round with tiles and in a cold winter also light fires to protect it from the effect of the cold. It is seldom recorded, but it has been seen occasionally, that the vessels have burst in a frost, leaving the wine standing in frozen blocks – almost a miracle, since it is not the nature of wine to freeze: usually it is only numbed by cold.

Pliny thinks that wine (normally) does not freeze, but reports that this extraordinary event occasionally happened in the neighbourhood of the Alps.

As to the wine and the Black Sea, Gellius presents us the Athenian philosopher Taurus debating with his dinner guests, Gellius himself being one of them, the question of why oil freezes often and readily, wine seldom and vinegar hardly ever. The motive for this debate is the fact that at that dinner (debate) about which Gellius reports, Taurus' slave-boy was unable to pour some oil into the pot because the oil flask was empty, but he was unaware of it and explained to the laughing guests that the oil congealed because it was cold in the morning.[56] While the boy went off to buy some oil, Taurus and his dinner guests started a conversation about frozen oil:[57]

---

53   Williams 1994, 10, note 19 refers to Gell. 17.8.16. Luck 1977, 212 ad Ov. trist. 3.10.23-24 refers to Plin. nat. 14.132 and Macr. sat. 7.12.28.

54   Cf. Fitton Brown 1985, 19; Amann 2006, 171-172; Florian 2007, 41; Bérchez Castaño2015, 29.

55   Plin. nat. 14.132. Translation adapted from Rackham's 1960, 273 Loeb edition, who reads *tegulisque* instead of the transmitted *tectisque*.

56   Cf. Gell. 17.8.1-8.

57   Gell. 17.8.8-10. Translation adapted from Rolfe's 1978, 231 Loeb edition.

[...] quoniam puer nunc admonuit solere oleum congelascere, consideremus cur oleum quidem saepe et facile, set vina rarenter congelascant?" Atque aspicit me et iubet quid sentiam dicere. Tum ego respondi coniectare me vinum idcirco minus cito congelascere, quod semina quaedam caldoris in sese haberet essetque natura ignitius, ob eamque rem dictum esse ab Homero αἴθοπα οἶνον, non, ut alii putarent, propter colorem.

[...] since the slave has just told us that oil is in the habit of congealing, let us consider why oil congeals often and readily, but wine rarely." And he looked at me and bade me give my opinion. Then I replied that I inferred that wine congealed less quickly because it had in it certain seeds of heat and was naturally more fiery, and that was why Homer called it αἴθοψ and not, as some supposed, on account of its color.

Not just Gellius, but also Taurus believes that wine is called αἴθοψ by Homer due to its fiery nature and warming effect.[58] However, Taurus points to the contradiction that, if those things or liquids which are warmer are frozen with greater difficulty and those which are colder freeze more readily, why does vinegar never freeze though it is the most cooling of all things?[59] Therefore, he proposes another theory: those things congeal more readily which are lighter and smoother.[60]

This theory leads him to another question, linked with the former discussion: the question of why rivers freeze, but not the sea. Taurus dismisses as highly unorthodox Herodotus' claim that the *mare Scythicum* in fact freezes:[61]

Praeterea id quoque ait quaeri dignum, cur fluviorum et fontium aquae gelu durentur, mare omne incongelabile sit. Tametsi Herodotus, inquit, historiae scriptor, contra omnium ferme qui haec quaesiverunt opinionem, scribit mare Bosporicum, quod Cimmerium appellatur, earumque partium mare omne quod Scythicum dicitur, gelu stringi et consistere.

Taurus says besides that it is also worth inquiring why the waters of rivers and streams freeze, while all the sea is incapable of freezing. "Although Herodotus," said he, "the writer of history, contrary to the opinion of almost all who have investigated these matters, writes that the Bosphoric sea, which is called Cimmerian, and of this side all the sea which is termed Scythian, is bound fast by the cold and brought to a standstill.

As we have seen, Herodotus says that the sea freezes (ἡ δὲ θάλασσα πήγνυται) and all of the Cimmerian Bosporus (καὶ ὁ Βόσπορος πᾶς ὁ Κιμμέριος), referring with ἡ θάλασσα to the Maeotian Lake (Sea of Azov) – and probably not additionally to the Black Sea – and with ὁ Βόσπορος πᾶς ὁ Κιμμέριος to the Strait of Yenikale in the north of the Black Sea,[62] which divides (or once divided) the Ukrainian Crimea from Russia. In Taurus' paraphrase, it is difficult to explain the *mare Scythicum*, because this expression might refer to the Maeotian Lake (Sea of Azov), which is normally

---

58   Cf. Gell. 17.8.10-11. Homer calls the wine αἴθοψ (cf. Hom. Il. 1.462; 4.259; *etc.*), which word etymologically means "fiery-looking" (αἰθός means "fire" and ὄψ "eye"). The exact meaning in Homer is unclear, because the word can mean "flashing, gleaming, sparkling" and, more concrete, "fiery/fiery-looking" or "black"; cf. LSJ s.v. αἴθοψ. According to Rolfe 1978, 230-231, note 2, Gellius is probably wrong if he suggests that the wine is called αἴθοψ because of its fiery nature. Rather, the meaning in Homer would be "sparkling". The Homeric scholia are divided between the assumption of the meaning "black" and "blazing"; cf. Kaster 2011, 256-257, note 101, with regard to Macr. sat. 7.12.28.

59   Cf. Gell. 17.8.12-14.

60   Cf. Gell. 17.8.15.

61   Gell. 17.8.16. Translation adapted from Rolfe's 1978, 233 Loeb edition.

62   Cf. Herodotus 4.28 (see footnote 44) and Rolfe 1978, 232-233, notes 2 and 3 to Gell. 17.8.16, according to whom ἡ θάλασσα refers to the Black Sea, too.

called the *Maeotis palus* or *lacus*, the Black Sea, or a gulf of the Caspian Sea that was called the Scythian gulf (*sinus Scythicus*).[63] As we will see below, the most probable answer is that in Taurus' view, Herodotus contends that the Maeotian Lake (Sea of Azov) freezes. Neither Herodotus nor Taurus talks about the frozen Black Sea. However, Taurus adds that according to Herodotus the *whole* Maeotian Lake (Sea of Azov) freezes (*mare omne quod Scythicum dicitur*), what Herodotus does not state explicitly and maybe does not even imply.

The reader of Gellius' anecdote would like to know now exactly what is the reason why these two phenomena (the liquids and the sea) do freeze or do not freeze, but Gellius reports at this point of his story that the discussion ended as the boy returned with the oil and the time had come to eat.[64] However, we learn from this conversation that intellectuals like Taurus and his guests hold the view that wine can freeze – although seldom – but all of the sea (we will return to the exact meaning of this expression) is incapable of freezing, and we will get to know the reasons in another passage that is based on this discussion – a clear case of intertextuality, unless the two texts depend on a third one unknown to us.

In Macrobius' *Saturnalia*, the characters again discuss the question of whether wine and the (Black) Sea can freeze.[65] First, they discuss and dismiss the theory that those things which are warmer are frozen with greater difficulty and those which are colder freeze more readily, because vinegar never freezes though it is the most cooling of all things.[66] Then, Dysarius proposes the theory that oil congeals more quickly because it is both smoother and thicker. This might be the solution because wine does not have that syrupy quality and is much more fluid than oil, while vinegar is the most fluid and harsher than the other liquids.[67] The sea provides an argument for this theory because the sea water is also harsh due to its bitterness and never freezes in frigid weather. With almost the same words as the Gellian Taurus, Dysarius dismisses as highly unorthodox Herodotus' claim that the *mare Scythicum* does in fact freeze.[68] However, this is not the whole truth:[69]

nam non marina aqua contrahitur, sed quia plurimum in illis regionibus fluviorum est et paludum in ipsa maria influentium, superficies maris, cui dulces aquae innatant, congelascit et incolumi aqua marina videtur in mari gelu, sed de advenis undis coactum.

Sea water does not freeze; however, because there are very many rivers and marshes in those regions that flow into the sea, the fresh water floats on the sea's surface and congeals, and though the seawater is unaffected, ice is seen in the sea, though it's really formed from the inflowing water.

According to this theory, the sea water does not freeze itself, but the sweet river water that flows into the sea and floats on its surface congeals. This effect can be seen in the Black Sea, too:[70]

hoc et in Ponto fieri videmus, in quo frusta quaedam et, ut ita dixerim, prosiciae gelidae feruntur, contractae de fluvialium vel palustrium undarum multitudine, in quas licet frigori, quasi levatiores marina.

---

63   For the *sinus Scythicus*, cf. Mela 3.38.
64   Cf. Gell. 17.8.17.
65   Cf. Macr. sat. 7.12.28-37.
66   Cf. Macr. sat. 7.12.28-29.
67   Cf. Macr. sat. 7.12.30.
68   Cf. Macr. sat. 7.12.31.
69   Macr. sat. 7.12.32. Translation adapted from Kaster's 2011, 259 Loeb edition.
70   Macr. sat. 7.12.33. Translation adapted from Kaster's 2011, 259-261 Loeb edition.

We see this happen in the Black Sea too: some chunks and, so to speak, slabs of ice are borne along, solidified out of a great mass of river and marsh water that's at the mercy of the cold, since it's smoother than sea water.

Indeed, there is much evidence for the theory that it is not the Black Sea's salt water that freezes, but the smoother river water that flows into it from many rivers:[71]

plurimum autem aquarum talium influere Ponto et totam superficiem eius infectam esse dulci liquore, praeter quod ait Sallustius mare Ponticum dulcius quam cetera est, hoc quoque testimonio, quod si in Pontum vel paleas vel ligna seu quaecumque natantia proieceris, foras extra Pontum feruntur in Propontidem atque ita in mare quod adluit Asiae oram; cum constet in Pontum influere maris aquam, non effluere de Ponto.

As evidence that a very great amount of such water flows into the Black Sea, whose entire surface is imbued with fresh water, we have not only Sallust's statement – "The Black Sea is fresher than all others" – but also the fact that if you throw wheat chaff or sticks or any floating material in the Black Sea, they're carried beyond the Black Sea and into the Sea of Marmara and from there into the sea that washes the coast of Asia Minor – though it is well known that the sea's water flows into the Black Sea, not out of it.

We learn from this discussion that the *mare Scythicum*, to which the Gellian Taurus and the Macrobian Dysarius refer, will be the Maeotian Lake (Sea of Azov), because it is opposed to and mentioned just before the Black Sea and the Sea of Marmara (*Propontis*) – and probably the adequate understanding of Herodotus' statements. Further, we understand in which respect these two characters contradict the Greek historian's account: when Herodotus writes that the Bosphoric and the Scythian Sea are bound fast by the cold and brought to a standstill, it sounds as if it was the salt water that freezes, but this is wrong. Less severe critics would have reproached Herodotus for giving an imprecise account and would have added that it is the fresh water that flows into the sea and freezes. However, Taurus is quite polemical when he says that the Greek historian has an opinion contrary to that of almost all who have investigated these matters. Moreover, he does not paraphrase him exactly when he adds that according to Herodotus the whole Maeotian Lake (Sea of Azov) freezes, because Herodotus writes that the sea (of Azov) freezes and all of the Cimmerian Bosporus.

Moreover, while it is unclear which perspective Herodotus takes (he seems to say that the whole surface of the narrow Cimmerian Bosporus is covered by ice so that it is a highway, while just a part of the Maeotian Lake has the same appearance), it is obvious that the Gellian Taurus and the Macrobian Dysarius do not wonder to which extent ice can form in the Maeotian Lake, *i.e.* if the whole lake is covered by ice. Their view is directed towards the two levels of water: on the one hand, the salt water at a greater depth, while on the other hand, the fresh water on the surface. Therefore, it does not really matter that they refer the word for "all" or "whole" (*omne*) to the wrong (part of the) sea, because the main difference is that they take it in the third and not in the second dimension: they talk about the depth and not the width.

The ancient discussion about the fact that all of the sea is incapable of freezing (*cur mare omne incongelabile sit*) is a debate about the fact that the salt water in the depth of the sea cannot freeze, while it is taken for granted that fresh water on the surface freezes – theoretically on the whole surface. As we will see below (see point 3.3), it will be important for us to take into account which perspective Ovid takes when he speaks about the frozen Black Sea, and we should be aware that this must not be our perspective which is usually directed at the surface and not into the depth.

---

71   Macr. sat. 7.12.34. Translation adapted from Kaster's 2011, 261 Loeb edition. For Sallust's statement, cf. hist. fr. 3.65.

3.2 Our modern world knowledge

Regarding the second approach, it is possible to distinguish at least between those scholars who think that especially Ovid's description of the frozen Black Sea is unrealistic or impossible, and those who contend that it corresponds to reality. The former view has recently been held by Amann, according to whom Ovid is seeking a humorous effect with the phantastic depiction (at least beginning in line 19 of trist. 3.10) of the Pontic winter.[72]

However, his discussion of the question also shows that the frosty winter is not completely phantastic, when he admits that even in our times, the temperature in modern Constanta (ancient Tomis) can fall below -20°C, that the coasts of the Black Sea can indeed freeze (to an extent of about 30-40 miles), and that strong winds are characteristic for the Dobrudja region during the winter.[73] Nonetheless, Amann considers Ovid's account as fictional because according to him, modern investigations have shown that it is impossible that the Black Sea is covered by masses of ice.[74] We will return to this point of text interpretation (see point 3.3) because it is problematic insofar as Ovid does not seem to pretend that (almost) the whole Black Sea freezes.

On the other hand, Helzle used meteorological data and pictures from recent decades to show that not only the Danube but also the western coast of the Black Sea freezes in severe winters.[75] Helzle is followed by Seibert, who adds that the popular argument that Tomis is situated on the same degree of latitude as central Italy is misleading, because the climate conditions in western and central Europe are different than in eastern Europe due to the gulf stream.[76]

While ongoing research motivated by the current climate change might allow us in the future to know more about the ancient climatic conditions,[77] it seems that – *rebus sic stantibus* – the latter view is much more plausible because it is based on modern meteorological data, and even Amann's discussion – although he favours the opposite view – emphasises that Ovid seems to be reliable when he tells us that the Danube and (parts of) the Black Sea freeze. The question of the dimension of ice building in the Black Sea will be considered in the context of other elegies in which Ovid speaks about the frosty Tomitan climate and which are analysed by Gahan, whose results corroborate the assumption that Ovid offers an accurate account of the Pontic winter.

3.3 Repetitions and authority

Gahan follows the premise that from the details Ovid chooses to include once more in the other elegies, we can determine more precisely the difference between facts and fictions.[78] However, without modification this procedure cannot be regarded

72   Cf. Amann 2006, 170-180, esp. 171-172.
73   Amann is partly relying on Danoff's 1962 important article about the Black Sea in the 'Real-Encyclopädie' that has a section about the climate (p. 938-949, here p. 944-945).
74   Cf. Amann 2006, 171-172, note 335. Following Fitton Brown 1985, 19, he takes into account the possible explanation of a climate change in the last 2,000 years, but rejects it because previous investigations could not confirm this assumption. Nonetheless, Amann does not exclude the possibility that Ovid's first winter at Tomis was exceptionally hard.
75   Cf. Helzle 2006, 141-142.
76   Cf. Seibert 2014, 53-54.
77   Bolikhovskaya *et al.* 2004 examine climate and environmental changes of the north-eastern Black Sea's coastal region during the middle and late Holocene, but these paleo-geographical examinations cover periods of at least hundreds, rather thousands of years.
78   Cf. Gahan 1978, esp. 198-199. Gahan is followed by Florian 2007, 41-46, who stresses that the question if Ovid's account is true cannot be decided on the basis of modern meteorological data. This is partly true. Nonetheless, if the modern meteorological data show that nowadays it is possible that parts of the Black Sea freeze, it will be possible or probable that this happened in antiquity, too, and that Ovid's account is true.

as a valid method to distinguish between facts and fictions, because a statement does not become (or continue to be) true if it is repeated several times. Nonetheless, Gahan's observations merit consideration because it is not just the fact that Ovid repeats – at least partly – the detailed depiction of the frosty winter in other elegies, but the contexts in which he does so point to the factuality of at least many of the details of the Pontic climate that Ovid presents us in trist. 3.10.[79]

In three elegies that belong to the fourth book of the *Epistulae ex Ponto* (composed between 13 and 16 AD), Ovid not just repeats – at least partly – the detailed depiction of the strong winter, but defends the veracity of his complaints about it, as he already did in trist. 3.10 in a passage not considered yet:[80]

vix equidem credar, sed, cum sint praemia falsi   35

  nulla, ratam debet testis habere fidem.

vidimus ingentem glacie consistere pontum,

  lubricaque inmotas testa premebat aquas.

nec vidisse sat est; durum calcavimus aequor,

  undaque non udo sub pede summa fuit.   40

I may scarce hope for credence, but since there is no reward for a falsehood, the witness ought to be believed. I have seen the vast sea stiff with ice; a slippery shell holding the water motionless. And seeing is not enough; I have trodden the frozen sea, and the surface lay beneath an unwetted foot.

Ovid claims that he is an eyewitness of the severe winter, and not only an eyewitness, but rather that as a protagonist of the narrated events he tested and experienced the frozen Black Sea with his own foots.[81]

In a similar way, in the fourth book of the *Epistulae ex Ponto* he reacts to the doubts that his account of the Pontic climate caused in the Roman readers, swearing that he tells the truth and refering to other witnesses who can support his statements. In an elegy addressed to Albinovanus Pedo (Pont. 4.10), Ovid begs his poet friend to believe him and take into account the reasons why the Black Sea freezes:[82]

hic agri infrondes, hic spicula tincta venenis,

  hic freta vel pediti pervia reddit hiems,

ut, qua remus iter pulsis modo fecerat undis,

  siccus contempta nave viator eat.

qui veniunt istinc, vix vos ea credere dicunt.   35

  quam miser est, qui fert asperiora fide!

crede tamen: nec te causas nescire sinemus,

  horrida Sarmaticum cur mare duret hiems.

---

79 More general relevant repetitions inside the exile elegies can be seen insofar, as Ovid mentions several times the freezing cold, not going into such detail as in trist. 3.10, but saying or implying that the harshness of the Tomitan winter is mentally depressing and physically harming; cf. trist. 3.3.7-8; 3.8.23; 3.4b.48; 3.2.8; 4.4.55; 2.189-190; 5.13.3-6. In some of these passages, Ovid uses the general term *caelum* ("weather") which must be understood in the sense of severe winter.

80 Trist. 3.10.35-40.

81 According to Amann 2006, 177 Ovid's argumentation why the readers should believe him (35-36) is empty. However, Ovid gives two good arguments why we should regard him as reliable: he is an eyewitness and there would be no profit for him in inventing things.

82 Pont. 4.10.31-38.

Here there are lands without a leaf, here are darts dyed in poison, here the winter makes even the sea a highway for one on foot, so that where the oar had but just now beaten a way through the waves, the traveller proceeds dryshod, despising boats. Those who come from your land report that you scarce believe all this. How wretched is he who endures what is too harsh for credence! Yet believe you must, nor shall I permit you to remain in ignorance of the reason why dread winter freezes the Sarmatian sea.

In the following, Ovid explains the reasons why the Black Sea freezes (39-64): The north wind is the source of the cold (39-44), and because so many rivers flow into the Black Sea (Ovid provides a catalogue of these rivers, 45-58), it is calmed (59-60). This then allows for the fresh water to float on the heavier salt water (63-64), and this water eventually freezes.[83] This argumentation, which has been interpreted as playful,[84] corresponds exactly to the ancient (scientific) discourse about frigid weather in foreign regions in which the wine and the (Black) Sea possibly freeze (see point 3.1), as can be seen especially in the following two lines:[85]

innatat unda freto dulcis leviorque marina est,

  quae proprium mixto de sale pondus habet.

The fresh water floats upon the flood, being lighter than the seawater which possesses weight of its own from the mixture of salt.

Ovid offers this explication also in trist. 3.10, where his main focus is the description of the frozen Black Sea. He tells us two alternative reasons for this extraordinary occurrence in just two lines that would be difficult to understand without the explanation given in Pont. 4.10:[86]

sive igitur nimii Boreae vis saeva marinas,

  sive redundatas flumine cogit aquas [...].

So whether the cruel violence of o'ermighty Boreas congeals the waters of the sea or the waters that overflowed from the river [...].

Although the Danube is mentioned in line 53, this will be a reference to the frozen Black Sea, and the meaning of the expression *redundatae flumine aquae* will be the alternative that much water flows from the rivers into the Black Sea where it congeals.

Therefore, this argumentation should be taken seriously: Ovid states that and explains why the Black Sea freezes, but he does not say that the whole surface of the

---

83 Cf. Gahan 1978, 201, note 11; Davisson 1982, 29-30.

84 Cf. Davisson 1982, 34-37, who holds the view that although the use of Lucretian terms (*causa*, 37; *rarus*, 44; *miscere*, 45 and 64; *pondus*, 64; *vis*, 42, 46, and 60; *adde quod*, 45; *quin etiam*, 61) and the length of the river catalogue suggest earnestness, Ovid seems to amuse himself with the figurative use of some words, and eventually to imply that he chose some details (rivers) of his proof arbitrarily. Davisson not just refers to figurative use of words (*domesticus*, 41; *adulterare*, 59), but also to stylistic ornamentation by the use of apostrophe (51, 52, and 58), personification (55 and 58), and periphrasis (55-56) and to „a decorative use of myth" (51, 52 and 55). This view is not convincing because the terms that she regards as Lucretian are no more Lucretian than normal Latin words, and neither this figurative use of words nor this stylistic ornamentation nor this use of myth nor this selection of details (rivers) shows that Ovid's (main) intention was to amuse his readers.

85 Pont. 4.10.63-64.

86 Trist. 3.10.51-52. Wheeler 1965, 139 translates *redundatae flumine aquae* with "or the full waters of the river", but this cannot be the meaning of this expression. Therefore, I propose "or the waters that overflowed from the river". For *redundatus* in active sense, cf. Ov. fast. 6.402 with Frazer's 1959, 349 translation: *amne redundatis fossa madebat aquis* ("a ditch was drenched with the water that overflowed from the river").

Black Sea congeals. Indeed, now we can understand better these statements and the Roman readers' doubts about them: they were sceptical about the account that the Black Sea freezes because they thought that only the fresh river water can freeze, but that it is impossible that the Black Sea's salt water congeals. Ovid explains to them that it is not the Black Sea's own water that freezes, but (a part of) the surface that is imbued with fresh water from the rivers that flow into the Black Sea. Contrary to the modern scholarship, the question of the extent to which the surface freezes is irrelevant to both Ovid himself and the Roman readers, as Pont. 4.7 and 4.9 will also show.

In the elegy Pont. 4.7, in which Ovid addresses Vestalis, who in an official mission – maybe as a *praefectus* or *legatus* – has reached the Pontic region and whose military prowess the poem praises,[87] Ovid defends the complaints he has made about Pontus and its climate:[88]

missus es Euxinas quoniam, Vestalis, ad undas,

    ut positis reddas iura sub axe locis,

aspicis en praesens quali iaceamus in arvo,

    nec me testis eris falsa solere queri.

accedet voci per te non inrita nostrae,   5

    Alpinis iuvenis regibus orte, fides.

ipse vides certe glacie concrescere Pontum,

    ipse vides rigido stantia vina gelu;

ipse vides onerata ferox ut ducat Iazyx

    per medias Histri plaustra bubulcus aquas.   10

Seeing that you have been sent to the Euxine waters, Vestalis, to dispense justice to those lands which lie beneath the pole, you behold face to face in what manner of country I am cast and you will bear witness that I am not wont to utter false complaints. My words will receive through you, young scion of Alpine kings, no idle support. You yourself see the Pontus stiffen with ice, you yourself see the wine standing rigid with the frost; you yourself see how the fierce Iazygian herdsman guides his loaded wagon over the middle of Hister's waters.

As Vestalis is present in the region, he can confirm as an eyewitness the veracity of Ovid's statement that the Danube, the Black Sea, and the wine in the winter freeze.

Likewise, Ovid addresses in the elegy Pont. 4.9 Graecinus, who is suspicious about his narratives, and tells him to ask his brother Flaccus, who as a soldier experienced the Pontic winter and can confirm that Ovid's account is true:[89]

quaere loci faciem Scythicique incommoda caeli

    et quam vicino terrear hoste roga.

[...]

mentiar, an coeat duratus frigore Pontus

    et teneat glacies iugera multa freti.

---

87   Cf Helzle's 1989, 156-157 commentary.
88   Pont. 4.7.1-10.
89   Pont. 4.9.81-82 and 85-86.

Question him about the face of this land, the rigours of the Scythian climate;
ask him about the terror that I suffer from the foe so close at hand [...] whether
I am a liar or the Pontus does indeed freeze with the cold and ice covers many
acres of the sea.

According to Gahan, from these three *Epistulae ex Ponto* another picture of winter
emerges that contains the following three elements: (1) wine, if left standing, becomes
frozen (Pont. 4.7.8; trist.3.10.23-24). (2) The Danube freezes so solidly that even carts
loaded with goods can be pulled across the ice (Pont. 4.7.9-10; trist. 3.10.33-34). (3)
Even the Black Sea freezes (Pont. 4.7.7; 4.9.81-86, esp. 85; 4.10.37-38; trist. 3.10.37-38)
over many acres of its surface (Pont. 4.9.81-86, esp. 86) so that, where boats once
floated, the traveller goes (Pont. 4.10.31-34; trist. 3.10.39-40 and 31, where a similar
comment is made of the Danube) with dry feet. This is what Gahan regards as the
basic and true picture of the winter at Tomis, because it is based on at least two,
sometimes three people's experience.[90]

   On the other side, two notable kinds of details present in trist. 3.10 are missing
from this revised weather picture and, Gahan concludes, cannot be regarded as
true: the extremes of climate, first of all, like continuous snows (13-16) and building-
razing winds (17-18), and secondly colourful descriptions like those of the natives
clad in skins and trousers with frosty hair and beards (19-22), of dolphins prevented
from jumping, or of fish totally imprisoned by the ice:[91]

> *tum neque se pandi possunt delphines in auras*
>
>> *tollere; conantes dura coercet hiems;*
>
> *et quamvis Boreas iactatis insonet alis,*   45
>
>> *fluctus in obsesso gurgite nullus erit;*
>
> *inclusaeque gelu stabunt in marmore puppes,*
>
>> *nec poterit rigidas findere remus aquas.*
>
> *vidimus in glacie pisces haerere ligatos,*
>
>> *sed pars ex illis tum quoque viva fuit.*   50

At such times the curving dolphins cannot launch themselves into the air; if
they try, stern winter checks them; and though Boreas may roar and toss his
wings, there will be no wave on the beleaguered flood. Shut in by the cold the
ships will stand fast in the marble surface nor will any oar be able to cleave the
stiffened waters. I have seen fish clinging fast bound in the ice, yet some even
then still lived.

In my view, Gahan has shown that Ovid's statements about the Pontic winter are
true that wine, if left standing, becomes frozen, that the Danube and even the
Black Sea freezes over many acres (*iugera multa*, Pont. 4.9.86) of its surface. This
last detail, that is found only here, is important for our adequate understanding of
trist. 3.10.35-40, too, because Ovid does not pretend that the whole surface of the
Black Sea freezes, as many critics paraphrase Ovid's statement, but that a part of
it congeals. From an ancient perspective, the freezing of the Black Sea itself is the
spectacular occurrence, while the question of the extent to which this happens is
largely irrelevant to the Roman readers.

---

90   Cf. Gahan 1978, 202.

91   Trist. 3.10.43-50; cf. Gahan 1978, 202 who assumes that Ovid was fanciful with regard to the ext-
       remes of climate, while the colourful pictures of the natives, the dolphins, and fish may or may
       not be true.

However, the limits that Gahan established between facts and fictions are probably not accurate, because the lacking veracity is just one possible and no necessary reason for the fact that Ovid utters a statement in trist. 3.10 which he does not repeat in the three *Epistulae ex Ponto* just mentioned (4.7, 4.9, and 4.10). Other reasons might be that Ovid wants to avoid this kind of monotony and that for reasons of variation he does not repeat always the same features even if he talks about the same or a similar topic.

As all of these elegies manifest and eyewitnesses can confirm, the winter climate at Tomis is characterised by extreme weather conditions to which the fact belongs that even the Black Sea freezes over many acres of its surface. Therefore, why should we think that other extremes of climate, the continuous snows (trist. 3.10.13-16) and storms (17-18), are fantasy products? If even the Black Sea freezes to a considerable extent and the wine becomes frozen in the jar, it is probable that it snows (continuously), and it is likely that windstorms damage or destroy towers and the roofs of buildings (*tecta* in line 18 should be taken in its literal meaning "roofs" and not in the metonymic sense of "houses" or "buildings", as many critics do). Moreover, other more or less historical sources confirm that snow and storms are typical for the Black Sea region, as we can see in Diodorus', Mela's and even in Theocritus' statements about the snow,[92] and in Theophrastus', Pliny's, and Xenophon's comments about winds and storms.[93] As to Ovid's statement that snow remains in many places for two years (16), we must probably understand this as a reference to higher regions, so that this assertion is not even an exaggeration.

Further, given this frosty winter, it is probable that the inhabitants wear trousers and skins to protect themselves from the cold, and it seems logical that their hair and beards are frosty, too. The former statement (and other details as well) has a parallel in Xenophon's *Anabasis*, where the author speaks about the winter that he passed with the other soldiers on the plain of the Thracian Thynians at the western coast of the Black Sea:[94]

ἦν δὲ χιὼν πολλὴ καὶ ψῦχος οὕτως ὥστε τὸ ὕδωρ ὃ ἐφέροντο ἐπὶ δεῖπνον ἐπήγνυτο καὶ ὁ οἶνος ὁ ἐν τοῖς ἀγγείοις, καὶ τῶν Ἑλλήνων πολλῶν καὶ ῥῖνες ἀπεκαίοντο καὶ ὦτα. καὶ τότε δῆλον ἐγένετο οὗ ἕνεκα οἱ Θρᾷκες τὰς ἀλωπεκᾶς ἐπὶ ταῖς κεφαλαῖς φοροῦσι καὶ τοῖς ὠσί, καὶ χιτῶνας οὐ μόνον περὶ τοῖς στέρνοις ἀλλὰ καὶ περὶ τοῖς μηροῖς, καὶ ζειρὰς μέχρι τῶν ποδῶν ἐπὶ τῶν ἵππων ἔχουσιν, ἀλλ οὐ χλαμύδας.

There was deep snow on the plain, and it was so cold that the water which they carried in for dinner and the wine in the jars would freeze, and many of the Greeks had their noses and ears frost-bitten. Then it became clear why the Thracians wear fox-skin caps on their heads and over their ears, and tunics not merely about their chests, but also round their thighs, and why, when on horseback, they wear long cloaks reaching to their feet instead of mantles.

Finally, if the Black Sea freezes over many acres of its surface, it is necessary that the dolphins are prevented from jumping on these parts of the Black Sea, and it seems possible what Ovid tells us about the fish (49). However, how do we have to understand this last statement (*vidimus in glacie pisces haerere ligatos*)? It is hardly believable that fish is imprisoned by the ice (as most critics paraphrase this statement) and that a part of them (or a part of the individual body) is still alive (50). We have already seen a passage in Strabo in which the author says that fish become caught in the ice and are obtained by digging with an implement called the

---

92   Cf. Diod. 1.41.7; Mela 3.59; Theokr. 22.28; Danoff 1962, 942.
93   Cf. Theophr. de vent. 9.54; Plin. nat. 2.126; Xen. anab. 5.7.7; Danoff 1962, 941-942.
94   Xen. anab. 7.4.3-4. Translation adapted from Dillery's 2006, 589 Loeb edition.

"gangame".[95] It is unclear what the gangame exactly is: some scholars suppose that it is a pronged instrument like a trident, other suggest that it is a net.[96]

A fishnet is explicitly mentioned by Juvenal in a context that might be relevant for a better understanding of the Ovidian passage:[97]

incidit Hadriaci spatium admirabile rhombi

ante domum Veneris, quam Dorica sustinet Ancon,   40

implevitque sinus; neque enim minor haeserat illis

quos operit glacies Maeotica ruptaque tandem

solibus effundit torrentis ad ostia Ponti

desidia tardos et longo frigore pingues.

[...] there turned up below the temple of Venus, which rests upon Doric Ancon, the incredible hulk of an Adriatic turbot. It filled the nets and there it stuck, just as big as the fish concealed by Azov's ice which, when the sun has finally broken up the ice, are poured down to the mouth of the Pontic flood, slow with inertia and bloated from the long cold.

The Adriatic turbot is caught in a net, and this is the most plausible explanation for Ovid's statement as well because he uses the verbs *haerere* ("hang, cling") and *ligare* (in the passive voice: "to be bound"): the fisher, after they broke the ice and fish filled the nets, extract them from the water beneath. A part of the fish is already dead, but some of them – and this is the surprising information, introduced with *sed* ("yet") – is still alive.[98] In Juvenal's comparision with the big fish concealed by Azov's ice, the size of the fish is the *tertium comparationis*, and the fish is said to survive under the frozen surface of the Maeotian Lake.

Conclusion

The elegies in which Ovid talks about the extreme winter at Tomis are not and cannot be a copy of reality, and we cannot prove definitely if especially the first winter depicted in trist. 3.10 was exactly as Ovid describes it. Nonetheless, all available methods that allow an investigation of these matters in terms of probability, point in the same direction and make it plausible that Ovid's account is true. Like the exile poems in general, this elegy might also contain some exaggerations, although they are easier to find in other poems, and it is one-sided because it focuses on the negative parts of Ovid's exile. However, Ovid does not seem to present invented events and descriptions to us, as especially points 3.1 and 3.3 have shown. His statements have to be seen against the background of the ancient discourse about frigid weather in foreign regions in which the wine and the (Black) Sea possibly freeze, not in the sense that Ovid imitates Virgil and that his account is a fictional story that originated in his fantasy or in other literary sources, but rather in the sense that he tells and

---

95   Cf. Strabo 7.3.18 (see footnote 45).

96   Cf. Radt 2007, 270-271 ad Strabo 7.3.18; Gajdukevič 1971, 125.

97   Iuv. 4.39-44. Translation adapted from Braund's 2004, 199-201 Loeb edition.

98   There is another strange story about the fish in the Black Sea that Pliny the elder reports, relying on Theophrastus (Plin. nat. 9.177): *eadem in Ponti regione adprehendi glacie piscium maxime gobiones non nisi patinarum calore vitalem motum fatentes.* (in Rackham's 1956, 283 translation: "In the same region of the Black Sea the fish most frequently caught in the ice is the goby, which is only made to reveal the movement of life by the heat of the saucepan.") The meaning of the expression *adprehendi glacie* will not be that the fish is "caught in the ice", but that the fish is grasped or gripped by the ice, *i.e.* that the goby is affected by the icy water in a higher degree than the other fish. The other fish, it is implied, is not so much affected by the icy water.

explains extraordinary events that he experienced. Moreover, Ovid is not the only eyewitness of the narrated events, but refers to two other persons who can confirm his statements. Finally, he stresses his authority not at an arbitrary point of his narrative, but at exactly those points where he anticipates or reacts to the conflict between the average Roman reader's knowledge about the (im-)possibility that the Black Sea can freeze and his more precise geographical insights.

There will be critics who will still contend that we should not take Ovid seriously and that we should regard him as playful, humorous, ironical, and unreliable even in those passages in which Ovid affirms that he says the truth. However, how does this assumption conform to the fact that Ovid was really banished by Augustus and tried to arouse the pity of his readers, especially of Augustus himself, in order to achieve his recall, as nearly all scholars believe? Why should he tell untrue things if there is, as he puts it, no reward for a falsehood (trist. 3.10.35-36)? How could Ovid give us a fictional account of the Pontic winter if there are eyewitnesses who could reject incorrect information? Finally, if not only his descriptions of the extreme winter are fictional stories but also these eyewitnesses are fictive, this would be a rather odd fiction.

References

Amann, M., 2006. *Komik in den Tristien Ovids*. Basel: Schwabe.

Bérchez Castaño, E., 2015. *El destierro de Ovidio en Tomis: realidad y ficción*. Valencia: Institució Alfons el Magnànim.

Besslich, S., 1972. Ovids Winter in Tomis. Zu trist. III 10. *Gymnasium*, 79, 177-191.

Bews, J.B., 1984. The Metamorphosis of Virgil in the *Tristia* of Ovid. *BICS*, 31, 51-60.

Bolikhovskaya, N., Kaitamba, M., Porotov, A. and Fouache, E., 2004. Environmental Changes of the Northeastern Black Sea's Coastal Region during the Middle and Late Holocene. *In*: E.M. Scott, A.Y. Alekseev and G. Zaitseva, eds. *Impact of the Environment on Human Migration in Eurasia*. Dordrecht: Springer, 209-223.

Braund, S.M., 2004. *Juvenal and Persius*. Cambridge, MA: Harvard University Press.

Chwalek, B., 1996. *Die Verwandlung des Exils in die elegische Welt. Studien zu den Tristia und Epistulae ex Ponto Ovids*. Frankfurt a.M: Peter Lang Verlag.

Claassen, J.-M., 1990. Ovid's Poetic Pontus. *Papers of the Leeds International Latin Seminar*, 6, 65-94.

Claassen, J.-M., 2008. *Ovid revisited. The Poet in Exile*. London: Duckworth.

Conte, G.B., 2017. *Stealing the Club from Hercules. On Imitation in Latin Poetry*. Berlin and Boston: De Gruyter.

Dan, A.-C., 2011. Quid melius Roma? Notes sur Rome et ses identités dans les *Tristes* et les *Pontiques* d'Ovide. *In*: M. Simon, ed. *Identités romaines: conscience de soi et représentations de l'autre dans la Rome antique (IVe siècle av. J.-C. – VIIIe siècle apr. J.-C.)*. Paris: Presses de l'École normale supérieure, 213-242.

Dana, M., 2011. *Culture et mobilité dans le Pont-Euxin. Approche régionale de la vie culturelle des cités grecques*. Paris and Bordeaux: Ausinius Editions.

Danoff, C.M., 1962. Pontos Euxeinos. *RE*, Supp. 9, 866-1175.

Davisson, M.T., 1982 Duritia and Creativity in Exile. Epistulae ex Ponto 4.10. *ClAnt*, 1, 28-42.

Dehon, P.-J., 1993. *Hiems latina. Études sur l'hiver dans la poésie latine, des origines à l'époque de Néron*. Brüssel: Peeters Publishers.

Evans, H.B., 1975. Winter and Warfare in Ovid's Tomis (*Tristia* 3.10). *CJ*, 70 (3), 1-9.

Feddern, S., 2013. *Die Suasorien des älteren Seneca. Einleitung, Text und Kommentar*. Berlin and Boston: De Gruyter.

Feddern, S., 2018. *Der antike Fiktionalitätsdiskurs*. Berlin and Boston: De Gruyter.

Fitton Brown, A., 1985. The unreality of Ovid's exile. *LCM*, 10, 19-22.

Florian, K., 2007. *Ovids Jahre am Pontus. Eine diachronische Analyse der Tristien und Epistulae ex Ponto als ein frühes Beispiel europäischer Exilliteratur.* Innsbruck, Wien and Bozen: Studien Verlag.

Frazer, J.G., 1959. *Ovid's Fasti.* Cambridge, MA: Harvard University Press.

Gahan, J.J., 1978. Ovid: The Poet in Winter. *CJ* 73, 198-202.

Gajdukevič, V.F., 1971. *Das Bosporanische Reich.* Berlin: Akademie Verlag.

Galfré, E., 2017. Mirum e fides. Meraviglia vs. credibilità nelle opere ovidiane dell'esilio. *SCO* 63, 187-218.

Gärtner, J.F., 2005. *Ovid, Epistulae ex Ponto. Book 1.* Oxford: Oxford University Press.

Godley, A.D., 2006. *Herodotus. Vol. 2: Books III – IV.* Cambridge, MA: Harvard University Press.

Goold, G.P. and Fairclough, H.R., 1999. *Virgil. Eclogues. Georgics.* Cambridge, MA: Harvard University Press.

Grebe, S., 2004. Rom und Tomis in Ovids *Tristia* und *Epistulae ex Ponto. In*: E. Christmann, ed. *Studia humanitatis ac litterarum trifolio Heidelbergensi dedicata. Festschrift für Eckhard Christmann, Wilfried Edelmaier und Rudolf Kettemann.* Frankfurt a.M.: Peter Lang Verlag, Internationaler Verlag der Wissenschaften, 115-129.

Helzle, M., 1989. *Publii Ovidii Nasonis Epistularum ex Ponto liber IV. A commentary on poems 1 to 7 and 16.* Hildesheim: Georg Olms.

Helzle, M., 2006. Fiktion und Realität in Ovids Exildichtung am Beispiel *Epistulae ex Ponto* IV 7. *WJA*, 30, 139-152.

Hinds, S., 1998. *Allusion and Intertext. Dynamics of Appropriation in Roman Poetry.* Cambridge: Cambridge University Press.

Hofmann, H., 1987. The unreality of Ovid's Tomitan exile once again. *LCM*, 12, 23.

Hofmann, H., 2001. Ovid im Exil?. *Mitteilungen des deutschen Altphilologenverbandes, Landesverband Baden-Württemberg*, 29, 8-19.

Holleman, A.W.J., 1985. Ovid's exile. *LCM*, 10, 48.

Holzberg, N., 1998. *Ovid. Dichter und Werk.* München: C.H. Beck.

Jones, H.L., 1983. *The Geography of Strabo. Vol. 3: Books VI – VII.* Cambridge, MA: Harvard University Press.

Kablitz, A., 2008. Literatur, Fiktion und Erzählung – nebst einem Nachruf auf den Erzähler. *In*: I.O. Rajewsky and U. Schneider, eds. *Im Zeichen der Fiktion. Aspekte fiktionaler Rede aus historischer und systematischer Sicht.* Stuttgart: Franz Steiner Verlag, 13-44.

Kaster, R.A., 2011. *Macrobius. Saturnalia. Vol. 3: Books 6-7.* Cambridge, MA: Harvard University Press.

Kettemann, R., 1999. Ovids Verbannungsort – ein *locus horribilis*?. *In*: W. Schubert, ed. *Ovid. Werk und Wirkung. Festgabe für Michael von Albrecht zum 65. Geburtstag. Vol. 2.* Frankfurt a.M.: Peter Lang Verlag, 715-736.

Klauk, T. and Köppe, T., 2014. Bausteine einer Theorie der Fiktionalität. *In*: T. Klauk and T. Köppe, eds. *Fiktionalität. Ein interdisziplinäres Handbuch.* Berlin: De Gruyter, 3–31.

Lamarque, P. and Olsen, S.H., 1994. *Truth, Fiction, and Literature. A Philosophical Perspective.* Oxford: Oxford University Press.

Lenz, L., 1993. Eis und Exil (Zu Tristien III 10). *In*: C. Neumeister, ed. *Antike Texte in Forschung und Schule. Fs. Willibald Heilmann.* Frankfurt a.M.: Diesterweg, 147-166.

Lozovan, E.,1959. Réalités pontiques et nécessités littéraires chez Ovide. *In:* E. Paratore, ed. *Atti del Convegno internazionale Ovidiano II.* Rome: Istituto di Studi Romani, 355-370.

Luck, G., 1977. *P. Ovidius Naso. Tristia. Vol. 2: Kommentar.* Heidelberg: Universitätsverlag Winter.

Maisuradze, G. and Schollmeyer, P., 2017. Tatsächlich trostlos? Ovids Exilort zwischen literarischer Fiktion und archäologischer Realität. *AW*, 48 (6), 30-33.

Martin, A.J., 2004. *Was ist Exil? Ovids Tristia und Epistulae ex Ponto*. Hildesheim: Georg Olms.

Naschert, G., 1998. Hyperbel. *In*: G. Ueding, ed. *HWR 4*. Tübingen: Max Niemeyer Verlag, 115-122.

Philbrick, R.S., 2016. *Hyperbole and the Hyperbolic Persona in Ovid's Exile Poetry*. Doctoral Thesis. Brown University.

Podossinov, A., 1987. *Ovids Dichtung als Quelle für die Geschichte des Schwarzmeergebiets*. Konstanz: Universitätsverlag Konstanz.

Rackham, H., 1956/1960. *Pliny. Natural History. Vol. 3: libri VIII – XI. Vol. 4: libri XII – XVI*. Cambridge, MA: Harvard University Press.

Radt, S., 2007. *Strabons Geographika. Vol. 6: Buch V–VIII: Kommentar*. Göttingen: S.L. Radt.

Reitz, C., 2013. Describing the invisible: Ovid's Rome. *Hermes*, 141, 283-293.

Rolfe, J.C., 1978. *The Attic Nights of Aulus Gellius. Vol. 3*. London and Cambridge, MA: Harvard University Press.

Schmitt, A., 2013. Exsul ludens. Ovids poetologische Exil-Geschichte zwischen Dichtung und Wahrheit. *AU*, 56 (4-5), 93-101.

Schmitzer, U., 2011. *Ovid*. Hildesheim: Georg Olms.

Seibert, S., 2014. *Ovids verkehrte Exilwelt. Spiegel des Erzählers – Spiegel des Mythos – Spiegel Roms*. Berlin and Boston: De Gruyter.

Trevizam, M. and de Avellar, J.B.C., 2016. Os citas e a Cítia em *Geórgicas* 3.349-383 e em *Tristia* 3.10: permanência de parâmetros e intertextualidade. *Phaos*. 16, 105-123.

West, D. and Woodman, A.J., eds., 1979. *Creative Imitation and Latin Literature*. Cambridge: Cambridge University Press.

Wheeler, S.M., 1965. *Ovid. Tristia. Ex Ponto*. London: William Heinemann Ltd.

Williams, G.D., 1994. *Banished Voices. Readings in Ovid's Exile Poetry*. Cambridge: Cambridge University Press.

Winterbottom, M., 1974. *The Elder Seneca. Declamations. Vol. 2: Controversiae, Books 7-10. Suasoriae*. Cambridge, MA: Harvard University Press.

Wulfram, H., 2008. *Das römische Versepistelbuch. Eine Gattungsanalyse*. Berlin: Verlag Antike.

Xenophon, 2006. *Anabasis. Translated by Carleton L. Brownson. Revised by John Dillery*. Cambridge, MA: Harvard University Press.

Zipfel, F., 2001. *Fiktion, Fiktivität, Fiktionalität. Analysen zur Fiktion in der Literatur und zum Fiktionsbegriff in der Literaturwissenschaft*. Berlin: Erich Schmidt Verlag.

Zipfel, F., 2014. Fiktionssignale. *In*: T. Klauk, and T. Köppe, eds. *Fiktionalität. Ein interdisziplinäres Handbuch*. Berlin: De Gruyter, 97–124.

A sea of wine and honey: Networks of narratives as resources for the negotiation of identities. A heuristic approach in the Hellenistic western Mediterranean

Raffaella Da Vela

Abstract

The formation of a new 'Mediterranean taste' and the introduction of new lifestyles within the local elites of the western Mediterranean during the Hellenistic period has frequently been labelled 'Hellenisation' or 'Romanisation'. Approaching consumptionscapes in the coastal cities as a semiotic network provides an empiric tool to overcome the concepts of 'Hellenisation' and 'Romanisation' as transcendent or immanent categories expressing changes in taste. The Mediterranean connections and sea routes can be considered not only from an economic perspective as the infrastructure of supply chains but also in their role for the circulation of ideas and shared strategies of social communication. The present contribution thus proposes a network approach to consider the multi-layered relationships between object mobility, semiotic values and narratives. A meshwork of objects and places on the western Mediterranean scale permits focusing on the selective adoption of international taste as a resource for managing local power relationships, focusing on the agency of local elites and bypassing the idea of colonial or ideological influences of supra-regional powers.

Affiliative networks, cultural transmission, consumptionscapes, distinction of taste

The Hellenistic western Mediterranean has been the focus of several consumption studies over the last four decades (Dietler 2005; Dietler 2006; Dietler 2010; Mullins 2011). In particular, the formation of new Mediterranean tastes and the introduction of new lifestyles within the local elite classes has been analysed in terms of dependence upon trade networks and the expansion of Roman overseas markets in form of direct or mediated circulation of goods (Tsirkin 1992, 231). Therefore, terms such as 'Hellenisation' and 'Romanisation', which had been adopted to indicate the influence of colonial or imperial power, have been progressively banned from scientific literature, reflecting a shift away from ideas of colonial or imperialistic influence emanating from the main supra-regional powers, and towards the concept of a more fluid diffusion of ideas and lifestyles (Bats 2017; Zuchtriegel 2016; Keay 2013, 300f.; Dietler 2010, 57; and more in general: Wallace-Hadrill 2008). This diffusion of ideas and lifestyles is a part of the entanglement of connections brought about by personal mobility and commercial exchange, and found a powerful agency in the mobility of objects (Hahn and Weiss 2013). This new approach embraces a greater complexity, implicating concepts such as social entanglements, mutual interaction between global and local networks, and different analytical scales (Hodos 2014, 250-252; Knappett 2011, 26-33; Pitts 2014, 89-92). These concepts – born within a post-colonial and post-processual debate – have evolved towards an archaeology of interaction or an archaeology of entanglement (Hodder 2011; Knappett 2011). The 'archaeology of interaction' refers to a theoretical framework that has developed out of a vast number of studies that have marked a significant change of direction in the archaeology of the western Mediterranean during the last ten years (Prag and Quinn 2013). While the archaeology of interaction approaches the complexity of (ancient) community connections (Bruhn 2011), local choices and orientations on matters of taste and consumption can only be explained by taking the sociocultural value of the objects within local communities into consideration. On the other hand, the supra-regional interactions across the western Mediterranean were themselves the result of a dialectic between local politics and the long-distance supply chain, since the demand of imported goods was frequently affected by the contingent needs of the local elites. These elites, who acted as the political ruling classes, but also as holders of economic power, were able to determine the value of imported objects, legitimating the objects' use to maintain or improve their own social status within local communities (Kistler 2017b, 195f.). This re-semantisation (Krämer 2022a, 97; Krämer 2022b, 400) or appropriation ('*Aneigung*': Hahn 2016) can be interpreted as a resource of the local elites to create or maintain the socio-political dynamics in their communities and finally to control the distribution of power within them.[1]

The power of social elites in legitimising the meaning and the value of objects manifested at the regulative level, with prescriptions for the use of these objects and impositions of taxation and limitations on their possession. It also manifested at the normative level, defining some objects and lifestyles as exclusive to certain classes, and thus giving them a diacritic function (Maguire 2019, 201) that made them attractive to other social segments (Dietler 1996, 98). A 'glocal view' on the diffusion of taste detects a huge variety of local reinterpretations of the value of objects, comparing different social meanings attributed to the same objects and assemblages in different contexts. Manipulations, re-semantisations or re-interpretations of these objects are common forms of local responses to 'global' models (Kistler 2017a; Da Vela 2016; Poux 2004). The attention to the interaction of global and local factors requires a re-evaluation of the gap between the circulation of objects on the market, conditioned by the laws of supply and demand, and the perception of value, use, and meaning of objects in local communities.[2]

The intriguing question concerning the local re-interpretation and use of consumption as a social and political resource for the local elites[3] is whether the

---

1   The circular process of semiotic evaluation between consumer behaviour and consumed objects is evocatively explained by Sophy Woodward as the way in which "*practices of consumption give objects meaning and objects give meaning to consumption practices*" (Woodward 2019, 168).

2   This 'in-between' dimension of connectivity is the focus of Tamar Hodos' contribution (Hodos 2014). An innovative approach to this dimension, defined as 'translocal', has been proposed for the other side of the ancient world, in Hellenistic Bactria, by Milinda Hoo (Hoo 2018).

3   The adopted conception of resources is based on a relational definition of them as every material and immaterial means that has a potential for the formation, conservation, and transformation of social identities: Hardenberg *et al.* 2017: 14-16.

narratives themselves circulated independently of the supply chain and could in fact have been 'triggers' for the adoption of global lifestyles and induce the consumption of imported objects. Regarding the social value of taste and behaviour in the western Mediterranean, the diffusion of these common narratives could provide an understanding of the use of objects or assemblages with a diacritical value for local elites in different geo-political contexts. For example, the use of jewellery modelled after that of the Macedonian kings and elites found in Hellenistic Campanian graves can be analysed as a specific strategy of self-representation related to local political choices, rather than a purely aesthetic trend linked to the wide diffusion of fashionable objects (Coen 2019, 67-70). From the other side, the narrative linking golden crowns to higher social status is in itself a kind of cultural import. This narrative is common not only among Etruscan elites, but also to other local contexts, with different needs for social representation; for example, in Magna Grecia.

The current contribution presents a methodological 'cut', and proposes to shift the focus of inquiry from the concrete trade and consumption of commodities into the social space of consumption (Bourdieu 2010, 120-125). The overall research question concerns the possibility of developing heuristic tools able to detect the formation of common narratives within the higher social segments of the Hellenistic (north) western Mediterranean from the 4th to the 2nd centuries by examining material culture. Such narratives are reflected in the objects consumed, as well as in the literary and iconographic production of the Hellenistic period (Sommer 2014, 187-191).

These narratives and shared social practices contributed to the expression of an upper social habitus[4], partly by referencing Mediterranean models. In many contexts these 'distinction strategies' (to use Bourdieu's terminology) determined specific patterns of local choices in the assemblage, usage, and meaning of the objects. Although the term Hellenistic *koinè* was born as a linguistic term to indicate a common Greek dialect, it has been used in archaeology to point out similarities in material culture. Recent studies applied globalisation theories to this phenomenon, and revised the concept of *koinè*, defining it as the interaction between global and local restructurings of political, economic, and cultural structures (Laftsidis 2019; Roselaar 2019, 167-169; Hoo 2018). These local responses to global restructuring can be considered under the interpretative categories of glocalism. The role of sea routes and connectivity thus expresses not only potential for commercial exchange, but also for the fluidity of ideas and political strategies. However, the formation of new consumptionscapes had a strong dependence upon pre-existing local conditions and power relationships (Costin and Earle 1989; Knappett 2011, 100-102). The levels of social communication inherent in consumption behaviours and the display of such behaviours are therefore numerous and complex (see Schweizer 2021, 310 f.). From a methodological point of view, studying the birth of a common narrative among the elites of the western Mediterranean presents one main advantage with respect to the analysis of the distribution of commercial ware. A vast amount of the available data comes from funerary contexts, which are not representative of the real consumption, but rather of an exhibited consumption aimed wholly at representation and heavily influenced by socio-cultural parameters. These funerary contexts and their related ceremonies are thus the space in which social representation and ideology find their maximal expression, in the form of conspicuous consumption (Krämer 2017, 530 with further bibliography). This fact, which is apparently seen as an obstacle in consumption studies, becomes a major advantage when studying the construction of social narratives, since the ostentatious consumption displayed in these limited contexts provides valuable information on those narratives that were considered

---

4   In this context, habitus refers to "the set of embodied dispositions that structure action in the world and consciously instantiate perception of identity and difference" (Dietler 2011, 179), see also Bourdieu 2010, 166.

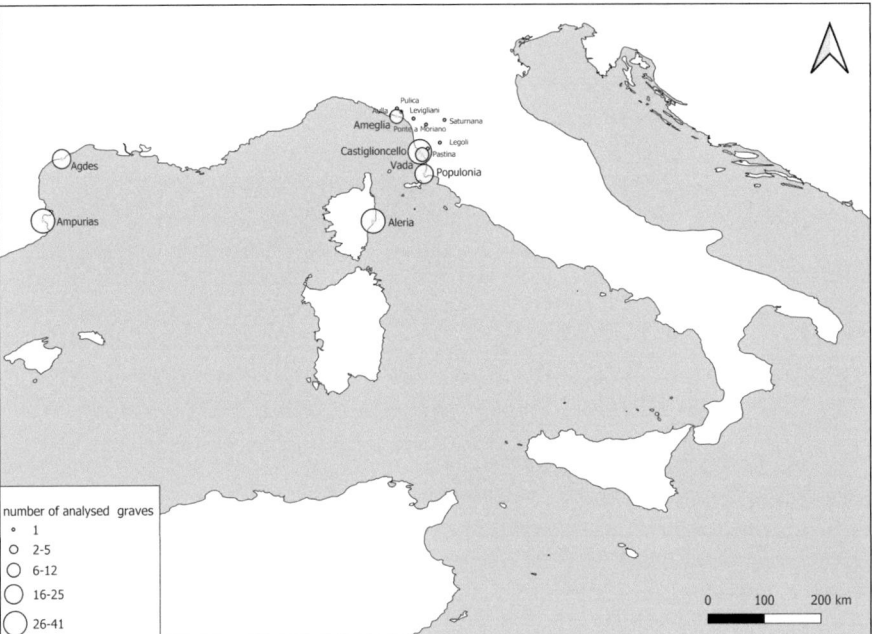

Figure 1. Distribution of the analysed grave assemblages. Software QGIS 3.8.3. Vectorial data: Natural Earth. Coordinate System WGS 84 EPSG: 4326.

worthy of representation. It is therefore possible to trace common narratives and the diffusion of semiotic associations in the archaeological record, by relating this to the communicative context and the social value of ostensive consumption (Dietler 2006, 222) in funerary assemblages.

The case study and its geo-political frame

From among the Hellenistic coastal necropoleis located in the western Mediterranean, I have chosen 171 grave assemblages from 14 different ancient local communities to use as an extended case study, and put this methodology to the test (Fig. 1).[5]

The geo-political frame of the analysis includes a plurality of political actors and growing economic interaction based on a well-established trade network that had connected the relevant cities for many centuries (Keay 2013; Gras 2010). Moreover, the political and economic restructuring of the western Mediterranean between the 4th and 2nd century BCE is reflected in many literary sources. These report exclusively conflictual events, such as the Punic Wars, Celtic invasions, Social Wars, the Roman conquest, and so on. The historical narratives of these events confirm the perception that some actors in our case study were part of an entangled western Mediterranean, but they also tend to reduce the interactions to oppositional pairs of actors: Celts *vs.* Locals; Roman *vs.* Etruscan and Italic allies, Roman *vs.* Iberian; Pro-Roman elites *vs.* Anti-Roman elites (Zuchtriegel 2016; Boissinot 2005). An archaeological approach that views consumptionscapes as local resources in the coastal centres reveals more articulated patterns of interactions.[6] The definition of the elite classes as Etruscan, Ligurian, Celtic or Iberian appears to indicate the social segments that retained economic and eventually political power at the local

---

5   References for the dataset: Aléria: Jéhasse and Jéhasse 1973; Agdes: Dedet and Schwaller 2010; 2018; Ameglia: Durante 1982; Ampurias: Almagro 1953; Castiglioncello: Gambogi and Palladino 1999; Populonia, Necropoli delle Grotte: Romualdi and Settesoldi 2009; Populonia, Casone e Buche delle Fate: Fedeli 1983; Baratti and Mordeglia 2005. Baratti and Mordeglia 2008; Pastina, Ponte a Moriano, Saturnana; Levigliani; Aulla: Ciampoltrini and Notini 2011; Vada: Massa 1974.

6   In the 1980s, the shared material culture of many coastal cities in the western Mediterranean was defined as the 'harbours' circuit' or 'harbours' facies' (Martelli 1981a, 171; 1981b, 426).

level, but this definition is mostly based on categories derived from Latin and Greek written sources, and these categories do not correspond to the local use of objects. It would therefore be more accurate in this context to talk about the elites of a specific location, rather than giving them a general 'ethnic' label.

Within the consumptionscapes of the selected necropoleis, some specific assemblages have been chosen to study the use of drinking and eating as diacritical practices. The choice of assemblages was made based on the theoretical frameworks established in the studies on feasting as a form of diacritical practice by Michael Dietler (Dietler 1996, 98) and in the work of the sociologist Pierre Bourdieu on the habitus and the distinction of taste (Bourdieu 2010 (1984), commented re-edition; for an archaeological application: Daveloose 2017; Da Vela 2022). Therefore, eating and drinking styles have been observed here as assumed parts of a commensal politics, in which the domestic economy becomes interlocked with global elements such as the production and supply chain, supra-regional trade networks and political affiliation. Since ancient funerary rituals were occasions for the public exhibition of the status and socio-economic power of local families, containers and other vases for the presentation and consumption of food and wine are indicative of the intention among elite families to display their habitus as an expression of their socio-economic capital (Dietler 1996, 89).

Semiotic networks and the distinction of taste

The presence of pottery related to the consumption of wine and other luxury goods in graves shows that the semiotics of wine and food consumption had a high social value. During the Hellenistic period, the expression of status and socio-economic power in different local communities along the coasts of the western Mediterranean shows a world of common references. Local funerary traditions progressively adopted supra-regionally appreciated objects and assemblages, shifting from the appropriation of prestigious objects to the appropriation of prestigious ideas. The accessibility of these goods – which was a consequence of trade over the commercial sea routes – is insufficient to explain the transformation of these objects and assemblages from targets of consumption to symbols of conspicuous consumption. Even the colonial encounters in Massalia, Agdes, or Ampurias (Dietler 2010; Dedet and Schwaller 2018), although they were powerful instances of cultural contact, cannot explain the comparable phenomena taking place in other regions, such as Etruria, where no Greek colonies were founded. The mobility of entrepreneurs, mercenaries and specialised workers, which is epigraphically attested in some coastal cities (Fentress 2013; Maggiani 2013; Cherici 2007), also cannot solely explain the wider and transcultural impact of some of these objects and assemblages. Furthermore, instances of collective elite feasting including both locals and strangers within emporia were occasions subject to precise rules of interaction (Krämer 2016; Gras 2010, 50-51). These strict social rules disqualify such events from being seen as strong triggers of the imitation and appropriation of symbols in terms of the consumption habitus and symbolic consumption-empowerment. The spread of the relevant narratives probably involved all of the aforementioned factors and can be seen as an articulated, fluid, and complex process, which requires specific methodologies if we are to approach it on a supra-local scale.

Semiotic networks of objects and places provide a suitable map for detecting subtle differences in the drinking and eating habitus of coastal elites without losing the relational dimension, which contributes to the sharing of this practice and the creation of common narratives. A semiotic network is an affiliative network constituted by two different groups of nodes, in our case grave assemblages, and objects and their relational ties (Knappett 2005, 50-52; Knappett 2012; Hyman 2007).

Grave/Object/o gg	skyphos T585 S	skyphos ferrara T585 N	oinochoe 5351	oinochoe 5371	oinochoe VII	cup 1472	cup 1524	cup 2152	cup 2154	cup 2534	cup 2536	cup 2538	cup 2522	coppa 2567	coppa 2574	coppa 2621	cup grey ware 2613	cup grey ware 2763	cup grey ware 2614	cup 2616	coppa 2672 ptest
ACB7a	0	0	0	0	0	0	0	0	0	0	0	0	0	0	0	0	0	0	0	0	0
ACB7b	0	0	0	0	0	0	0	0	0	0	0	0	0	0	0	0	0	0	0	0	0
ACB7c	1	0	0	0	0	0	0	0	0	0	0	0	0	0	0	0	0	0	0	0	0
ACJ54a	0	0	0	0	0	0	0	0	0	0	0	0	0	0	0	0	0	0	0	0	0
ACJ54b	0	0	0	0	0	0	0	0	0	0	0	0	0	0	0	0	0	0	0	0	0
ACJ54c	0	0	0	0	0	0	0	0	0	0	0	0	0	0	0	0	0	0	0	0	0
ACJ54ext	0	0	0	0	0	0	0	0	0	0	0	0	0	0	0	0	0	0	0	0	0
ACL2	0	0	0	0	0	0	0	0	0	0	0	0	0	0	0	0	0	0	0	0	0
ACR28	0	0	0	0	0	0	0	0	0	0	0	0	0	0	0	0	0	0	0	0	0
ACT40	0	0	0	0	0	0	0	0	0	0	0	0	0	0	0	0	0	0	0	0	0
AL1	0	0	0	0	0	0	0	0	0	0	0	0	0	0	0	0	0	0	0	0	0
AL10	0	0	0	0	0	0	0	0	0	0	0	0	0	0	0	0	0	0	0	0	0
AL11	0	1	0	0	0	0	0	0	0	0	0	0	0	0	0	0	0	0	0	0	0
AL12	0	0	0	0	0	0	0	0	0	0	0	0	0	0	0	0	0	0	0	0	0
AL13	0	0	0	0	0	1	0	0	0	0	0	0	0	0	0	0	0	0	0	0	0
AL14	1	0	0	0	0	1	0	0	0	0	0	0	0	0	0	0	0	0	0	0	0
AL15	0	0	0	0	0	1	0	0	0	0	0	0	0	0	0	0	0	0	0	0	0
AL16	0	0	0	0	0	0	0	0	0	0	0	0	0	0	0	0	0	0	0	0	0
AL17	0	0	0	0	0	0	0	0	0	0	0	0	0	0	0	0	0	0	0	0	0
AL18	0	0	0	0	0	0	0	0	0	0	0	0	0	1	0	0	0	0	0	0	0
AL19	0	0	0	0	0	0	0	0	0	0	0	0	0	0	0	0	0	0	0	0	0
AL2	1	0	0	0	0	1	1	0	0	0	0	0	0	0	0	0	0	0	0	0	0
AL20	0	0	0	0	0	1	0	0	0	0	0	0	0	0	0	0	0	0	0	0	0
AL21	0	0	0	0	0	1	0	0	0	0	0	0	0	0	0	0	0	0	0	0	0
AL22	0	0	0	0	0	1	0	0	0	0	0	0	0	0	0	0	0	0	0	0	0
AL23	0	0	0	0	0	0	0	0	0	0	0	0	0	0	0	0	0	0	0	0	0
AL24	0	0	0	0	0	0	0	0	0	0	0	0	0	0	0	0	0	0	0	0	0
AL25	0	0	0	0	0	1	0	0	0	0	0	0	0	0	0	0	0	0	0	0	0
AL26	0	0	0	0	0	0	0	0	0	0	0	0	0	0	0	0	0	0	0	1	0
AL27	0	0	0	0	0	1	0	0	0	0	0	0	0	0	0	0	0	0	0	0	0
AL28	0	0	0	0	0	0	0	0	0	0	0	0	0	0	0	0	0	0	0	0	0
AL29	0	0	0	0	0	0	0	0	0	0	0	0	0	0	0	0	0	0	0	0	0
AL3	0	0	0	0	0	1	0	0	0	0	0	0	0	0	0	0	0	0	0	1	0
AL30	0	0	0	0	0	0	0	0	0	0	0	0	0	0	0	0	0	0	0	0	0
AL31	0	0	0	0	0	0	0	0	0	0	0	0	0	0	0	0	0	0	0	0	0
AL32	0	0	0	0	0	0	0	0	0	0	0	0	0	0	0	0	1	1	0	0	0
AL33	0	0	0	0	0	0	0	0	0	0	0	0	0	0	0	0	0	1	0	0	0
AL34	0	0	0	0	0	0	0	0	0	0	0	0	0	0	0	0	0	0	0	1	0
AL35	0	0	0	0	0	0	0	0	0	0	0	0	0	0	0	0	0	0	0	0	0
AL36	0	0	0	0	0	0	0	0	0	0	0	0	0	0	0	0	0	0	0	0	0
AL37	0	0	0	0	0	0	0	0	0	0	0	0	0	0	0	0	0	0	0	0	0
AL38	0	0	0	0	0	0	0	0	0	0	0	0	0	0	0	0	0	0	0	0	0
AL39	0	0	0	0	0	0	0	0	0	0	0	0	0	0	0	0	0	0	1	0	0
AL4	0	0	0	0	0	0	0	0	0	0	0	0	0	0	0	0	0	0	1	0	0
AL40	0	0	0	0	0	0	0	0	0	0	0	0	0	0	0	0	0	0	0	0	0
AL5	1	1	0	0	0	0	0	0	0	0	0	0	0	0	0	0	0	0	0	0	0
AL6	1	1	0	0	0	0	0	0	0	0	0	0	0	1	0	0	0	0	0	0	0
AL7	0	0	0	0	0	0	0	0	0	0	0	0	0	0	0	0	0	0	0	0	0
AL8	0	0	0	0	0	0	0	0	0	0	0	0	0	0	0	0	0	0	0	0	0

Figure 2. Excerpt of the asymmetric matrix in Excel.

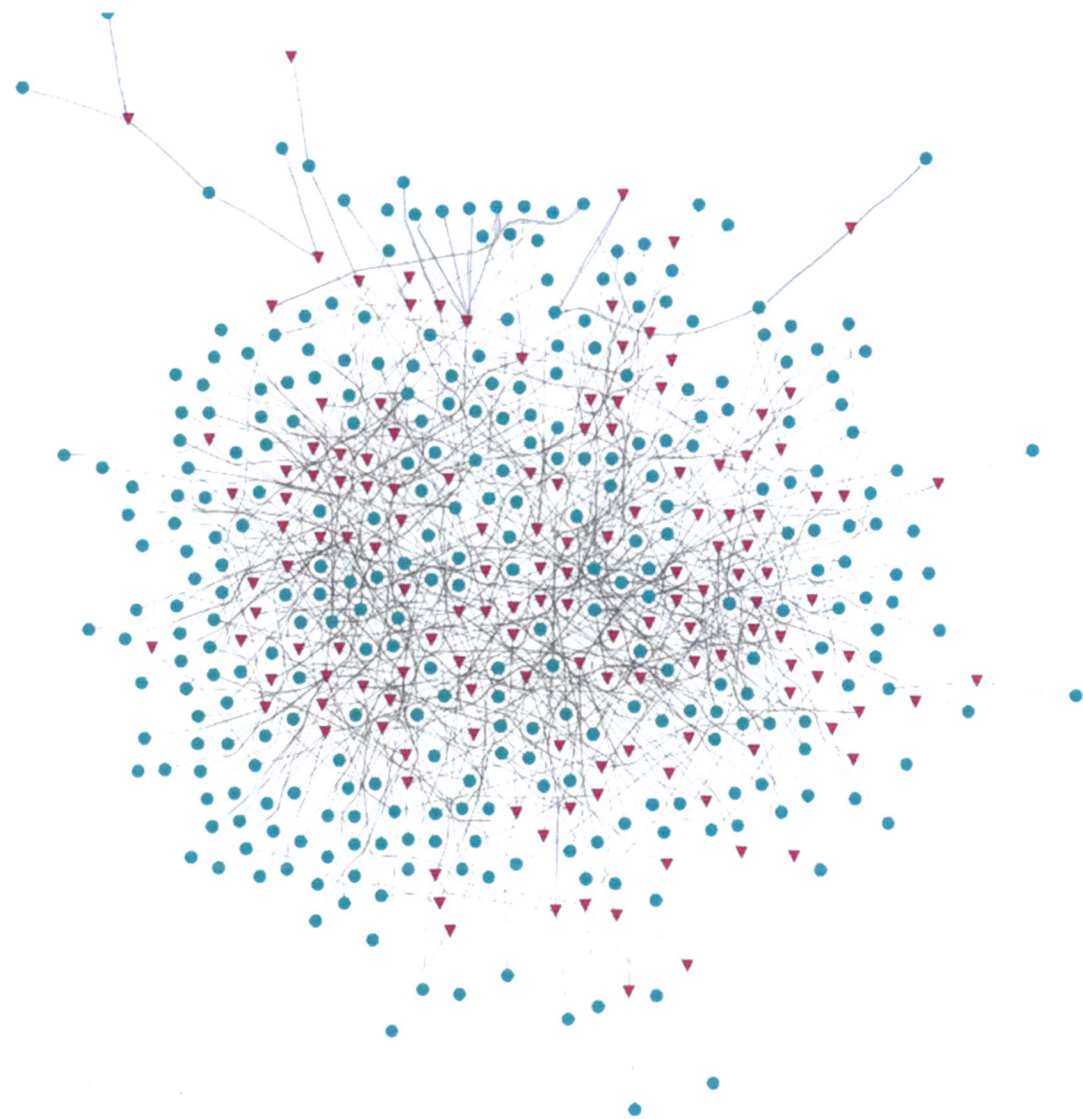

The selected grave assemblages have been inserted into an asymmetric matrix, including all grave goods present in the assemblages and not only the drinking and eating vessels selected for the analysis.[7] The matrix comprises 171 graves arranged in rows, and 312 different typologies of objects arranged in columns, wherever one of them is present in one or more graves, and in different association with other objects. The two-mode network maintains the connections within objects and contexts, allowing us to trace the association within the assemblages (Fig. 2). Working with typologies is a first step, as this allows us to understand the distribution of particular luxury goods in these coastal contexts and relate them to commercial maritime trade. A change in the qualitative scale of the network is necessary to progress from an analysis of the spread of objects and assemblages to the spread of narratives in the form of local imitation, selection, or appropriation of Mediterranean models and ideas.

Figure 3. Overview of the semantic network. Software Visone 2.18.

7 The analysis and the visualisation have been performed using the open-source SNA-Software Visone (Brandes and Wagner 2004).

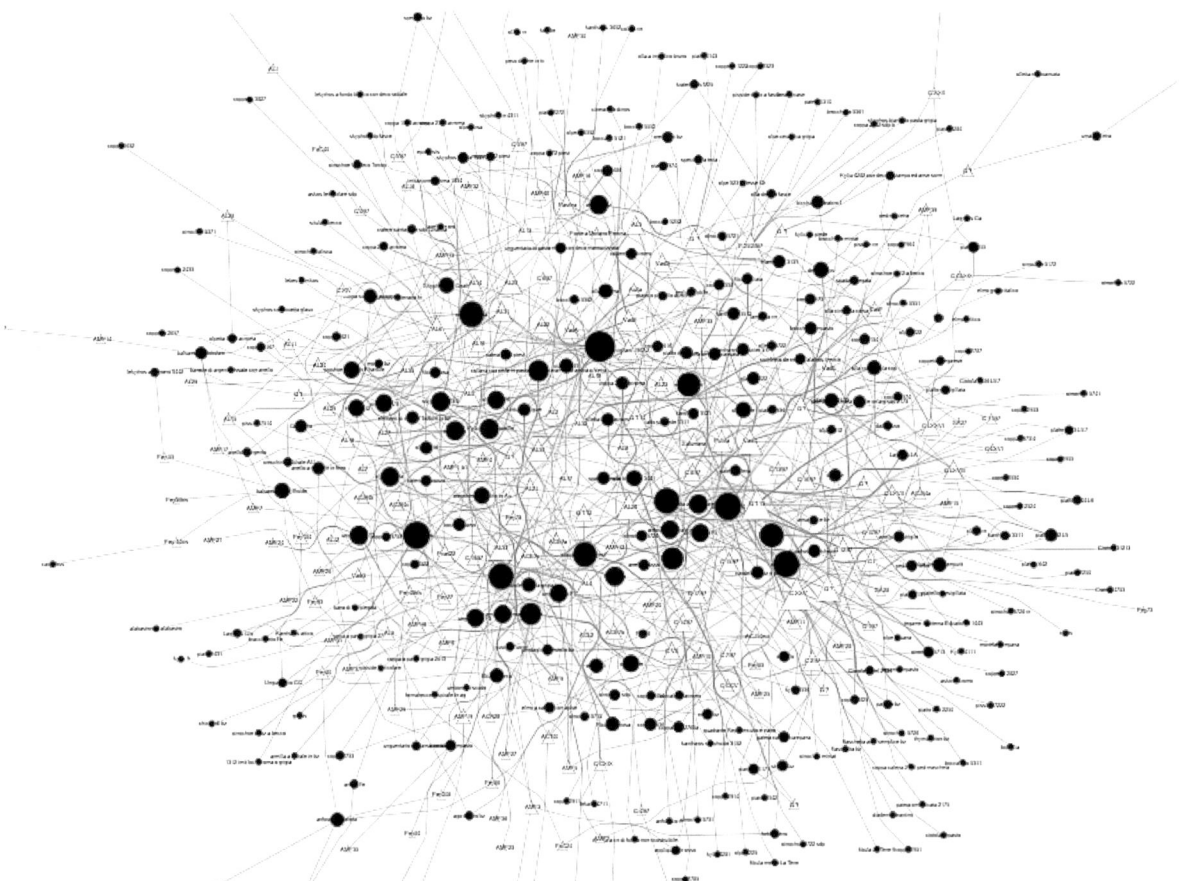

Figure 4. Overview of the semiotic network with measurement of the degree value of prestige objects. Software Visone 2.18.

In the second step of the analysis, the focus has therefore been shifted from object typologies to morpho-functional entities. Here, morpho-functional refers to objects that have a specific shape combined with a functional determination. This means that amphoras in the context of *symposion* assemblages have been considered separately from amphoras used as cinerary urns, but amphoras of the same typology can be present in both groups, just as many different typologies can also be included in each group. The definition of morpho-functional groups follows a hierarchical order, starting with the shape and then considering shifts in function in relation to the primary use. In this way, a second simplified two-mode network is obtained. The qualitative change in scale results in a new two-mode network linking places and morpho-functional entities (Fig. 3). Within this network, it is possible to choose targeted grave goods that relate to eating and drinking behaviours, and analyse the degree of their nodes.[8] In the semiotic network of Hellenistic western Mediterranean – for example – cups and skyphoi present a particularly high degree value (Fig. 4). These objects seem to have had a high ranking in different geo-cultural areas and consequently to have a shared value in the conversion of economic capital into social capital. The glocal function of these grave goods can be verified by selecting their context of association within the network. The identification of recurrences in the network role of the objects, and their specific use in context,

---

8   The degree of a node is the number of ties (relationships) of this node – a higher degree corresponds to more connections. In the case of a semiotic two-mode network, whose nodes form two separated groups constituted respectively by objects and people/contexts, the analysis of the degree of the nodes in the group of objects indicates the 'popularity' of an object in different contexts, and finally the spread of its consumption.

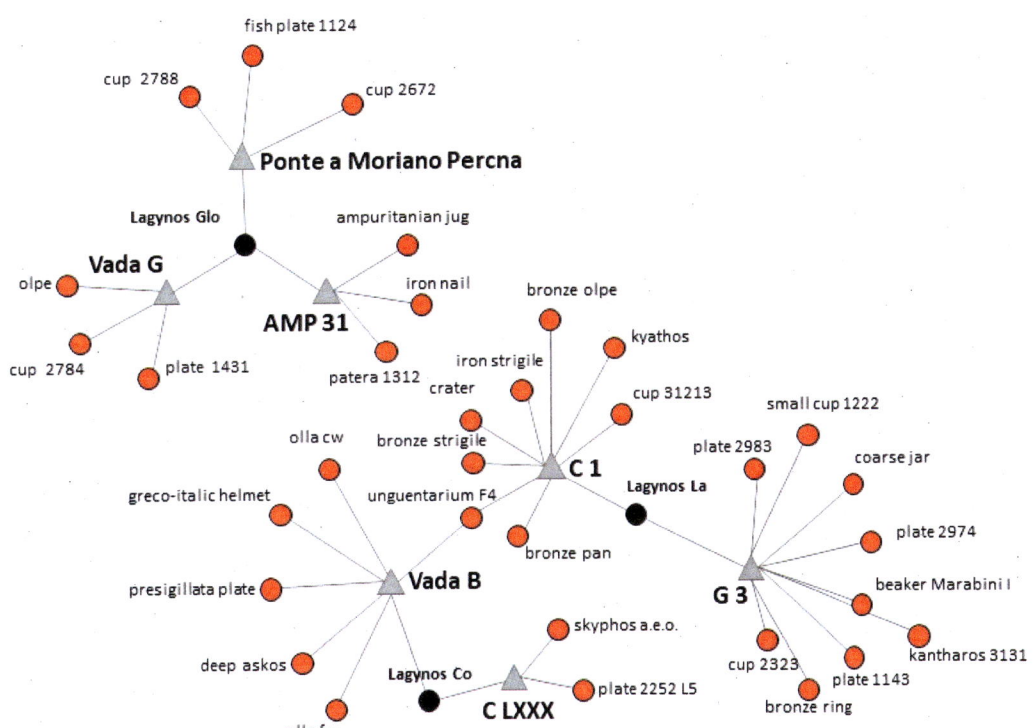

both function to individuate 'subtle differences' arising from specific needs in self-representation linked to contingent situations in local communities.

The proposal made here comprises using semiotic networks as an exploratory tool. However, the aim of their application is not to detect clusters or patterns of consumption, which could be easily done with other multivariate statistical tools (such as the cluster analysis), but rather to use these networks as a working tool, detecting local choices within generalised behaviours. This methodology presents the advantage of preserving the visibility of single assemblages, and specific and peculiar choices within them. Coming to our examples, it is easy to notice that the context and position of amphoras in different geo-cultural regions can strongly vary since they are normally part of a *symposion* narrative, but could also be used as cinerary urns in Ligurian graves. In this case, the narrative of wine consumption became secondary, demoted by the new meaning (Da Vela 2016; Hahn 2014, 102). The geographical and chronological differences in the use of amphoras in funerary contexts (as well as the probable differences in their secondary meanings) presents a challenge for understanding their value as vehicles of self-representation for the elites: this value can also be multi-layered. The same observation can be applied to other objects with high nodal degree, such as the later lagynoi or Iberian kalathoi. The lagynoi, as the first class of sampled objects, include a vast spectrum of typologies, with some of them acting as proxies for geographical traditions or chronology. Therefore, their introduction in the wine-set marks a significant innovation in the tradition of drinking and in the composition of the banquet-set, since the use of a bottle indicates the possibility of pouring wine, rather than mixing it in the crater and serving it with a ladle (Sciarma 2005). The second class of sampled objects are Iberian kalathoi, also called 'sombreros de copa'. The use of these large vases, with a height of about 30 centimetres and a large mouth, has been the subject of wide and lively discussion. The most common hypothesis is that they served as containers for food supply, particularly Iberian honey, but other interpretations as containers of dried fruit or salted fish have been proposed as well (Persano 2016, 18; Puppo 2016a).

Figure 5. Semiotic networks excerpt with the association of lagynoi within the necropoleis. Software Visone 2.18.

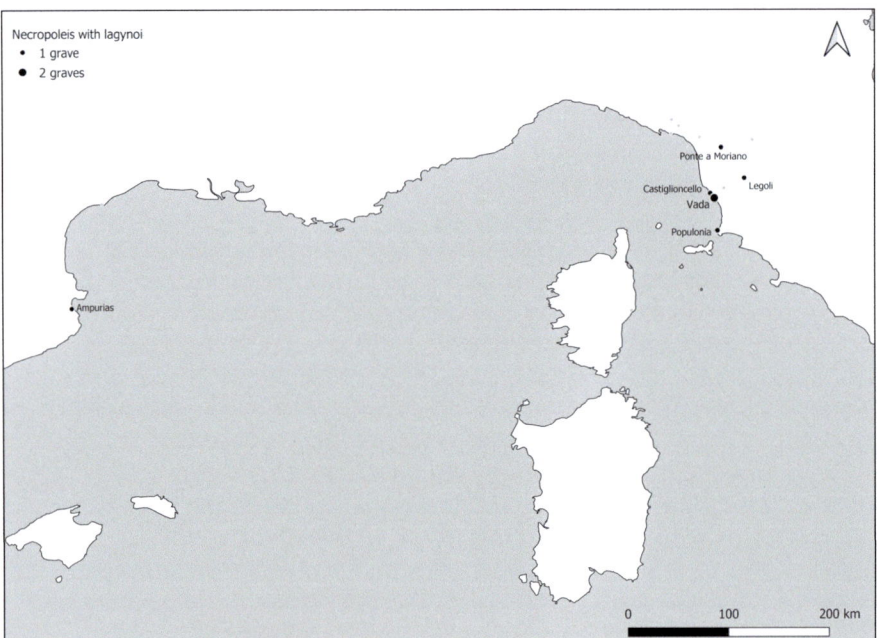

Figure 6. Distribution of Lagynoi
in the analysed dataset. Software
QGIS 3.8.3. Vectorial data:
Natural Earth. Coordinate
System WGS 84 EPSG: 4326.

Figure 7. Castiglioncello, Grave
Assemblage LXXX images
provided concessione del
Museo Archeologico Nazionale
di Firenze (Direzione regionale
Musei della Toscana).

10 cm

Semiotic networks can also be applied to detect semiotic systems, while considering the concurrence of assemblages of different objects within the case study; for example, the assemblage of oinochoe-cup-skyphos or of jug(olpe)-cup-kantharos. The observation of such concurrences indicates the diffusion of narratives of representation across the consumptionscapes of different geo-political regions or within different chronologies relating to the use of prestige assemblages rather than that of single prestige objects (Fig. 5).

Once we have identified the objects and assemblages that have contributed more to creating a common narrative of self-representation, it is opportune to proceed with an interpretation of them in their function as vehicles of social distinction for their owners, while framing these objects within their geo-political context. In this way, we can consider which grave assemblages are using these objects within a necropolis, and what comprises their contextual frame (structure, topographic and social position of the grave in the local community). For example, the lagynoi – as a class of objects – were largely produced in the eastern and western Mediterranean with a wide distribution along the sea routes, since almost the middle Hellenistic period (Fig.6). Their presence in grave assemblages has been frequently connected to the diffusion of religious ceremonies linked to Dionysian cults (Bessi 2005). Therefore, if we observe the composition of the assemblages and the position of lagynoi within the elite graves of the early Hellenistic phase, it becomes clear that the connotation of these bottles is frequently not so far removed from its contemporary usage as a banquet vase, as the grave assemblage associations with cups, askoi, craters, and glasses indicates (Fig. 7). For example, this is visible in Etruscan contexts of coastal and sub-coastal regions as in Legoli or Castiglioncello. The observations of the lagynoi's coastal and internal distribution show that the dynamics of

Figure 8. Castiglioncello, Grave Assemblage LXVIII images provided concessione del Museo Archeologico Nazionale di Firenze (Direzione regionale Musei della Toscana).

appropriation of this object – which imply the introduction of a different attitude towards the traditional consumption of wine – are more closely linked to complex interaction between coastal and internal regions than the widespread distribution of these objects along maritime trade routes. Within the Hellenistic assemblages, it is possible to notice a progressive popularisation of these bottles, which probably corresponds to their re-semantisation from a wine container to a ritual vase.[9]

Similar analyses can be conducted on many different meaningful objects found in western Mediterranean coastal necropoleis and related to the consumption of wine and luxury goods. In the case of the Iberian Kalathoi (Fig. 8), the production centres in Catalonia have been clearly individuated, in particular those in Fontscaldes near Tarragona and Ampurias (Guérin 1993, 89f.), with some rare imitation in pottery workshops of other regions; for example, in Languedoc (Ensérune: Guérin 1993: 90) and Mediolanum (Casini and Tizzoni 2010). Regarding our research question, it is possible to notice clusters of attestation of these materials in specific local communities, rather than in specific regions. The question of the social meaning and motivation attached to their widespread distribution is therefore different to that of the lagynoi. The hypothesis that the kalathoi found in the graves of immigrated celt-iberic mercenaries had an identitarian function (Puppo 2016b) could be an interpretative key for explaining their presence in coastal Etruscan, Alerian and Sicilian necropoleis, where they were frequently associated with further Iberian pottery, such as jugs. The comparison of these two classes of objects reveals a high variability in the construction of narratives of power and social identity through similar objects set in different geographical, socio-economic, and chronological contexts. The contexts of the assemblages with Iberian kalathoi locate these containers in specific consumptionscapes. In these consumptionscapes, the kalathoi and their contents are utilised in the social positioning of 'diverging' social groups in possession of a certain level of wealth and economic power. However the degree of political inclusion for these groups remains an open question for now. By comparing the networks of selected morpho-functional classes of objects in this way, it is possible to understand differences in their usage within narratives related to social, economic, or ethnic identities, even within the same local community.

Discussion

This proposal for the application of a semiotic two-mode network to individuate the use of Mediterranean narratives as a resource of power for local elites presents a high potential for glocal analyses but still requires some refinement. Some aspects in particular should be taken into account for the future development of this methodology.

First, it will be necessary to establish some parameters for an homogeneous positioning of the social segments adopting Mediterranean narratives within local communities. The significant geo-political and cultural differences in the coastal cities of the western Mediterranean are the results of centuries of *local* development within a context of continuous interactions. This fact makes it particularly difficult to precisely compare the roles of these narratives at the local, social level. In this context, it would be interesting to introduce a weighted parameter into the network, with indications of the quantity of consumed objects, which could be useful for understanding whether the attestation of lifestyle patterns in drinking and eating

---

9   Use of *lagynoi* as ritual vases is particular evident in late Hellenistic contexts in inland Etruria, *e.g.* in Chiusi and Perugia, where *lagynoi* have been deposited in loculi-graves outside the closure of each niche, associated with cups deposited upside-down and used for libations or similar functions in the hypogeic chamber or loculi tombs outside of each cinerary urn (see Faralli 2014; Feruglio 2002).

was linked to competitive social interactions based on commensal politics and hospitality between social elites or rather to hospitality or patronage between parties of unequal social standing. The observed narratives on possession and consumption of drinking pottery can thus be seen as an expression of different forms of social interaction. A multiplication of the drinking vessels could be a materialisation of the competition between elite members of society, which consequently leads to an ostentatious display of wealth. The presence of single objects or of modest assemblages could instead indicate other kind of interaction; for example, gifts given by patrons, or a synthesis of a different banquet narrative, one that indicates the acceptance of non-elite members into a distinctive social circle by invitation.

A second aspect that may prove fruitful is a longitudinal (diachronical) analysis of the networks. The individuation of the diachronic relationships between narratives in different geo-cultural areas could help to overcome a linear diffusionist approach, and consider the complex socio-political and cultural entanglements occurring fluidly across the three centuries under analysis.

Moreover, the analysis of these two aspects could permit us to differentiate nuances of habitus and status, and identify turnstile or trickle-down effects at the local level (Dietler 1996, 98). At the global or supra-regional level, this could also allow for inquiry into inducted consumption behaviours (Dietler 2006, 228). The progressive influence of political and cultural powers on consumptionscapes could prove a rich resource for controlling broader geo-economic spaces.

Conclusion

Approaching consumptionscapes in the coastal cities of the western Mediterranean as a semiotic network provides a means to overcome the concepts of 'Hellenisation' and 'Romanisation' as transcendent or immanent categories expressing changes in taste. The comparison between the presence of globally distributed status-symbols and their specific communicative function within local communities allows us to understand the 'glocal dimension' of this diffusion of taste. The symbolic and collective value of these objects and behaviours is variable, dependent upon local traditions and local social structures, which are the primary references for the acquisition or maintenance of social power. The insurgence of shared Mediterranean narratives functioning as a form of socio-political communication in the funerary contexts of different regions can be visualised and analysed in a semiotic two-mode network. This methodology shows strong potential as a tool to detect which objects are contributing to the formation of common narratives of social representation in the western Mediterranean. Through observation of the relative positioning of widely distributed objects in specific contexts, it is possible to detect strategies of social representation used by some social segments within local communities. Not only single prestige objects, but also the association of these objects in assemblages (semiotic prestige systems) show the impact of globally diffused consumption models on local habitus and consumptionscapes. The detection of supra-regional consumption communities, coalescing via the shared habitus of certain social classes in different regions, suggests the high value of shared narratives as a means of social differentiation within local communities. The visualisation of relationships and interactions within a semiotic network offers the possibility to trace the local contexts of globally-shared narratives and understand how these narratives became resources for establishing (local) power relationships. The common narrative of elites in the western Mediterranean was primarily a resource in the negotiation of corporative social identities, able to convert economic capital into political power, and based on the groups' access to and possible localised control of the supply chain. The local specificity and variability of the meanings of these objects and assemblages derives from different strategies of social communication, such as the re-semantisation of imported objects and their appropriation, both of which were means for manipulating the social validation of prestige objects (Dietler 2006, 227-229). The adoption of global narratives reflected in the ostentatious consumption of funerary objects occurred across traditional geographic and cultural boundaries, and at the same time created new social boundaries within local communities. However, the new social boundaries were also permeable and fluid, and progressively allowed other social groups access to these Mediterranean tastes and lifestyles by emulating the appropriation of objects. In the face of the fluidity of these mechanisms of distinction operating in Hellenistic local communities of western Mediterranean, local narratives of power proved more resilient, and the social classes retaining power used their maritime commercial and cultural connections to introduce new elements and narratives of social distinction, as resources to maintain their power.

Acknowledgements

I would especially like to thank Anya Rutter for inviting me to participate in the publication project and for her helpfulness during the editorial process of my contribution, in the difficult times of the COVID-19 pandemics. I would also like to thank Robinson Krämer for the interesting and sometime challenging discussions on the topic of ancient consumption and Rubymaya Jaeck-Woodgate, who performed the linguistic and stylistic editing of the English text. The study has been partially funded by the Deutsche Forschungsgemeinschaft (DFG, German Research Foundation) within the collaborative research center SFB 1070 ResourceCultures Project number 215859406 (research project B04). In the present article, the interesting contribution of Beat Schweizer (2021), published shortly after the final version of the manuscript was sent, could not be discussed.

References

Almagro, M., 1953. *Las nécropolis de Ampurias*. Barcelona: Diputación de Barcelona.

Bats, M., 2017. "In principio fu l'acculturazione". Parcours et modèls pour penser l'interculturalité. *In*: Istituto per la Storia e l'Archeologia della Magna Grecia, ed. *Ibridazione e integrazione in Magna Grecia. Forme, modelli, dinamiche, Atti del Conquantaquattresimo Convegno di Studi sulla Magna Grecia, Taranto 25 – 28 settembre 2014.* Taranto: Istituto per la Storia e l'Archeologia della Magna Grecia, 55-71.

Baratti, G. and Mordeglia, L., 2005. Nuove indagini a Populonia, la necropoli di Buche delle Fate. *In*: Bartoloni, G., ed. *Populonia. Scavi e ricerche dal 1998 al 2004*. Rome: Editrice Ateneo, 62-66.

Baratti, G. and Mordeglia, L., 2008. Necropoli di Buche delle Fate. Corredo di una ricca tomba del II sec. a.C. *Materiali per Populonia*, 7, 287-302.

Bessi, B., 2005. Il lagynos. Una forma dionisiaca. *Atti dell'Accademia Nazionale dei Lincei. Classe di Scienze Morali, Storiche e Filologiche*, 16, 241-275.

Boissinot, P. 2005. Sur la Plage emmêlés. Celtes, Ligures, Grecs et Ibères dans la confrontation des textes et de l'archéologie. *MCV*, 35 (2), 13-43.

Bourdieu, P., 2010. *Distinction. A Social Critique of the Judgment of Taste*. London and New York: Routledge.

Brandes, U. and Wagner, D., 2004. Analysis and visualization of social networks. *In*: M. Jünger and P. Mutzel, eds. *Graph Drawing Software. Mathematics and Visualization*. Berlin and Heidelberg: Springer, 321-340. Available from: doi:10.1007/978-3-642-18638-7_15

Bruhn, J.G., 2011. *The Sociology of Community Connections*. Dordrecht, Heidelberg, London and New York: Springer.

Casini, S. and Tizzoni, M., 2010. Kalathoi iberici e loro imitazioni nella Mediolanum celtica. *Notizie Archeologiche Bergomensi*, 18, 165-178.

Cherici, A., 2007. Sulle rive del Mediterraneo centro-occidentale: aspetti della circolazione di armi, mercenari e culture. *In*: G.M. Della Fina, ed. *Etruschi, Greci, Fenici e Cartaginesi nel Mediterrraneo centrale*. Atti del XIV Convegno Internazionale di Studi sulla storia e l'archeologia dell'Etruria, Annali della Fondazione per il Museo "Claudio Faina" 14. Rome: Edizioni Quasar, 221-269.

Ciampoltrini, G. and Notini, P., 2011. *La fanciulla di Vagli. Il sepolcreto ligure-apuano della Murata a Vagli di Sopra*. Lucca: I segni dell'Auser.

Coen, A., 2019. Ornarsi alla greca, ornarsi all'Etrusca. Oreficerie in Campania tra tardo arcaismo e primo ellenismo. *Polygraphia*, 1, 57-72.

Costin, C.L. and Earle, T., 1989. Status Distinction and Legitimation of Power as Reflected in Changing Patterns of Consumption in Later Prehispanic Peru. *American Antiquity*, 54, 691-714.

Da Vela, R., 2016. Cultural Transmission and Semantic Change of Ceramic Forms in Grave Goods of Hellenistic Etruria. *Continuities and Changes of Meaning, Distant World Journal*, 1, 27-53. Available from: doi:10.11588/dwj.2016.1.30153

Da Vela, R., 2022. Consumption Behaviors and Economic Mentalities of Migrants in Hellenistic Etruria. *In*: R. Da Vela, ed. *The Economic Contribution of Migrants to Ancient Societies. Technological Transfer, Integration, Exploitation and Interaction of Economic Mentalities, Panel 1.3, Proceedings of the AIAC-ICCA Convention in Cologne and Bonn 2018*. Heidelberg: Propylaeum, 67-86.

Daveloose, A., 2017. Funerary Culture in Hellenistic Chiusi: A Socio-Cultural Shift Towards less Expenditure and Ostentatious Display. *PBSR*, 85, 37-69.

Dedet, B. and Schwaller, M., 2010. Les pratique funéraires in Languedoc et en Provence du Ve au milieu du II^{e}siècle av. J.-C. *In*: P. Barral, B. Dedet, F. Delrieu, P. Giraud, I. Le Goff, S. Marion and A. Villard-Le Tiec, eds. *Gestes funéraires en Gaule au second Âge du Fer, Annales littéraires 883, Environnement société et archéologie 14*. Besançon: Presses universitaires de Franche-Comté, 269-290.

Dedet, B. and Schwaller, M., 2018. *Grecs en Gaule du Sud. Tombes de la Colonie d'Agathe (Agde, Hérault, IVe- IIe siècle av. J.-C.). Études massaliètes* 15. Arles: Errance.

Dietler, M., 1996. Feasts and Commensal Politics in the Political Economy. Food, Power and Status in Prehistoric Europe. *In*: P. Wiessner and P. Schiefenhövel, eds. *Food and the Status Quest. An Interdisciplinary Perspective*. Oxford: Berghahn, 87-125.

Dietler, M., 2005. *Consumption and Colonial Encounters in the Rôhne Bassin of France. A Study of Early Iron Age Political Economy*. Lattes: CNRS (Centre National de la Recherche Scientifique).

Dietler, M., 2006. Culinary Encounters Food Identity, and Colonialism. *In*: K.C. Twiss, ed. *The Archaeology of Food and Identity*. Occasional Paper 34. Carbondale: Center for Archaeological Investigations, 218-242.

Dietler, M., 2010. *Archaeologies of Colonialism. Consumption, Entanglement and Violence in Ancient Mediterranean France*. London and Los Angeles: University of California Press.

Dietler, M., 2011. Feasting and Fasting. *In*: T. Insoll, ed. *The Oxford Handbook of the Archaeology of Ritual and Religion*. Oxford: Oxford University Press.

Durante, A., 1982. La necropoli preromana di Ameglia. *Rivista di Studi Liguri*, 48, 148-164.

Faralli, S., 2014. Aspetti del rito funerario nella necropoli di Balena. *In*: M. Salvini, ed. *Etruschi e Romani a San Casciano dei Bagni. Le Stanze Cassianensi*. Rome: Edizioni Quasar, 42-45.

Fedeli, F., 1983. *Populonia. Storia e territorio*. Firenze: All'Insegna del Giglio.

Fentress, E., 2013. Strangers in the city: élite communication in the Hellenistic central Mediterranean. *In:* J.R.W. Prag and G.C. Quinn, eds. *The Hellenistic*

West. Rethinking Ancient Mediterranean. Cambridge: Cambridge University Press, 157-178.

Feruglio, A.E., 2002. La tomba dei Cai Cutu e le urne cinerarie perugine di età ellenistica. *In*: G.M. Della Fina, ed. *Perugia etruscsa. Atti del IX Convegno Internazionale di Studi sulla Storia e l'Archeologia dell'Etruria.* Annali della Fondazione per il Museo 'Claudio Faina' 9. Rome: Edizioni Quasar, 475-495.

Gambogi, P. and Palladino, S., eds., 1999. *Castiglioncello. La necropoli ritrovata. Cento anni di scoperte e scavi (1896 – 1997).* Rosignano Solvay: Museo Civico Archeologico.

Gras, M., 2010. Empória ed emporía: riflessioni sul commercio greco arcaico in Occidente. *Hesperia*, 25, 47-56.

Guérin, P., 1993. Le sombrero de copa: quelques résultats récents. *Documents d'Archéologie Méridionale*, 16, 88-92.

Hahn, H.-P., 2014. Praktiken und Transformationen. *In*: S. Samida, M.K.H. Eggert and H.P. Hahn, eds. *Handbuch Materielle Kultur. Bedeutungen, Konzepte, Disziplinen.* Stuttgart and Weimar: J.B. Metzler, 97-104.

Hahn, H.-P., 2016. Aneignung und Domestikation. Handlungsräume der Konsumenten und die Macht des Alltäglichen. *In*: D. Hohnsträter, ed. *Konsum und Kreativität.* Konsumästhetik. Bielefeld: Transcript, 43-60.

Hahn, H.-P. and Weiss, H., 2013. Introduction: Biographies, travels and itineraries of things. *In*: H.-P. Hahn and H. Weiss, eds. *Mobility, Meaning & Transformations of Things. Shifting contexts of material culture through time and space.* Oxford: Oxbow Books, 8-24.

Hardenberg, R., Bartelheim, M. and Staecker, J., 2017. The ‚Resource Turn'. A Socio-Cultural Perspective on Resources. *In*: A.K. Scholz, M. Bartelheim, R. Hardenberg and J. Staecker, eds. *ResourceCultures. Socio-Cultural Dynamics and the Use of Resources – Theories, Methods, Perspectives.* RessourcenKulturen 5. Tübingen: University Press, 13-24.

Hodder, I., 2011. Wheels of Time: Some Aspects of Entanglement Theory and the Secondary Products Revolution. *Journal of World Prehistory*, 24, 175-187.

Hodos, T., 2014. Global, Local and in between. Connectivity and the Mediterranean. *In*: M. Pitts and M.J. Versluys, eds. *Globalisation and the Roman World. World History, Connectivity and Material Culture.* Cambridge: Cambridge University Press, 240-253.

Hoo, M., 2018. Ai-Khanum in the Face of Eurasian Globalisation. A Trans-Local Approach to a Contested Site in Hellenistic Bactria. *AWE*, 17, 161-186.

Hyman, M.D., 2007. Semantic Networks: A Tool for Investigating Conceptual Change and Knowledge Transfer in the History of Science. *In*: H. Böhme, C. Rapp and W. Rösler, eds. *Übersetzung und Transformation.* Berlin: De Gruyter, 355-367.

Jéhasse, J. and Jéhasse, L., 1973. *La nécropole préromaine d'Aléria (1960-1968).* Gallia Suppl. 25. Besançon: CNRS (Centre National de la Recherche Scientifique).

Keay, S., 2013. Were the Iberian Hellenized? *In*: J.R.W. Prag and J.C. Quinn, eds. *The Hellenistic West: Rethinking the Ancient Mediterranean.* Cambridge: Cambridge University Press, 300-319.

Kistler, E., 2017a. Lokal divergierende Antworten auf die Krater-isierung West- und Mittelsiziliens (6./5. Jh. v. Chr.) – Perspektiven des Binnenlandes. *In*: L. Cappuccini, C. Leypold and M. Mohr, eds. *Fragmenta Mediterranea. Contatti, tradizioni e innovazioni in Grecia, Magna Grecia, Etruria e Roma. Studi in onore di Christoph Reusser.* Firenze: All'Insegna del Giglio, 111-131.

Kistler, E., 2017b. Feasts, Wine and Society. Eighth – Sixth Centuries BCE. *In*: A. Naso, ed. *Etruscology.* Berlin and New York: De Gruyter, 195-206.

Knappett, C., 2005. *Thinking Through Material Culture. An Interdisciplinary Perspective.* Philapelphia: University of Pennsylvania Press.

Knappett, C., 2011. *An Archaeology of Interaction. Network perspectives on Material Culture and Societies.* Oxford: Oxford University Press.

Knappett, C., 2012. Meaning in Miniature: Semiotic Networks in Material Culture. In: N.M. Johannsen, M.D. Jessen and H.J. Jessen, eds. *Excavating the Mind. Cross-sections through culture, cognition and materiality.* Aarhus: Aarhus University Press, 87-110.

Krämer, R.P., 2016. Trading Goods – Trading Gods. Greek Sanctuaries in the Mediterranean and their Rome as emporia and 'Ports of Trade' (7th – 6th Century BCE). *Distant World Journal,* 1, 75-98. Available from: doi:10.11588/dwj.2016.1.30154

Krämer, R.P., 2017. *What is Dead May Never Die.* Pratiche sacrificali per la divinizzazione del defunto in Etruria e nel Lazio nell'età orientalizzante e età arcaica. Un approccio di economia politica. *Scienze dell'Antichità,* 23 (3), 517-538.

Krämer, R.P., 2022a. *Etruskische Heiligtümer des 8.–5. Jhs. v. Chr. als Wirtschaftsräume und Konsumptionsorte von Keramik.* Italiká 8. Wiesbaden: Reichert.

Krämer, R.P., 2022b. Sacred-consumptionscapes in Northern Etruria (7th to 5th cent. BCE). Consumption and re-semantization of pottery in sactuaries. *In:* L. Cappuccini and A. Gaucci, eds. *Officine e Artigianato Ceramico nei siti dell'Appennino Tosco-Emiliano tra VII e IV sec. a.C.* Atti del I Convegno Internazionale di studi sulla cultura materiale etrusca dell'Appennino (Arezzo 18 ottobre 2019 – Dicomano 19 ottobre 2019), Biblioteca di Studi Etruschi 66. Rome: Giorgio Bretschneider Editore, 399–419.

Laftsidis, A., 2019. *The Hellenistic "Koine" as a Linguistic and Ceramic Concept.* Oxford: Oxford University Press.

Maggiani, A., 2013. Mercenari liguri? *In*: G.M. Della Fina, ed. *Mobilità geografica e mercenariato nell'Italia preromana.* Atti del XX Convegno Internazionale di Studi sulla storia e l'archeologia dell'Etruria, Annali della Fondazione per il Museo "Claudio Faina" 20. Rome: Edizioni Quasar, 233-255.

Maguire, J.S., 2019. Chapter 9. Taste, Legitimacy and the Organization of Consumption. *In*: F.F. Wherry and I. Woodward, eds. *The Oxford Handbook of Consumption.* Oxford: Oxford University Press, 197-216.

Martelli, M., 1981a. Scavo di edifici nella zona "industriale" di Populonia. *In*: A. Neppi Modona, ed. *L'Etruria Mineraria.* Atti del XII Convegno di Studi Etruschi e Italici, Firenze, Populonia, Piombino, 16-20 giugno 1979. Firenze: L.S. Olschki, 161-172.

Martelli, M., 1981b. Populonia: cultura locale e contatti con il mondo greco. *In*: A. Neppi Modona, ed. *L'Etruria Mineraria.* Atti del XII Convegno di Studi Etruschi e Italici, Firenze, Populonia, Piombino, 16-20 giugno 1979. Firenze: L.S. Olschki, 399-427.

Massa, M., 1974. Tombe tardo-repubblicane di Castiglioncello e Vada. *Rivista di Studi Liguri,* 60, 25-74.

Mullins, R.P., 2011. The Archaeology of Consumption. *Annual Review of Anthropology,* 40 (2011), 133-144. Available from: doi:10.1146/annurev-anthro-081309-145746

Persano, P., 2016. Vasi da miele in Etruria. Confronti archeologici ed etnografici per le 'olle stamnoidi a colletto'. *Archivio Español de Arqueología,* 89, 9-24.

Poux, M., 2004. *L'âge du vin. Rites de boissons, festins et libations en Gaule indépendeante.* Montagnac: Éditions Monique Mergoil.

Prag, J.R.W. and Quinn, G.C., eds., 2013. *The Hellenistic West. Rethinking Ancient Mediterranean.* Cambridge: Cambridge University Press.

Pitts, M., 2014. Globalisation, Circulation and Mass Consumption in the Roman World. *In*: M. Pitts and M.J. Versluys, eds. *Globalisation and the Roman World. World History, Connectivity and Material Culture.* Cambridge: Cambridge University Press, 69-98.

Puppo, P., 2016a. Trade Exchanges in the Western Mediterranean: The Distribution of sombreros de copa. *In*: S. Japp and P. Kögler, eds. *Traditions and Innovations.*

Tracking the Development of Pottery from the Late Classical to the Early Imperial Periods. Proceedings of the 1st Conference of IARPotHP Berlin, November 2013, 7th-10th. Wien: Phoibos Verlag, 87-98.

Puppo, P., 2016b. Il *kalathos* Iberico del museo civico di Cuneo. Il *séma* di un mercenario ispanico? *Quaderni del Museo Civico di Cuneo*, 4, 22-26.

Romualdi, A. and Settesoldi, R., eds., 2009. *Populonia, la necropoli delle Grotte. Lo scavo dell'area della Cava 1997/1998.* Pisa: Edizioni ETS.

Roselaar, S.T., 2019. *Italy's Economic Revolution. Integration and Economy in Republican Italy*. Oxford: Oxford University Press.

Schweizer, B., 2021. Wine as a Key Resource in the Fifth Century BC. Substances and Things, Body and Emotion in Dyonisian Practices. *In*: T. Schade, B. Schweizer, S. Teuber, R. Da Vela, W. Frauen, M. Karami, D. K. Ohja, K. Schmidt, M. Sieler and M.S. Toplak, eds. *Exploring Resources. On Cultural, Spatial and Temporal Dimensions of the ResourceCultures*. RessourcenKulturen 13. Tübingen: Tübingen University Press, 307-328.

Sciarma, A., 2005. La diffusione delle lagynoi nelle tombe etrusche tardo-ellenistiche. *Ostraka*, 14, 209-277.

Sommer, M., 2014. OIKOYMENH. Long Durée Perpectives on Ancient Mediterranean 'Globality'. *In*: M. Pitts and M.J. Versluy, eds. *Globalisation and the Roman World. World History, Connectivity and Material Culture*. Cambridge: Cambridge University Press, 175-197.

Tsirkin, J.B., 1992. Romanization of Spain. Socio-Political Aspects. *Gerión*, 10, 205-242.

Wallace-Hadrill, A., 2008. *Rome's cultural revolution*. Cambridge: Cambridge University Press.

Woodward, S., 2019. Chapter 7. Meaningful Objects and Consumption. *In*: F.F. Wherry and I. Woodward, eds. *The Oxford Handbook of Consumption*. Oxford: Oxford University Press, 165-178.

Zuchtriegel, G., 2016. Colonization and Hybridity in *Herakleia* and its Hinterland (Southern Italy) 5th-3rd century BC. *Mélanges de l'École Française de Rome*, 128 (1), 170-186.

Part 2: Connectivity by sea and networking of seafarers

Seafaring songs in Pindar's *Epinikia* and *Enkomia*

Thomas Kuhn-Treichel

Abstract

One of the most salient features of the poetic 'I' articulated in Pindar's poetry can be seen in his ability to establish connections between otherwise disconnected entities, *e.g.* between persons separated by time or space, between the dead and the living, or between humans and gods. When it comes to people separated by space, the act of connecting is often represented as a movement of either the poetic 'I' or the poem itself. Some remarkable cases of the latter kind involve the sea. This paper discusses Pindar's *Pythian* 2.67sq., *Nemean* 5.1-3, and *Enkomion* fr. 124ab Maehler, focusing on three interlacing questions: how the passages construct connectivity, how they define the role of poetry, and how they shape the identities of the persons involved. Although the passages describe different types of connections, in all of them the song itself plays a pivotal role. The poetic 'I' can or must be imagined as stationary, but his seafaring song enables him to establish connections across the Mediterranean. In different ways, the idea of seafaring also affects the identity of the addressees, all of whom lived on islands: the songs replicate and inscribe themselves into the real world of the addressees.

Pindar, epinikia, enkomia, seafaring, connectivity

It has become a commonplace that the poems of Pindar – the most famous Greek lyric poet of the 5th cent. BCE – are distinguished by a particularly prominent speaking voice, or – as I prefer to describe it – a particularly overt poetic 'I'.[1] Among the special powers characterising this poetic 'I', I would contend that one of the most crucial ones is that of establishing connections between otherwise disconnected

---

1   Cf. *e.g.* Lattmann 2017, 123: 'One of the most salient features of Pindar's epinician odes, it might seem, is the voice of Pindar himself, a swift bee loving to boast about its superior poetic powers ...' For an extensive discussion of the poetic 'I' (conceptualised as an intradiscursive figure blending poet and choir), see Kuhn-Treichel 2020 (cf. also Kuhn-Treichel 2018). Recent important contributions on this issue (apart from Lattmann) include D'Alessio 1994, Morrison 2007, Calame 2010, Currie 2013, Maslov 2015, Stehle 2017, and Budelmann 2018.

entities. Pindar's poetic 'I' can connect persons separated by time or space, humans and gods, or even the dead and the living.[2] Perhaps the most obvious way of creating such connections are apostrophes to different figures in the same poem, but other self-referential statements can serve similar purposes. When it comes to people separated by space, the act of connecting is often represented as a movement of either the poetic 'I' or the poem itself. Some remarkable cases of the latter kind involve the sea, and this makes them relevant for the topic of this volume. In this paper, I wish to discuss three passages and focus on three interlacing questions that arise from them: how the passages construct connectivity, how they define the role of poetry, and how they shape the identities of the persons involved.[3] My first two cases are taken from the victory odes, the genre Pindar is best known for, and the third one from the less well preserved but no less intriguing genre of *enkomia.*

Before turning to the individual texts, it has to be stressed that the motif of seafaring songs forms part of a broader and more complex phenomenon. Song-journey motifs are not only common in Pindar, but in all of early Greek poetry. The journeys are accomplished by various means of transport, but travel by ship is anything but an exception. René Nünlist has collected no less than 164 journey images in early Greek poetry, 27 of which he assigns to the category 'by ship'.[4] Vedic parallels suggest that the 'ship of song' dates back to an Indo-European or at least Graeco-Aryan tradition of poetological imagery.[5] It should also be kept in mind that early Greek poetry uses maritime imagery in quite different contexts; other notable stock metaphors include the 'ship of state' and the 'ship of symposiasts'.[6] What distinguishes the cases that I will discuss is precisely the sense of connectivity they convey: the motif of seafaring songs implies a sender and a recipient, both of whom can remain stationary but are linked through (and in some sense also defined by) the sea.

Pythian 2: The song as merchandise

In Pindar's *Pythian* 2, composed for Hieron of Syracuse, movement across space and especially across the sea features prominently, but in different forms. The opening of the poem is based on the so-called arrival motif.[7] The poetic 'I' addresses the city of Syracuse, claiming to be coming from Thebes, which evidently involves a sea voyage (*P.* 2.1-4):[8]

---

2   I discuss all of these categories in Kuhn-Treichel 2020, 161-248. Connections between the dead and the living are probably least obvious, but nevertheless attested in some poems, cf. Segal 1985.

3   I understand identity in a broad sense as a set of characteristics or attributions distinguishing a person or group from others. The most recent discussion of identity in Pindar is Lewis 2019 (with general remarks on pp. 25-27).

4   Nünlist 1998, 228-283. The fundamental study on the image of the way into early Greek literature is Becker 1937; the idea of sending is treated comprehensively by Tedeschi 1985. For recent positions on journey imagery in Pindar, see Sigelman 2016, 50-85 and Spelman 2018, 23f.; recent studies on imagery in Pindar more generally include Patten 2009, Lattmann 2010, and Kirichenko 2016. On space in Pindar, see now Neer/Kurke 2019.

5   See Nünlist 1998, 265 and West 2007, 40f. for examples from the *Rig Veda.* Nünlist adds remarkable examples from Egyptian literature, which, however, do not come as close to the images used by Greek poets.

6   For the 'ship of state' cf. *e.g.* Brock 2013, 53-67; for the 'ship of symposiasts', Nünlist 1998, 317-325. Some other usages of nautical imagery in antique literature are collected by Kaiser 1953. Cf. also the contributions by Maria Noussia-Fantuzzi and Ippokratis Kantzios in this volume.

7   The term was coined by Bundy 1962, 23. 27f.; for further examples, see Nünlist 1998, 229-238.

8   Whether Thebes is mentioned as the site of the victory or merely as Pindar's home city, remains disputed, cf. Cingano in Gentili *et al.* 1995, 366 (one of the most detailed discussions is Most 1985, 61-65, who argues for the former option). I quote Pindar from Maehler's edition; the translations follow Race (modified in the case of fr. 124ab).

Μεγαλοπόλιες ὦ Συράκοσαι ...

ὔμμιν τόδε τᾶν λιπαρᾶν ἀπὸ Θηβᾶν φέρων

μέλος ἔρχομαι ἀγγελίαν τετραορίας ἐλελίχθονος ...

O great city of Syracuse ..., to you I come from shining Thebes bearing this song and its news of the four-horse chariot that shakes the earth ...

In the second half of the poem, the journey motif is taken up once again. This time it appears with an explicit reference to a 'garlanded ship' which the poetic 'I' is going to embark upon (P. 2,62sq.):

εὐανθέα δ' ἀναβάσομαι στόλον ἀμφ' ἀρετᾷ

κελαδέων.

I shall embark upon a garlanded ship to celebrate your excellence.

Just a little later, the journey motif occurs for the third time, but now the focus has shifted to the poem that is moving across the Mediterranean. The lines in question – which form the first of my three examples of the seafaring song motif – begin with an address to Hieron (P. 2.67sq.):

χαῖ-

ρε· τόδε μὲν κατὰ Φοίνισσαν ἐμπολάν

μέλος ὑπὲρ πολιᾶς ἁλὸς πέμπεται ...

Farewell. This song is being sent like Phoenician merchandise over the grey sea ...

I will not discuss – unlike some commentators – whether this description matches what actually happened while the preceding statements about the poetic 'I' are purely fictional or metaphorical.[9] What I am interested in is the scenario created in the text and – more specifically – the interplay between the poem, the poetic 'I', and the 'grey sea'. The sentence is based on what is often called the sending motif. Nonetheless, who is actually sending and who is receiving the poem is not as clear as one might suppose. An obvious interpretation would be to supply the poetic 'I' (which does not speak in the first person but is implied in the address χαῖρε) as the sender and Hieron, the primary addressee, as the receiver. In this case, the poetic 'I' himself would remain stationary, but bridge the distance to Hieron by means of his seafaring song, in this way establishing a one-to-one connection across the Mediterranean. If we infer Thebes as the starting point (as suggested by lines 1-4, albeit with a different concept of movement), we might visualise this movement as an arrow stretching from Thebes to Syracuse (Fig. 1).[10] In this context, the metaphor of Phoenician merchandise could have a double implication: first, of course, it evokes the model of a seafaring nation *par excellence*, thus illustrating the poem's long sea journey; second, it might hint at the fact that the victory ode was, just like

---

9   Cf. Cingano in Gentili *et al.* 1995, 390: '*alla metafora del viaggio del poeta per nave (v. 62 sg.) e all'annuncio fittizio dell'arrivo a Siracusa nel proemio (v. 3 sg.) si contrappone ora la menzione reale dell'invio dell'ode per mare*' (with reference to Tedeschi 1985, 32ff.). Contrast Nünlist 1998, 229 n. 3, who questions this distinction in general (cf. also Spelman 2018, 23f.). Sigelman 2016, 57 explains the logical discrepancies by attributing them to 'Pindar's fondness for ever-changing imagery'.

10   It is important to note that Thebes as the starting point is only a plausible possibility. Thebes also suggests itself as Pindar's hometown, but identifying the poetic 'I' with Pindar is an interpretation, too. I will return to the underdetermination of the sending images in the conclusions.

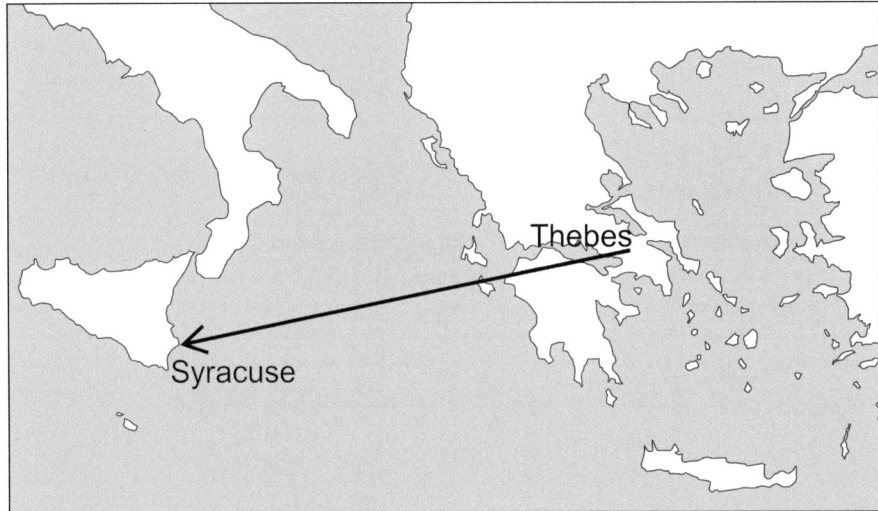

Figure 1. Pythian 2.67sq., interpretation a (one-to-one connection). Map material from the Ancient World Mapping Center (http://awmc.unc.edu/ awmc/applications/alacarte/); modifications by author.

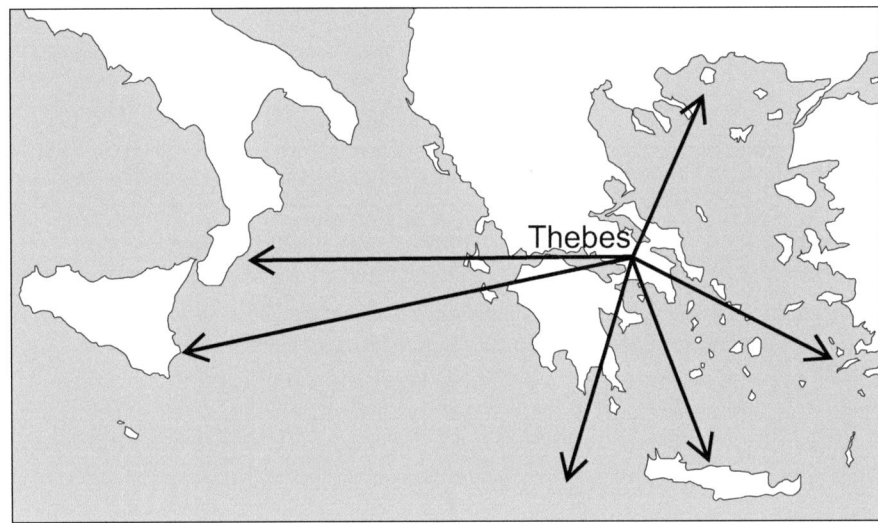

Figure 2. Pythian 2.67sq., interpretation b (one-to-many connection). Map material from the Ancient World Mapping Center (http://awmc.unc.edu/ awmc/applications/alacarte/); modifications by author.

the precious goods the Phoenicians dealt in, something to be paid for by the person celebrated in the poem.[11]

However, this is not the only interpretation the text yields.[12] Pointing to the fact that the verb πέμπεται is not accompanied by a dative, Nünlist has argued that the song is not 'delivered' to Hieron, but '(potentially) to all the word'.[13] This would turn the one-to-one into a one-to-many relationship, which could be illustrated by a multitude of arrows spreading from Thebes (if we retain this as the starting point) and going in various exemplary directions across the sea (Fig. 2). According to this interpretation, the sending motif would allude to the various secondary audiences which were supposed to receive the ode after its primary performance, be it through reperformances or in written form (both possibilities are frequently discussed in

11 For the trade metaphor and its implications, see especially Steiner 2011, 240f.; cf. also Péron 1974, 152; Cingano in Gentili *et al.* 1995, 391.

12 The general interpretive ambiguity of the passage is also noted by Fearn 2017, 252: 'The poem or song is a pseudo-visual phenomenon, but Pindar provides no material-cultural or other imaginistic framework, beyond the idea of song traded as cargo.'

13 Nünlist 1998, 274: '*Das Lied wird wie phoinikisches Handelsgut (potentiell) in die ganze Welt 'geliefert'.*'

recent scholarship).[14] The metaphor of Phoenician merchandise would also work in this context, albeit with a shift in meaning: the focus would not be on payment but on the fact that the Phoenicians traded their products all across the Mediterranean. As to the sender, the passive form πέμπεται is equally inconclusive. The idea of the poetic 'I' sending the poem may seem most natural, but it is not impossible to imagine the poetic 'I' as the instance of discourse that is being sent with the poem.

This ambiguity does not just reduce the contrast with the preceding statements, but it also provides a general insight. Whether conceived of as moving or stationary, it is mainly through his poem that the poetic 'I' is able to establish connections to remote people. The poetic 'I' *can* present himself as embarking on a ship (as in lines 62sq.), but even if he does not explicitly do so (as in lines 67sq.) he can aspire to a high degree of connectivity because his poem gives him a range on a par with one of the most famous seafaring nations in antiquity. In the world of his poetry, distances seem to shrink and the sea becomes a trade route for poetic communication. All of this bestows a sort of cosmopolitan aura on both the sender and the recipient(s): both parties are demonstrated to be part of a pan-Hellenic elite, whose members can be connected through the song because they are already linked by their shared identity.[15]

Nemean 5: The song sailing the seas

In the case of *P.* 2.67sq., I would argue that a one-to-many relationship is only one possible interpretation of an intentionally ambiguous statement. A more explicit example of such a relationship can be found in the famous beginning of *Nemean* 5, composed for Pytheas of Aigina (*N.* 5.1-3):[16]

Οὐκ ἀνδριαντοποιός εἰμ', ὥστ' ἐλινύσοντα ἐργά-

  ζεσθαι ἀγάλματ' ἐπ' αὐτᾶς βαθμίδος

ἑσταότ'· ἀλλ' ἐπὶ πάσας

  ὁλκάδος ἔν τ' ἀκάτῳ, γλυκεῖ' ἀοιδά,

στεῖχ' ἀπ' Αἰγίνας διαγγέλλοισ', ὅτι ...

I am not a sculptor, so as to fashion stationary statues that stand on their same base. Rather, on board every ship and in every boat, sweet song, go forth from Aigina and spread the news that ...

Here, the focus is unambiguously placed on the secondary audiences that are going to read or hear the song after its first performance on Aigina. The recipients are consciously unspecified, but it is potentially everybody who can be reached by ship, which creates a situation analogous to Figure. 2, albeit with a different starting point (Fig. 3). The contrast between the stationary statue and the seafaring song

---

14 One of the most important studies is Spelman 2018, esp. 13-43. For the dissemination of Pindar's poems more generally, see Hubbard 2004 and 2011; recent papers on reperformances include Morrison 2012 and Budelmann 2017.

15 This accords with the thesis developed by Hubbard 2001, who argues that the *epinikia* can function as 'public relations' advertisement for 'individuals or states whose positions within the broader Greek world were problematic and thus in need of public relations' (as summarised in Hubbard 2004, 74).

16 Recent discussions include Dougherty 2001, 40-42, Hornblower 2004, 226f., Burnett 2005, 63f., Männlein-Robert 2007, 22f., Morgan 2007, 230f., Pavlou 2010, Kowalzig 2011, 129-131, Kirichenko 2016, 19-22, and Fearn 2017, 16-28, the majority of which focus on the comparison with the statue rather than the idea of seafaring (Dougherty, Hornblower, and Kowalzig are among the exceptions). Cf. also the commentary by Pfeijffer 1999, 62 and 101f.

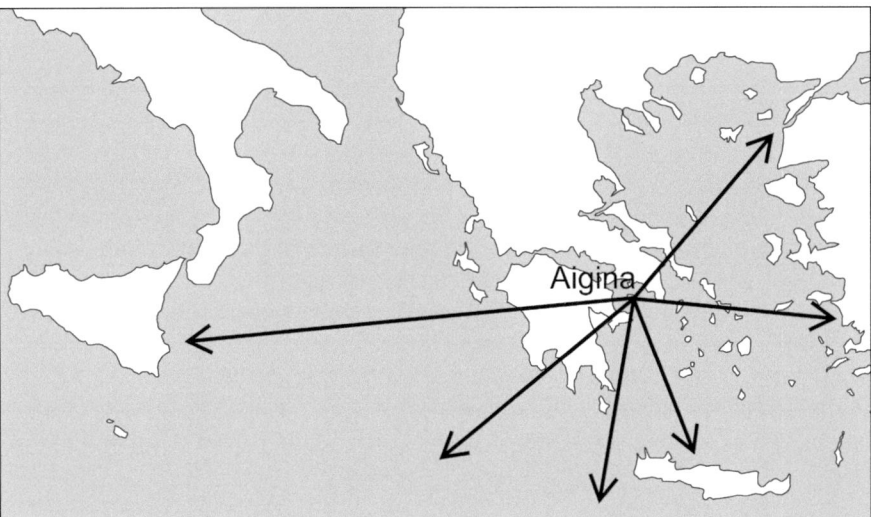

Figure 3. Nemean 5.1-3 (one-to-many connection). Map material from the Ancient World Mapping Center (http://awmc.unc.edu/awmc/applications/alacarte/); modifications by author.

highlights the advantages of poetry: the poem is supposed to be superior to material art precisely because it can cross the sea and thus reach people who would not come on their own.[17] From an archaeological perspective, one might also object that statues were transported across the sea, although this would miss Pindar's point.[18] It is important to note that the song is portrayed as an active participant: the song itself is imagined to 'go forth' (στεῖχ') and 'spread news' (διαγγέλλοισ'). In this case, it is obvious that the poetic 'I', who addresses the poem, is the sender. According to the scenario created in the lines, the song sails the seas on its own while the poetic 'I' remains behind (although in some sense, of course, the poetic 'I' is transported wherever the poem goes).

The poetic 'I' is probably best understood as the originator of a self-evolving dissemination: his power to establish connections to people throughout the Mediterranean is not so much rooted in his own travelling but in his ability to craft a song that can use 'every ship and every boat' as its means of transport and extend the scope of connectivity on its own.[19] Again, this affects not only the poetic 'I' but also the victor and the Aiginetans more generally. The fact that the poem can embark on any ship to spread news is of course due to the Aiginetan's extended commercial relations.[20] The exhortation to the song draws attention to this cultural background. On a semi-metaphorical level, the song is inscribed into the Aiginetan's trade connections and in this way made to illustrate their identity as merchants on a pan-Hellenic scale.

Enkomion fr. 124ab: Seafaring and the symposion

The third passage I want to discuss presents a slightly dubious, but all the more rewarding case. The poem in question, a fragmentary piece composed for Thrasyboulos of Akragas, is commonly assigned to the *enkomia*, a genre that is, at

---

17   Whether or not this implies a general conceit of sculpture remains debated, cf. Fearn 2017, 18.
18   Burnett 2005, 63 suggests that the 'the performance ... takes place just as the Aiakid replacements were being set into the pediments of the Aphaia temple'. In this case, the contrast would have of course been evident (cf. also Pavlou 2010, 3f.).
19   The historical background the lines allude to is the dissemination of Pindar's poems in written form; cf. the literature listed in n. 14 above (especially Spelman 2018, 39-43).
20   Discussed at length by Kowalzig 2011; cf. also Hornblower 2004, 212-217.

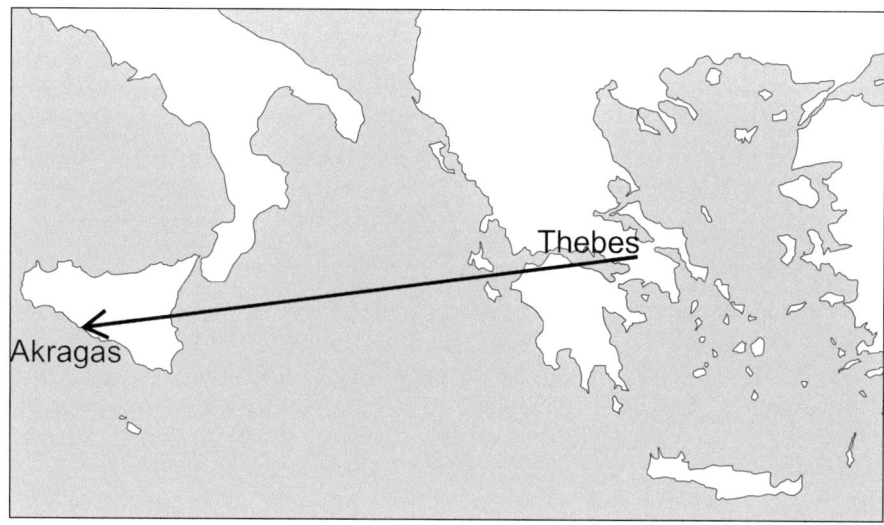

Figure 4. Fragment 124ab.1sq. Maehler (one-to-one connection). Map material from the Ancient World Mapping Center (http://awmc.unc.edu/awmc/applications/alacarte/); modifications by author.

least in part, defined by its close association with the symposion.[21] In the beginning of the song we find another instance of the sending motif (fr. 124ab.1sq. Maehler):

Ὦ Θρασύβουλ', ἐρατᾶν ὄχημ' ἀοιδᾶν
τοῦτό ⟨τοι⟩ πέμπω μεταδόρπιον.
O Thrasyboulos, I am sending you this vehicle of lovely songs for after dinner.

The verb πέμπω ties the passage especially to *P.* 2.67sq., where we find the passive counterpart πέμπεται. However, the active voice in this passage makes the situation much more explicit than there. Here, it is unmistakably the poetic 'I' who is sending the poem, and if we accept the conjecture τοι, it is unmistakably Thrasyboulos whom it is being sent to. In other words, as in the first interpretation of *P.* 2.67sq., we have a one-to-one relationship spanning across the Mediterranean. The starting point is not made explicit, but if we supply Pindar's hometown Thebes and assume that that the symposion takes place in Akragas (neither of which is cogent), we would obtain a visualisation very similar to Figure 1 (Fig. 4).

One complicating factor is the vehicle metaphor. The term ὄχημα can designate any means of transport. The fact that the Sicilian city of Akragas is obviously separated from the Greek mainland by the sea might suggest that the intended vehicle is a ship.[22] On the other hand, interpreters have favoured a chariot, not only because this meaning is more frequent with ὄχημα,[23] but also because Thrasyboulos's father Xenokrates had repeatedly won chariot victories (celebrated by Pindar in *P.* 6 and *I.* 2), a fact that might be alluded to here.[24] There is nothing in the text to suggest that ὄχημα should be restricted to one of the two meanings here. In any case, we are to imagine a song moving across the sea and that makes the passage relevant for our topic.

What distinguishes the quoted lines from those discussed so far is the last word of the sentence. The 'vehicle of songs' is being sent 'for after dinner' (μεταδόρπιον),

---

21   The status of the ἐγκώμια as a genre is partly problematic. In Pindar's own time, songs associated with the symposion were rather called σκόλια, and it is not quite clear whether the Alexandrian book title ἐγκώμιον simply replaces this term or forms a wider category; cf. Harvey 1955, 162f., Carey 2009, 31f. and Budelmann 2012, 174f.

22   Cf. the passages listed in LSJ s. v. II.2 (though in most of the cases ὄχημα is specified in some way).

23   LSJ s. v. II.1; Slater s. v. ὄχημα ('mulecart'). Cf. also Nünlist 1998, 264 and Fearn 2007, 39. I have changed Race's translation 'chariot' to the more general 'vehicle' in order not to prejudice the question. The term ὄχημα is nowhere attested in Pindar's epinicia, but occurs in fr. 106.7 Maehler (in a concrete sense, probably 'mulecart') and fr. 140b.8 Maehler (poetologically, otherwise unspecified: [ὄ]χημα λιγ[υ).

24   Cf. van Groningen 1960, 86 and 96.

i.e. for a symposion. A reference to such a specific destination is a remarkable feat in itself, for as far as I see, there is nothing similar to be found in the song-journey motifs of Pindar's *epinikia*. However, more significantly, the symposium motif appears linked to the idea of seafaring in the following lines (fr. 124ab.2-8 Maehler):

ἐν ξυνῷ κεν εἴη

συμπόταισίν τε γλυκερὸν καὶ Διωνύσοιο καρπῷ

καὶ κυλίκεσσιν Ἀθαναίαισι κέντρον·

ἁνίκ᾽ ἀνθρώπων καματώδεες οἴχονται μέριμναι   5

στηθέων ἔξω· πελάγει δ᾽ ἐν πολυχρύσοιο πλούτου

πάντες ἴσα νέομεν ψευδῆ πρὸς ἀκτάν·

ὃς μὲν ἀχρήμων, ἀφνεὸς τότε, τοὶ δ᾽ αὖ πλουτέοντες ...

Amid the company may it (the vehicle of songs) be a sweet goad for your drinking companions, for the fruit of Dionysos, and for the Athenian drinking cups, when men's wearisome cares vanish from their breasts, and on the sea of golden wealth we all alike swim to an illusory shore; then the pauper is rich, while the wealthy ...

Here it is not the poem that is moving on the sea, but the symposiasts. Interestingly, the poetic 'I' presents himself as part of this group by using a verb in the first-person plural (νέομεν, line 7), which contrasts with the sending motif of the first two lines. It may be helpful to note that lines 5-8 show traits of generalisation, starting with ἀνθρώπων in line 5 and continuing with πάντες ἴσα in line 7. These generalising traits do not just affect the semantics of the first-person plural, but also the interpretation of the passage as a whole. As the text suggests, the experiences described here can be had in any drinking party. In other words, we are presented with an ideology of symposion which seems to be based on common motifs, several of which are also found in an *enkomion* by Bacchylides (fr. 20B Maehler).[25]

The crucial point for my paper is that this ideology involves maritime imagery that links it to the opening sentence. Just as the sea (without being mentioned) connects the poetic 'I' and Thrasyboulos in the first lines, so it connects the symposiasts (including the poetic 'I' and Thrasyboulos) with each other a little later. Apart from the shared idea of moving on the sea, the two cases are, of course, quite different: while the song seems to be sent directly and successfully to its receiver, the symposiasts head towards an 'illusory shore' (ψευδῆ πρὸς ἀκτάν, line 7), and while the song is moving in or as a vehicle of some sort, the symposiast are literally said to be swimming (νέομεν, line 7). The sea, it becomes clear, is also a dangerous place, a place that has to be mastered. Crossing the sea is an achievement in its own right, and the fact that the song is successfully sent to Sicily instead of floating on the sea hints at the superior power of its sender.

As noted in the introduction, Pindar is not the only author to describe the symposion in terms of maritime imagery. Under the heading 'the ship of symposiasts', Nünlist adduces quite a number of early Greek poets who employ nautical images in the context of the symposion, and one could even add non-Greek texts like the

---

25   The correspondences between the two poems are discussed by van Groningen 1960, 100f. and Fearn 2007, 37-41. B. fr. 20B was probably commissioned in the 490s (Maehler 2004, 245; cf. Fearn 2007, 55f. with n. 94), thus possibly predating Pi. fr. 124ab; however, direct imitation is far from certain since both poems seem to use *topoi* (Maehler 2004, 248f.; Fearn 2007, 37f.). Whether the book of the Alexandrian edition containing poems like B. fr. 20B was actually entitled ἐγκώμια is not quite clear (cf. Maehler 2004, 238f.; Fearn 2007, 27f. n. 2; D'Alessio 2016); at any rate, the poems in question are closely connected with Pindar's 'ἐγκώμια'.

song about the drunkard in Proverbs 23:29-35.[26] Even Bacchylides' *enkomion* fr. 20B, although it does not use maritime metaphors, mentions ships as part of the symposiast's imagination.[27] All of this suggests that the maritime imagery in Pi. fr. 124ab can be understood as an expression (and corroboration) of an overarching sympotic identity. One of the original features of the poem is the juxtaposition of sympotic seafaring with the seafaring song: we might go so far as to say that the song is not only sent across the Mediterranean; in some sense, it is also launched into the metaphorical sea of the symposiasts, thus inscribing itself into their shared identity.

Conclusions

The three passages discussed in this paper represent but a small selection from the broader spectrum of poetological seafaring imagery in Pindar and other early Greek poets. Other notable examples include Pindar's *Pythian* 10, where the poetic 'I', imagining his poem as a sea journey, summons himself to 'hold the oar and quickly plant the anchor in the earth from the prow as a safeguard against the jagged reef',[28] and *Olympian* 9, where the poetic 'I' goes so far as to boast that he will send his announcement 'more swiftly than either a high-spirited horse or a winged ship'.[29] In Bacchylides, one might think of the beginning of *Dithyramb* 2.[30] That being said, the three instances of the seafaring song motif have proven to be particularly instructive cases in terms of connectivity. The last of the three examples constructs a one-to-one connection between the poetic 'I' and the recipient, the second one a one-to-many connection, and the first one allows for both interpretations. The maps inserted above can help to illustrate the different types of connectivity, although it has to be kept in mind that none of the three passages specifies both the starting point and the destination. Rather than delineating a precise route, we might say that the passages convey the idea of connectivity, which goes beyond arrows on a map.[31] In all of the cases, the song itself plays a pivotal role: the poetic 'I' can or must be imagined as stationary, but his seafaring song enables him to establish connections across the Mediterranean.

Interestingly, the idea of the seafaring song combines a Panhellenic and a local perspective. One the one hand, the metaphors highlight the shared identity connecting the sender and the recipient(s) across the Mediterranean. On the other hand, at least to some degree, the passages draw attention to the hometown of the addressee, which is envisaged either as the starting point or as the destination.[32] It is conspicuous that all three of the addressees live on islands. This is not to say that there is a rule for Pindar to employ maritime imagery only when the addressee is an islander, as poems like *Pythian* 10 or

---

26 Nünlist 1998, 317-325 ('*Das Schiff des Symposiasten*'); cf. also Slater 1976 and Fearn 2007, 39 with n. 32. The relevant part of Prov 23:29-35 is v. 34 (English Standard Version: 'You will be like one who lies down in the midst of the sea, like one who lies on the top of a mast').

27 B. fr. 20B.14-16 (ed. Maehler): πυροφ‚όροι δὲ κατ' αἰγλάεντ‚α πό‚ντον / νᾶες ἄγο‚υσιν ἀπ' Αἰγύπτου μέγιστον / πλοῦτον· ὡς ‚πίνοντος ὀρμαίνει κέαρ ('and wheat-bearing ships bring great wealth from Egypt over a dazzling sea. Such are the musings of the drinker's heart', transl. Campbell).

28 Pi. P. 10.51sq.: κώπαν σχάσον, ταχὺ δ' ἄγκυραν ἔρεισον χθονί / πρῴραθε, χοιράδος ἄλκαρ πέτρας.

29 Pi. O. 9.23-25: καὶ ἀγάνορος ἵππου / θᾶσσον καὶ ναὸς ὑποπτέρου παντᾷ / ἀγγελίαν πέμψω ταύταν. Cf. also the hypothetical sea journey in Pi. P. 3.68sq.: καί κεν ἐν ναυσὶν μόλον Ἰονίαν τάμνων θάλασσαν / Ἀρέθοισαν ἐπὶ κράναν παρ' Αἰτναῖον ξένον ... ('And I would have come, cleaving the Ionian sea in a ship, to the fountain of Arethusa and to my Aetnaean host ...').

30 B. Di. 2.1-4: [...]ιου . ιο[...]ἐπεὶ / [ὀλκ]άδ' ἔπεμψεν ἐμοὶ χρυσέαν / [Πιερ]ίαθεν ἐ[ὕθ]ρονος [Ο]ὐρανία, [πολυ- / φ]άτων γέμουσαν ὕμνων ... ('..., since fine-throned Urania has sent me from Pieria a golden cargo-boat laden with glorious songs ...').

31 Both points are mentioned in P. 2.1-4, but here we do not have a 'seafaring song'.

32 Most obviously N. 5 (Aigina as point of departure). In P. 2.67sq., Syracuse is not mentioned, but the address to Hieron (χαῖρε) suggests it as a possible destination; fr. 124ab does not mention a particular city, but the symposion is in all likelihood to be imagined as taking place in Thrasyboulos' home town.

Olympian 9 (both mentioned above) exemplify the opposite. Nevertheless, in the cases discussed in this paper, the poetological metaphors correspond to the addressee's geographical situation, and one can even suggest that they illustrate an insular identity.[33]

However, seafaring was naturally an important cultural technique not only for islanders, but for a majority of the ancient Greeks. What makes the cases discussed above so intriguing is the fact that this cultural technique is so artfully intertwined with the realm of poetry. In different ways, the song replicates and inscribes itself into the real world of the addressees. We find landscapes created in the texts, but the distances seem to shrink as they are overcome by the poem. The poetic 'I' may remain at his place, although as the originator of seafaring songs, he can lay claim to a scope of connectivity on a par with – if not superior to –[34] the famous seafaring nations of antiquity. In some sense, this also makes himself – and Pindar, as the historical author – a master of the sea.

References

Primary literature

Pindarus, *Ps. I. Epinicia*, post B. Snell ed. H. Maehler, Lipsiae [8]1987; *Ps. II. Fragmenta. Indices*, ed. H. Maehler, Lipsiae 1989.

Pindar, *2 Vol.*, ed. and transl. by W.H. Race, Cambridge/London 1997.

Bacchylides. *Carmina cum fragmentis*, ed. H. Maehler, Monachii/Lipsiae [11]2003.

Greek Lyric, Volume 4: Bacchylides, Corinna, and others, with an English translation by D.A. Campbell, Cambridge/London 1992.

Secondary literature

Becker, O., 1937. *Das Bild des Weges und verwandte Vorstellungen im frühgriechischen Denken*. Berlin: Weidmann.

Brock, R., 2013. *Greek political imagery from Homer to Aristotle*. London and New York: Bloomsbury Academic.

Budelmann, F., 2012. Epinician and the symposion. A comparison with the encomia. *In*: P. Agócs, C. Carey and R. Rawles, eds. *Reading the victory ode*. Cambridge: Cambridge University Press, 173-190.

Budelmann, F., 2017. Performance, reperformance, preperformance. The paradox of repeating the unique in Pindaric Epinician and beyond. *In*: R. Hunter and A. Uhlig, eds. *Imagining reperformance in ancient culture. Studies in the traditions of drama and lyric*. Cambridge: Cambridge University Press, 42-62.

Budelmann, F. 2018. Lyric minds. *In*: F. Budelmann and T. Phillips, eds. *Textual events. Performance and lyric in ancient Greece*. Oxford: Oxford University Press, 235-256.

Bundy, E.L., 1962. *Studia Pindarica*. Berkeley and Los Angeles: University of California Press (reprint 1986).

Burnett, A.P., 2005. *Pindar's songs for young athletes of Aigina*. Oxford: Oxford University Press.

Calame, C., 2010. Das poetische Ich. Enuntiative und pragmatische Fiktion in der griechischen Lieddichtung am Beispiel von Pindar, Ol. 6. *RhM*, 153, 125-140.

Carey, C., 2009. Genre, occasion and performance. *In*: F. Budelmann, ed. *The Cambridge companion to Greek lyric*. Cambridge: Cambridge University Press, 21-38.

Currie, B., 2013. The Pindaric first person in flux. *ClAnt*, 32, 243-282.

---

33 This is particularly evident in *P.* 2, where poetological seafaring images occur several times (see above), and in *N.* 5, whose strong maritime character is regularly pointed out in scholarship (cf. *e.g.* Hornblower 2004, 226f. with further literature).

34 Especially *O.* 9.23-25 suggests an even superior power which borders on divine abilities (one may think of Homeric gods rushing across land and sea).

D'Alessio, G.B., 1994. First-person problems in Pindar. *BICS,* 39, 117-139.

D'Alessio, G.B., 2016. Bacchylides' banquet songs. *In*: V. Cazzato, D. Obbink and E.E. Prodi, eds. *The cup of song. Studies on poetry and the symposion.* Oxford: Oxford University Press, 63-84.

Dougherty, C., 2001. *The raft of Odysseus. The ethnographic imagination of Homer's Odyssey.* Oxford: Oxford University Press.

Fearn, D., 2007. *Bacchylides. Politics, performance, poetic tradition.* Oxford: Oxford University Press.

Fearn, D., 2017. *Pindar's eyes. Visual and material culture in epinician poetry.* Oxford: Oxford University Press.

Gentili, B., Bernadini, P.A., Cingano, E. and Giannini, P., eds., 1995. *Pindaro. Le Pitiche.* Rome and Milano: Fondazione Lorenzo Valla/Arnoldo Mondadori Editore.

Harvey, A.E., 1955. The classification of Greek lyric poetry. *CQ,* 5, 157-175.

Hornblower, S., 2004. *Thucydides and Pindar. Historical narrative and the world of epinikian poetry.* Oxford: Oxford University Press.

Hubbard, T.K., 2001. Pindar and Athens after the Persian war. *In*: D. Papenfuß and V.M. Strocka, eds. *Gab es das griechische Wunder? Griechenland zwischen dem Ende des 6. und der Mitte des 5. Jahrhunderts v. Chr.* Mainz: Verlag Philipp von Zabern, 387-400.

Hubbard, T.K. 2004. The dissemination of epinician lyric. Pan-hellenism, reperformance, written texts. *In*: C.J. Mackie, ed. *Oral performance and its contexts.* Leiden and Boston: Brill, 71-93.

Hubbard, T.K., 2011. The dissemination of Pindar's non-epinician choral lyric. *In*: L. Athanassaki and E. Bowie, eds. *Archaic and classical choral song. Performance, politics and dissemination.* Berlin and Boston: De Gruyter, 347-363.

Kaiser, K.H., 1953. *Das Bild des Steuermannes in der antiken Literatur.* Doctoral Thesis. Erlangen.

Kowalzig, B., 2011. Musical merchandise 'on every vessel': Religion and trade on Aegina. *In*: D. Fearn, ed. *Aegina. Contexts for choral lyric poetry. Myth, history, and identity in the fifth century BC.* Oxford: Oxford University Press, 129-171.

Kirichenko, A., 2016. The art of transference. Metaphor and iconicity in Pindar's Olympian 6 and Nemean 5. *Mnemosyne,* 69, 1-28.

Kuhn-Treichel, T., 2018. Relationale Rollenbestimmung durch ‚Ich aber'-Formulierungen bei Pindar. *RhM,* 161, 113-135.

Kuhn-Treichel, T., 2020. *Rollen in Relation. Das poetische Ich in verschiedenen Gattungen bei Pindar.* München: Verlag C.H. Beck.

Lattmann, C., 2010. *Das Gleiche im Verschiedenen. Metaphern des Sports und Lob des Siegers in Pindars Epinikien.* Berlin and Boston: De Gruyter.

Lattmann, C., 2017. Pindar's voice(s). The epinician persona reconsidered. *In*: N.W. Slater, ed. *Voice and voices in antiquity.* Leiden and Boston: Brill, 123-148.

Lewis, V.M., 2019. *Myth, locality, and identity in Pindar's Sicilian odes.* Oxford: Oxford University Press.

Maehler, H., 2004. *Bacchylides. A selection.* Cambridge: Cambridge University Press.

Männlein-Robert, I., 2007. *Stimme, Schrift und Bild. Zum Verhältnis der Künste in der hellenistischen Dichtung.* Heidelberg: Universitätsverlag Winter GmbH Heidelberg.

Maslov, B., 2015. *Pindar and the emergence of literature.* Cambridge: Cambridge University Press.

Morgan, C., 2007. Debating patronage. The cases of Argos and Corinth. *In*: C. Morgan and S. Hornblower, eds. *Pindar's poetry, patrons, and festivals. From archaic Greece to the Roman empire.* Oxford: Oxford University Press, 213-263.

Morrison, A.D., 2007. *The narrator in archaic Greek and Hellenistic poetry.* Cambridge: Cambridge University Press.

Morrison, A.D., 2012. Performance, re-performance and Pindar's audiences. *In*: P. Agócs, C. Carey and R. Rawles, eds. *Reading the victory ode*. Cambridge: Cambridge University Press, 111-133.

Most, G.W., 1985. *The measures of praise. Structure and function in Pindar's Second Pythian and Seventh Nemean Odes*. Göttingen: Vandenhoeck & Ruprecht.

Neer, R. and Kurke, L., 2019. *Pindar, song, and space. Towards a lyric archaeology*. Baltimore: Johns Hopkins University Press.

Nünlist, R., 1998. *Poetologische Bildersprache in der frühgriechischen Dichtung*. Stuttgart and Leipzig: B.G. Teubner.

Patten, G., 2009. *Pindar's metaphors. A study in rhetoric and meaning*. Heidelberg: Universitätsverlag Winter GmbH Heidelberg.

Pavlou, M., 2010. Pindar Nemean 5: Real and poetic statues. *Phoenix*, 64, 1-17.

Péron, J., 1974. *Les images maritimes de Pindare*. Paris: Librairie Klincksieck.

Pfeijffer, I.L., 1999. *Three Aeginetan odes of Pindar. A commentary on Nemean V, Nemean III, & Pythian VIII*. Leiden: Brill.

Segal, C., 1985. Messages to the underworld. An aspect of poetic immortalization in Pindar. *AJPh*, 106, 199-212.

Sigelman, A.C., 2016. *Pindar's poetics of immortality*. Cambridge: Cambridge University Press.

Slater, W.J., 1976. Symposion at sea. *HSPh*, 80, 161-170.

Spelman, H., 2018. *Pindar and the poetics of permanence*. Oxford: Oxford University Press.

Stehle, E., 2017. The construction of authority in Pindar's Isthmian 2 in performance. *In*: E.J. Bakker, ed. *Authorship and Greek song. Authority, authenticity, and performance*. Leiden and Boston: Brill, 8-33.

Steiner, D., 2011. Pindar's bestiary. The 'coda' of Pythian 2. *Phoenix*, 65, 238-267.

Tedeschi, A., 1985. L'invio del carme nella poesia lirica arcaica: Pindaro e Bacchilide. *SIFC*, 3a (3), 29-54.

van Groningen, B.A., 1960. *Pindare au banquet. Les fragments des scolies édités avec un commentaire critique et explicative*. Leiden: Sijthoff.

West, M.L., 2007. *Indo-European poetry and myth*. Oxford: Oxford University Press.

Maritime cultural landscapes of fishing communities in Roman Cyprus

Maria M. Michael, Carmen Obied

Abstract

This paper explores the tradition of fisheries and fishing techniques on the island of Cyprus during the Roman period. The maritime cultural landscape indicates fishing activities were important in the utilisation of maritime space in the Roman Mediterranean. Regarding archaeological, iconographical and written evidence, fishing could be characterised as a small-scale activity for supporting a fisher's family, or as an organised societal activity.

The research presented here aims to demonstrate how perceptions of the maritime cultural landscape on the island of Cyprus can help to interpret the role the Mediterranean region played in the cultural, technological and ideological developments of traditional fishing activities in Cyprus. Maritime communities relied on accumulated cognitive knowledge and mental maps of the landscape, often preserved through oral traditions, to navigate and identify key fishing grounds. As with ancient navigation, landmarks and toponyms played an important structural role in the fisher's perceptions of the coastal landscape. Thus, this research attempts to examine how the physical Mediterranean environment determines the presence or absence of fishing activities within its maritime landscape, and in turn to further understand the relationship between fishers and their maritime environment through fishing activity.

To achieve this aim, the research intends to examine archaeological data of the fishing methods from archaeological sites in Cyprus in an attempt to acquire a better general understanding of the formative phases of fisheries on the island during the Roman period. The fish bone assemblages, the iconographic and written sources and the environmental and ethnographic data are a supporting class of evidence. This research forms part of an ongoing project that will contribute towards a more holistic understanding of the relationship between fishers and their maritime cultural landscape diachronically.

Roman, fishing, Cyprus, maritime cultural landscape

Introduction

This paper aims to demonstrate the perceptions of maritime cultural landscapes in the natural and archaeological context of Cyprus based on the results developed during two PhD research projects (Obied 2016; Michael 2020). It mainly focuses on the maritime cultural landscape of fishing communities on the island of Cyprus during the Roman period, which is a part of a wider ongoing PhD research project on fishing activities and techniques in Cyprus diachronically (Michael 2020).

Fishing is an activity that dates from the appearance of human civilisation in the Mediterranean regions and beyond, as their inhabitants explored and exploited the rich resources of the sea and rivers for their survival (Farrugio *et al.* 1993, 106; Van Neer *et al.* 2005, 131; Marzano 2013, 15). However, fishing seems to be a research topic that for a long time was left out of discussions within the archaeological context of Cyprus (Frost 1985, 169). Scholars believed that it was not a profitable topic of research due to the lack of archaeo-ichthyologic evidence or conceptions such as fishing being an emergency resource, a poor and unstable occupation that Cypriots preferred to not do (Dikaios 1961, 290; Egoumenidou and Michaelides 2000, 112; Ionas 2001, 217; Knapp 2018, 151). However, is this view really acceptable regarding the maritime cultural landscape of Cyprus during the Roman period?

Thus, this paper aims to explore how the physical Mediterranean environment determines the presence or absence of fishing activities within the Cypriot maritime cultural landscape. It attempts to understand if Cypriots accepted the influence from their maritime environment regarding the development of fishing activity or distanced themselves from it; In other words, this paper attempts to understand the relationship between fishers and their maritime environment and how this relationship affected the technological and ideological development of fishing activity in Cyprus in the past. Furthermore, it aims to examine if the value of the development of fishing activities in Cyprus is the same as in the Mediterranean Sea during the Roman period.

To achieve these objectives, a multi-disciplinary approach is adopted, in which maritime archaeo-ichthyologic data from fifteen archaeological sites in Cyprus, ancient textual sources, iconographical representations and geospatial analysis are applied. Ethnographic data is combined with the archaeological evidence, in order to illuminate aspects that are invisible in archaeological records, and help further our understanding of fishers' mental maps.

To sum up, in this paper, the perceptions of the maritime cultural landscape are first presented to define the theoretical background on which this research is developed. This presentation also defines the ways of accessing and understanding how the maritime cultural landscape is defined. Second, the maritime environment of the Mediterranean and the development of fishing activity during the Roman period are briefly discussed to provide some information on the wider context in which Cypriots lived, interacted and developed fishing activity. This also helps to understand how the pace and scale of development of fishing activity in Cyprus compared to other regions in the Mediterranean basin during the Roman period. Third, different types of data sets (archaeological, ichthyologic, descriptive and ethnographic evidence) are analysed to elucidate the material, social and cognitive aspects of fishing activity in Cyprus during the Roman period. Finally, some preliminary results of this ongoing research are presented.

Perceptions of the maritime cultural landscape

Prior to focusing on the case study of fishing communities of Cyprus, it is useful to clarify some of the perceptions of the maritime cultural landscape to establish an effective background against which a new methodological approach can be developed.

Fishing is an activity that is still mainly conducted by populations that inhabit coastal areas and who use a variety of gear to exploit the physical features of coastlines and sea to catch the fish or develop aquaculture (Rose 1994, 53, 101-102; Ayodeji 2004, 51-52; Marzano 2013, 199-205; Ford 2014, 771). The coast can be defined as the parts of the land adjoining or near the sea which are involved in maritime activities since ancient times and where marine processes such erosion, deposition and storm surges influence terrestrial and vice versa (Ford 2011, 764; Ford 2014, 764-766; Michael 2016). Consequently, its archaeological records must be taken into account along with harbours and shipwrecks to reconstruct an accurate picture of fishing activity in the past.

The term *"maritime cultural landscape"*, coined by Christer Westerdahl (1992, 5-6; 2007; 2011a; 2011b) in his studies of coastal Scandinavia, comprises:

> *'the whole network of sailing routes with ports and harbours along the coast, and its related constructions and remains of human activity, underwater as well as terrestrial'.*

Consequently, the study of the maritime cultural landscape within the case study of fishing activities referred to the exploration of all kinds of human relationships to the sea or any large body of water. In other words, this study aims to explore how people perceived the landscape of fishing, the landscape of transport and communications, including routes, harbours and landmarks or seamarks, and the cognitive landscape, including the ritual and symbolic landscape (fishers' mental maps) as expressed in oral traditions (Westerdahl 2007, 215-216; 2011a, 733-762).

Fishers have to make decisions based on where, when, what and how to fish, if they aim to achieve a good quantity of caught fish. These decisions are affected by various factors such as their origin, personality, beliefs and personal preference, manpower, gender, age and their social status and knowledge (Parker 2001, 33-41 Mylona 2008, 67). In addition, fishers would rely on the use of mental maps for navigating through the landscape, locating optimal fishing grounds and resources and creating fishing equipment. For instance, meteorological, ecological and biological knowledge, navigational skills, as well as fishing skills and the availability of resources are some broadly-defined categories of the specialised knowledge (cognitive knowledge and mental maps) that fishers have (Acheson 1981, 290-291; Wilson 1990, 28; McNiven 2003, 330-332; Westerdahl 2007, 207-208; Morales-Muñiz 2010, 28-29; Duncan 2011, 273). Consequently, this suggests that a multi-disciplinary approach is a better approach to be adopted, because these factors and aspects are not detectable only from the maritime archaeological data.

Thus, terrestrial and underwater archaeological data of fishing activities from fifteen sites in Cyprus are combined with ancient textual and iconographic sources and geospatial analysis to acquire a better general understanding of the formative phases of fisheries on the island during the Roman period. The methodological approaches to elucidate cognitive aspects of landscape formation and perception include oral histories, folklore, superstition, toponymy, symbology and local traditional knowledge networks. To truly be able to comprehend the practices and culture of a maritime community, it is imperative to try to first better appreciate the mindset of the individuals and groups that formed it. Oral histories, toponymy, and folklore offer powerful additional avenues of insight into how communities lived and interacted, which might be used to interpret archaeological sites and use of the local environment (Duncan 2011). Oral histories and folklore also provided significant observations of complex social and cognitive aspects of the fishing community that had never been recorded elsewhere (Duncan 2011).

Having briefly explained the theoretical background and the relative methodological approach that are used in this paper, the examination of the maritime environment of the specific case study shall follow.

Maritime environment of Mediterranean and the development of fishing activity during the Roman period

Cyprus is the third largest island in the eastern Mediterranean and a precariously sea-connected island just before and during the early Holocene, and again from the 2nd millennium BCE onward (Broodbank 2013, 599; Fig. 1). It has experienced over 4,000 years of intervening parochialism, as it became internally self-sufficient, but it escaped its insularity when the outside world learned of its copper (Broodbank 2013, 599). Therefore, an overview of the maritime environment of the Mediterranean Sea is essential to comprehend the maritime cultural landscape of fishing activity during the Roman period.

The Mediterranean is a semi-enclosed sea and one of the most oligotrophic ocean regions in the world, with poor productivity, but high biodiversity and endemism in coastal areas and continental shelves (Coll *et al.* 2000, 1-3, 25; Bariche 2012, 9; Demetropoulos and Hadjichristophorou 2017, 433). In the eastern part of Mediterranean, its oligotrophic character mainly depends on the high temperatures, evaporation, high salinity and inflow of fresh water, which is very limited due to the absence of large rivers (Coll *et al.* 2000, 1-3, 25; Bariche 2012, 9; Demetropoulos and Hadjichristophorou 2017, 433). However, about 400 indigenous fish species in small quantities have been recorded in the eastern Mediterranean (Golani *et al.* 2006, 9). This number was increased based on the phenomenon of the Lessepsian Migration since the opening of the Suez Canal in 1869 and the invasion of tropical species through the Strait of Gibraltar and by ship transportation (Coll *et al.* 2000, 24-25; Golani *et al.* 2006, 9-10; Bariche 2012, 7; Ioannou and Michaelides 2015, 4).

Consequently, the Mediterranean provided a wide variety of resources to the people living on its shores, and evidence shows that the Romans did exploit these to the extent allowed by the technology available (Bekker-Nielsen 2010; Marzano 2013, 7). According to archaeo-ichthyological evidence and written and iconographic evidence, it is proven that fishing was ubiquitous in the Roman Mediterranean and was practised on different levels. Fishery mainly aimed to support fishers' families or the subsistence of farmers occasionally supplementing their diet by fishing. (Trakadas 2006, 260-261; Bekker-Nielsen 2010, 187; Marzano 2013, 15; Marzano 2020, 277).

On the other hand, the studies of fishing in coastal lagoons by using traps, the evidence of aquaculture and the development of tuna fishing also prove that large-scale fishing activity developed in the Mediterranean during the Roman period (Marzano 2013, 52-78, 199-234; Marzano 2020). Fishers organised in associations who worked in collaboration with the fish-salting establishments or the fishmongers (Marzano 2013, 15, 51-88; Lytle 2016, 113-114; Marzano 2020, 290-292). The numerous fish-processing sites (*e.g.* for fish sauce and salted, smoked, dried or pickled fish and trade) and fish-salting establishments known mainly in the western Mediterranean also indicate that fishing was systematically practised on a medium or large scale and organisation beyond subsistence levels (Trakadas 2005; Marzano 2020; 285).

Although fishing was a humble occupation, didactic literary works on fishing or depictions of fishing in mosaics of elegant houses and villas found an interested elite audience due to a long philosophical tradition centred on the investigations of the nature of animals (Reese 2002; Monteagudo 2010; Marzano 2013, 49; Lytle 2016, 114-115). In other words, it takes place within a wide-ranging and complex pattern

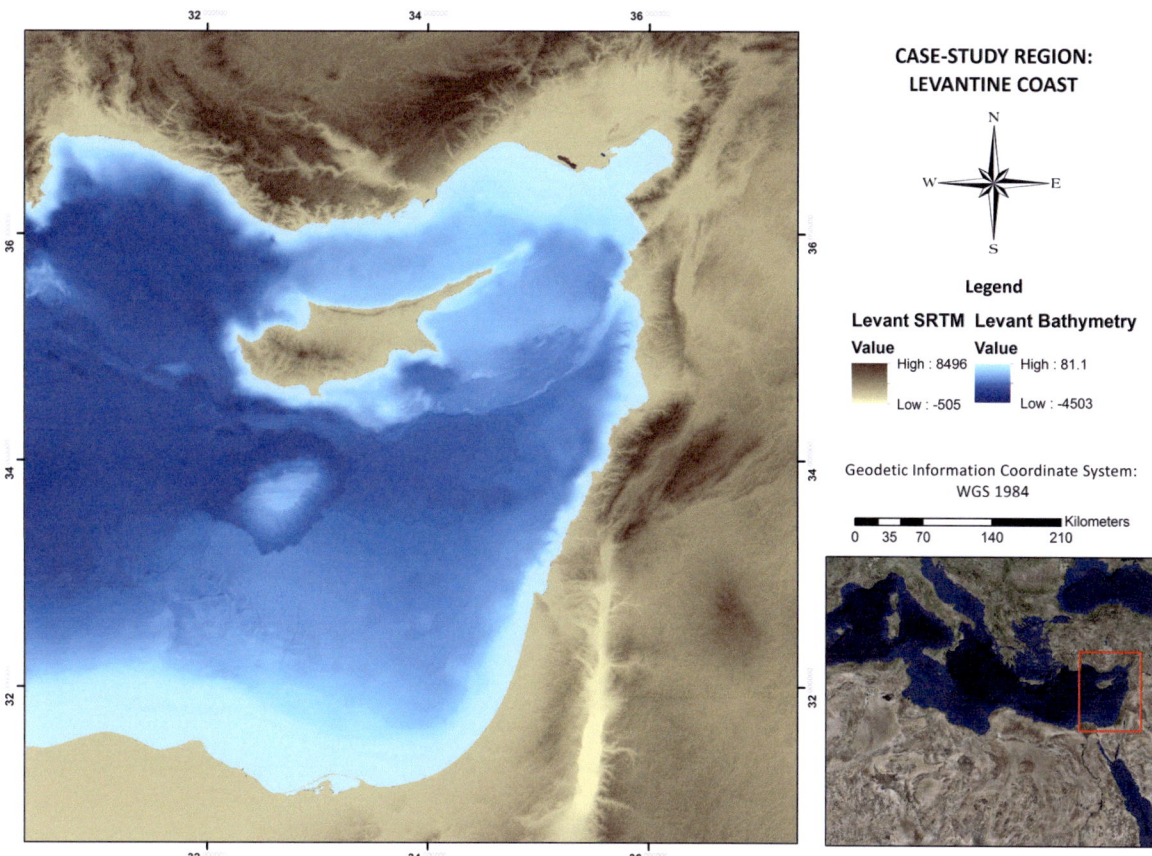

Figure 1. Map of Cyprus and the eastern Mediterranean. Map produced by C. Obied on ArcGIS10.2.2. (Source for layers: DEM: SRTM_1km, Bathymetry: Emodnet).

of interaction involving social, economic, cultural, biological and environmental aspects (Bekker-Nielsen 2010, 187).

According to Roman legal theory, anyone was free to exploit the resources of the sea. A number of legal texts affirm that the sea and its resources *a priori* belong to no one and that he who catches them owns them (Bekker-Nielsen 2010, 195-196; Marzano 2013, 235-300; Lytle 2016, 107). Nevertheless, the perception and usage of the sea in antiquity is not static. Economic and social changes had real effects on the way its inhabitants conceived the Mediterranean and its resources (Lytle 2016, 107, 121-124).

Having briefly described the maritime environment of the Mediterranean Sea and the development of fishing activity in its wider context during the Roman period, next the examination of the fishing activity in Cyprus during the Roman period based on archaeo-ichthyologic evidence, written, iconographic and ethnographic sources shall follow.

Fishing activity in Cyprus during the Roman period

Before discussing the evidence that is essential for the reconstruction of the landscape of fishing and communication and the cognitive landscape of fishing communities in Roman Cyprus, it is essential to provide a brief description of the chronological context of the case study.

During the Hellenistic period, Cyprus formed part of the Ptolemaic Kingdom of Egypt. In 58 BCE, Cyprus was annexed by the Roman Empire and it was first administered by Cicero and then by Mark Antony and Cleopatra VII (Michaelides 1996,

142; Christodoulou 2018, 143). In 31 BCE, Cyprus officially became part of the Roman world, after Octavian's victories over Antony and Cleopatra VII. However, Rome did not make a concrete effort to Romanise the island, although – as is natural – many aspects of the Roman way of life, culture and traditions gradually filtered into the culture of Cyprus.

The landscape of Roman Cyprus was occupied by a web of settlements that stretched across the island (Rautman 2000, 317). However, inland cities seemed to have been abandoned and cities were developed along the coastline, indicating that Cypriots were not afraid of any external threat (Michaelides 1996, 143). The island was divided into four districts for the purposes of local government: Salamis in the east, Lapithos in the north, Paphos in the west and Amathus in the south (Christodoulou 2018, 144, 155). The cities appear to have been much more autonomous in their internal affairs than under the Ptolemies, while they were supported by smaller rural villages and cities (Hunt 1982; Christodoulou 2018, 144, 155).

The literary evidence regarding Roman Cyprus is rather limited, but it is indicated that Greek continued to be the official language on the island (Hunt 1982, 129-130; Runciman 1982, 138; Christodoulou 2018, 145). The lack of interest in Cyprus on the part of writers can be attributed to the fact that the island, enjoying considerable prosperity under Roman rule, created no problems to the central government and there was thus no need to talk about it. Moreover, with the eastern Mediterranean now united under the Pax Romana, Cyprus lost its strategic importance (Hunt 1982, 121, 131; Michaelides 1996, 140-142; Christodoulou 2018, 143). The transfer of the imperial seat to Constantinople on 11th May 330 AD is the moment that Cyprus becomes entwined with that of the Christian Byzantine Empire and the Orthodox Church, and the Roman period ended in Cyprus (Runciman 1982, 134; Panayides 2018, 180).

Archaeological evidence related to fishing activity and fish bone assemblages

It is self-evident that a researcher attempting to examine the fishing activities in the past should consider fish remains. Fish is the main reason for the establishment of these activities because people would not develop any technique or industry if they did not need them, in order to catch the different marine creatures and process them. In addition, fishing technology such as hooks, harpoons, net weights and traps that were developed to achieve the best capture of fish species is also an important indicator of fishing activity. Due to the perishable nature of most of the archaeological evidence, the most interesting attestations related to fishing tend to be either indirect archaeological evidence, such as installations for fish-salting, documentary and epigraphic texts and iconographical sources. In certain cases, evidence for specific individuals involved in professional fishing can be attested archaeologically by the study of human bones.

There are fifteen Hellenistic and Roman sites confirming the existence of fishing activities on the island (Tab. 1 and Fig. 2). The finds were mainly recovered on archaeological sites located along the coast, as only one (Anogyra Vlou) is inland (Fig. 2). In addition, two shipwrecks (Kerynia, Mazotos) have been found in the northern and southern offshore areas of Cyprus (Fig. 2). Although their origin might not be Cypriot, their crew fished in the region of Cyprus; as a result, they could be good comparative examples for the classification of fishing gear and techniques from these periods.

As already mentioned, fish remains are the main indicator of fishing activities. The amount of fish remains identified at archaeological sites in Cyprus are negligible and unidentified (Table 1) because their study is characterised as problematic. Fish remains were rarely photographed or their analysis is not detailed, as they appeared chiefly in appendices of final publications of archaeological sites, rather than as the

Site Name	Date	Location (District)	Site Type	Archaeological Finds	Fish Bone Samples	Reference
Agia Irene	Roman	Nicosia		A potential fish-tank. A small, rectangular rock-cut vat with two channels used to fill and empty water. Foot walls or mid-tidal gates are not detectable. Grooves on the rocks used for placing the gates are not detectable, either.		Quilici Gigli, 1971: 14, 22.
Agios Phylon	Hellenistic, Roman and Early Christian period	Karpasia, Famagusta		A potential complex of fish-tanks. Du plat Taylor mentions that a number of rock-cut fish tanks can still be seen along the rocky shore, to the east of the town (Du plat Taylor, 1980: 154). Michael (current author) has not located these features during her fieldwork. In addition, it seems that quarrying activity existed in the area; as a result, these features might be remains of a quarry.		Du Plat Taylor, 1980: 154.
Agora (Nea Paphos)	Roman	Paphos	Agora	1 fragmentary bronze fish hook. 2 stone net weight. 3 potential conical lead line sinkers.		Unpublished. Thanks to Dr Evdoxia Papuci-Wladyka for the permission.
Amathus	Hellenistic, Roman, Early Byzantine period	Limassol	Building complex	1 bronze fish hook (lower city). 1 bronze fish hook (eastern necropolis). 1 lead folded net sinker (tunnel-sanctuary). 14 bronze small fish hooks (probably from tomb 252).	Unidentified fish bones (tunnel sanctuary)	Christou, 1998a: 63-64. The fourteen bronze small fish hooks are unpublished and they are stored in the British Museum. Thanks to Dr Thomas Kiely and Dr Ross Thomas for the permission.
Amathus	Hellenistic and Roman	Limassol	Harbour (underwater find)	1 potential lead line sinker. 17 lead folded net sinkers. 6 lead line sinkers. 4 lead fish hooks.		Michael, 2018a: 79-118. Michael, 2018b: 191-196.
Anogyra Vlou	Hellenistic or Roman	Limassol	Occasional finds in the area of a Hellenistic building complex and a Roman rural sanctuary.	1 potential ceramic net weight. 1 potential bronze needle. 3 potential round limestone net weights.		Goroncharovskiy, 2017: 687-716.
House of Dionysos	Roman	Paphos	Villa	Deep reservoir used for keeping fish (fish pond).		Nicolaou, 1967: 101.
House of Orpheus	Roman	Paphos	Villa	2 bronze fish hooks. 6 lead folded net sinkers.		Unpublished. Thanks to Dr Demetrios Michaelides for the permission.
Kition Bamboula	Hellenistic	Larnaca		1 fragmentary bronze fish hook.	4 fish bones: The vertebrae might be silurid imported from Egypt. Vertebrae of Arius thalassinus.	Desse, 1993:104-105. Salles and Chavane, 1993: 333.

Table 1. All materials presented in this table are part of the ongoing doctoral research of Maria M. Michael.

Site Name	Date	Location (District, Toponym)	Site Type	Archaeological Finds	Fish Bone Samples	Reference
Kourion	Roman	Limassol	House (known as the Earthquake House from the earthquake of the 365AD)	2 bronze fish hooks (room 14: kitchen and room 28: small shop). 38 lead folded net sinkers. 185 bone pins/bobbins possibly using for making fishing nets.	Unidentified fish remains (cistern, room 14: kitchen)	Soren and James, 1988: 127-128, 139, 142. Bon, 1989.
Kourion	Early Christian	Limassol	Basilica	1 bronze fish hook.	Unidentified fish remains	Megaw, 2007: 533.
Lapithos	Roman	Kerynia		A complex of fish-tanks.		Nicolaou, and Flinder, 1976: 133-141.
Polis Peristeries	Hellenistic, Roman and Early Christian periods	Paphos	Sanctuary/Basilica	1 bronze fish hook. 1 lead fish hook. 1 potential lead conical net weight. 1 potential ceramic spherical net weight. 2 potential lead cylindrical net weights.		Database of archaeological mission (unpublished). Thanks to Dr Joanna Smith, Dr Nancy Serwint and Dr Willy Childs for the permission.
Salamis	Hellenistic, Roman and Early Christian	Famagusta		1 damaged bronze fish hook. 1 bronze fish hook. 1 sandstone net weight. 1 bronze shuttle used on a loom to run the thread of the weft between the warp threads. 1 bronze net needle. 1 lead folded net sinker. 2 net stone weights.	Unidentified fish remains	Chavane, 1975: 109-114.
Soli	Hellenistic and Roman	Nicosia	Room X of the temple B	1 net bronze needle		Unpublished. On the website of Medelhavetmuseet (Sweden).
Tombs of Kings	Hellenistic	Paphos	Monumental tombs		Unidentified fish remains.	Karageorghis, 1989: 830.
Yeronisos Island	Hellenistic	Paphos		Pierced ceramic sherds probably re-used as fish net-weights. 2 lead folded net sinkers. 1 bronze fish hook.		Christou, 1998a: 58-59. Christou, 1998b: 67-68.

Table 1. continued.

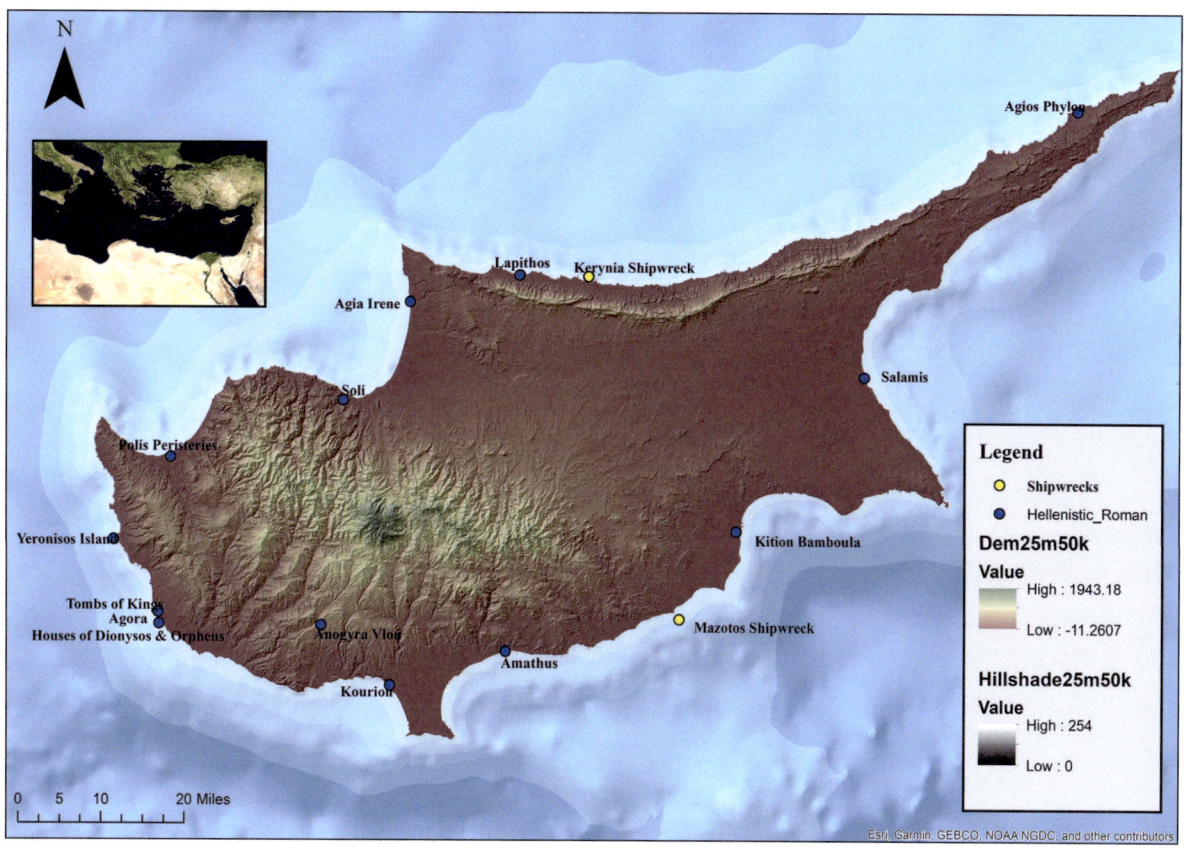

Figure 2. Map of Cyprus presenting the archaeological sites with finds of fishing gear and fishbone assemblages. Map produced by M.M. Michael on ArcGIS10 2.2. (Source for layers of Digital Elevation Model, Hillshade, Coastline, Rivers and Salt Lakes: Department of Lands and Surveys, Cyprus; Source of the basemap: Esri Garmin, NCAA NGDC, and other contributors; Layer of archaeological sites produced by M.M. Michael).

subject of detailed analysis in their own right. Furthermore, the limited or non-existent usage of sieving in conjunction with the absence of precise and integrated reference collections affects the precise identification of fish species. This is the key reason that many of the fish remains are unidentified and cannot provide any information regarding the fish species and fishing techniques or grounds but they do indicate only the existence of fishing activity and fish consumption. Furthermore, it is not easy to recognise if there was small, medium or large-scale fishing activity in the island as with other areas along the Mediterranean coasts.

However, some vertebrae recovered on the archaeological site of Kition were identified as *Arius thalassinus* known as giant sea catfish (Desse 1993, 103-105). This fish species certainly originates from the Red Sea, and rarely enters freshwater (Froese and Pauly 2019). The recovery of its remains on an archaeological site in Cyprus leads to the interpretation that it was imported from Egypt, and that fish trade was developed between Cyprus and other areas of the eastern Mediterranean during the Roman period.

The other key indicator of fishing activities in the past is the archaeological finds of fishing gear. The majority of the recovered archaeological finds are lead line and net sinkers, stone net weights and fish hooks (Tab. 1 and Fig. 3). This shows the usage of fishing nets such as gillnets and entangling nets (trammel nets) and set long lines or vertical lines, which can be multi-hooked or carry only one hook attached at the end of the line (Von Bradt 1964; Nédélec and Prado 1990; Department of Fisheries and Marine Research, Cyprus, 2009). However, the number of these finds is limited, in order to lead to accurate interpretations about the nature of fishing activity in Cyprus.

Figure 3. Fishing gear: Fish hooks and weights. (Michael, 2018a: 109, Fig. 3, © A. Athanasiou, Archives of École française d' Athènes).

The usage of these techniques is also identified by iconographic evidence recovered in Cypriot archaeological context. An ivory plaque (MP1936/64 A/A catalogue 1312) recovered in a Hellenistic II-Roman Tomb (no.5/68) during the rescue excavation for a pit by the Public Works Department in the yard of the police station in Paphos demonstrates a very detailed fishing scene. A person with a beard and wearing a mariner's/fisher's hat sits fishing by using a fishing rod. The fishing rod comprises a wooden rod where and a line with a hook fastening. Aside from this detailed scene of fishing, iconographic sources in Cyprus are limited compared with other regions in the Mediterranean basin, as already mentioned.

As already mentioned, the number of written sources relating to fishing on the island are also restricted. Furthermore, if written sources exist, they are not detailed, as with a dedicatory inscription from a fisher to the god Opaon Melathios at Amargeti in the Paphos district, which does not provide any information about the fishing as an occupation (Hadjioannou 1980, 89; Michaelides 1998, 26).

In addition, evidence of aquaculture has been recovered on the northern coast of the island (Tab. 1 and Fig. 2). The fact that fish-tanks have been recovered in the northern part of Cyprus dictates that their systematic study is not possible due to the Turkish occupation since 1974. However, their existence in this area probably proves their usage for fish farming aquaculture, as in many other coasts along the Mediterranean Sea (Auriemma and Solinas 2009, 136; Marzano 2013, 205-233; Morhange and Marriner 2015, 148-149; Evelpidou and Karkani 2018, 3).

The fish-tanks from Lapithos are very large and likely indicate intensive fishing activity in the area (Fig. 4). Furthermore, Lapithos was one of the four administrative districts of the island during the Roman period; as a result, it seems that fishing activities in this area were likely to be organised and under the control of the Roman administration. According to textual and archaeological evidence recovered in the wider region of the Mediterranean basin, such installations are known during the Roman period and were built free-standing above the shore or cut into rock or incorporated into a maritime villa (Cato and Varro, *De Re Rustica* 3.5.12; Columella, *De Re Rustica* 8.16-17; Trakadas 2006, 261; Lytle 2016, 126-127). These installations were mainly treated as private property (Columella, *De Re Rustica* 8.16.6; Trakadas 2006, 268; Lytle 2016, 126-127; Marzano 2020, 278).

To sum up, it seems that the archaeo-ichthyologic evidence is limited for reconstructing a real, holistic view of fishing activity in Cyprus during the Roman period. However, the existence of this evidence proves that Cypriots were involved in fishing during this period. In addition, the presence of fish-tanks along the northern coast of the island also proves that fishing was not simply a secondary activity in the lifestyle of Cypriots or an occupation for poor people, but they make a special effort to construct these installations and exploit the marine environment of the island.

Fishers' mental maps: Social and cognitive landscape

Figure 4. Fish Ponds at the archaeological site of Lapithos. (© M.M. Michael 2018).

As mentioned earlier, maritime communities likely relied on accumulated cognitive knowledge and mental maps of the landscape, often preserved through oral traditions, to navigate and identify key fishing grounds. As with ancient navigation, navigational markers such as landmarks, toponyms, oral histories and folklore would have played an important structural role in shaping the fishers' behavioural patterns and perceptions of the coastal landscape.

It became evident during the present research that recent oral histories were a central data source for accessing and understanding fishing landscapes, as much of this information was/is never written down or recorded historically. Oral history evidence detailed the nature and extent of fishing grounds, along with the intricacies of the equipment used. Oral histories are evidenced; for example, by many Cypriot fishers who mentioned that the seabed of the northern part of Cyprus is far richer in different fish species in comparison to the southern part, due to it not being sandy and muddy, but rather composed of rocky and seagrass meadows, which offers optimal growing conditions, as a result of which fish can find nutrition (CRC/OTA 94, 218, 356, 522, 609, 933, 1243, 1329, 1333, 1467 1568, 1627, 2487, 2496, 2552, 2882, 3136, 3137). This might be the reason that Roman fish-tanks were constructed along the northern coast of the island. In addition, they evidenced fishing techniques such as fish poisoning and baited basket trap known as *"Skarka"* in Cyprus (Fig. 5), which did not survive in the archaeological finds due to its untraceable or perishable nature (CRC/OTA 356, 522, 609, 728, 1243, 1329, 1333, 2552; Ionas 2001, 223-224).

Furthermore, specialist knowledge existed as to how to exploit individual fish species, their favoured habitat conditions and bait, along with its seasonal availability and individual characteristics. For instance, some local fishers mentioned that the *Spicara smaris* (Picarel/Marida) forms large groups and they recommended to catch it before the breeding season, which takes place once a year, around March (CRC/OTA 522, 1329, 1568, 1627, 2552). Local fishers also mentioned that the Mediterranean parrotfish *Sparisome cretense* (Mediterranean parrotfish/ Skaros) can be caught by using basket traps and noted that they prefer the leaves from the syringe plant (Persian lilac) as bait (CRC/OTA 218, 356, 522, 933, 1243, 1333,

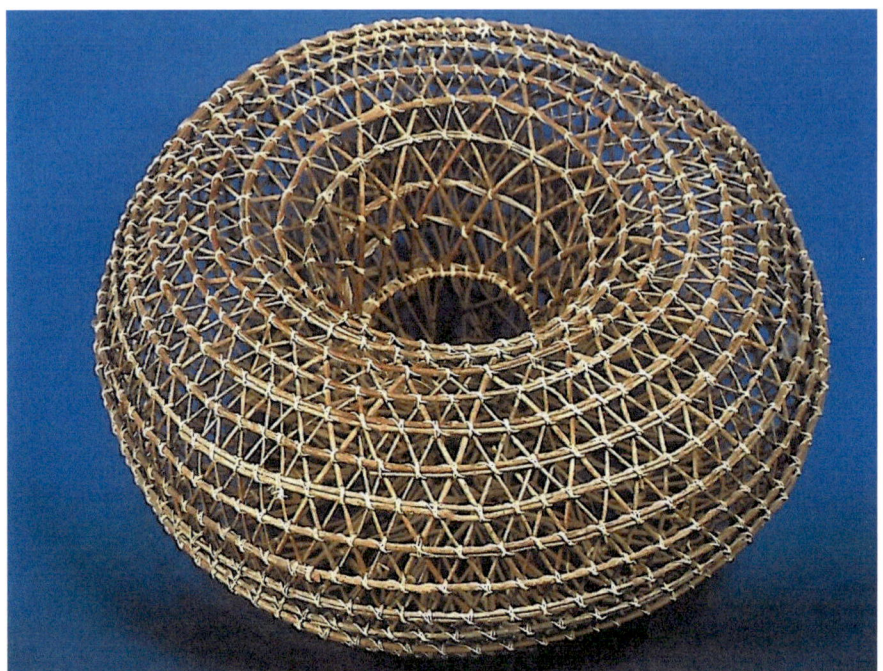

Figure 5. Fishing trap known as "Skarka", made of widthe. It was found at Lapithos, Kerynia. (Papademetriou, 1999: 75).

2487, 2882, 3136, 3137). By contrast, the *Mugil cephalus* (Flatched mulet/Cephalos) can be caught by using line fishing techniques and that they prefer small fish as bait, such as *Sardina pilchardus* (European pilchard/Sardela) (CRC/OTA 356, 1333, 1568, 2552, 2487, 3137). Consequently, these types of examples of oral histories reflect how fishers carefully observed, adapted and utilised their knowledge of the environment and animal behaviour to their advantage (Marzano 2013, 2).

Furthermore, a traditional nautical technique of fishers for orientation at sea, especially for locating fishing spots in a fishing ground, was described to clarify an aspect of the relationship between fishers and their sea environment through fishing activity. A navigator or fisher, as is well-known, pays constant attention to some points of orientation to discern from time to time where they are at sea (Obied 2016). The navigators or fishers watch a fixed landmark or a pair of landmarks, which are familiar to them and observe how the landmarks look from their boat to enable them to know their present position. With the help of two pairs of landmarks for triangulation, if available, they can bring their boat with considerable accuracy to a given spot. Determining how to locate a fishing spot by lining up one landmark behind another therefore depends on the topography of the island(s) or bays being referred to and varies from one fishing ground to another.

Thus, to locate the fishing grounds, Cypriot fishers relied on landmarks such as churches/sanctuaries or particular buildings (*e.g.* towers, forts/lookouts), distinctive elevations or mountaintops (*e.g.* Stavrovouni, Fig. 6), a tree or a promontory (CRC/OTA 728, 3134; Goodchild 1953, 75; Ionas 2001, 219-220; Morton 2001, 203; Davis 2009, 176). Promontory shrines of Phoenicians, Greeks and Romans prevail in classical authors for coastal sites of the eastern Mediterranean to the Atlantic (Thuc., Pel.War 3.94.2, 6.3.1-2/44.2-3, 7.26.2). They often also served as indicators of fresh water sources (Semple 1927; Morton 2001, 203). These promontory temples would have been visible to mariners and fishers moving along this coast, acting as key navigational markers (Semple 1972, 379):

'The ancient east-west sailing route may be traced by these promontory temples, set up like milestones at every port of call, all the way from Cyprus past Crete and Malta to the Pillars of Hercules.'

Figure 6. Different perspectives of the Levant demonstrating the contrasting elevations along the coastline, which divide the landscape into a series of distinguishable reference points. The mountaintops that fishers used as landmarks are distinguishable. Map produced by C. Obied on QGIS. (Source for basemap: ©Bing Aerial Layer; DEM: SRTM_1km).

Moreover, they served defensive and religious purposes, connecting mariners with their holy patrons that guided them along their sea journeys (Semple 1972, 383-384):

> 'The promontory gods who were expected to rescue men from dire peril were appeased by offerings of cattle and even of human lives. (...) similar features characterised the cult of Apollo on the Curias promontory in southwestern Cyprus, long under Phoenician influence. There anyone who touched the altar of the god was cast into the sea to propitiate the deity. (Euripides, Iphigenia in Tauris, 34-41, 380-405).'

In addition, marine deities had special links to seafarers and fishers. Poseidon was a protector of Greek sailors (Herodotus VII.192), and numerous temples and shrines were dedicated to this deity of the sea and marine winds, on headlands and in ports throughout Greece and its overseas territories (Semple 1927; Morton 2001). Similarly, Roman mariners and fishers worshipped Neptune, the Latin god of both fresh waters and the sea whose maritime symbols included the tuna, dolphin, and trident fishing spear (Brody 2008, 2; McCann 1987). The Greek and Roman protector of garden fertility, Priapus, was also a patron of sailors, maritime trade, and fishers (Bassett 1885; Brody 2008, 3; Neilson 2002).

To sum up, it has become evident that cognitive and navigational markers were a central data source for accessing and understanding fishing landscapes and developing mental maps of the maritime cultural landscape, as much of this information was/is never written down or recorded historically. It is also fundamental to discuss ethnographic data relating to traditional fisheries, in order to benefit the reconstruction of fishing techniques in the earlier periods.

Conclusion

Overall, this paper highlights fishing as an activity that can contribute towards enhancing our knowledge in the studies of Ancient Mediterranean connectivity and mobility, as it seems that people from different communities along its region and over time apply similar sets of fishing techniques, in order to catch the different fish species. Furthermore, the recovery of fish remains belonging to no local fish species in Cypriot archaeological sites probably indicates that there was mobility in the Mediterranean basin diachronically.

Furthermore, the opinion that Cypriots did not engage in fishing activities during the Roman period seems to be negated, as the physical environment and the archaeological and faunal evidence determine the presence of fishing activities in its maritime landscape. The maritime cultural landscape also indicates fishing activities were important in the utilisation of maritime space in the Roman Mediterranean. In addition, previous research on the environment of island and coastal areas has demonstrated that erosion, alluvial coverage of harbours, increased sedimentation and tectonic uplift substantially affected coastal archaeological site preservation and led to the loss of important information regarding past trade and maritime activities, such as fishing (Andreou *et al.* 2017, 197). This probably is one of the reasons that evidence of fishing is limited, and until now scholars assumed that fishing had not been developed on the island of Cyprus in the past.

According to ethnographic data and the archaeological evidence of fish-tanks along the north coast of Cyprus, it seems that Cypriot fishers were more active in the north part of the island, as the fishing grounds were more profitable. However, Turkish occupation limits the potential for further research, to recover and record the remaining evidence related to fishing activity. In addition, Cypriot fishers, mariners and merchants could include illiterate people with limited or no access to written sources. Fishery in Cyprus was mainly a small-scale artisanal industry targeting a diverse range of seafood with catches predominantly consumed by fishers' families or sold fresh in local markets. Fishing methods can also be classified into three major categories: 1) manual collection without tools; 2) passive fishing based on the use of natural and human-made devices that capture fish using natural fish mobility; and 3) active fishing, based on attacking aquatic creatures by human-made devices. On the other hand, it seems that fishing activities could also be organised and under the control of Roman administration. However, large-scale fishing activity has not been developed in Cyprus, unlike in other areas.

Finally, the study of fishers' practical experience and mental mapping potentially offers insights into a different way of perceiving the *oikoumene*. Broodbank (2013), and Horden and Purcell (2000) both emphasise that the short local-scale trips undertaken every day are mainly the source of the maritime knowledge that gives rise to the longer journeys, the inter-regional trade and the maritime connectivity within the Mediterranean basin. As already suggested, fishing was a fundamental activity along the coasts of Mediterranean during the Roman period because it is such a readily and legally accessible subsistence resource to everyone. Therefore, fishers seem to have been the people who interacted with the maritime environment and navigated the seas and coasts to find the best fishing grounds every day. Thus, they developed and nurtured the local maritime knowledge, which was the starting point of exploring the wider environment of the Mediterranean Sea and causing the maritime connectivity.

Consequently, the activity of fishing in a seafaring sense is likely to be an underpinning piece of maritime activity for most Mediterranean coastal societies. Thus, the study of fishing activity and fishers' interaction with their maritime landscape is important for understanding the fundamental maritime activity that supports and expands the wider Mediterranean connections that attract the interest from scholars. Accordingly, further and more elaborate research in this field of study will not only enhance our knowledge about fishing activity in the Mediterranean basin, but it will also allow for some more detailed conclusions about long-distance connectivity.

Acknowledgements

We would like to express our gratitude to the organisers for allowing us to participate in this well-organised conference. This work would not have been possible without the endless support of the Honor Frost Foundation, and Dr. Lucy Blue. We are also grateful to the Cypriot Department of Antiquities, all directors of archaeological excavations, and David Reese for granting access to the archaeological finds related to fishing. Finally, immense gratitude also goes to reviewers, supervisors, and specifically to Dr Julian Whitewright, friends and colleagues, as this publication would not have been completed without their guidelines and help.

References

Primary sources: Literary

Cato and Varro. *De Re Rustica. In*: *Cato and Varro on Agriculture*, with an English translation by W.D. Hooper and H.B. Ash. LCL 283. Cambridge MA 1934.

Columella, *De Re Rustica. In*: *Columella on Agriculture, Books 5-9*, with an English translation by E.S. Forster and E.H. Heffner. LCL 407. Cambridge MA 1954.

Herodotus VII.192, Godley, A.D. (trans.), 1920-1925. *Herodotus. The Histories*, 4 vols. London and Cambridge, MA.

Thucydides. *The History of the Peloponnesian War, Books 1-2*, with an English translation by C.F. Smith. LCL 108. Cambridge MA 1919.

Ethnographic sources: Oral tradition archive in the Cyprus Research Centre

CRC/OTA, Registration Number 218, Famagusta, (Yialousa 3). Testimony P. Xioutas (8.12.1990).

CRC/OTA, Registration Number 356, Famagusta, (Rizokarpaso 13). Testimony E. Zachariou (14.1.1991).

CRC/OTA, Registration Number 522, Kerynia, (Kerynia 94). Testimony A. Pateras Toumanis (20.3.1991).

CRC/OTA, Registration Number 609, Kerynia, (Ayios Amvrosios 18). Testimony K. Pessiogkes (22.4.1991).

CRC/OTA, Registration Number 728, Kerynia, (Karavas, 78). Testimony A. Pagdatis (22.5.1991).

CRC/OTA, Registration Number 933, Kerynia, (Kerynia 111). Testimony K. Elissaiou (23.9.1991).

CRC/OTA, Registration Number 1243, Famagusta, (Rizokarpaso, 57). Testimony N. Lampi (30.10.1991).

CRC/OTA, Registration Number 1329, Kerynia, (Lapithos, 94). Testimony K. Gabriel (20.1.1991).

CRC/OTA, Registration Number 1333, Famagusta, (Yialousa, 22). Testimony P. Patriotis (15.1.1992).

CRC/OTA, Registration Number 1467, Famagusta, 11. Testimony A. Hadjigeorgiou (16.2.1992).

CRC/OTA, Registration Number 1568, Famagusta, (Akanthou, 17). Testimony P. Hadjipavlis (13.3.1992).

CRC/OTA, Registration Number 1627, Kerynia, (Kerynia 134). Testimony M. Economoy (21.3.1992).

CRC/OTA, Registration Number 2487, Famagusta, (Yialousa 35). Testimony A. Ch. Yiasemidou (28.1.1993).

CRC/OTA, Registration Number 2496, Kerynia, (Livera, 15). Testimony T. Mathaiou (3.2.1993).

CRC/OTA, Registration Number 2552, Kerynia (Agios Avrosios 38). Testimony V. and E. Hapeshi (8.2.1993).

CRC/OTA, Registration Number 2882, Famagusta, (Rizokarpaso 69). Testimony I. Hadjisolomou (unknown date).

CRC/OTA, Registration Number 3134, Famagusta 50. Testimony G. Kountounos (10.09.1993).

CRC/OTA, Registration Number 3136, Famagusta (Davlos, 16). Testimony Z. Hadjikyriakou and E. Hadjikyriakou (20.9.1993).

CRC/OTA, Registration Number 3137, Famagusta (Davlos, 17). Testimony M. Tziminis (24.9.1993).

Secondary literature

Acheson, M.J., 1981. Anthropology of Fishing. *Annual Review of Anthropology*, 10, 275-316.

Andreou, G.M., Opitz, R., Manning, S.W., Fisher, K.D., Sewell, D.A., Georgiou, A. and Urban, T., 2017. Integrated methods for understanding and monitoring the loss of coastal archaeological sites: The case of Tochni-Lakkia, south-central Cyprus. *Journal of Archaeological Science: Reports*, 12, 197-208.

Auriemma, R. and Solinas, E., 2009. Archaeological remains as sea level change markers: A review. *Quaternary International*, 206, 134-146.

Ayodeji, K., 2004. *Fishing Equipment and Methods in the Roman World*. Doctoral Thesis. Royal Holloway, University of London.

Bariche, M., 2012. *Field Identification Guide to the Living Marine Resources of the Eastern and Southern Mediterranean*. Rome: Food and Agriculture Organisation of the United Nations.

Bassett, F., 1885. *Legends and Superstitions of the Sea and of Sailors*. Chicago and New York: Belford, Clarke & Co.

Bekker-Nielsen, T., 2010. Fishing in the Roman World. *In*: T. Bekker-Nielsen and D. Bernal-Casasola, eds. *Ancient Nets and Fishing Gear. Proceedings of the International Workshop on "Nets and Fishing Gear in Classical Antiquity: A first approach" Cadiz, November 15-17, 2007*. Aarhus: Aarhus University Press, 187-204.

Bon, S., 1989. *Bone Bobbins from Fourth Century Cyprus*. Draft manuscript.

Broodbank, C., 2013. *The Making of the Middle Sea. A history of the Mediterranean from the Beginning to the Emergence of the Classical World*. London: Thames and Hudson.

Chavane, M.J., 1975. *Salamine de Chypre. VI: Les Petits Objets*. Paris: Diffusion de Boccard.

Brody, A.J., 2008. The Specialized Religions of Ancient Mediterranean Seafarers. *Religion Compass*, 2 (4), 444-454.

Childs, A.W., Smith, S.J. and Padgett, M., 2012. *City of Gold. The archaeology of Polis Chrysochous, Cyprus*. New Haven and London: Princeton University Press.

Christodoulou, S., 2018. Κεφάλαιο Στ' „Ρωμαϊκή Κύπρος". *In*: Σ. Νεοκλέους, ed. Ιστορία της Κύπρου. Τόμος Α': 11000 π.Χ.-649 μ.Χ. Αθήνα: Μέλαθρον Οικουμενικού Ελληνισμού: Συλλεκτική Έκδοση, 143-177.

Christou, D.,1998a. *Annual Report of the Department of Antiquities for the year 1992*. Nicosia: Antiquity Department Government Publications, Foundation Anastasios G. Leventis.

Christou, D., 1998b. *Annual Report of the Department of Antiquities for the year 1993*. Nicosia: Antiquity Department Government Publications, Foundation Anastasios G. Leventis.

Christou, D., 2013. Ανασκαφές του Κουρίου, 1975-1998. Τόμος Α'. Λευκωσία: Department of Antiquities, Cyprus.

Coll, M., Piroddi, C., Steenbeek, J., Kaschner, K., Lasram, F., Aguzzi, J., Ballesteros, E., Bianchi, C.N., Corbera, J., Dailianis, T., Danovaro, R., Estrada, M., Froglia, C., Galil, B.S., Gasol, J.M., Gertwagen, R., Gil, J., Guilhaumon, F., Kesner-Reyes, K., Kitsos, M.-S., Koukouras, A., Lampadariou, N., Laxamana, E., López-Fé de la Cuadra, C.M., Lotze, H.K., Daniel, M., Mouillot, D., Oro, D., Raicevich, S., Rius-Barile, J., Ignacio Saiz-Salinas, J., San Vicente, C., Somot, S., Templado, J., Turon, X., Vafidis, D., Villanueva, R. and Voultsiadou, E., 2000. The Biodiversity of the Mediterranean Sea: Estimates, Patterns, and Threats. *PLoS ONE*, 5 (8): e11842. Available from: doi:10.1371/journal.pone.0011842 [Accessed: 15 June 2020].

Davis, D.L., 2009. *Commercial Navigation in the Greek and Roman World*. Doctoral Thesis. University of Texas at Austin.

Demetropoulos, A. and Hadjichristoforou, M., 2017. Η θαλάσσια ζωή της Κύπρου – Κατάσταση και προοπτικές. *In*: Κ. Δημητριάδης, Α. Κλ.Σοφοκλέους, and Π. Αργυρίδης, eds. Γεωγραφία της Κύπρου. Λευκωσία: Γεωγραφικός Όμιλος Κύπρου, 431-450.

Department of Fisheries and Marine Research, Cyprus, 2009. Επαγγελματικές μέθοδοι αλιείας της Κύπρου. Λευκωσία: Γραφείο Τύπου και Πληροφοριών.

Desse, J., 1993. "Les vestiges osseux du basin 417" in J.-F. Salles and O. Callot "Chapitre IV: Le Chantier Sud". *In*: J.-F. Salles, ed. *Kition-Bamboula IV: Les Niveaux Hellénistiques*. Paris: Editions Recherche sur les Civilisations, 103-105.

Dikaios, P., 1961. *The Stone Age in Cyprus. Volume IV. 1A*. Lund: The Swedish Cyprus Expedition.

Duncan, B., 2011. "What do you want to catch?": Exploring the Maritime Cultural Landscapes of the Queenscliff Fishing Community. *In*: B. Ford, ed. *The Archaeology of Maritime Landscapes*. New York: Springer, 267-289.

Du Plat Taylor, J., 1980. Excavations at Ayios Philon, the ancient Carpasia. Part I: The Classical to Roman periods. *Report of the Department of Antiquities, Cyprus,* 152-216.

Egoumenidou, E. and Michaelides, D., 2000. Gathering, hunting, fishing. The procurement of food from the non-domesticated animal kingdom in Cyprus through the ages. *In*: P. Lysaght, ed. *Food from Nature. Attitudes, Strategies and Culinary Practices. Proceedings of the 12th conference of the International Commission for Ethnological Food Research, Umea and Frostviken, Sweden, 8-14 June 1998*. Uppsala: The Royal Gustavus Adolphus Academy for Swedish Folk Culture, 111-120.

Evelpidou, N. and Karkani, A., 2018. Archaeology and Sea-Level change. *In*: C.W. Finkl and C. Makowski, eds. *Encyclopedia of Coastal Science*. Cham: Springer International Publishing AG, 1-7.

Farrugio, H., Oliver, P. and Biagi, F., 1993. An overview of the history, knowledge, recent and future research trends in Mediterranean fisheries. *Scientia marina*, 57 (2-3), 105-119.

Ford, B., 2011. Introduction. *In*: B. Ford, ed. *The Archaeology of Maritime Landscapes*. New York: Springer, 1-9.

Ford, B., 2014. Coastal Archaeology. *In*: A. Catsambis, B. Ford and D.I. Hamilton, eds. *The Oxford Handbook of Maritime Archaeology*. Oxford: Oxford University Press, 763-785.

Froese, R. and D. Pauly, eds., 2019. *FishBase*. World Wide Web electronic publication [online]. Available from: www.fishbase.org [version 12/2019].

Frost, H., 1985. Appendice 2: Fishing Tackle: Three Limestone Weights. *In*: M. Yon and A. Caubet, eds. *Kition-Bamboula 3. Le Sondage L-N 13 (Bronze récent et géométrique I)*. Paris: ʃEtudes et Recherche sur les Civilisations, 169-171.

Golani, D., Öztürk, B. and Başusta, N., 2006. *Fishes of the Eastern Mediterranean.* Istanbul: Turkish Marine Research Foundation.

Goodchild, R.G., 1953. The Roman and Byzantine limes in Cyrenaica. *Journal of Roman Studies*, 43, 65-76.

Goroncharovskiy, A.V., 2017. Anogyra-Vlou Archaeological Survey (2008) and Excavation preliminary report (2009-2012). *Report of the Department of Antiquities, Cyprus*, 687-716.

Hadjioannou, K., 1980. Η Αρχαία Κύπρος εις τας Ελληνικάς Πηγάς. Τόμος Δ'-Μέρος Α': Συμπληρώματα εκ των ελληνικών επιγραφών και των λατινικών κειμένων. Λευκωσία: Εκδόσις Ιεράς Αρχιεπισκοπής Κύπρου.

Horden, P. and Purcell, N., 2000. *The Corrupting Sea. A study of Mediterranean History.* Oxford: Blackwell Publications.

Hunt, D., 1982. The Roman period 30 B.C.-A.D. 330. *In*: D. Hunt, ed. *Footprints in Cyprus. An illustrated history*. London: Trigraph, 120-131.

Ioannou, G. and Michaelides, N., 2015. Τα 100 σημαντικότερα είδη ψαριών των κυπριακών θαλασσών. Λευκωσία: Γραφείο Τύπου και Πληροφοριών για το Τμήμα Αλιείας και Θαλάσσιων Ερευνών.

Ionas, I., 2001. Παραδοσιακά Επαγγέλματα της Κύπρου. Nicosia: Center for Scientific Research.

Karageorghis, V., 1989. Chronique des fouilles et decouvertes archeologiques a Chypre en 1988. *Bulletin de Correspondance Hellenique*, 113 (2), 789-853.

Knapp, B., 2018. *Seafaring and Seafarers in the Bronze Age Eastern Mediterannean.* Sidestone Press. Available from: https://www.sidestone.com/books/seafaring-and-seafarers-in-the-bronze-age-eastern-mediterranean [Accessed 01 October 2018].

Lytle, E., 2016. Status beyond law: ownership, access and the ancient Mediterranean. *In*: T. Bekker-Nielsen and R. Gertwagen, eds. *The Inland Seas. Towards an Ecohistory of the Mediterranean and the Black Sea.* Stuttgart: Franz Steiner Verlag, 107-136.

Marzano, A., 2013. *Harvesting the Sea. The Explotation of Marine Resources in the Roman Mediterranean.* Oxford: Oxford University Press.

Marzano, A., 2020. A Story of Land and Water. Control, Capital, and Investment in Large-Scale Fishing and Fish-Salting Operations. *In*: P. Erdkamp, K. Verboven and A. Zuiderhoek, eds. *Capital, Investment, and Innovation in the Roman World.* Oxford: Oxford University Press, 275-306.

McCann, A.M., 1987. The Lagoon Temple. *In*: A.M. McCann, J. Bourgeois, E.K. Gazda, J.P. Oleson and E.L. Will., eds. *The Roman Port and Fishery of Cosa: A Center of Ancient Trade.* Princeton, NJ: Princeton University Press, 129-136.

McNiven, I.J., 2003. Saltwater People: Spiritscapes, Maritime Rituals and the Archaeology of Australian Indigenous Seascapes. *World Archaeology*, 35 (3), 329-349.

Megaw, A.H., 2007. *Kourion. Excavations in the Episcopal Precinct.* Washington: Dumbarton Oaks Research Library and Collection.

Michael, M.M., 2016. Reconstructing the Maritime Cultural Landscape: the case study of coastal landscape of Larnaca on the island of Cyprus in the Late Bronze Age. *In*: R. Castillo Belinchón, A. Ramírez Pernía and L.Á. Torres Sobrino, eds. *Proceedings of the 5th International Congress on Underwater Archaeology. A heritage for mankind, Cartagena, October 15th-18th, 2014.* Cartagena: Ministerion de Educación, Cultura Y Deporte, 479-495.

Michael, M., 2018a. The Hellenistic metallic artefacts found in Amathus harbour. *In*: J.-Y. Empereur, ed. *The Hellenistic Harbour of Amathus. Underwater Excavations, 1984-1986. Volume 2. Artefacts found during excavations.* Athens: EFDA, 79-118.

Michael, M., 2018b. The Late Roman metallic artefacts found in Amathus harbour. *In*: J.-Y. Empereur, ed. *The Hellenistic Harbour of Amathus. Underwater Excavations, 1984-1986. Volume 2. Artefacts found during excavations.* Athens: EFDA, 191-196.

Michael, M.M., 2020. Who is fishing and how?: The case study of fishing communities in Cyprus through time. *In*: M. Michael and B. Holtzman, eds. *Maritime Archaeology Graduate Symposium 2019, 29th-31st March 2019, Short Reports Series*. Available from: doi:10.33583/mags2019.05

Michaelides, D., 1996. The economy of Cyprus during the Hellenistic and Roman periods. *In*: V. Karageorghis and D. Michaelides, eds. *The Development of the Cypriot Economy from the Prehistoric Period to the Present day*. Nicosia: Lithographica, 139-152.

Michaelides, D., 1998. Food in ancient Cyprus. *In*: P. Lysaght, ed. *Food and the Traveller. Migration, Immigration, Tourism and Ethnic Food. Proceedings of the 11th Conference of the International Commission for Ethnological Food Research, Cyprus, June 8-14 1996*. Nicosia: Intercollege Press, 22-43.

Monteagudo, L.G., 2010. Nets and Fishing Gear in Roman Mosaics from Spain. *In*: T. Bekker-Nielsen and D. Bernal-Casasola, eds. *Ancient Nets and Fishing Gear. Proceedings of the International Workshop on "Nets and Fishing Gear in Classical Antiquity: A first approach" Cadiz, November 15-17, 2007*. Aarhus: Aarhus University Press, 161-186.

Morales-Muñiz, A., 2010. Inferences about Prehistoric Fishing Gear based on Archaeological Fish Assemblages. *In*: T. Bekker-Nielsen and D.B. Casasola, eds. *Ancient Nets and Fishing Gear. Proceedings of the International Workshop on "Nets and Fishing Gear in Classical Antiquity: A first approach", Cádiz, November 15-17, 2007*. Aarhus: Aarhus University Press, 25-53.

Morhange, C. and Marriner, N., 2015. Chapter 9: Archaeological and biological relative sea-level indicators. *In*: I. Shennan, A. J. Long and B.P. Horton, eds. *Handbook of Sea-level Research*. Hoboken, NJ: John Wiley & Sons, Ltd., 146-156.

Morton, J., 2001. *The role of the physical environment in ancient Greek seafaring*. Leiden, Boston, Köln: Brill.

Mylona, D., 2008. *Fish-Eating in Greece from the fifth century B.C. to the seventh century A.D. A story of impoverished fishermen or luxurious fish banquets?* BAR International Series 1754. Oxford: British Archaeological Reports Oxford Ltd.

Nédélec, C. and Prado, J., 1990. *Definition and Classification of fishing gear categories*. FAO Fisheries Technical Paper 222.1. Rome: Food and Agriculture Organisation of the United Nations.

Neilson, H.R., 2002. A Terracotta Phallus from Pisa Ship E: More Evidence for the Priapus Deity as Protector of Greek and Roman Navigators. *The International Journal of Nautical Archaeology*, 31 (2), 248-253.

Nicolaou, K., 1967. Excavations at Nea Paphos. The house of Dionysos. Outline of the Campaigns 1964-1965. *Report of the Department of Antiquities, Cyprus*, 100-125.

Nicolaou, K. and Flinder, A., 1976. Ancient fish-tanks, Cyprus. *The International Journal of Nautical Archaeology and Underwater Exploration*, 5 (2), 133-141.

Obied, C.T., 2016. *Rethinking Roman Perceptions of Coastal Landscapes: A case- study of the Levant*. Doctoral Thesis. University of Southampton.

Papademtriou, E., 1999. *Cyprus Folk Art. The Cyprus Folk Art Museum – Society of Cypriot Studies*. Nicosia: Cultural Centre of the Popular Bank.

Panayides, P., 2018. Κεφάλαιο Ζ': Βυζαντινή Κύπρος I: Ύστερη Αρχαιότητα και Πρώιμη Βυζαντινή περίοδος. *In*: Σ. Νεοκλέους, ed. Ιστορία της Κύπρου. Τόμος Α': 11000 π.Χ.-649 μ.Χ. Αθήνα: Μέλαθρον Οικουμενικού Ελληνισμού: Συλλεκτική Έκδοση, 179-242.

Parker, A.J., 2001. Maritime Landscapes. *Landscapes*, 2 (1), 22-41.

Quilici Gigli, S., 1971. Prima perlustrazione topografica. *In*: Istituto per gli Studi Micenei ed Egeo-Anatolici, ed. *Studi Ciprioti E Rapporti di Scavo, Consiglio Nazionale delle Ricerche Istituto per gli Studi Micenei ed Egeo-Anatolici*. Rome: Istituto per gli studi micenei ed egeo-anatolici, 13-34.

Rautman, M. L., 2000. The busy countryside of Late Roman Cyprus. *Report of the Department of Antiquities of Cyprus*, 317-331.

Reese, D.S., 2002. Fish Evidence from Specimens, Mosaics, Wall Paintings, and Roman Authors. *In*: W. Jashemski and F. Meyer, eds. *The Natural History of Pompeii*. Cambridge: Cambridge University Press, 274-291.

Rose, M.J., 1994. *With Line and Glittering Bronze Hook: Fishing in the Aegean Bronze Age*. Doctoral Thesis. Indiana University.

Runciman, S., 1982. The Byzantine Period A.D. 330-1191. *In*: D. Hunt, ed. *Footprints in Cyprus. An illustrated history*. London: Trigraph, 134-162.

Salles, J-F. and Chavane, M.-J., 1993. Chapter XIV: Les petits objects. In: J-F. Salles, ed. *Kition – Bamboula IV: Les Niveaux Hellenistiques*. Paris: Editions Recherche sur les Civilisations, 81-346.

Semple, E.C., 1927. The Templed Promontories of the Ancient Mediterranean. *The Geographical Review*, 17 (3), 353-386.

Soren, D. and James, J., 1988. *Kourion. The search for a lost Roman City*. New York: Anchor Press.

Trakadas, A., 2005. The Archaeological Evidence for Fish Processing in the Western Mediterranean. *In*: T. Bekker-Nielsen, ed. *Ancient Fishing and Fish Processing in the Black Sea. Proceedings of an interdisciplinary workshop on marine resources and trade in fish products in the Black Sea region in antiquity, University of Southern Denmark, Esbjerg, April 4-5, 2003*. Aarhus: Aarhus University Press, 47-82.

Trakadas, A., 2006. "Exhausted by Fishermen's Nets". Roman Sea Fisheries and their Management. *Journal of Mediterranean Studies*, 16 (1/2), 259-272.

Van Neer, W., Zohar, I. and Lernau, O., 2005. The emergence of fishing communities in the Eastern Mediterranean región: A survey of evidence from Pre- and Protohistoric periods. *Paléorient*, 31 (1), 131-157.

Von Bradt, A., 1964. *Fish Catching Methods of the World*. London: Fishing News (Books).

Westerdahl, C., 1992. The maritime cultural landscape. *International Journal of Nautical Archaeology*, 21 (1), 5-14.

Westerdahl, C., 2007. Fish and ships: towards a theory of maritime culture. *Deutsches Schiffahrtsarchiv*, 30, 191-236.

Westerdahl, C., 2011a. The Maritime Cultural Landscape. *In*: A. Catsambis, B. Ford and D.L. Hamilton, eds. *The Oxford Handbook of Maritime Archaeology*. Oxford: Oxford University Press, 733-762.

Westerdahl, C., 2011b. Conclusion: The Maritime Cultural Landscape Revisited. *In*: B. Ford, ed. *The Archaeology of Maritime Landscapes*. New York: Springer, 331-344.

Wilson, J., 1990. Fishing Knowledge. *Land Economies*, 66 (1), 12-29.

Sea storms and aristocratic identity in Alcaeus

Ippokratis Kantzios

Abstract

In his nautical poems, Alcaeus displays enhanced awareness of the figurative possibilities of the sea by incorporating it into his larger political themes. Although the civic meaning of Alcaeus' sea storms has been questioned, the presence in them of the same sociolect that characterises his exhortations for the overthrow of the tyranny strongly suggests that these storms are political. In fr. 208, the ship of state/*hetaireia* is relentlessly assaulted by waves rolling from all directions, but the language used mainly seems to refer to the turbulence in Mytilene. Similarly, in fr. 6, the ship endures the raw forces of the agitated sea, but the text is coloured by aristocratic didacticism which highlights the crew's ancient pedigrees of nobility and their duty of resilience in the face of a destructive enemy. The replacement of urgently needed practical advice with a discourse in which the crew/*hetairoi* are presented as part of a long aristocratic tradition that must be honoured and perpetuated again points towards the metaphorical nature of Alcaeus' storms. The islander audience – intimately familiar with maritime life – must have had no difficulty in recognising the lack of realism in these poems and thus their allusiveness to the political troubles of Mytilene.

Alcaeus, Mytilene, sea storms, aristocratic identity

In many ways, Alcaeus' nautical discourse is conventional, in the sense that he follows his poetic predecessors in perceiving the sea as a place of adventure, danger and death. Homer uses sea imagery not only to convey its potential for terrifying sailors with its immensity and raw power (*e.g. Od.* 5.291-332, 9.67-81), but also to create psychological landscapes that express the pathos, loneliness and despair of his characters.[1] Archilochus uses similar imagery: in fact, he seems to develop it further into full-fledged allegories, as in fr. 105 W, in which he depicts the agitated sea and the threatening clouds as figures for the fear of war.[2] Alcaeus follows the same steps, but with enhanced awareness of the figurative possibilities of the sea, as he integrates them into his narrative of the declining fortunes of the aristocracy in early-sixth-century Mytilene. By endowing his nautical metaphors with civic meaning, the poet assimilates them into his larger political discourse, centred on the overthrow of the tyranny and the reestablishment of his *hetaireia* in its privileged place. The political nuances of Alcaeus' sea storms have been recognised in modern scholarship, although often as a means to adduce or corroborate later biographical and historical information.[3] In this paper, I will discuss the sea storms by drawing attention to their ethopoietic function and their contribution to the demarcation of the ideological parameters of the poet's elite group. By incorporating into his sea storms certain fundamental aristocratic precepts, the poet offers his listeners an occasion to reflect upon their past and act accordingly in the present, just as he does in the explicitly political poems. The calls to action in a nautical setting may, in fact, have been inspired by the political situation in Alcaeus' insular city, a situation as shifting and unpredictable as the sea itself.

The notion that Alcaeus' sea storms fall within his larger civic discourse can be seen by the presence of the same sociolect that characterises his core political poems, for instance, fr. 140, which was probably performed in exile.[4] Here Alcaeus transforms the great hall into an idealised space that exudes the military valour of his *hetaireia*. The epic-sounding weapons on the wall, mentioned in detail and with affection, although not ancient,[5] direct to an earlier, more prosperous age and inevitably force a juxtaposition between a glorious past and a degraded present under tyranny. Through the vividness (ἐνάργεια) of his words, the poet enables his listeners to see the banquet hall with the eyes of their imagination (φαντασία),[6] stating with confidence that it is simply impossible to forget it, and underlining this impossibility by setting the whole poem in vivid historical present. The weapons – symbols of the cause – have now been engraved on the minds of his listeners in perpetuity, shaping and articulating their vision and ambitions.

Fr. 140, with its focus on the aristocratic banquet hall, a place epitomising stability and continuity on *terra firma*, paradoxically finds its counterpart in the sea storm poems, because they, too, are preoccupied with similar concerns, although now amidst the ferocity of the elements and the ever-present danger of death. In fr.

---

1   In *Il.* 1.350, Achilles, sitting at the shore (θῖν' ἔφ' ἁλὸς πολιῆς), gazes at the sea (ὁρόων ἐπὶ οἴνοπα [or probably ἐπ' ἀπείρονα, Aristarchus] πόντον) in a way that intensifies the anguish of the previous verse. In *Od.* 5.13-7, at Calypso's island, Odysseus looks at the open ocean (εὐρέα νῶτα θαλάσσης) contemplating his isolation. See also *Il.* 1.327, 9.182, 23.59, *Od.* 5.312. For the ominous aspects of the sea, cf. *Il.* 2.144-6, 208-10 and 2.394-7, in which the army's thunderous shout is compared to the roar of waves that crash on a steep cliff.

2   Heraclitus (*Alleg. Hom.* 5) thinks that here the poet speaks metaphorically: τὸν πόλεμον εἰκάζει θαλαττίῳ κλύδωνι ("He likens the war to a sea storm"). For the allegorical nature of fr. 105 W, Strauss Clay 1982, 201-4. For the sinister side of the sea in Archilochus, cf. also frr. 13.3-4, 24.12 W.

3   For the correspondence between the particulars of the sea storms and specific historical events, cf. Gentili 1988, 199: "If allegory is an extended metaphor – or metaphorical narrative – it is obvious that every element must convey a piece of information; and comprehensibility is a prerequisite for credibility within the circle of *hetairoi*." Thus, fr. 6 has been taken as indicating: Alcaeus' advice to his companions not to allow Myrsilus to become tyrant of Mytilene; his warnings about the difficulty of removing the tyrant once in power; or his exilic experiences. For the various views, see Liberman 1999, 204-5.

4   Marzullo 2009, 149-52; Kantzios 2019, 326-8.

5   Kantzios 2019, 328.

6   Ekphrastic descriptions, especially in the Greco-Roman era, were favoured by orators because they facilitated persuasion, cf. Webb 2009, 39-60; hence Heraclitus' admiration for Alcaeus' ability to recreate the sea storms with great naturalism (τίς οὐκ ἂν εὐθύς...νομίσειε;).

208, the ship of state/*hetaireia*[7] is relentlessly assaulted by waves rolling from this side and that, but the vocabulary used also seems to allude to the political turbulence in Mytilene. In fr. 6, the ship endures the savage forces of the agitated sea, but, again, the poem is coloured by aristocratic didacticism. Heraclitus – a grammarian of the first century CE – notices the double register of these poems and warns the reader not to take them literally, but rather as allegories for the dangers caused by the tyranny:

τίς οὐκ ἂν εὐθὺς ἐκ τῆς προτρεχούσης περὶ τὸν πόντον εἰκασίας ἀνδρῶν πλωιζομένων θαλάττιον εἶναι νομίσειε φόβον; ἀλλ᾽ οὐχ οὕτως ἔχει· Μύρσιλος γὰρ ὁ δηλούμενός ἐστι καὶ τυραννικὴ κατὰ Μυτιληναίων ἐγειρομένη σύστασις.

Who would not suppose right away from the previous depiction of the sea that this is its fear by those sailing? But this is not so. For it is Myrsilus who is signified and tyrannical conspiracy being prepared against the Mytileneans.

Heraclit. *Alleg. Hom.* 5 (vis-à-vis fr. 208)

Modern scholarship has followed this interpretation, although not without exceptions. William Slater – for instance – rejects the political nature of Alcaeus' sea storms, understanding them instead as references to sympotic practices, especially in their association with Dionysus at sea.[8] A different type of scepticism has been expressed recently by Anna Uhlig.[9] Her discussion is inspired by a theoretical approach known as "surface reading," according to which we should avoid construing elements in a text as symbolic of something concealed. "One can resist this type of treasure-hunt by privileging those features that can be discerned at the surface of the text and by adopting an interpretative disposition that situates symbolic meaning along, rather than against, the grain of the text."[10] According to Uhlig, the sea storms in Alcaeus are just that: sea storms, the description of which creates (I assume) a cathartic pleasure to his islander audience located now in the comfort of the banquet hall.

The notion that the sea was a quintessential part of the lives of Alcaeus' listeners can be taken for granted.[11] The citizen-sailors of Mytilene were intimately familiar with both the technical details of seamanship and the hardships of maritime life, and would doubtless have enjoyed listening to songs about their adventures on the open water. However, it is precisely their familiarity with the sea that gives force to the metaphorical argument, as they would have been able to recognise the lack of realism in some of these poems. Let us illustrate this point by discussing fr. 6:

τόδ᾽ αὖτε κῦμα τὼ προτέρω ᾽νέμω

στείχει, παρέξει δ᾽ ἄμμι πόνον πόλυν

ἄντλην, ἐπεί κε νᾶος ἔμβαι

]. ὀμεθ᾽ ἐ[4

]..[..].[

---

7   Alcaeus understands "state" and "*hetaireia*" as tightly intertwined.
8   Slater 1976, 161-70. For earlier scholars reluctant to accept the allegorical character of Alcaeus' sea storms, see Page 1955, 182.
9   Uhlig 2018, 63-92.
10   *Ibid.* 82.
11   In Alcaeus' corpus there are at least 22 fragments that mention the sea. In fr. 296b, the speaker mentions exile, sailing into a dangerous storm and perhaps death at the bottom of the sea. Text uncertain: ἐ]ξέφυγον πολλ . [/ ν . ν. [ἀ]νεμωλ[/]ας[.]δος[.]ς πυθμ[εν ("I went into exile... much... wind...bottom [of the sea?]"). It would be unreasonable to suggest that every nautical poem is an allegory: a sailor's life is more complex than his political activities. Frr. 34 A and 249, *e.g.* flow naturally without resorting to metaphorical meaning. For the need of internal evidence, see Wilamowitz (cited by Uhlig 2018, 73).

[   ]

φαρξώμεθ' ὠς ὤκιστα [

ἐς δ' ἔχυρον λίμενα δρό[μωμεν,   8

καὶ μή τιν' ὄκνος μόλθ[ακος

λάβη· πρόδηλον γὰρ· μέγ[

μνάσθητε τῶν πάροιθε ν[

νῦν τις ἄνηρ δόκιμος γε[νέσθω.   12

καὶ μὴ καταισχύνωμεν [

ἔσλοις τόκηας γᾶς ὔπα κε[ιμένοις·

...

ἔοντε[ς ἔσθλοι] κὰπ πατέρων μάθος   17

τῶν σφ[ῶν ὁ δ'] ἄμμος θῦμ[ος¹²

...

μοναρχίαν δ . [

μ]ηδὲ δεκωμ[¹³   28

This wave again comes like the previous one

and will give us much toil to bale out

when it enters the ship's...   3

Let us secure the ... as soon as possible

and let us run into a safe harbour.   8

And let soft fear not seize

anyone. For it is obvious: ...

Remember our previous...

Now let every man be steadfast.   12

And let us not shame

our brave fathers, lying under the earth...

Being brave, their learning (came)   17

from their own fathers, and our courage...¹⁴

tyranny...   28

nor let us accept...

12   Lines 17-8 appear as reconstructed by Ferrari and Pontani 1996: 1-4.
13   For Alcaeus, enumeration and text (except fr. 6.17-8) by Voigt 1971. All translations are mine.
14   For ἄμμος θῦμος, 18, I follow Rösler 1980, 133 n.55 *'unser Mut.'*

Although the mutilated text depicts only one aspect of the storm – its dangerous waves – we may easily complete the picture, taking hints from fr. 208, by also imagining the howl of the gale, sickening instability of the vessel, disorder, screams, rain and wind slapping the faces of the crew, cargo dislocated and tossed around, sails torn. In such circumstances, Alcaeus' sailor-listeners know what the captain's words to the crew would have been: "Hang in there, young men! Do the things you must! Slacken and you are dead!" This is not a moment for grand statements of aristocratic pride, but for staying alive by keeping the ship afloat. Instead, the poet delivers exhortations loaded with explicit political meaning, exhortations totally improbable under the circumstances. And yet, Uhlig, a supporter of "surface reading," namely a reading that looks for realism in the text, finds nothing strange here: "There is nothing unusual in calling on young men to uphold the honour of those who have preceded them."[15] True, but not when one is drowning. The absence of urgently needed practical advice and the creation of a diachronic setting in which the *hetairoi* become part of an intergenerational sequence are indicative, I think, of the figurative nature of these storms.[16] The temporally comprehensive view of the crew elucidates the importance of being a δόκιμος ἀνήρ, 12 ("steadfast man"), a quality which Alcaeus envisions for every man on the ship. The term stems from δοκέω and δέκομαι[17] and is associated with acceptance, approbation and successful trial by the community, all of which are of paramount significance in a shame culture. However, in an archaic aristocratic milieu, acceptance only comes when one's conduct conforms to the standards of the past, namely when it follows the practices of the ἐσθλοί τόκηες (14). Emulation and transmission of ancestral excellence presuppose that it must be learned, and Alcaeus points this out in lines 17-8, as the convincing reconstruction by Franco Ferrari and Filippomaris Pontani suggests. This emphasis on μάθος follows in the steps of the *Iliad*: Hector – for instance – confides to Andromache that he "*learned to be brave... winning great glory for his father and himself*" (μάθον ἔμμεναι ἐσθλός / ...ἀρνύμενος πατρός τε μέγα κλέος ἠδ' ἐμὸν αὐτοῦ, 6.444-6), while some lines later he expresses his hope that his son will also distinguish himself and prove even better than his father in battle (πατρός γ' ὅδε πολλὸν ἀμείνων, 6.476-80). Like the great heroes of Troy, who show reverence to their ancestors by proving equal or superior to them, so do Alcaeus' men model themselves after their own forefathers and do not shame them through ἀνανδρία ("unmanliness").[18] μάθος ensures not only effective transmission of ἀρετή, but also proper honour for the past generations.

Learning, however, is meaningless unless it is retained, hence underlining the importance of memory. The correlation between the two is such that in the *Iliad*, (learned) military ἀρετή is a content of μνημοσύνη, and the warrior's performance in battle depends on his degree of recollection of the former.[19] Homer contains a whole array of memory-based phrases that indicate the fusion of the two concepts, but the poets of martial exhortation, are also aware of their connection and its effects on fighting. In fr. 6, the direct object of μνάσθητε (11) has not survived, but it must have referred to some praiseworthy deed that could function as an inspiration in the current difficult situation.[20] It is the remembrance of that event that will reignite the resolution of the companions to resist the forces of the sea storm, in this case, the

15 Uhlig 2018, 88.
16 Cf. Page 1955, 185 on lines 9-14: "For the sailor labouring in a storm, when death appears imminent, the warning against 'hesitation' and the appeal 'not to disgrace ancestors' are inept."
17 Beekes 2010, 1: 345. δοκιμάζω ("to try," "approve") and δοκιμασία ("test") are denominatives. For δόκιμος in a military sense (*i.e.* μάχιμος), Frisk 1960, 1: 405.
18 For αἰδώς as a motivator for ἀνδρεία, cf. Martin 1989, 14. In the exhortation of *Il.* 15.561-3, Ajax employs the term three times in just three lines. In Alcaeus, shame culture is revealed mostly through the frequent use of αισχ- derivatives: καταισχύνωμεν, 6.13; αἶσχος, 117b.31, 75.5; ὠναίσχυντος, 68.5; αἴσχυν, 298.1. See also αἴδετ[, 306h.2 and αἴδως, 331.
19 Collins 1998, 78-125; Bakker 2002, 70.
20 In line 11: perhaps "Remember our previous (hardships or words)?" Either of Hunt's supplements μόχθων, μύθων would be appropriate here. The ν at the end of the line in Voigt's text may be a μ.

tyranny of Myrsilus, as suggested by the presence of his name in the margin of the page.[21] Indeed, just as in Homer, memory turns the events of the past into an actual experience in the present,[22] so in fr. 6 recollection of prior achievements summons the courage of the forebears and becomes a means to save the ship/state in its present moment of crisis. Here Alcaeus assumes an authoritative role,[23] as his words embody the essential values of his aristocratic *hetaireia* and instil in its members a sense of civic ethics that demands that they address the current challenges properly (μοναρχίαν δ . [/ μ]ηδὲ δεκωμ[, 26-7), having learned from their ἐσθλοί ancestors.

In fr. 6, then, the sea storm provides an occasion for the crew to display, even under duress, their virtues, which, *mutatis mutandis*, at a political level could be equated to perseverance, loyalty and tactical savvy. In another nautical fragment, 208, the poet's exhortations are conveyed more obliquely (no imperatives or hortatory forms), but again their allusions to the public arena of Mytilene are discernible:

ἀσυν<ν>έτημμι τῶν ἀνέμων στάσιν,

τὸ μὲν γὰρ ἔνθεν κῦμα κυλίνδεται,

τὸ δ' ἔνθεν, ἄμμες δ᾽ ὂν τὸ μέσσον

νᾶϊ φορήμεθα σὺν μελαίναι 4

χείμωνι μόχθεντες μεγάλωι μάλα·

πὲρ μὲν γὰρ ἄντλος ἰστοπέδαν ἔχει,

λαῖφος δὲ πὰν ζάδηλον ἤδη,

καὶ λάκιδες μέγαλαι κὰτ αῦτο, 8

χάλαισι δ' ἄγκυραι, <τὰ δ᾽ ὀήϊα>

[   ]

. [. . .] . [–   ]

τοι πόδες ἀμφότεροι μένο[12

ἐ<ν> βιμβλίδεσσι· τοῦτό με καὶ σ[άοι

μόνον· τὰ δ᾽ ἄχματ᾽ ἐκπεπ[.] . άχμενα

I do not understand the direction of the winds:

one wave is rolling in from this side

another from that, and we in the middle

are carried along with the black ship 4

much toiling in the great storm.

The bilge-water swallows up the masthold

And the entire sail is already tattered

and there are large holes in it. 8

The anchors are slackening, <and the rudders>

[   ]

21   See Voigt 1971: 181.
22   Bakker 1997: 16; 2002: 67-73.
23   Kantzios 2019: 325.

both feet remain... (entangled in)   12

[   ]

the ropes. It is this alone that saves me.

The cargo (shifts... above)...

At first sight, the poem depicts the terrifying experience of men who battle the elemental forces of a sea storm while their lives are hanging by a thread. And yet the poem is more than just a realistic depiction of a frightful event. Indeed, even apart from Heraclitus' explicit note about the poem's allegorical character, there are elements in the text that lead us in that direction.

The first such element is the term στάσις, a *double entendre* meaning "direction" (here "of winds") but also "civil war" or "strife" (fr. 130b.11). The verb ἀσυν<ν>έτημμι, 1 ("I do not understand") suggests that στάσις should be rather taken in its political sense, for otherwise the whole statement is a platitude: sea storms never come upon a ship in an orderly fashion but are always confusing and overpowering, not allowing the sailors the luxury of being analytical.[24] On the other hand, the confounding political landscape of Mytilene offers Alcaeus many an occasion to "not understand" it, the most important being Pittacus' betrayal of the poet's *hetaireia*. Such a betrayal turns Alcaeus' world upside down. Trustworthiness and loyalty, two fundamental values of the aristocratic groups throughout their history,[25] now receive a grievous blow as Pittacus abandons his companions to join the tyrants, blurring on the way the distinction between φιλία and ἐχθρότης, nobility and baseness. However, in addition to Pittacus' perfidy, there are other instances that baffle the poet, such as the discord among the various aristocratic clans, cf. λύας and ἐμφύλω μάχας (fr. 70.10-11), signifying internal strife and infighting. The speaker is frustrated at the inability of his fellow aristocrats to recognise that such behaviour is detrimental to their goals, as it makes their political restitution doubtful and helps Pittacus solidify his power.[26] ἀσυν<ν>έτημμι τὼν ἀνέμων στάσιν seems to be an expression of the poet's aporia about the incomprehensibility of the political winds of Mytilene rather than those of the open sea.

The second element that suggests the figurative nature of fr. 208 appears more discreetly in line 12. In the midst of the violent storm, the speaker highlights that the crew's salvation depends on their resolution – in this case, on whether they succeed in keeping both of their feet, entangled in the ropes, on the deck (πόδες ἀμφότεροι μένοισιν). This firmness of the πόδες on the ship's deck (the nautical equivalent to the ground) brings to mind martial exhortations, especially Tyrtaeus, frr. 10.31-2 and 11.21-2 W, in which the poet admonishes the aristocratic warrior to remain steadfast in battle by planting his feet on the earth (ἀλλά τις εὖ διαβὰς μενέτω ποσὶν ἀμφοτέροισι / στηριχθεὶς ἐπὶ γῆς). But there is more nuance here, since it is difficult for Alcaeus' audience to hear about feet without thinking of Pittacus' own: his perjury and political betrayal were depicted in a memorable

---

24 For the confusing nature of winds during sea storms, see, *e.g.*: *Il.* 2.396-7: τὸν δ' οὔ ποτε κύματα λείπει / παντοίων ἀνέμων, ὅτ' ἂν ἔνθ' ἢ ἔνθα γένωνται ("[A high cliff] which the waves of all sorts of winds never leave alone, when they come from this direction or that"); *Od.* 5. 295-6: σὺν δ' Εὖρός τε Νότος τ' ἔπεσον Ζέφυρός τε δυσαὴς / καὶ Βορέης αἰθρηγενέτης, μέγα κῦμα κυλίνδων ("Together the East Wind and the South Wind fell upon him, and the stormy West Wind and the North Wind, born in the clear sky, rolling a great wave"); *Od.* 5.304-5: ἐτάραξε δὲ πόντον, ἐπισπέρχουσι δ' ἄελλαι / παντοίων ἀνέμων ("And he has stirred up the sea, and the blasts of every kind of wind rage furiously").

25 Cf., *e.g.* the persistent motif of πιστὸς φίλος ἑταῖρος in the *Theognidea* or even Hipponax's fantasising of a gruesome death for a disloyal *hetairos*, fr. 115 W.

26 ἐκ δὲ χόλω τῶδε λαθοίμεθ . . [/ χαλάσσομεν δὲ τὰς θυμοβόρω λύας / ἐμφύλω τε μάχας, τάν τις Ὀλυμπίων / ἔνωρσε, δᾶμον μὲν εἰς ἀυάταν ἄγων / Φιττάκω<ι> δὲ δίδοις κῦδος ἐπήρ[ατ]ον, 9-13. ("And may we forget this anger... Let us relax the heart-devouring strife and internal battles, which one of the Olympians has raised, leading the people to ruin but giving Pittacus desirable glory.")

image of trampling on his oaths to overthrow the tyranny.[27] Thus the whole drama of Mytilene is condensed into two correlated images: on the one hand, the *hetairoi* try desperately to save the ship/state by keeping their feet firmly on its deck, while on the other, Pittacus destroys the city by stepping on his oaths. Elsewhere the tyrant, being a figure at odds with the community, is treated as a φαρμακός (cf. stoning in frr. 298 and 68), whose presence alone brings pollution. Distant and godforsaken, he is sharply contrasted to the crew/*hetairoi*, who are depicted cohesively in "we" terms and, even storm-tossed, can claim both fraternal camaraderie and a privileged bond with the divine, especially with gods associated with the aristocracy like the Dioskouri (fr. 34 A).[28] Alcaeus thus creates an opposition between his own *hetaireia* and his political enemy, who, by assuming the form of a sea storm, is transformed into a force that belongs not only outside the polis, but outside humanity itself.[29]

It is noteworthy that in fr. 208, the ship is not mentioned simply in passing, but in minute detail that reveals it as a piece of *techne.* The poet provides a close topography of its body, mentioning the masthold, walls, sails, anchor, rudders, ropes, and even the cargo itself, to the point that he has been accused by at least one modern scholar of artificial display of nautical knowledge.[30] Nonetheless, Alcaeus' insistence on detail may be connected more with his perception of the ship as an emulation of the city, not only in terms of institutions and transactional relationships, but also technological advances. Civilisation is the domain of the polis.[31] And just as in Alcaeus' polis the aristocrats are found at its centres of power, protecting it from tyranny, here, too, the crew fights for the ship's survival while they stand at its centre (ὂν τὸ μέσσον νᾶϊ, 3).

This bond of the aristocratic *hetairoi* that ties them together in moments of crisis is also observed in the symposion,[32] and, in fact, Alcaeus' extant corpus contains two fragments, 58 and 73, that fuse sea and drinking. The former (58) is obscure and enigmatic.[33] The latter (73), although incomplete and lacuna-riddled, does have a detectable line of argument. The poet begins with the recurring image of the "ship of state" in distress,[34] but soon he proposes to change his subject by "forgetting" political matters and turning his attention to the pleasures of drinking. *Lethe* becomes a desirable commodity, ironically in an environment – the symposium – which produces most of archaic monody, the major manifestation of aristocratic *mnemosyne*. What is

---

27 ἀλλὰ βραϊδίως πόσιν / ἔ]μβαις ἐπ᾽ ὀρκίοισι δάπτει / τὰν πόλιν ἄμμι, fr. 129.22-4.

28 Cf. Burnett 1983, 129 with relevant ancient references.

29 Elsewhere the tyrants' savagery is conveyed through comparisons to a beast devouring the wealth of the city (fr. 70.7; δαπτέτω used mostly of wild animals) and fire destroying everything in its path (fr. 74).

30 Burnett 1983, 154: "As if the singer's chief pleasure lay in his knowing use of nautical terms."

31 For the equation of life outside the limits of the polis to feral existence, see fr. 130b.

32 See, *e.g.* fr. 38, in which the loss of sympotic camaraderie is understood as equivalent to death (1-4). In the last decades, the Greek *symposion* has become the focus of great interest both as a social institution and a venue for the performance of archaic poetry. For a detailed bibliography, see Yatromanolakis 2016.

33 Liberman 1999, 42 describes fr. 58 as "un poème unique," in which "la situation mise en scène par le poète n'apparaît pas clairement." Drinking at sea is a strange setting, even if we take it as an allusion to the tipsiness of the symposiasts, which feels like the lurch of sailors. It may reveal, however, a desire on the part of the participants to distance themselves from *hoi polloi* and secure a self-contained space for their undisturbed congregation where they can contemplate politics and seek respite from their everyday toils. Fr. 58 is mutilated, but we can still recognise drinking activity and isolated words like κατθάνη[and δόμοις. We have too few clues to determine the theme of the poem, but the reference to "death" in a nautical context may be advice for caution and vigilance at a political level rather than a sympotic jest. Instead of the destabilising yet innocuous waves that strike later convivial ships, the poet may be introducing once again the sinister tempest of tyranny. But all this is uncertain.

34 πὰν φόρτι[ο]ν δ . . [/ δ᾽ ὄττι μάλιστασάλ[/ καὶ κύματι πλάγεισ[αν / ὄμβρω<ι> μάχεσθαι . . [/ φαῖσ᾽ οὐδὲν ἰμέρρη[ν, ἀσάμωι] / δ᾽ ἔρματι τυπτομ[έναν, 73.1-6 ("The entire cargo... as much as possible... and struck by a wave... She [the ship]) says she has no desire to fight against the rain, but hitting a hidden reef...").

especially noteworthy in fr. 73, however, is the dramatic transformation of the ship: the tempests have taken their toll on it, as Pittacus solidifies his power and the elite clans find themselves increasingly marginalised. From the symbol of a proud aristocratic Mytilene, it has now become the image of a wrecked city. In fact, if fr. 306 i refers to fr. 73,[35] as is likely, the ship is not only decrepit but also diseased. For the tyrant, being a violator of divine laws (fr. 129), is a polluter, who, like a φαρμακός not yet cast out, inevitably infects the state. Moreover, the ship is described in female anatomical terms suggestive of sexual penetration.[36] In his discussion of the fragment, Bruno Gentili effectively highlights the semantic nexus ship-prostitution-inflammation-city.[37]

I would like to end by returning to fr. 140, the "land" poem I started with, pairing it with the sea storm fragments, because together they articulate Alcaeus' vision of the *hetaireia* in complementary ways. Although at first sight one sees primarily the differences between the two (the stability of the land *vs.* the inconstancy of the sea; the unhurried glance at the past *vs.* the manic preoccupation with an emergency at hand), they both are permeated by the thread of μνήμη, a fundamental aspect of aristocratic identity and a precondition for a companion's becoming a δόκιμος ἀνήρ ("steadfast man"). Moreover, they both exhort the *hetairoi* discreetly but firmly not to fall short of the expectations of the community and their family traditions. Alcaeus' poetic sea storms, like his larger political discourse, are harnessed in the efforts of his *hetaireia* to overthrow the tyranny and reestablish itself in its rightful place. While, however, elsewhere the poet adopts direct political language, here he uses extended nautical metaphors, confident that his audience of experienced sailors will understand that his storms have to do more with things on land than at sea.

References

Bakker, E., 1997. Storytelling in the Future: Truth, Time, and Tense in Homeric Epic. *In*: E. Bakker and A. Kahane, eds. *Written Voices, Spoken Signs, Tradition, Performance, and the Epic Text.* Cambridge, MA: Harvard University Press, 11-36.

Bakker, E., 2002. Remembering the God's Arrival. *Arethusa*, 35, 63-81.

Beekes, R.S.P., 2010. *Etymological Dictionary of Greek, vol. 1.* Leiden and Boston: Brill.

Burnett Pippin, A., 1983. *Three Archaic Poets.* Bristol: Harvard University Press.

Campbell, D.A., 1982. *Sappho and Alcaeus.* Loeb Classical Library. Cambridge, MA: Harvard University Press.

Collins, D., 1998. *Immortal Armor: The Concept of* Alkē *in Archaic Greek Poetry.* Lanham: Rowman & Littlefield.

Frisk, H., 1960. *Griechisches Etymologisches Wörterbuch, vol. 1.* Heidelberg: Winter Universitätsverlag.

Ferrari, F. and Pontani, F., 1996. Alcaeus' Grandfathers: A Note on Fr. 6, ll. 17-20 V. *ZPE*, 113, 1-4.

---

35 Fr. 306 i contains several quotes from perhaps two different poems, to each of which the commentator appends a brief explanation.

36 οἶα δὲ σκέλη ἤδη κεχώρηκε αὖται (14-5)· καὶ τὰ σκέλη αὐτῆς πεπαλαίωται[ι (14-6)· συνουσίας (26). ("Because it [*sc.* the sand] has already entered through her legs; and her legs have become old … intercourse"). Merkelbach and Trumpf (in Koniaris 1966, 395) understand the poem as a political allegory, reflecting the realities of exile, as Alcaeus and his companions observe the city from afar. In their inability to reignite fighting, the poet advises Bycchis to at least enjoy the *symposion* until the conditions for the *hetaireia* improve. Koniaris' 1966, 395 objection that this type of allegory with a "hybrid double manifest subject" is not found in archaic poetry does not create unsurpassable difficulties. For the "ship of state" is so well established in the poetry of Alcaeus that an expansion of its imagery to make it a "ship of state-prostitute" is only a small step that renders its hybrid nature anything but shocking.

37 Gentili 1988, 206-12. On occasion, Mytilene is treated as a living organism, see fr. 348, in which, having fallen under the spell of Pittacus, it is described as ἄχολος, "gutless" (Campbell's 1982 translation). The term is medical ("relieving bile"), found in authors like Hippocrates and Aristotle.

Gentili, B., 1988. *Poetry and Its Public in Ancient Greece*. Baltimore and London: Johns Hopkins University Press.

Kantzios, I., 2019. Memory and Forgetfulness in Alcaeus. *CP*, 114, 322-43.

Koniaris, G.L., 1966. Some Thoughts of Alcaeus' Frs. D 15, X 14, X 16. *Hermes*, 94, 385-97.

Liberman, G., ed. 1999. *Alcée: Fragments*. Paris: Les Belles Lettres.

Marzullo, B., 2009. *Il 'Miraggio' di Alceo*. Berlin: De Gruyter.

Martin, R.P., 1989. *The Language of Heroes: Speech and Performance in the Iliad*. Ithaca and London: Cornell University Press.

Page, D., 1955. *Sappho and Alcaeus*. Oxford: Clarendon Press.

Rösler, W., 1980. *Dichter und Gruppe: eine Untersuchung zu den Bedingungen und zur Historischen Funktion Früher Griechischer Lyrik am Beispiel Alkaios*. München: Fink.

Slater, W., 1976. Symposium at Sea. *HSCP*, 80, 161-70.

Strauss Clay, J., 1982. ΑΚΡΑ ΓΥΡΕΩΝ: Geography, Allegory, and Allusion (Archilochus Fragment 105 West). *AJP*, 103: 201-4.

Voigt, E.-M., ed., 1971. *Sappho et Alcaeus. Fragmenta*. Amsterdam: Athenaeum – Polak & Van Gennep.

Webb, R., 2009. *Ekphrasis, Imagination and Persuasion in Ancient Rhetorical Theory and Practice*. Surrey: Ashgate Publishing Ltd.

Uhlig, A., 2018. Sailing and Singing: Alcaeus at Sea. *In*: F. Budelmann and T. Phillips, eds. *Textual Events: Performance and the Lyric in Early Greece*. Oxford: Oxford University Press, 63-92.

Yatromanolakis, D., 2016. Greek Symposion. *Oxford bibliographies* [online]. Available from: https://www.oxfordbibliographies.com/view/document/obo-9780195389661/obo-9780195389661-0210.xml [Accessed 08 March 2021].

The ideology of seafaring in the *Odyssey* and Telemachos' hanging of the slave girls (*Od.* 22,461-474)[1]

Hauke Schneider

Abstract

This article offers a new interpretation of the much-debated hanging of the unfaithful maidservants by Telemachos in book 22 of the *Odyssey*. It is based upon a historical approach to the Homeric Society (7th century BCE), which attached integral importance to the representation of one's social rank, and an analysis of the Homeric Society's perception and evaluation of the sea, showing why the seafaring man was held in high esteem. Both aspects are combined with a close reading of the scene in question to demonstrate that the extreme punishment of the maids is unavoidable and that Telemachos' hanging of the slave girls – which is a change from Odysseus' original order to decapitate them – is a well-calculated act by a young man who has increased his personal prestige by the successful overseas voyage and therefore needs to demonstrate his new standing symbolically. It is thus shown how fundamentally the mastering of the sea – with all of the difficulties involved and resulting profits – is the essential element in the *Odyssey* and in this particular scene.

Telemachos, Homeric society, hospitality networks, prestige and representation

Odysseus, the most intelligent and cleverest of all Greek heroes, is the protagonist of the *Odyssey*, one of the oldest pieces of Greek literature.[2] The well-known ruler of the island Ithaca invented the famous wooden horse, outplayed the gigantic

---

1 Thanks are due to Prof. Lutz Käppel, Dr. Kleoniki Rizou, Prof. Andreas Luther, Prof. Ernst-Richard Schwinge, PD Dr. Thomas Kuhn-Treichel, Lasse Felgendreher and Swaantje Otto, all of whom listened to and commented on my ideas. I am especially grateful to Laura Schmidt, who drew my attention to some important points, and to Hannah Goldbeck who generously supplied me with desperately needed literature from her private library during the Covid-Crisis. I owe the greatest debt to my wife Luisa, who is not only the instructor of the best course on the *Odyssey* ever but as my first reader has supported and encouraged me constantly, sharp-witted and warmhearted.
2 The question of origin, transmission and dating of the *Odyssey* has most recently been summarised by Pulleyn 2018, 36-45.

Cyclops Polyphemos and, having finally returned home, defeated the suitors who importuned his loyally waiting wife Penelope.[3] While Odysseus takes his last steps home after ten years of fighting in Troy and another ten of wandering around the Mediterranean Sea (and possibly beyond), his son Telemachos undertakes a sea voyage to his father's old comrades to gather information about the absentee and win himself fame. Back home in Ithaca, he encounters his in the meantime likewise returned father. Together they kill the suitors, who in the absence of Odysseus had lived recklessly at his expense, plotted to murder Telemachos and violated the right to hospitality protected by Zeus when they maltreated Odysseus himself who entered his own palace in the disguise of a beggar to evaluate the situation there beforehand. Thus, generally little offence is taken at their deaths,[4] whereas Odysseus' order to decapitate the maidservants who had sex with the suitors, and even more that Telemachos changes this order and hangs the girls instead, causes horror and moral indignation to this day.[5]

The execution of these slaves is our starting and focal point, so we begin with a close look at the scene in question. After killing the suitors Odysseus advises his nurse Eurykleia to summon the twelve servant maids whose infidelity she witnessed over the past years. He then tells his comrades, his son Telemachos and the two loyal herdsmen Eumaios and Philoitios, to let these slaves clean the hall of the remains of the bloody battle with the suitors. After the clearing-up the maids are to be put to death due to their disloyal sexual relationships with the suitors. Odysseus concretises:

'αὐτὰρ ἐπὴν δὴ πάντα δόμον κατακοσμήσησθε,	440
δμῳὰς ἐξαγαγόντες ἐϋσταθέος μεγάροιο	441
θεινέμεναι ξίφεσιν τανυήκεσιν, εἰς ὅ κε πασέων	443
ψυχὰς ἐξαφέλησθε καὶ ἐκλελάθωντ' ἀφροδίτης,	
τὴν ἄρ' ὑπὸ μνηστῆρσιν ἔχον μίσγοντό τε λάθρηι.'	445
[...]	
τοῖσι δὲ Τηλέμαχος πεπνυμένος ἦρχ' ἀγορεύειν·	461
'μὴ μὲν δὴ καθαρῶι θανάτωι ἀπὸ θυμὸν ἑλοίμην	
τάων, αἵ δὴ ἐμῆι κεφαλῆι κατ' ὀνείδεα χεῦαν	
μητέρι θ' ἡμετέρηι, παρά τε μνηστῆρσιν ἴαυον.'	
ὣς ἄρ' ἔφη, καὶ πεῖσμα νεὸς κυανοπρώιροιο	465
κίονος ἐξάψας μεγάλης περίβαλλε θόλοιο,	
ὑψόσ' ἐπεντανύσας, μή τις ποσὶν οὖδας ἵκοιτο.	

3 Odysseus is already in the first line of the poem called by the epithet πολύτροπος, 'of many turns', which makes his cunning intelligence one of the most prominent motifs of the epic. On this see *e.g.* West 1988, ad loc.; Pulleyn 2018, ad loc. Cf. Odysseus' famous self-characterisation: εἴμ' Ὀδυσεὺς Λαερτιάδης, ὃς πᾶσι δόλοισιν / ἀνθρώποισι μέλω, καί μεο κλέος οὐρανὸν ἵκει ('I am Odysseus, son of Laertes, renowned among men for all manner of wiles, so that my prestige extends to heaven', 9,19-20).

4 See *e.g.* Clay 1983, 213-39; Rutherford 1986; Hölscher 1988, 259-71; Dietz 2000, 197-9; Grethlein 2017, 213-27. But see now Loney 2019.

5 Fernández-Galiano 1992, 296 (ad 441-73) calls this 'strange and unwarranted cruelty'. Cf. his remarks ad 22,462 and ad 22,463. Likewise Thalmann 1998b, 219: 'Telemakhos exceeds his father's orders in the savagery and rage with which he punishes Melanthios and the disloyal slave-women [...] – hardly an example of Odyssean self-restraint.' Allan 2010, 24-5 interprets the hanging as an immature emotional outburst, which is contrasted by Odysseus' rational calculation. Similarly also Felson/Slatkin 2014, 215. Osborne 2004, 214 sees here 'the most ethically questionable part of Odysseus' revenge'. Seeck 2004, 270 denounces this as *atavistisch anmutende Sittenstrenge*. There is no lack of psychological analyses. Clarke 1989, 40 thinks that Telemachos' deed is 'part of a deep-seated reaction against an adolescence spent among women.' Wöhrle 1999, 138 interprets the act as overcompensation of pent-up feelings of inferiority, while Felson-Rubin 1994, 91 understands the hanging as a cleaning from 'animosity toward women' which results from sexual refusal. For a more differentiated approach see *e.g.* Merkelbach 1951, 129; Hölscher 1988, 259; Heath 2001, 151-2.

ὡς δ' ὅτ' ἂν ἢ κίχλαι τανυσίπτεροι ἠὲ πέλειαι
ἕρκει ἐνιπλήξωσι, τό θ' ἑστήκηι ἐνὶ θάμνωι,
αὖλιν ἐς ἰέμεναι, στυγερὸς δ' ὑπεδέξατο κοῖτος,   470
ὣς αἵ γ' ἐξείης κεφαλὰς ἔχον, ἀμφὶ δὲ πάσαις
δειρῆισι βρόχοι ἦσαν, ὅπως οἴκτιστα θάνοιεν·
ἤσπαιρον δὲ πόδεσσι μίνυνθά περ, οὔ τι μάλα δήν.

'But when you have set all the house in order,   440
lead the women forth from the well-built hall   441
and cut them down with your long swords, until   443
you have taken away the life from them all, and they forget the love
which they enjoyed under the suitors, when they lay with them in secret.'   445
[Telemachos and the faithful herdsmen Eumaios and Philoitios lead the maids
out of the hall and into the courtyard]
Amongst them wise Telemachos spoke first and said: 461
'Let me not by a clean death take the lives of these,
who have poured reproaches on me
and my mother and passed the nights with the suitors.'
So he spoke, and he tied the cable of a dark-prowed ship   465
to a high column and flung it round the roundhouse,
stretching it high up, so that none could touch the ground with her feet.
And as when long-winged thrushes or doves
get entangled in a snare, which has been set in a thicket,
as they seek to reach their roost but an abominable bed welcomes them,   470
even so they held their heads in a row, and round the necks
of all nooses were laid, so that they might die most pitiable.
And they writhed a little with their feet, but not for long. (22,440-74, omitted
are 446-60)[6]

We see that Odysseus issues a precise order regarding the location and the form
of the women's execution: Telemachos and the herdsmen are to decapitate them
outside the hall. He also gives the reason for this extreme punishment: Their secret
sexual relationships with the suitors. The men do as they are told and after the
cleaning is done, they lead the slaves out of the hall and into the courtyard. But
then Telemachos deliberately deviates from his father's orders. Emphasising that
their behaviour dishonoured him and his mother, he wishes the maids not to be
decapitated but hanged instead. The arrangement of the gallows and the hanging
itself, although described at some length, cannot satisfactorily be reconstructed and
we are left with the assumption that this is a rather fanciful picture than a realistic
account.[7] The concluding simile illustrates the execution and the comparison with
thrushes, a bird often connected with female sexuality, insinuates the women's
misdemeanour.[8]

    There seem to be three crucial questions for the explanation of this scene: (i)
Why does Odysseus wish the maids to be punished although the suitors are already
dead? (ii) Why does Telemachos disobey his father's order by changing the execution
method? (iii) Why does the poet use more than half a verse to state explicitly that

---

6   Line 22,442 (= 22,459) is since van Leeuwen's deletion rightly regarded as spurious and left out of
     this text, which follows Martin West's Teubner edition. The only instance where I departed from
     his text is verse 467, where I retain the otherwise generally accepted ἐπεντανύσας instead of the
     slightly changed ἐπαντανύσας accepted by West, for which see his *apparatus criticus*. – All line
     numbers, unless otherwise stated, refer to the *Odyssey*. The translations are my own.
7   See Fernández-Galiano 1992, 215-7. 296-7 (ad 441-73). For further details see also Fulker-
     son 2002, 337-41.
8   See Fulkerson 2002, 339.

Telemachos chooses 'the cable of a dark-prowed ship' (πεῖσμα νεὸς κυανοπρώιροιο, 465) to hang the maids?

I want to approach these questions from two different sides: From the historical perspective of the Homeric Society, thus trying to look at the described action with the poet's audience's perspective,[9] and – like Odysseus and Telemachos – from the sea, more precisely by analysing the Homeric Society's perception of the sea and seafaring.

There are now some general agreements about the controversially discussed Homeric Society.[10] While the heroes and their deeds are seen as archaised, exaggerated and purely mythic,[11] the social and historical background, in front of which the epic storyline develops, has successfully been reconstructed. It is generally placed into the time of the written composition of the *Iliad* and the *Odyssey*, that is the seventh century BCE.[12] This agrarian society[13] is organised in *oikoi*, households, which are ruled by men, who are politically organised in public meetings.[14] However, far from an established democracy as known from fifth's century Athens or a hereditary monarchy, the sovereignty, that is the rank of the *basileus*, the first man, is a matter of competition.[15] The social status results from personal prestige, the *time*.[16] It is neither determined by birth, nor static, but correlates with individual power, based upon influence, wealth and esteem and, above all, individual *aretai*, qualities of a wide range like fighting power, athletic skills, but also prudence, far-sightedness, the competence to establish order, artistic skills, craftmanship and agrarian activity.[17] The *time* awarding instance is the public.[18] Since wealth can be acquired by everybody via raids or wars, an essential signum of this society is the social mobility.[19] To save and extend their own status the *basilees* compete among one another for supremacy, for which the conflict between Agamemnon and Achilles in the *Iliad* is paradigmatic.[20] Therefore, especially the *basilees* but essentially every member of the Homeric Society strives to represent and increase his *time*, for which – due to the missing of an institutionalised fixation – symbols that strikingly depict the status are essential.[21] A central institution in this context is the ceremonial banquet, for which *e.g.* Agamemnon as leading *basileus* invites the other Greek leaders. To participate at such an exquisite event demonstrates per se one's high rank and *time*.[22] A special

---

9   For this need see *e.g.* Hölscher 1988, 259.
10   For a brief overview of the discussion since Moses Finley's groundbreaking *The World of Odys-seus* (1977, first published 1954) see Ulf 2011, 257-8.
11   See *e.g.* Raaflaub 1998, esp. 175-6.
12   See Ulf 1990, 213-68; Raaflaub 1998; Osborne 2004, 216-8; Ulf 2011, 276-7. For an earlier dating (ninth/eighth centuries BCE) see Raaflaub 1997, 625-8.
13   See Richter 1968. Cf. Ulf 1990, 175-212; van Wees 1992, 49-53; Donlan 1997, 654-61; Raaflaub 1998, 630-1; Osborne 2004, 214-5.
14   See the two assemblies in Ithaca in the *Odyssey* (2,6-257. 24,420-66) and in the *Iliad* the assemblies of the Greek army at Troy (2,84-394. 9,9-79. 14,109-27) and the Trojan one (7,345-79). They are mirrored by the assemblies of the Gods in both epics. Cf. van Wees 1992, 31-40; Raaflaub 1997, 641-5; Raaflaub 1998, 629-33; Osborne 2004, 212; Ulf 2011, 270-1.
15   See Ulf 1990, 85-125. Cf. Raaflaub 1997, 633-5 and especially for the *Odyssey* Halverson 1986.
16   See Ulf 1990, 4-12; Yamagata 1994, 121-44; Adkins 1997, 702-6. Cf. Ulf 2011, 260-1.
17   For the last ones see *e.g.* Achilles, who sings the *klea andron* (*Il.* 9,189), Odysseus, who carpentered his one-of-a-kind marital bed (*Od.* 23,189-201) and his father Laertes who works in his orchard (*Od.* 24 *passim*, cf. 18,365-75). Cf. Polydamas' 'catalogue' of *aretai* in *Il.* 13,170-1. See in general Ulf 1990, 12-49. Cf. Ulf 2011, 271-2.
18   See Ulf 1990, 41-9. Cf. Raaflaub 1997, 635-6; Ulf 2011, 271.
19   The most prominent example for this is given by the 'Cretan' Odysseus, who tells Eumaios that he rose from a moderate position to power and renown through nine successful raids he undertook (*Od.* 14,199-234). See Donlan 1997, 665; Ulf 2011, 263-4.
20   See Ulf 1990, 85-117. Cf. Osborne 2004, 213; Ulf 2011, 274-5.
21   See Ulf 1990, 48-9; van Wees 1992, 101-25. Cf. Osborne 2004, 213; Ulf 2011, 274-5.
22   See Ulf 1990, 193-202; van Wees 1992, 44-8.

form of indicating and increasing one's *time* is the honorific gift.[23] This can be a particular piece of meat, like the chine of the sacrificed bull Agamemnon gives to Ajax after his duel with Hector (*Il.* 7,313-20), or a cup of wine or a precious material artefact (often made of gold, silver, iron or cloth, in general called *keimelia*), often objects which have a long history and an honourable, often mythical provenance.[24] These social ties, based on gifts, strengthen the powerful positions of the involved persons and symbolise the reciprocal relationship between the giving and the receiving *basileus*. Such symbols of *time* are of special importance for the children of a *basileus* if they want to earn a high rank themselves because a father does not bequeath his social status automatically to his offspring.[25]

This is exactly Telemachos' situation before he undertakes his sea voyage. He is the son of a renowned man, a hero and *basileus* of Ithaca, but as social prestige and *time* are not passed from a father to his children, he has to prove his qualifications, his *aretai*, before he is regarded as a worthy successor of Odysseus and a leading figure in Ithaca.[26] Before he sets sail neither his mother's suitors have regarded him as a man of appropriate *time* (2,199-200. 2,323-36), nor his mother, who forbade him to rule over the women (22,426-7), nor the nurse Eurykleia, who, like Penelope, did not think him capable of the voyage across the sea (2,361-70. 4,707-28. 4,804-23),[27] nor the disloyal servant maids, who had intercourse with the suitors despite Telemachos' presence (16,108-9. 18,324-5. 20,6-8. 22,37-8).[28] The pervasive possibility that children can indeed be of lower quality than their parents is emphasised by Athena/Mentor when s/he tells Telemachos that the outcome of his overseas voyage will prove his worth.[29]

---

23   See the comprehensive study of Wagner-Hasel 2000. Cf. Finley 1977, esp. 61-6. 95-8 and *passim*; Ulf 1990, 202-12; Donlan 1997, 663-5; Osborne 2004, 213.
24   See Grethlein 2008, who lists in an appendix (47-8) all of these objects mentioned in the *Iliad* and the *Odyssey*.
25   See Halverson 1986; Ulf 1990, 114-7.
26   Ulf 1990, 115: 'Die Möglichkeit, Basileus zu werden, hat aber der Sohn des Odysseus nur dann, wenn er sich den Rivalen als überlegen erweisen sollte. Auch ihm nützt seine Herkunft nicht.'
27   Cf. Eumaios' reaction to the returned Telemachos, 16,22-4 = Penelope's reaction, 17,39-42.
28   Cf. Melantho's behaviour against the disguised Odysseus in 18,320-42. 19,65-95. Fulkerson 2002, 347 n. 60 rightly emphasised that the disloyal slaves would have been Telemachos' concern (as well as Eurykleia's before the return of Odysseus).
29   Cf. Heath 2001, 144.

παῦροι γάρ τοι παῖδες ὁμοῖοι πατρὶ πέλονται,
οἱ πλέονες κακίους, παῦροι δέ τε πατρὸς ἀρείους.

Few sons are indeed the equal of their fathers.
Most are inferior, and few surpass their father. (2,276-7)

If the just prospective heir to the ruling position wants to be seen as the future leading *basileus* of Ithaca, he has to demonstrate his claim to power and the appropriate *time* in the face of potential rivals, but also in the face of the members of Odysseus' *oikos*, who have regarded him until then as an underage youth.

Earning *time* is, besides gathering information about his father, the decided purpose of his voyage to Pylos and Sparta (1,93-5 [= 3,78][30]. 13,422-3). Telemachos succeeds in either respect. He overcomes his initial fear in interacting with the big men (3,21-4) and receives ritual hospitality from his father's comrades. He eats at Nestor's dinner table (3,34-42), gets a place to sleep (3,395-403), is washed by one of the *basileus*' daughters (3,464-8), partakes at a ceremonial feast (3,430-74) and receives a carriage to visit Menelaos (3,475-97). Here too Telemachos is welcomed hospitably, is washed (4,47-51), receives a place at the *basileus*' table (4,52-67. 15,133-42), a place to sleep (4,296-302) and prestigious gifts: a silver mixing-bowl from Menelaos and a precious garment from Helena, which is destined for Telemachos' future wife (4,589-619. 15,99-132). On his way back to Pylos he is hospitably entertained by Diokles (15,186-8). Before he leaves for Ithaca one Theoklymenos, pursued by the relatives of a man he had killed at Argos, calls on Telemachos and Odysseus' son receives him as a *hiketes* (15,223-86). Not only in this situation but throughout the whole journey Telemachos acts as the leader of the crew, which accompanies him (see esp. 15,495-549). Aboard the ship the men become Telemachos' *hetairoi* (2,383-435). Odysseus' son now has everything he needs to take over the rule over the *oikos* and Ithaca as soon as his father retires (like Laertes) or dies – or leaves his *oikos* and dominion at least temporarily again, as at least the hearer/reader knows from Teiresias' prediction he will to atone for the killing of the suitors and eventually reconcile Poseidon (11,118-31. 23,266-86). Telemachos not only gathered information about his father but by visiting his father's *hetairoi* he activated this hospitable network for himself and is accepted into the exclusive circle of *basilees*. Odysseus' former companions act as his first positive male role models, who demonstrate to him how to act as a *basileus* and how important symbolic-ritual actions are for the representation of one's *time*.[31] The successful sea voyage had an effect on Telemachos' maturity and can be seen as an initiation.[32] Telemachos gives proof of his *basileus* qualities by managing his ship like an *oikos*. His crew obeys his orders and he receives a suppliant, a highly ritual deed typically done by *basilees*. Telemachos' newly-gained power and *time* is confirmed by the suitors' plot to murder him on his way back to Ithaca (4,638-73).[33] They did not take his words seriously when he announced his voyage but immediately recognise the returning young man as a threat to their own powerful position, as a future *basileus* surpassing them all in respect of *time*.[34] This becomes immediately evident by one of the leading suitors speech: Having learned about Telemachos' journey and imminent return Antinoos addresses his fellow suitors.

---

30   Line 3,78 is most likely interpolated, cf. West 1988, ad loc.
31   See Heath 2001, 140-3. Cf. also Schmiel 1972.
32   Against Wilamowitz' point of view, who maintains that throughout the *Odyssey* there is no development of Telemachos' character 1927, *e.g.* 106, see the seminal interpretations of Scott 1917 and Austin 1960. See further Heath 2001, 129, with note 1, who offers a good overview over the major contributions here since then. For the aspect of initiation see especially Eckert 1963, whose anthropological outlook, for example when he interprets the hanging of the maids as a ritual 'mock rejection of the mother' (52), I do not always share. Cf. also Olson's criticism (1995, 66 note 2). See furthermore Moreau 1992; Toher 2001.
33   For the plot see West 1988, ad 4,672.
34   Cf. West 1988, ad 4,638-40; Ulf 1990, 47.

ὣ πόποι, ἦ μέγα ἔργον ὑπερφιάλως ἐτελέσθη
Τηλεμάχωι ὁδὸς ἥδε· φάμεν δέ οἱ οὐ τελέεσθαι.
εἰ τοσσῶνδ' ἀέκητι νέος πάϊς οἴχεται αὔτως   665
νῆα ἐρυσσάμενος κρίνας τ' ἀνὰ δῆμον ἀρίστους,
ἄρξει καὶ προτέρω κακὸν ἔμμεναι· ἀλλά οἱ αὐτῶι
Ζεὺς ὀλέσειε βίην, πρὶν ἡμῖν πῆμα γενέσθαι.
ἀλλ' ἄγε μοι δότε νῆα θοὴν καὶ εἴκοσ' ἑταίρους,
ὄφρα μιν αὐτὸν ἰόντα λοχήσομαι ἠδὲ φυλάξω   670
ἐν πορθμῶι Ἰθάκης τε Σάμοιό τε παιπαλοέσσης,
ὡς ἂν ἐπισμυγερῶς ναυτίλεται εἵνεκα πατρός.'

'Outrageous. Truly a mighty deed has been insolently completed
by Telemachos, this journey, and we said that he would not be successful.
With all of us against him the young lad is gone without more ado,   665
launched a ship and chose the best men from the populace.
He is going to give us still more trouble. But hopefully
Zeus may destroy his might before he becomes our bane.
But come on, give me a fast ship and twenty comrades,
that when he comes, I may lay for him in ambush   670
in the strait between Ithaca and rugged Samos,
so that his voyage in search of his father ends in misery.' (*Od.* 4,663-72)

This speech, which is praised by the other suitors (4,673), shows that their consideration to kill Telemachos is fundamentally encouraged by his successful overseas voyage to Pylos and Sparta.[35] They realise that their fear, which is in broad contrast to their initial contempt (2,199-200), is perfectly reasonable, when Telemachos' foresees their ambush (thanks to Athena, 15,27-35) and manages to evade them (15,296-300). Their resulting horror culminates in an even bolder plan to kill him in Ithaca (16,342-448), but they are forestalled by the arrival of Odysseus, Telemachos and their companions. Back home again the next step is for Telemachos to help his father defeat the suitors.

In the course of the well-known bow contest, the disguised Odysseus reveals his true identity to the suitors, starts the fight and finally kills them. Thus, his status within his *oikos* is re-established for two reasons. First, there are no more suitors who court his wife and challenge his rule. Second, the suitors' corpses are deposited in an exposed position, namely the courtyard, the *aule*, near the main entrance leading to the road (23,49), a place everybody who enters or leaves the *oikos* has to pass. In this way, the dead suitors become an immediately intelligible symbol of the returned *basileus*' insuperable power and mark the *oikos* as being again under his rule.

(i) *So why, after Odysseus' position of power is so undoubtedly re-established and symbolically demonstrated, is the punishment of the servant maids necessary?*

They committed two serious crimes by telling the suitors about Penelope's secret plan to delay her new marriage (2,107-9. 19,154) and by sleeping with them (16,108-9. 18,324-5. 20,6-8. 22,37-8).[36] They are loyal to the suitors and therefore most disloyal to

---

35 Cf. again Ulf 1990, 47.

36 The originality of the last passage has been questioned because of the unparalleled παρευνάζομαι and the claim that the servant maids were forced by the suitors into having sex with them, although they are otherwise presented as visiting the suitors happily and of their own free will. Cf. Fernández-Galiano 1992, ad 22,37, who rightly points to *Od.* 5,119 παρ' ἀνδράσιν εὐνάζεσθαι. There is little point in splitting hairs here, since it is just that the 'sexual guilt is made to attach both to the suitors and to the maids.' Thus West 2014, 284 (cf. his remarks on the same issue on p. 68), who does not express any reservation against the verses or the verb anyway.

Penelope, but also to Telemachos, Odysseus and the whole *oikos*.[37] Since sex with the wife of the master of the house is, as we see in Aegisthus' occupation of Agamemnon's ruling position through Klytaimestra's bed, the final step in usurping his position of power, the maids let the suitors come, at least symbolically, very close to Penelope's bed by having intercourse with them, although they are also sexually the property of the *oikos*-ruler.[38] Since every member of the *oikos* has witnessed their deeds, they would become a symbol of the disordered house under the suitors' dominance and Telemachos' (and Penelope's) powerlessness if they would stay alive. That would be even more the case be it that one of the maids would be pregnant by a suitor. The story of the swineherd Eumaios, told by him to Odysseus (15,415-84), serves as a foil depicting the dangerousness of unfaithful servants. Himself a *basileus*' son he was kidnapped by a servant maid, who was seduced by Phoenician pirate-traders and sold as a slave to Odysseus' father.[39] Therefore it is quite evident that Odysseus is left with little choice but to execute the maids, which is more an annihilation of signs which undermine his rule than a mere punishment.[40]

(ii) Why, then, does Telemachos disobey his father's order and changes the execution method?

Unlike Odysseus Telemachos yet needs to demonstrate the *time* he gained through his overseas voyage, and prove himself the worthy successor of his father in the face of the members of the *oikos*. Since the displayed corpses of the suitors serve clearly as a symbol for Odysseus' rule there are only the disloyal maids left, with whose execution Telemachos can create a sign of power for himself. In fact, he creates an immediately intelligible symbol as he does not decapitate but hang the girls.[41] Their dangling corpses are arranged near the suitors' and therefore in a likewise exposed position, so that next to Odysseus' power Telemachos' ability to put the *oikos* upright is shown symbolically to everyone who leaves or enters the *oikos* – as the suitors and maids had done so freely.[42] The execution is thus not an instrumental but a highly symbolical act, which has even a performative character, because an emblematic act publicly staged in this way binds its witnesses, and here every one who beholds the hanged maids, to respect what is symbolically established – here Telemachos' position of power in the *oikos* – and behave accordingly in the future. The public character of the demonstration is furthermore insinuated when Telemachos' speech is said to be held τοῖσι 'amongst them', *i.e.* Philoitios and Eumaios, in the formulaic line 22,461. As Fernández-Galiano notices the expression is appropriate to meetings

---

37 *Pace* Fernández-Galiano 1992, ad 22,463, who understands Telemachos' anger at the serving-women's behaviour as 'a sign of his youthful immaturity.' For the inseparability of the honour of the house and his ruler see *e.g.* Saïd 2011, 360-2. For the absolute necessity of servants' loyalty see in our context Olson 1992.

38 That slaves are also sexually the property of their owner is clearly stated in the *Odyssey*. Laertes is said to have abstained from intercourse with Eurykleia, because he feared that his wife might be indignant with him (1,427-33). When Telemachos arrives in Sparta he witnesses a double wedding of Menelaos' and Helen's daughter Hermione and of Menelaos' son Megapenthes, whose mother is said to be a slave woman (4,12). See generally Thalmann 1998b, 70-4; Thalmann 1998a, esp. 30-1; Hunnings 2011, 60-4. See further Fulkerson 2002. *Pace* Grethlein 2017, 218-9, who considers the suitors' sexual behaviour as a mere bagatelle.

39 Cf. Olson 1995, 120-39, esp. 137; Thalmann 1998b, 73-4 and generally Segal 1994, 164-83. See also Lane Fox 2008, 326-9. For the Phoenician pirate-merchants see Latacz 1990; van Wees 1992, 242; Winter 1995; Donlan 1997, 653; Dougherty 2001, 46-7. 112-7.

40 Cf. Levine 1987, 24; Rankine 2011, 40; Horn 2014, 312-3, who, however, attaches no importance to Telemachos' independent and unauthorised action.

41 There is no hint that Telemachos might not be involved in the execution itself as suggested by Fernández-Galiano 1992, 297 (ad 441-73).

42 Cf. Fulkerson 2002, 346-7; Hunnings 2011, 64-5.

or assemblies.[43] This is furthermore corroborated by the term ἦρχ' ἀγορεύειν, which is always used of one speaker among other speakers.[44] However, Fernández-Galiano fails to see that the two herdsmen are the first members of the Odyssean *oikos* and the Ithacan public to witness his power.[45] Both Eumaios and Philoitios have heard Odysseus' original order and can (and will) spread the word that the maids have been executed by Telemachos, who thus demonstrates that he has grown into his epithet, πεπνυμένος 'wise' (461), which means that he now has the ability to put his words into action, which is an integral quality of the adult and powerful man in the Homeric Society.[46] Beyond that he demonstrates that he is not only familiar with the repertoire of symbols representing authority, which are integral for the Homeric Society, but also that he is able and ready to use these symbols for the establishment of his own rule.[47] This might also be the reason why Telemachos makes Odysseus spare the suppliants Phemios and Medon, the bard and the herald (22,330-80): Both are predestined to spread the news about Odysseus' return and Telemachos' newly-gained power and thereby, of course, increase their *time*.[48] Odysseus then demands explicitly this from Medon:

θάρσει, ἐπεὶ δή σ' οὗτος ἐρύσσατο καὶ ἐσάωσεν,
ὄφρα γνῶις κατὰ θυμόν, ἀτὰρ εἴπησθα καὶ ἄλλωι,
ὡς κακοεργίης εὐεργεσίη μεγ' ἀμείνων.

Have courage, because this one rescued and saved you,
so that you know by heart and also tell others
that well-doing is far better than wickedness. (22,372-4)

Moreover, Medon – addressing the people of Ithaca at the end of book 24 – indeed reports that Odysseus is supported by the gods themselves and scares the suitors' enraged relatives of the returned *basileus*' power (24,439-51).[49] Accordingly, Odysseus' acceptance of the changed order is hardly surprising. He has demonstrated his own power well enough by killing and exhibiting the suitors so that nobody will question his rule although Telemachos executed the women in a different way from the original instruction. Moreover, his son's high reputation may be of his very own interest.[50]

---

43 Fernández-Galiano 1992, ad loc.
44 See Heath 2001, 153.
45 See Heath 2001, 152-3.
46 For this see Heath's excellent analysis (2001), who interprets the changing of the execution method as a further indication of Telemachos' maturity. Cf. also Penelope's words at 19,160-1 and 19,530-4, recognising her son's changed status.
47 *Pace* Grethlein 2017, 76-9, who does not see Telemachos acting on his own authority but standing on the threshold of adulthood not passing it throughout the epic. He recognises an initiation in the *Telemachy* but no inner ripening of Odysseus' son.
48 See *e.g.* Pulleyn 2018, ad 154. Beyond that Medon must be credited with the loyal act of revealing the suitors' plot to murder Telemachos to Penelope, 4,675-714, cf. 16,412.
49 The originality of this speech has been questioned prominently by Wilamowitz 1884, 71-2, whose position has recently been supported by West 2014, 303. But Heubeck 1992, ad 24,443-9, has plausibly argued for its authenticity, to which, I daresay, my point has added further plausibility.
50 *Pace* Fernández-Galiano 1992, ad 22,462. Laura Schmidt pointed out to me that Odysseus accepted a change of his plan proposed by Telemachos prior to this. When he wanted to inquiry the loyalty of all his servants, male and female, Telemachos objected that ascertaining the male ones, peasants scattered round the countryside, would take far too long (16,301-20). As Hoekstra 1989, ad 16,316-9 notes, 'an inquiry into the loyalty of the men would have been impossible from a compositional point of view.' Likewise West 2014, 249, who in addition refers to a remark of Wilamowitz 1927, 146, who remarks that Odysseus lacks an appropriate number of followers (λαοί) for this kind of undertaking. These considerations are undoubtedly right, but the poet shows us nevertheless a self-confident and far-sighted Telemachos whose advise is not ignored by his father.

There is some discussion about the meaning of καθαρῶι (462). In the Homeric epics this adjective does not yet have the religious sense it later acquired, but denotes either a clean and empty space (*Il.* 8,491 [= 10,199]. 23,61) or freshly laundered clothes (*Od.* 4,750 = 17,48 ~ 4,759 = 17,58. 6,61).[51] Moreover Telemachus cannot suppose a death free from ritual pollution since the bloodshed of a decapitation would indeed be polluting and require further purification. Fernández-Galiano admits that 'we are left with the idea of a 'clean', in the sense of 'quick and easy' death.'[52] However, Fulkerson rightly stresses that the following simile of the thrushes suggests that the hanging is exactly this, quick and easy.[53] This is additionally supported by the only other instance of a hanging in the Homeric epics, the suicide of Oidipus' mother, here called Epicasta, who encounters Odysseus during his *katabasis* (*Od.* 11,271-80) and whose death is described as accomplished by a βρόχον αἰπύν, a 'precipitous noose' (*Od.* 11,278).[54] Both Fulkerson and Fernández-Galiano endeavour to fathom if death by hanging is more honourable than by decapitating. Drawing on examples from tragedy they end diametrically opposed. Fernández-Galiano points to men who kill themselves by hanging and concludes that this is not dishonourable, whereas Fulkerson maintains that hanging at least in Classical Athens and in later times was a dishonourable means of death:[55] 'The difference between death by sword and by rope is one of honor.'[56] Instead of contributing to this controversial and in the context of the *Odyssey* rather anachronistic discussion, I want to propose a solution that does not refer to texts of other genres from 5th century Athens but is in accordance with the genuine Homeric semantic. As noted above, καθαρός in the Homeric epics denotes either a clean and empty space or freshly laundered clothes: in the *Iliad*, Hector assembles the Trojans at a place devoid of corpses (8,491), an expression repeated in the interpolated *Doloneia* to describe the place where the Greek leaders congregate ([10,199]). Furthermore, the adjective specifies the appearance of the part of the shore which is washed clean by the waves, where Achilles falls asleep and dreams of the recently-deceased Patroclus (23,61). In the *Odyssey* καθαρός is used five times to denote freshly laundered, clean clothes, four times that worn by Penelope after she had taken a bath (4,750 = 17,48 ~ 4,759 = 17,58) and once the clothes Nausikaa launders at the shore before she meets Odysseus (6,61). Therefore, generally speaking, καθαρός is used in both epics to denote physical rather than religious or moral cleanliness. Applied to Telemachos' speech this would characterise the women's death as physically clean. Since this cannot refer to the spilling or not-spilling of blood, it could be referred to the corpses. Were the maids decapitated, their corpses would probably be thrown onto the pile of the remains of the suitors. In this case they would in a way vanish, disappearing in the heap, and leave the courtyard, where they were executed, *empty*. Their corpses would not remain visible and could not serve as a specific sign for Telemachos. It thus seems plausible that Telemachos, when he tells the women that their death shall not be καθαρός, has in mind to display their corpses in the courtyard. This is accomplished by the hanging which provides the opportunity to leave the corpses dangling and thereby becoming a sign of Telemachos' power over the *oikos*. This interpretation has the advantage of being congruent with the semantic of καθαρός we find especially in the *Iliad*.

---

51 See van der Mije 1991. Cf. *h.Ap.* 121 ἁγνῶς καὶ καθαρῶς in connection with the washing of the newborn Apollo, with Richardson's notes ad loc. 2010, 99-100.
52 Fernández-Galiano 1992, ad 22,462.
53 Fulkerson 2002, 341.
54 See Fulkerson 2002, 341-2.
55 Fernández-Galiano 1992, ad 22,462; Fulkerson 2002, 341-3.
56 Fulkerson 2002, 343. See also Hunnings 2011, 64 and Felson/Slatkin 2014, 214-5. Thus already a scholiast ad *Od.* 22,462: τὸν διὰ ξίφους θάνατον τοῦ ἠγχονισμένου θανάτου ἐνόμιζον καθαρώτερον (Death by the sword was considered to be cleaner than death by strangulation, ed. Dindorf).

(iii) After he has symbolically given proof of his ability to maintain order in the oikos, *why does Telemachos use a ship's cable to execute the maids, which the poet emphatically illustrates?*

Perpetual references throughout the epic make it possible to show that the sea was perceived highly ambivalent by the Homeric Society: Unbreachable and separating except for seafaring men. However, even for them the sea was extremely dangerous. There were windstorms, hostile peoples at various shores and pirates, not to mention the dangers a not always obedient crew might create:[57] Odysseus himself is of course the best example. When he finally comes home, he has lost his ship and his entire crew in consequence of all of these dangers. Nonetheless, who crosses the sea successfully has the chance to expand his knowledge and achieve wealth and fame, an essential task for members of the Homeric Society.[58] A suitable example is Menelaos who gathered great wealth during his return from Troy and learned from the sea god Proteus about Odysseus' fate (4,81-518), information he can pass on to Telemachos who crossed the sea himself to learn about his father's fortune.[59] The renown and wealth which can be acquired by means of seafaring become evident in Odysseus, too. He is πολύτροπος (1,1) because he got to know many peoples and their dispositions (1,3).[60] Although this causes him much trouble, he cannot resist to reveal his real name to Polyphemos, that it was not *Outis*, a nobody, who blinded and outplayed him, but Odysseus from Ithaca, the son of Laertes (9,502-5). Now the Cyclops can tell his father Poseidon exactly whom he wishes to be punished (9,522-36), but everyone who ever encounters Polyphemos or hears about the deed will know the name of Odysseus and that will increase his renown.[61] Odysseus' *time* is enormous due to the deeds, like the defeat of the Cyclops, he did during his sea voyages, respectively at Troy, a region he could only reach because he is able to cross the sea. The riches he carries with him to Ithaca, given to him by the Phaeacians, he could only acquire thanks to his successful seafaring, and, one might argue, it is due to their ability to do successful seafaring that the Phaeacians are so rich that they can give so generously to Odysseus.

These negative and positive aspects of Mediterranean seafaring were rated so highly that seafaring itself became an important criterion to judge people's culture and power.[62] This becomes most evident in the comparison between the Cyclopes and the Phaeacians.[63] The uncivilised Cyclopes live their lives as loners in sparse caves scattered over their island. They produce food only for their own subsistence and do not make contact with other peoples (9,106-15). Polyphemos refuses Odysseus and his crew the right to hospitality. He offers them neither food, nor the possibility to wash themselves, nor a place to sleep, nor a gift but devours them instead

---

57   For a general account of seafaring in Homeric times see Lane Fox 2008.

58   Cf. Mark 2005, 24, whose analysis of the maritime trade in the Homeric Society (17-24) is otherwise superficial and in part speculative. See rather Casson 1991, 44-54; van Wees 1992, 238-48; Donlan 1997, 651-4; Foxhall 1998; van Wees 2009, 457-60. See also Dougherty 2001, 46-50.

59   Cf. Dougherty 2001, 106-7 with note 19.

60   For the causal connection between travel and knowledge and wisdom respectively in our context see in general Dougherty 2001, 3-7 and *passim*.

61   Telling his real name to Polyphemos can therefore not be regarded as Odysseus' mistake, as *e.g.* Segal 1994, 95-8 puts it. The Homeric hero is, so to say, socialised to behave in these *time*-seeking ways.

62   Dougherty 2001, esp. 161-76 analysis this from the view of colonisation and presents Odysseus as a kind of prototype colonist: 'The ability to sail is part of what distinguishes the colonist from the native inhabitant [...] and so nautical skill comes to represent the triumph of civilization over nature, that of the colonist over native inhabitants' (165-6).

63   Cf. Mondi 1983, esp. 25-8; Heubeck 1989, ad 9,106-15; Segal 1994, 30-3. 202-15; Raaflaub 1997, 645-6; Dougherty 2001, 122-42; Alden 2017, 231-3; Grethlein 2017, 127-41. Particularly with regard to the Cyclopes see also Shaw 1982/3, 5-31.

(9,250-344). An important signum of the Cyclopes is that they are not seafaring people (9,125-30). The Phaeacians, who are said to be the Cyclopes neighbours (6,5), on the contrary, live in a well fit society and show highly developed agricultural skills. Their *basileus* Alkinoos resides in a richly decorated palace, where he treats Odysseus with hospitality and presents him with treasures surpassing even those, he brought with him from Troy (7-8. 13,1-125). The most important achievement of the Phaeacians is their grand expertise in seafaring, which enables them to get in contact with the peoples of the surrounding islands. They finally carry Odysseus home safely on one of their extraordinary ships (13,70-125).

How fundamentally the idea of successful seafaring as a sign of a highly developed culture and general superiority is persistent throughout the Odyssey becomes strikingly manifest in the hanging of the disloyal maidservants. Telemachos not only establishes a sign of his newly-gained *time*, but also uses a πεῖσμα νεὸς κυανοπρώιροιο (22,465) a ship's cable for the strangulation (and subjugation) of the maids, which is not just 'another piece of nautical equipment which happens to be lying about in the αἴθουσα'[64] but rather a distinct symbol of his superiority. In Homer, a πεῖσμα in all but one instance describes a ship's cable that is used for mooring. Only in *Od.* 10,167 is it a rope used that Odysseus makes to tie up a stag he had hunted down.[65] However, this is told within the description of the disembarkation at Aiaia, so Odysseus clearly acts here in his role of the seafaring man. Thus, by hanging the maids with a ship's cable Telemachos' *time* is symbolically linked with its source, his successful overseas voyage and the thereby obtained initiation into the exclusive circle of the mightiest *basilees* of the Greek Mediterranean. He thus bears resemblance to his father who overbears his enemies thanks to his nautical skills.[66] Furthermore, this resemblance, which of course heightens Telemachos' prestige, becomes most evident in the description of the act of hanging. After the ship's cable has been fastened, Telemachos 'stretches it high up, so that none could touch the ground with her feet' (22,467). The stretching of the πεῖσμα is described with the participle ἐπεντανύσας. In book 21 the verb τανύω is used nine, ἐντανύω fourteen times to denote the drawing of Odysseus' bow.[67] This peculiar analogy shows that as Odysseus succeeds in drawing his famous bow and kill his opponents with it Telemachos succeeds in stretching the ship's cable and kill his opponents with it.[68] He demonstrates that he is indeed one of the children of great men who match their father's abilities and renown and proves himself worthy of the leading position he aspires to and presents himself as the genuine successor of his father.[69]

Let me conclude. Telemachos' deliberate change of the execution method demonstrates his newly-gained *time* to the whole *oikos*, the ship's cable symbolises the source of this new *time*-based social rank and power. Besides this reasonable interpretation of the usage of the ship's cable in the execution of the servant maids – and therefore besides the explanation of little more than half a verse of the *Odyssey's* about 12,000 verses – a few other aspects have at least been slightly touched. The perspective of the Homeric Society with its focus on gaining and representing *time* has shown an act which has up to now often been condemned for its repulsive cruelty

---

64   Fernández-Galiano 1992, ad 22,465.

65   Cf. Morrison/Williams 1968, 57, who falsely write that Odysseus hangs the maids; Kurt 1979, 180-1; Mark 2005, 154, who also believes that it is Odysseus who executes the women. See also Fernández-Galiano 1992, ad 22,465.

66   See Dougherty 2001, 164-7. Odysseus for example compares his blinding of Polyphemos to a shipwright boring timber (9,384-5). For the act see Merry 1880, ad 9,382.

67   See Fernández-Galiano 1992, ad 22,467.

68   Fulkerson 2002, 337, argues that the πεῖσμα and other materials used for the hanging symbolise Odysseus' return and his restoration of order in his *oikos*. This may be one aspect but, as I have tried to demonstrate, is not the main significance of the ship's cable here.

69   Cf. *e.g.* Fulkerson 2002, 347. *Contra* Allan 2010, who stresses the differences between Telemachos and Odysseus to conclude that the son will never match his father.

to be well considered and meaningful. The same perspective may shed new light on other epic scenes. The gained insight into the general perception of the sea and seafaring as highly dangerous on the one hand but as an extraordinary possibility to gain knowledge, wealth and fame and to secure and extend one's influence through broad *hetairoi* networks on the other hand and the inherent cultural categorisation of men and peoples based on their ability for seafaring may be found useful for the understanding of the Homeric epics beyond this single scene. The legitimation of the *basileus'* power and rule through seafaring accessories is for example also important in the task Odysseus has to fulfil to expiate the killing of the suitors and to reconcile the offended sea god Poseidon: He is supposed to carry an oar on his shoulder while walking inland until he meets people who have never seen the sea or ships and hence oars and who ask him what a peculiar winnowing fan he is carrying. There he has to build an altar for Poseidon and make sacrifices to the god (11,118-31. 23,266-86). This shows that the social system based upon prestige is valid in the world of the gods as well, who fight for *time* as much as humans do.[70] By the establishment of an altar in a region to which the god of the sea is unknown Poseidon's might and therefore his *time* is extended. Hence, Odysseus not only founds a sacred place but also establishes a new cult, which again shows an ideology of the cultural superiority of the seafaring man.[71] This superiority is the fundament for Odysseus' victory over the suitors, who did not participate in the Trojan expedition and therefore did not excel in seafaring, and for Telemachos' gained maturity and is thus far beyond the Homeric epics of great importance for the Homeric Society in general. In an agrarian culture seafaring is an extraordinary possibility to gain wealth and fame and to secure and extend one's influence through broad connective *hetairoi* networks throughout the Mediterranean.

References

Adkins, A.W.H., 1997. Homeric Ethics. *In*: I. Morris and B. Powell, eds. *A New Companion to Homer*. Mnemosyne Suppl., 163. Leiden, New York, Köln: Brill, 694-713.

Alden, M., 2017. *Para-Narratives in the Odyssey. Stories in the Frame*. Oxford: Oxford University Press.

Allan, A.L., 2010. Generational Degeneration. The Case of Telemachus. *Scholia*, 19, 14-30.

Austin, N., 1960. Telemachos Polymechanos. *California Studies in Classical Antiquity*, 2, 45-63.

Ballabriga, A., 1989. La prophétie de Tirésias. *Métis*, 4, 291-304.

Casson, L., 1991. *The Ancient Mariners. Seafarers and Sea Fighters of the Mediterranean in Ancient Times*. Princeton: Princeton University Press.

Clarke, H.W., 1989. *The Art of the Odyssey*. Bristol: Bristol Classical Press.

Clay, J.S., 1983. *The Wrath of Athena. Gods and Men in the Odyssey*. Princeton: Princeton University Press.

Dietz, G., 2000. *Menschenwürde bei Homer. Vorträge und Aufsätze*. Bibliothek der Klassischen Altertumswissenschaften, N.F., 2. Reihe, 108. Heidelberg: Winter Universitätsverlag.

Donlan, W., 1997. The Homeric Economy. *In*: I. Morris and B. Powell, eds. *A New Companion to Homer*. Mnemosyne Suppl., 163. Leiden, New York and Köln: Brill, 649-667.

---

70   Cf. the Phaeacians' ship which is turned into stone by Poseidon because he felt that they violated his prohibition to help Odysseus. The ship thus becomes the most permanent sign of Poseidon's insuperable power and *time*. See Ulf 1990, 7 n. 26.

71   Cf. Dougherty 2001, 172-6. See also Ballabriga 1989; Segal 1994, 187-94.

Dougherty, C., 2001. *The Raft of Odysseus. The Ethnographic Imagination of Homer's Odyssey*. Oxford and New York: Oxford University Press.

Eckert, C.W., 1963. Initiatory Motifs in the Story of Telemachus. *The Classical Journal*, 59, 49-57.

Felson, N. and Slatkin, L., 2014. *Nostos, Tisis,* and two Forms of Dialogism in Homer's *Odyssey. In*: M. Christopoulos and M. Païzi-Apostolopoulou, eds. *Crime and Punishment in Homeric and Archaic Epic. Proceedings of the 12th International Symposium on the Odyssey, Ithaca, September 3-7, 2013.* Ithaca: Publications of the Centre for Odyssean Studies of Ithaca, 211-222.

Felson-Rubin, N., 1994. *Regarding Penelope. From Character to Poetics*. Princeton: Princeton University Press.

Fernández-Galiano, M., 1992. Books XXI-XXII. *In:* J. Russo, M. Fernandez-Galliano and A. Heubeck, eds., 1988-1992. *A Commentary on Homer's Odyssey. Vol. III.* Oxford: Clarendon Press, 131-310.

Finley, M.I., 1977. *The World of Odysseus*. London: Chatto & Windus.

Foxhall, L., 1998. Cargoes of the Heart's Desire. The Character of Trade in the Archaic Mediterranean World. *In*: N.R.E. Fisher and H. van Wees, eds. *Archaic Greece. New Approaches and New Evidence.* London: Classical Press of Wales, 295-309.

Fulkerson, L., 2002. Epic Ways of Killing a Woman. Gender and Transgression in Odyssey 22,465-72. *The Classical Journal*, 97, 335-350.

Grethlein, J., 2008. Memory and Material Objects in the *Iliad* and the *Odyssey. The Journal of Hellenic Studies*, 128, 27-51.

Grethlein, J., 2017. *Die Odyssee. Homer und die Kunst des Erzählens.* München: C.H. Beck.

Halverson, J., 1986. The Succession Issue in the *Odyssey. Greece & Rome*, 33, 119-128.

Heath, J.R., 2001. Telemachus pepnymenos. Growing into an Epithet. *Mnemosyne*, 54, 129-157.

Heubeck, A., 1989. Books IX-XII. *In*: A. Heubeck and A. Hoekstra, eds., 1988-1992. *A Commentary on Homer's Odyssey. Vol. II.* Oxford: Clarendon Press, 3-143.

Heubeck, A., 1992. Books XXIII-XXIV. *In*: J. Russo, M. Fernandez-Galliano and A. Heubeck, eds., 1988-1992. *A Commentary on Homer's Odyssey. Vol. III.* Oxford: Clarendon Press, 313-418.

Hoekstra, A., 1989. Books XIII-XVI. *In*: A. Heubeck and A. Hoekstra, eds., 1988-1992. *A Commentary on Homer's Odyssey. Vol. II.* Oxford: Clarendon Press, 147-287.

Hölscher, U., 1988. *Die Odyssee. Epos zwischen Märchen und Roman.* München: C.H. Beck.

Horn, F., 2014. *Held und Heldentum bei Homer. Das homerische Heldenkonzept und seine poetische Verwendung.* Classica Monacensia, 47. München: Narr Verlag.

Hunnings, L., 2011. The Paradigms of Execution: Managing Slave Death from Homer to Virginia. *In*: R. Alston, E. Hall and L. Proffitt, eds. *Reading Ancient Slavery*. London and New York: Bristol Classical Press, 51-71.

Kurt, C., 1979. *Seemännische Fachausdrücke bei Homer. Unter Berücksichtigung Hesiods und der Lyriker bis Bakchylides.* Zeitschrift für vergleichende Sprachforschung, Ergänzungsheft, 28. Göttingen: Vandenhoeck & Ruprecht.

Lane Fox, R., 2008. *Travelling Heroes. Greeks and their Myths in the Epic Age of Homer.* London: Penguin Books.

Latacz, J., 1990. Die Phönizier bei Homer. *In*: U. Gehrig and H.G. Niemeyer, eds. *Die Phönizier im Zeitalter Homers*. Mainz: Verlag Philipp von Zabern, 11-20.

Levine, D.B., 1987. Flens Matrona et Meretrices Gaudentes. Penelope and her Maids. *The Classical World*, 81, 23-27.

Loney, A.C., 2019. *The Ethics of Revenge and the Meanings of the Odyssey.* Oxford, New York: Oxford University Press.

Mark, S., 2005. *Homeric Seafaring.* Texas: Texas A&M University Press.

Merkelbach, R., 1951. *Untersuchungen zur Odyssee.* Zetemata 2. München: C. H. Beck.

Merry, W.W., ed., 1880. *Homer, Odyssey, Books I-XII with Introduction, Notes, Etc.* Oxford: Clarendon Press.

van der Mije, S.R., 1991. καθαρός. *In*: Thesaurus Linguae Graecae, ed. *Lexikon des Frühgriechischen Epos. Vol. 2.* Göttingen: Vandenhoeck & Ruprecht, 1272.

Mondi, R., 1983. The Homeric Cyclopes: Folktale, Tradition, and Theme. *Transactions of the American Philological Association*, 113, 17-38.

Moreau, A., 1992. Odyssée XXI, 101-139. L'examen de passage de Télémaque. *In*: A. Moreau, ed. *L'initiation. Actes du colloque international de Montpellier, 11-14 avril 1991. Vol. 1.* Montpellier: Universtité Paul Valéry, 93-104.

Morrison, S.J., Williams, R.T., 1968. *Greek Oared Ships, 900-322 B.C.* Cambridge: Cambridge University Press.

Olson, S.D., 1992. Servants' Suggestions in Homer's *Odyssey. The Classical Journal*, 87, 219-227.

Olson, S.D., 1995. *Blood and Iron. Stories and Storytelling in Homer's* Odyssey. Mnemosyne Suppl. 148. Leiden, New York and Köln: Brill.

Osborne, R., 2004. Homer's Society. *In*: R. Fowler, ed. *The Cambridge Companion to Homer*. Cambridge: Cambridge University Press, 206-219.

Pulleyn, S., 2018. *Homer, Odyssey, Book 1. Edited with an Introduction, Translation, Commentary and Glossary*. Oxford: Oxford University Press.

Raaflaub, K.A., 1997. Homeric Society. *In*: I. Morris and B. Powell, eds. *A New Companion to Homer*. Mnemosyne Suppl. 163. Leiden, New York and Köln: Brill, 624-648.

Raaflaub, K.A., 1998. A Historian's Headache. How to read 'Homeric Society'? *In*: N. Fisher and H. van Wees, eds. *Archaic Greece. New Approaches and New Evidence.* London: Classical Press of Wales, 169-193.

Rankine, P., 2011. Odysseus as Slave: The Ritual of Domination and Social Death in Homeric Society. *In*: R. Alston, E. Hall and L. Proffitt, eds. *Reading Ancient Slavery.* London and New York: Bristol Classical Press, 34-50.

Richardson, N., 2010. *Three Homeric Hymns. To Apollo, Hermes, and Aphrodite, Hymns 3, 4, and 5*. Cambridge: Cambridge University Press.

Richter, W., 1968. *Die Landwirtschaft im homerischen Zeitalter*. Archaeologica Homerica, H. Göttingen: Vandenhoeck & Ruprecht.

Rutherford, R., 1986. The Philosophy of the Odyssey. *The Journal of Hellenic Studies*, 106, 145-162.

Saïd, S., 2011. *Homer and the Odyssey*. Translated by R. Webb. Oxford: Oxford University Press.

Schmiel, R., 1972. Telemachus in Sparta. *Transactions of the American Philological Association*, 103, 463-472.

Scott, J.A., 1917. The Journey Made by Telemachus and its Influence on the Action of the Odyssey. *The Classical Journal*, 13, 420-428.

Seeck, G.A., 2004. *Homer. Eine Einführung*. Stuttgart: Reclam.

Segal, C., 1994. *Singers, Heroes, and Gods in the* Odyssey. Myth and Poetics. Ithaca and London: Cornell University Press.

Shaw, B.D., 1982/3. 'Eaters of Flesh, Drinkers of Milk'. The Ancient Mediterranean Ideology of the Pastoral Nomad. *Ancient Society*, 13/14, 1-31.

Thalmann, W.G., 1998a. Female Slaves in the Odyssey. *In*: S.R. Joshel and S. Murnaghan, eds. *Women and Slaves in Greco-Roman Culture. Differential Equations.* London and New York: Routledge, 22-34.

Thalmann, W.G., 1998b. *The Swineherd and the Bow. Representations of Class in the Odyssey*. Myth and Poetics. Ithaca and London: Cornell University Press.

Toher, M., 2001. Telemachus' Rite of Passage. *La Parola del Passato*, 56, 149-168.

Ulf, C., 1990. *Die homerische Gesellschaft. Materialien zur analytischen Beschreibung und historischen Lokalisierung*. Vestigia 43. München: C.H. Beck.

Ulf, C., 2011. Homerische Strukturen: Status – Wirtschaft – Politik. *In*: A. Rengakos and B. Zimmermann, eds. *Homer-Handbuch. Leben – Werk – Wirkung*. Stuttgart and Weimar: J.B. Metzler, 257-277.

Wagner-Hasel, B., 2000. *Der Stoff der Gaben. Kultur und Politik des Schenkens und Tauschens im archaischen Griechenland*. Campus historische Studien 28. Frankfurt and New York: Campus Verlag, Frankfurt am Main.

van Wees, H., 1992. *Status Warriors. War, Violence and Society in Homer and History*. Dutch Monographs on Ancient History and Archaeology 9. Amsterdam: J.C. Gieben.

van Wees, H., 2009. The Economy. *In*: K.A. Raaflaub and H. van Wees, eds. *A Companion to Archaic Greece*. Blackwell Companions to the Ancient World. Malden: Wiley-Blackwell, 444-467.

West, M.L., 2014. *The Making of the Odyssey*. Oxford: Oxford University Press.

West, S., 1988. Books I-IV. *In*: A. Heubeck, S. West and J.B. Hainsworth, eds., 1988-1992. *A Commentary on Homer's Odyssey. Vol. I*. Oxford: Clarendon Press, 33-245.

Wilamowitz-Moellendorff, U. v., 1884. *Homerische Untersuchungen*. Berlin: Weidmann.

Wilamowitz-Moellendorff, U. v., 1927. *Die Heimkehr des Odysseus. Neue homerische Untersuchungen*. Berlin: Weidmann.

Winter, I.J., 1995. Homer's Phoenicians. History, Ethnography, or Literary Trope? (A Perspective on Early Orientalism). *In*: J. B. Carter and S. P. Morris, eds. *The Ages of Homer. A Tribute to Emily Townsend Vermeule*. Austin: University of Texas Press, 247-271.

Wöhrle, G., 1999. *Telemachs Reise. Väter und Söhne in Ilias und Odyssee oder ein Beitrag zur Erforschung der Männlichkeitsideologie in der homerischen Welt*. Hypomnemata 124. Göttingen: Vandenhoeck & Ruprecht.

Yamagata, N., 1994. *Homeric Morality*. Mnemosyne Suppl. 131. Leiden: Brill.

Malta's connections and cultural identity: Remarks on the architectural language in the western Mediterranean in the 4th and 3rd centuries BCE

Francesca Bonzano

Abstract

The article discusses the architectural language attested in the late 4th and early 3rd century BCE in Malta, in the Tas-Silġ sanctuary. It is a composite idiom that shows affinity with the decorative motifs found elsewhere in the Punic Mediterranean but also exhibits striking originality. This period – characterised by great cultural vivacity and exchange – is variously defined by writers as Late Punic, Punic or Punic-Hellenistic, which underlines the uncertainty underlying our interpretation of the Punic Mediterranean in the Hellenistic period. This is linked to the question of the alleged "Hellenisation" of the Punic world, manifested in architecture through the adoption of decorative motifs of Greek tradition. The Tas-Silġ remains are considered in the light of these more general problems and evaluated in relation to the specific local context. On the one hand, it was fully integrated into the circulation of goods, people and ideas in the western Mediterranean. On the other hand, the locality possessed a distinctive cultural identity, evident in the continued use of Late Neolithic structures and the employment of "mixed" architecture that stands out for its originality and stylistic quality compared to other traditions known from the Carthaginian eparchy.

Archaeology of Malta, archaeology of cult places, Punic architecture, religious architecture, Tas-Silġ sanctuary

Introduction

This paper discusses the architectural language attested in the sanctuary of Astarte in Tas-Silġ (Malta) in the 4th to 3rd century BCE. It is a composite idiom which, although adopting elements that are widespread and shared with other settlements in the Carthaginian eparchy, also features specific elements that are distinctive.

The topic addressed in this workshop concerns primarily the movement of "objects" interpreted as architectural models and consequently linked with ideas and people; these were "objects" which could be accessed during contacts with the rest of the Mediterranean but also "objects" to which the local community was exposed and in which it recognised itself. The architectural landscape was an integral part of the local cultural identity.

The complexity and variety of the cultural exchanges that underlay the development of these practices are manifest in the academic uncertainty concerning the definition of this period – Late Punic, Hellenistic, or Punic-Hellenistic – and its cultural manifestations. Each alternative emphasises what is taken to be the major interacting component, based on considerations that do not necessarily reflect the profundity of its influence.

These reflections set out in the section on terminology are not limited to Malta but apply to the Punic Mediterranean in general during the 4th and 3rd centuries BCE. The architecture of this period shows original developments characterised by the addition to more properly Punic elements of motifs of Greek, Alexandrian and Near Eastern origin, whose presence in Malta is due to its important role in Mediterranean sea routes (see the section on composite architectures).

Within this field, more detailed consideration is given to the "hellénisation de Carthage" controversy, the main points of which are presented in an overview. The concluding observations assess the relationship between architecture and cultural identity, that is the product of external overseas relations and traditional components rooted in local culture.

The substantial silence of ancient sources, at least those that have come down to us, regarding the Maltese archipelago has occasionally led to an underestimation of Malta's role within the great Mediterranean circuits, from which the island might be thought to have been excluded until the Roman conquest. However, it was also of considerable interest to Carthage (see Bonzano 2021). Nonetheless, Malta's central position in the middle of the Mediterranean and the emphasis in surviving documents on the favourable conformation of its coasts and its natural ports suggest that the archipelago played an important role in the flux of trade, people and ideas that distinguished the western Mediterranean during the Hellenistic period.

Late Punic, Hellenistic or Punic-Hellenistic: Just a question of terminology? (Fig. 1)

The spatial, chronological and cultural characteristics of the areas subject to the influence of Carthage in the 4th and 3rd centuries are defined in diverse ways: they may be referred to as Late Punic, Hellenistic or Punic-Hellenistic, not only according to which aspect is being highlighted but also depending on the training of the writer who addresses the topic.

Recent contributions to the theme of defining the Punic (and) Hellenistic Mediterranean are two collective volumes focused on the Hellenistic West (Prag and Crawley Quinn 2013b) and the Punic Mediterranean (Crawley Quinn and Vella 2014b). Both express the need to adopt a new approach in order to respectively "rethink the ancient Mediterranean" and establish "the identity" of the centres analysed from the time of Phoenician settlement to the Roman conquest. From these works emerges the desire to overcome obsolete historiographic traditions like Greek East *vs.* Roman West by means of a redefinition of the concept of Western Hellenism.

The term *Hellenismus* was of course used by Johann Gustav Droysen to indicate the fusion between Greek and non-Greek elements, in the period in which – between Alexander's death and the birth of Christ – the boundaries between East and West had disappeared. The German scholar devoted more space to Western Hellenism

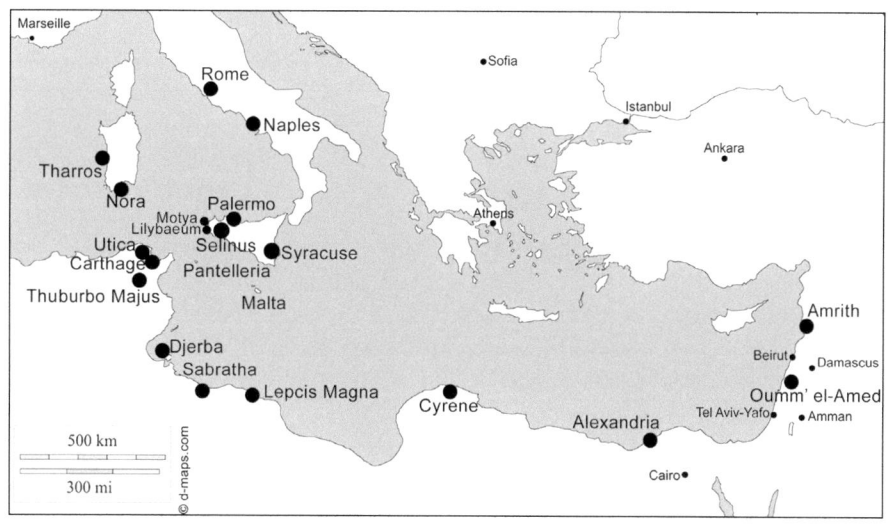

Figure 1. The Mediterranean basin with main sites mentioned in the text. https://d-maps. com/carte.php?num_ car=4861&lang=en, reworked.

than had any previous history of the Hellenistic world, with a "pan-Mediterranean" vision that clashes with recent historiographical trends.[1] The treatment given to the West in the Hellenistic era has often been sectorial and fragmented, with little inclination to evaluate from a unified perspective – while also taking account of the distinctive features of the different contexts – the cultural events and languages of this part of the Mediterranean.

The recent increase in Phoenician and Punic studies[2] has not significantly affected the East/West dichotomy, partly given that the Punic world is often perceived as a phenomenon of limited scope, essentially focused on Carthage; the isolation of these studies is not only linked to the ideological presumption of the pre-eminence of "Classical" culture, but also involves the priority given to texts and written evidence.[3] In fact ancient authors saw a hiatus between the Eastern and Western Greeks; the latter would naturally have been inclined to βαρβαρίζειν: the geo-political situation, which placed them in close contact with non-Greek populations, was responsible for an inclination towards unsatisfactory behaviour like luxury and indolence – and above all for their inability to repel the barbarians, as the Attalid rulers – for example – had been able to do.[4] Even Hieron, who had raised Syracuse to

---

1   J. Prag and J. Quinn explain Droysen's "open" vision as being due to the political and cultural context of the time, which allowed events in Rome and Carthage to be treated on the same level, combining Carthaginian politics with the model of English imperialism (Prag and Crawley Quinn 2013a, 7, 9). On the origin and meaning of the term *Hellenismus* used by Droysen see also Canfora 1987; Marcone 2013. A clarification of the historiographic trends regarding Italy and Sicily in the Hellenistic period is given in Dench 2003, 297: '*One of the remaining problems of modern scholarship is that these sophisticated studies of Sicily and Italy have had little impact on major narratives and collected works on the Hellenistic world as a whole: there is still a tendency to privilege the Hellenistic kingdoms of the East on the one side, and the coming of Rome, somewhat decontextualized from Italy, on the other side*'.

2   Prag and Crawley Quinn 2013a, 7. A number of publications, mostly covering lengthy periods, have recently focused on Carthage (see Aounallah and Mastino 2018; Russo *et al.* 2019) and the Punic world (see Guirguis 2017b; Fariselli and Secci 2018), in particular Sardinia (see Del Vais *et al.* 2019; also the *corpora* of Sardinian Antiquities, especially Guirguis 2017a).

3   Prag and Crawley Quinn 2013a, 7-8; on the importance of the Punic world's role in the context of Western Hellenism, see also Wallace-Hadrill 2013, 39; for a view that evaluates the history of Carthage within the Hellenistic *koiné* see Melliti 2016, 185-224.

4   Erskin 2013, 29, 32. Luxury was associated with western Greek cities even before the Hellenistic period. Taranto became the first example of life of *luxuria*; the decadence that ancient writers attributed to these towns also explained their defeat: when Syracuse was taken by the Romans, it was because the inhabitants were drunk (Pol. VIII, 37).

the dignity of a genuine Hellenistic kingdom, had to compromise by allying himself with the Romans.[5]

This historiographical trend has favoured the East/West dichotomy, and furthermore it has discouraged modern research from seeing the populations that shared the Mediterranean Sea as participating in the same cultural climate. However, the need to evaluate the Mediterranean as a whole and its ability to make connections have recently been underlined, with particular attention to border areas and passageways: *"zones of ambiguity, where different milieux abutted, acquire a new prominence, and, in categorization of the large spaces of historical comparison, new attention is being given to the effect on each zone of the nature of its edges"* (Purcell 2014, 61).

Then again, the "Hellenisation" interpretative model is often inadequate to express the dynamics of *cross-pollination* between the different areas.[6] Archaeological research shows that areas such as Sicily – for which it is also difficult to propose a uniform body of 3rd century evidence, partly given that the extraordinary late 2nd – 1st century BCE building surge made the preceding phases difficult to understand (see Campagna 2011a, especially 165-166) – show a multifaceted picture within which it may be misleading to try and identify opposing categories such as Greek/Punic, earlier/later.[7] Sicily is an obligatory reference point due to its relations with both Carthage and Egypt; with regard to the Punic metropolis, interactions are documented with the Sicilian elites, which maintained strong contacts with their mother country as a trading enclave but at the same time strengthened their positions through prudent marriage policies; Hamilcar who led the Carthaginian army was in fact the son of a woman from Syracuse.[8]

While the relations between Sicily (especially Syracuse) and Alexandria are known, the nature and extent of relations between Carthage and Alexandria are less clear, although the political ties must have been quite solid, as evidenced by the fact that Ptolemy Philadelphus did not give assistance to Pyrrhus against the Carthaginians. For its part, Carthage hoped to obtain a loan of 2000 talents from Alexandria to finance the continuation of the Punic Wars but according to Appian, the capital of the Ptolemaic kingdom refused to conserve good relations with Rome (see Melliti 2016, 207). These connections corresponded with economic and cultural relationships: in Carthage, there was a temple dedicated to Isis from at least the 3rd century BCE, and the city was among those which received priests sent

---

5   Erskin 2013, 30. There is an ample bibliography on Hieron and the building programme he undertook; for an overview see Portale 2017.

6   The term is used in Prag and Crawley Quinn 2013a, 13. On the concept of Hellenisation of the Punic world, see also below.

7   For a picture of Sicily in the 3rd century, see most recently Wilson 2013; Portale 2015; Portale 2017 with bibliography. A good example is Selinunte, where the Punic era acropolis phase has been discussed by Sophie Helas, who recognised its structure and urban organisation (Helas 2011). However, as Portale has highlighted, the tendency to confidently construe certain residential and monumental constructions on an ethnic basis risks creating interpretative *impasses*. An example is Temple B, built around 300 with a "Greek" typology and therefore referable to a particular historical moment (the passage of Agathocles or the backing of Pyrrhus) – or to a possible Punic client who built a cult building for a Greek divinity and thus "acquired" its rituality. More likely, according to the scholar, the explanation lies in a mixed social structure, which also determined adherence to the cause of Pyrrhus (Portale 2015, 716-718).

8   Fentress 2013, in particular 157-158. Already in the late 5th century, Diodorus tells of Agrigentans who sell wine and oil in Carthage (Diod. XIII, 81, 4); the historian also wrote about groups of Greeks who resided in Carthage (Diod. XIV, 77, 5), as well as the property that some Carthaginians owned in Syracuse in about 406 BCE (Diod. XIV, 46, 1). The coexistence between Greeks and Phoenicians in Sicily is illustrated by the existence of pro-Phoenician groups in most of the island's Greek cities (see Melliti 2016, 209-210), as well as the "Phoenicians who lived among them" in Syracuse, an expression that presupposes a peaceful and accepted coexistence (Peri 2003, 145-146). Different sources, both literary and archaeological, indicate a similar scenario at the Punic centre of Mozia, where the famous statue of the young charioteer may have been dedicated to "Greek dealings with Motye… or by a local, wealthy merchant" in about 470-460 BCE (Marconi 2014, 444-445).

from Memphis to introduce the cult of Egyptian gods into the Mediterranean (see Ensoli 2016, 56-57).

Returning to the Punic Mediterranean, scholars have asked themselves what "Punic" really means: a question tied in turn to issues regarding the existence (or non-existence) of a "Punic world", its possible coherence and its relationship with the Phoenician domain (see Crawley Quinn and Vella 2014a, 3). A confusing variety of this denomination is found in modern usage, at times employed to indicate a geographical area like Phoenician settlements in the western Mediterranean, in an ethnic sense, or even in reference to Carthage alone. More traditionally, Punic territories were those in the western Mediterranean under Carthage's political and cultural influence[9], to which is often added a chronological restriction: the term Punic is applied from the 6th century onwards, while before this Phoenician is used, also in the west.[10]

For these reasons, defining the cultural aspects of the areas of Punic influence in the West in the 4th and 3rd centuries BCE is rather complex, since the concepts of "Punic" and "Hellenistic", if used rigidly, risk being misleading; in reality these two cultural worlds were not separate, nor is there evidence that they were perceived as such in ancient times (see Crawley Quinn 2013, 190). This is shown by the way in which the protagonists presented and represented themselves: although later in date, the behaviour of Massinissa and characteristics of the Numidian world – with regard to which the concept of "Hellenisation" has been repeatedly invoked – are good examples.[11]

The Punic world also had contacts with the Italian peninsula – its conflict with Rome certainly did not imply the absence of commercial relations between them: recent studies have confirmed that the Campanian A pottery produced in Cales reached Carthage, where the production of Black-Glazed Ware is testified by the "Byrsa 661" class, from the 4th-3rd century and that amphorae containing wine from the Gulf of Naples were widespread at this time in the coastal sites of Sicily, up to the Punic metropolis.[12] Similarly, amphorae from Paestum dating to the first half of the 3rd century BCE have been identified in Palermo, Pantelleria, Djerba and Carthage, as well as in Malta at the site of Zejtun, not far from the Tas-Silġ sanctuary (see Bechtold 2018).

In partial contrast with traditional interpretations is a recent monograph on the history of Carthage which outlines the events of the *métropole méditerranéenne*, with a focus on the Carthaginian state's affirmation in the 4th century BCE (see Melliti 2016, 25-61). The work highlights the eparchy's role in the wider economic and cultural

---

9   For some scholars, however, the "Punic world" focuses on the cultural and economic ties between North Africa, western Sicily, southern Sardinia, Ibiza and southern Spain without necessarily implying military supremacy or political control by Carthage (see Van Dommelen and López Bertran 2013, 273).

10   Crawley Quinn and Vella 2014a, 5-6. This temporal discrimination coincides with a time of significant cultural transformations, for example the transition from cremation to inhumation, and expansion of Carthaginian control. On the other hand, there are no substantial linguistic differences between "Punic" and "Phoenician", and calling these peoples Phoenicians involves the application of a term which they never used themselves (see Bondì 2014, 50-60).

11   Coarelli and Thébert 1988. Apart from the question of tower-like funerary monuments – also at the centre of a lively debate regarding their attribution of a specific cultural sphere – the methods adopted by the king to display his power were similar to those of "traditional" Hellenistic monarchs, as indicated by his donations on the island of Delos (Griesbach 2010; Griesbach 2013) and meeting with Ptolemy VIII Evergete II, which perhaps took place in Cirta, as recounted by Athenaeus (Athen. VI, 15 [229d]; XII, 16 [518f-519a]; Laporte 2012).

12   These new data are mainly based on a re-examination of the cargo of the Secca di Capistello shipwreck, which sank between 300 and 280 BCE and included Type V Greek-Italic amphorae and Black-Glazed Ware (see Olcese 2015, 190-192). Cales pottery is also present in the late 4th – early 3rd century tombs at Lilybaeum, on the route between Carthage and Rome, although in small quantities (see Olcese 2015, 174-175, 187).

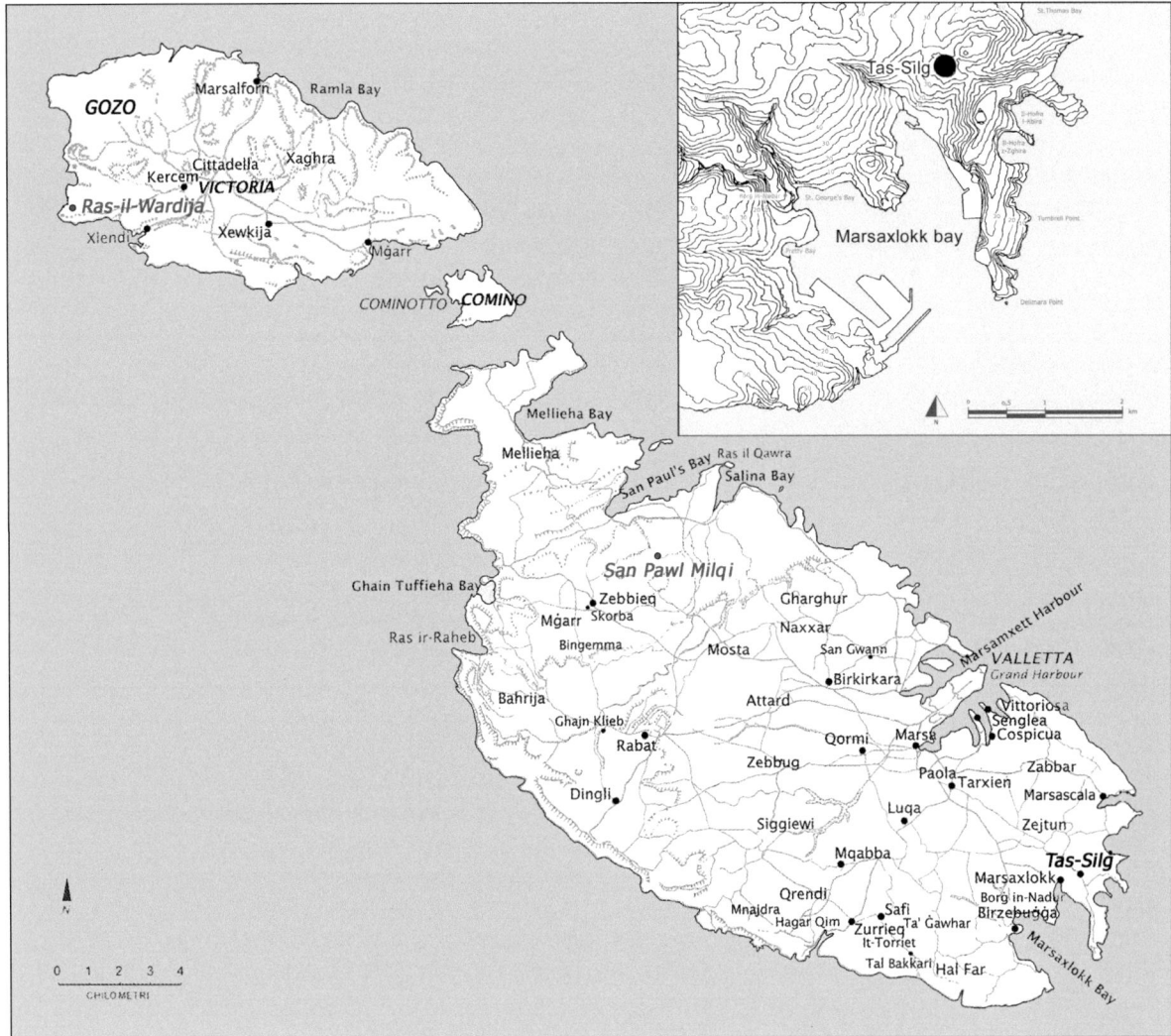

Figure 2. The Maltese archipelago, plan. Bruno 2004, Fig. 3.

world of Hellenic origin, closing significantly with a chapter dedicated to the "golden age" in the first half of the 2nd century BCE, on the eve of what Melliti calls the *troisième guerre romaine*, rather than the usual Third Punic War.[13] Notwithstanding the reservations that have been expressed regarding the actual scale of these influences, the generality of certain critical opinions and some archaeological gaps, the importance of this overall vision that goes beyond the separation of the Greek East and the Punic or Roman West has been stressed. It points to the existence of a Punic commonwealth led by Carthage and integrated in the Greek commercial *koiné* (see Melliti 2016, 221-224; D'Andrea 2017).

---

13   See the section *"Une ouverture plus affirmée à la* koiné *culturelle et commerciale grecque"* (*ibid.,* 93-111), the chapter *"L'insertion de Carthage dans la* koiné *hellénistique"* (*ibid.,* 185-224) and the section *"L'après-Cannes: la consécration de la politique hellénistique"* (*ibid.,* 352-362), contained within an account of the Second Punic War; and the last chapter *"Un âge d'or à l'ombre de la* mare nostrum *romaine"* (*ibid.,* 423-466).

Examples of composite architectures in the Malta archipelago (Fig. 2)

In an already inhomogeneous panorama, Malta rarely finds an adequate location: work on the archipelago before it became part of a Roman province is usually exclusive in nature and focused on the characteristics of Maltese material culture. On the one hand, the significant but "cumbersome" legacy of prehistoric monuments – the focus of scholars and local authorities for a long time – weighs heavily,[14] while on the other, studies have often highlighted Malta's particular situation in comparison with other colonies, which had led to a sort of autonomy with respect to Carthage.[15] In addition, ancient remains have not yielded a clear archaeological picture, both because many surveys are dated and because there are too many isolated discoveries, disproportionately funerary in nature (see Sagona 2002). In this context, the Tas-Silġ sanctuary itself is also isolated with respect to the surrounding territory, but it throws light on Malta's economic and cultural relations with the main centres in the Mediterranean.[16] It is no coincidence that N. Purcell, in a recent work on the Ancient Mediterranean, quotes the passage from Diodorus Siculus concerning Malta and its "connective vocation" which led in some instances to the development of craft activities (Diod. V, 12; Purcell 2014, 63-64). He also notes that "Malta has many harbours, various in their advantages"; it was these natural features above all that caused the growth of the archipelago's role in trade.

The Tas-Silġ sanctuary has been investigated since the early 1960s by the Italian Archaeological Mission, and since the end of the 1990s also by the University of Malta (Fig. 3).[17] This religious site – located on the main island at one of Malta's most important harbours, the port of Marsaxlokk – was built during the Late Neolithic and was in use throughout the Bronze Age and the Early Iron Age. When Phoenicians colonised the archipelago, the megalithic building was still visible and the site was frequented (Fig. 4.1). Thus, re-utilising the previous sanctuary in part, they established an international place of worship dedicated to Astarte, as attested by numerous votive inscriptions in Phoenician; this preservation of the principal megalithic temple is a tangible sign of the conservatism that characterised the site throughout the historical period. The themes of continuity and links with external

14 The temples were seen as symbols of the young nation, which became independent only in 1964 but whose history stretches back thousands of years (see Gilkes and Vella 2001, especially 377-379).

15 Vidal González 1996; Aubet 2009, 249: "*La influencia de Cartago en Malta es muy escasa. Por razones que desconocemos, la isla perdió su función estratégica durante la fase púnica, al quedar marginada de los circuitos principales del Mediterráneo hasta la conquista de Roma a finales del siglo III a.C.*" Of the same opinion are Bondì et al. 2009, p. 157; "*il fatto che il passaggio di Malta sotto Roma segua di quasi un venticinquennio l'abbandono della Sicilia da parte di Cartagine mostra a sufficienza la marginalità anche strategica della regione maltese in questa fase storica*". In the aforementioned work by Melliti, the Maltese archipelago is not given much space in accounts of the eparchy, with a brief mention in the narration of the Second Punic War (see Melliti 2016, p. 310).

16 On Punic era remains see Bruno 2004, pp. 106-107, 115-116, 127, 131-133,139-140 regarding the sites of Tas-Silġ and San Pawl Milqi and the circulation of containers for goods; Bonanno 2005, pp. 86-123 *et passim* for site descriptions; Sagona 2015, pp. 218-263. The term "Hellenistic" is rarely used for the material culture of this period, "Late Punic" being preferred, *e.g.* with regard to the pottery vessels found in funerary contexts (Sagona 2002, p. 23: "*new fabrics were introduced from North Africa and Sicily; they faced swift change with commercial relationships with Sicily*"). A different perspective is adopted in the work of B. Bechtold, which instead examines the various productions within extensive regional frameworks (see Bechtold 2018 with bibliography).

17 An up-to-date account of excavations is given in Bonzano 2017a; the results of excavations by the University of Malta conducted in the southern portion of the site (south of the modern road that crosses the archaeological area) were published in 2015 (Bonanno and Vella 2015). A volume covering all the Italian Mission's excavations from the 1960s up to the present is due to be published soon (Rossignani *et al.,* in press).

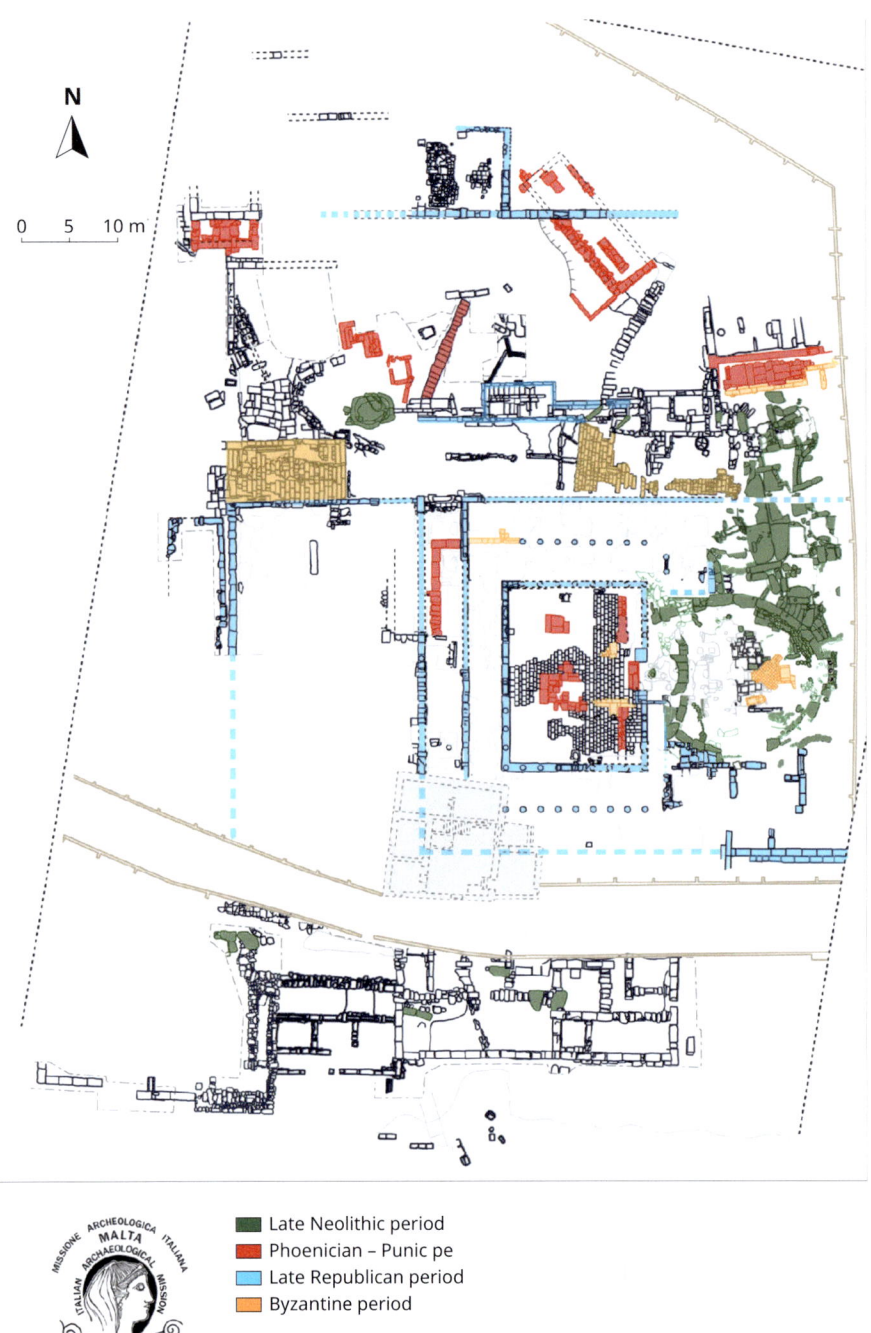

N

0   5   10 m

- Late Neolithic period
- Phoenician – Punic pe
- Late Republican period
- Byzantine period

Figure 3. Tas-Silġ, the multiphase sanctuary plan. Italian Archaeo-logical Mission Archive.

influences constitute a *leitmotiv* in the sanctuary's history, conditioned not just by the size of the plot, but more so by the location of the temple – the international dimensions of which are evident even in the meagre remains found of inscriptions from the Republican period (see Bruno 2004, 18-19; Cassia 2008). Starting from the late 4th – early 3rd century BCE, an important monumental transformation was enacted, with the construction of the building that lasted until the beginning of the 1st century BCE, when the sanctuary underwent an overall rebuilding (see Bonzano 2017a) (Fig. 3).

The architectural remains belonging to this phase are few in number, but extremely significant in a scenario open to external influences but at the same time

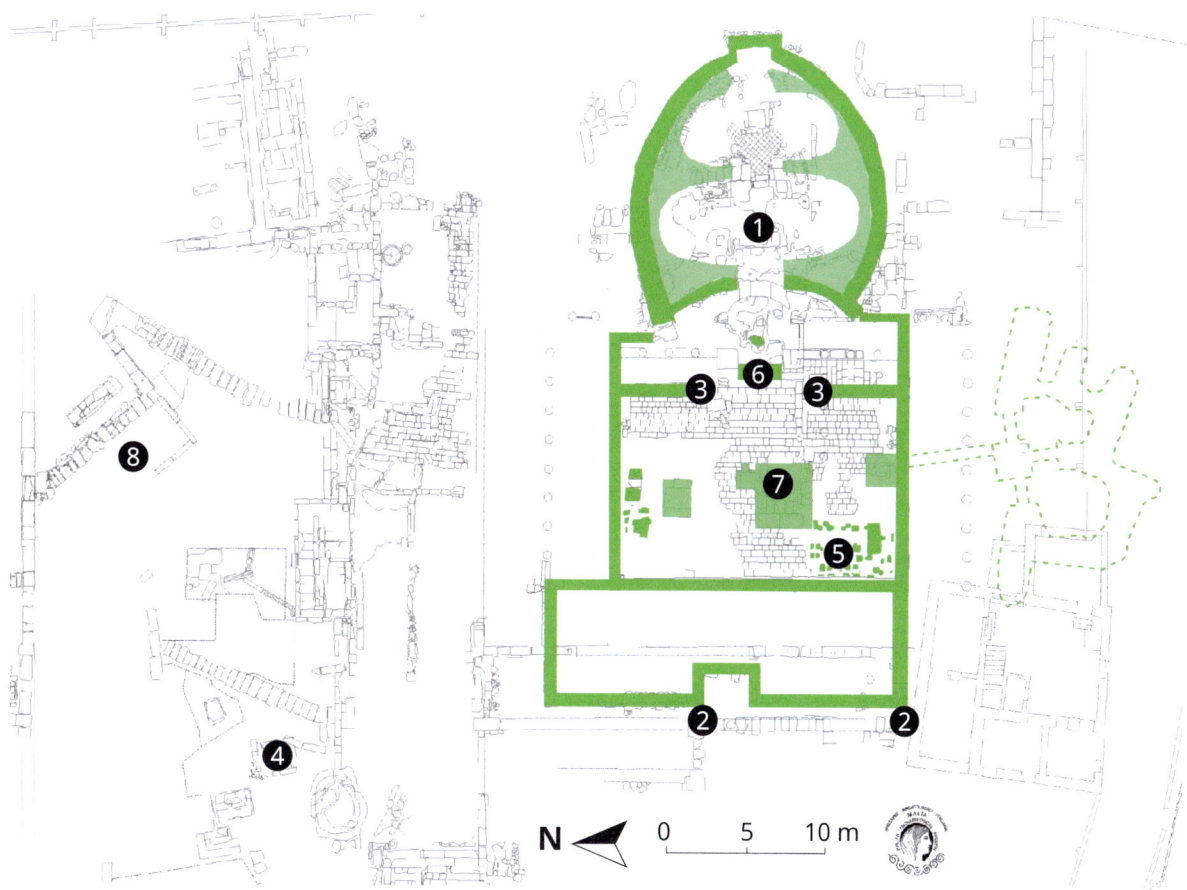

Figure 4. Tas-Silġ, the central area of the sanctuary during Punic-Hellenistic period. Italian Archaeological Mission Archive, reworked.

capable of reworking different 'languages' in an original way, adapting them to the context (see Bonzano 2021).

Prominent among these are the decorative elements of Alexandrian heritage, that is the large Aeolian pilaster capitals that I have suggested were placed at corners to emphasise the edges of the walls leading to the central area (Fig. 4.2; Ciasca 1972, 21-22, tav. 11, 2; Cagiano de Azevedo 1973, Fig. 45, 3). Compared to other contemporary examples of this type, these pieces stand out for their abundant decorative features and stylistic refinement (Fig. 5b, d). At present, the closest parallel is Sabratha Mausoleum B, in respect to which the Maltese specimens show greater formal complexity and a softer and more refined rendering of the ornamentation (Fig. 5a; Di Vita 1968, 16-31, Figs. 2-9; Di Vita 1976; Di Vita 1983, 357-360, Fig. 3; Di Vita 2010, 9; Prados Martínez 2008, 144-149).

Figure 5. Aeolic pilaster capitals: a – Sabratha, Mausoleum B; b – Malta, Tas-Silġ; c – Tharros, so-called temple with Doric half-columns; d – Malta, Tas-Silġ. a – Di Vita 1968, (b – Cagiano de Azevedo 1973, tav. 45, 3; c – Acquaro 1991a, Fig. 6; d – Italian Archaeological Mission Archive).

Figure 6. a, b – Amrith, pilasters crowned with double-grooved capital; c – Malta, Tas-Silġ, double-grooved capital; d – Malta, Tas-Silġ, composite block (a, b – Dunand and Saliby 1985, Fig. 4, Pl. XXXIII, 1-2; c – Italian Archaeological Mission Archive; d – Ciasca 1969, tav. 5, 1).

The Sabratha pieces date to the very early 2nd century BCE (see Bessi 2009, 15-18, 24), while the Tas-Silġ capitals, found reused in the late Republican structures, seem to have come from the 4th – 3rd century phase.[18] Given that the type known from Carthage is different, it is possible that the Maltese exemplars and subsequently those of Sabratha were derived from an Alexandrian prototype without the mediation of Carthage. Similar, although much simplified in terms of rendering and structure, is the pilaster capital used in the basement of the "Temple with Doric Columns" in Tharros (Fig. 5c).[19]

A certain originality is also displayed by the decorations of Egyptian tradition, in particular the capital with double-grooved Egyptian mouldings (Fig. 6c), which (together with another of unknown whereabouts) perhaps crowned the pillars that concluded the "archaic antas" [20] (Fig. 4.3; Cagiano de Azevedo 1973, 98-99; Caprino 1973, 51, 3, tav. 38,2, 39, 1-2). The latter are masonry walls located inside the sacrificial area that subdivide it. There are few parallels for such objects; in the temple of Amrith in Syria, the monumental phase of which is dated to the Persian period, pilasters and rectangular pillars crowned with similar capitals were found in the north-western corner of the complex, although they are more schematic in form; their original location has not been identified (Figs. 6a-b; Dunand – Saliby 1985, 16-17, Fig. 4. Pl. XIX, 1; XXXIII, 1-2; LXI, n. 22). Another capital, in this case with a simple moulding, is present on a composite element, a pillar that was part of the side wall of a tank (Figs. 4.4; 6d; Ciasca 1969, 40, tav. 5, 1-2). In this interesting piece, the Egyptian moulding motif is present on a capital that surmounts a fluted pilaster. No

---

18 Excavations conducted in the central area of the sanctuary have not brought to light late 4th/3rd – late 2nd/early 1st century BCE building phases that might plausibly have incorporated such large components (height 63.4 cm; width 46.2 cm; max. depth 52 cm).

19 As yet a precise reconstruction of the appearance of the monument's Punic phase has not been proposed (see Pesce 1961; Acquaro 1991a; Floris 2014-2015).

20 Ciasca initially assigned this piece from Malta to the Phoenician phase (Ciasca 1976-1977, 169, fig. 2), but later to the "Hellenistic" phase on the basis of comparison with Amrith (Ciasca 1991, 757).

a

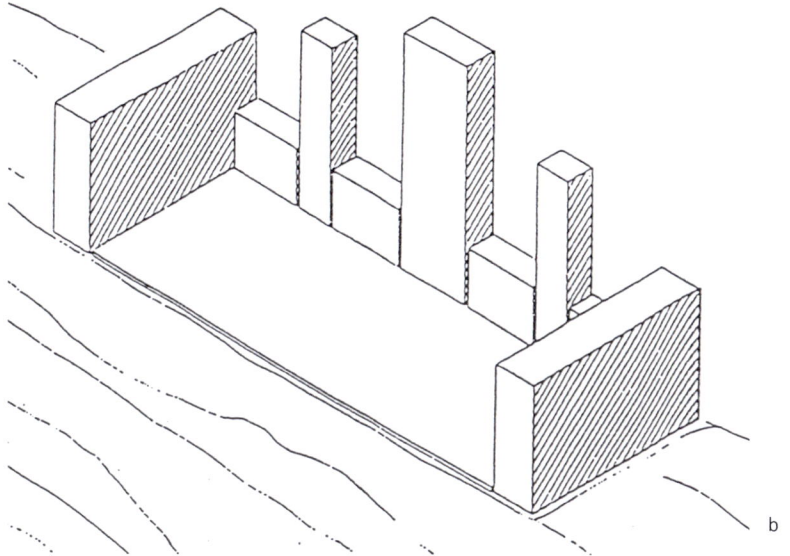

b

Figure 7. a – So-called ground altar, monolithic stone slab; b – so-called ground altar, hypothetical reconstruction (a – Rossignani 2012, Fig. 2; b – Ciasca 1993, Fig. 2).

precise parallels are known: a wall moulding with base and an Ionic pilaster come from Thuburbo Maius (Lézine 1961, 111-113, Fig. 60, Pl. XVII, 108); more generally, the presence of Egyptian forms and Greek mouldings on Aeolian pilaster capitals is also found in the Temple with Doric Columns in Tharros.

The presence of Greek forms constitutes another distinctive feature of the sanctuary's Punic era architecture, as shown by the presence of a Doric capital; although with due caution since this element has only been classified by its profile, it seems to closely resemble a piece in Carthage, from the *Quadergebäude* in Rue Ibn Chabaat (see Ferchiou 1989, 81-82, n.III.IB5, Fig.12d, Pl. CIV a; Rakob 1991, 70, Abb. 11, 3-4, Taf. 19, 1-3; Mancini 2010, 47, Fig. 4). This is not the earliest Doric find

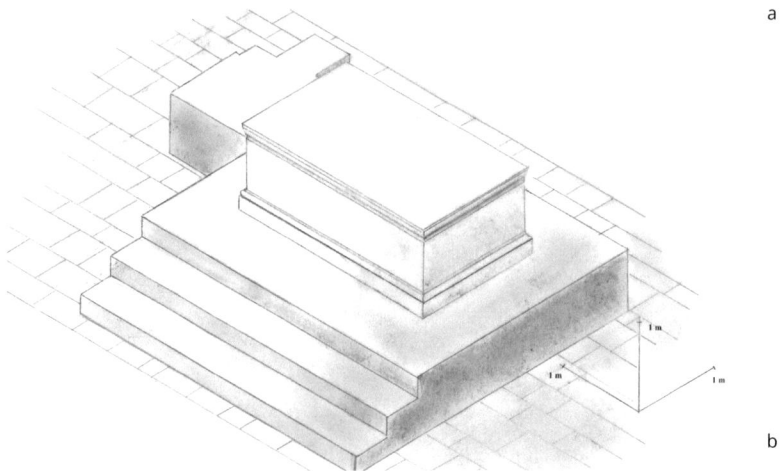

Figure 8. a – Table altar area, cuts in the beaten-earth floor; b – table altar, hypothetical reconstruction (a – Italian Archaeological Mission Archive; b – Bonzano 2004-2005, Fig. 10).

in the Maltese sanctuary; based on stylistic comparisons, a Doric capital seems to be attributable to the mid-5th century BCE (Caprino 1972, 42, Fig. 29,1).[21] If this date is correct, this attestation predates the arrival of Doric capitals in Carthage in the beginning of the 4th century by several decades (see Rakob 1996; Mancini 2010, 47). This situation may certainly be explained by Malta's proximity to and economic and cultural contacts with Greek Sicily, whose key role in the transmission of decorative models and motifs has been demonstrated (see Rakob 1996). The presence of *kymatiom* mouldings decorated with Ionic *kyma* is also interesting, found on memorial stones and votive objects originally placed in large numbers around one of the two altars in the central area (Figs. 4.5; 8a).[22] In front of the temple entrance stands the "ground altar", dating to the Phoenician epoch (Figs. 4.6; 7a): this monolithic stone slab, without a base, has three recesses on its long side. According to Ciasca, these would have held vertical stones known as baetyls (Ciasca 1976-1977, 166; Ciasca 1993, 228-229). From the Punic era there was also a table altar characterised by Greek forms and surrounded by votive objects (Figs. 4.7; 8b; Bonzano 2004-2005). The *kymatiom* bears a fragmentary inscription in the Phoenician language "... altar

21   The profile is more similar to some examples in Magna Graecia dated between 480 and the second half of the 5th century (Mertens 2006, 271-272, 276-277, 288-289, 390, 396, 417).

22   In late Republican times, these were removed from their locations and shattered; the preparation levels of the paving slabs cover the remains of this dismantling operation, the ritual character of which is indicated by a layer of ash.

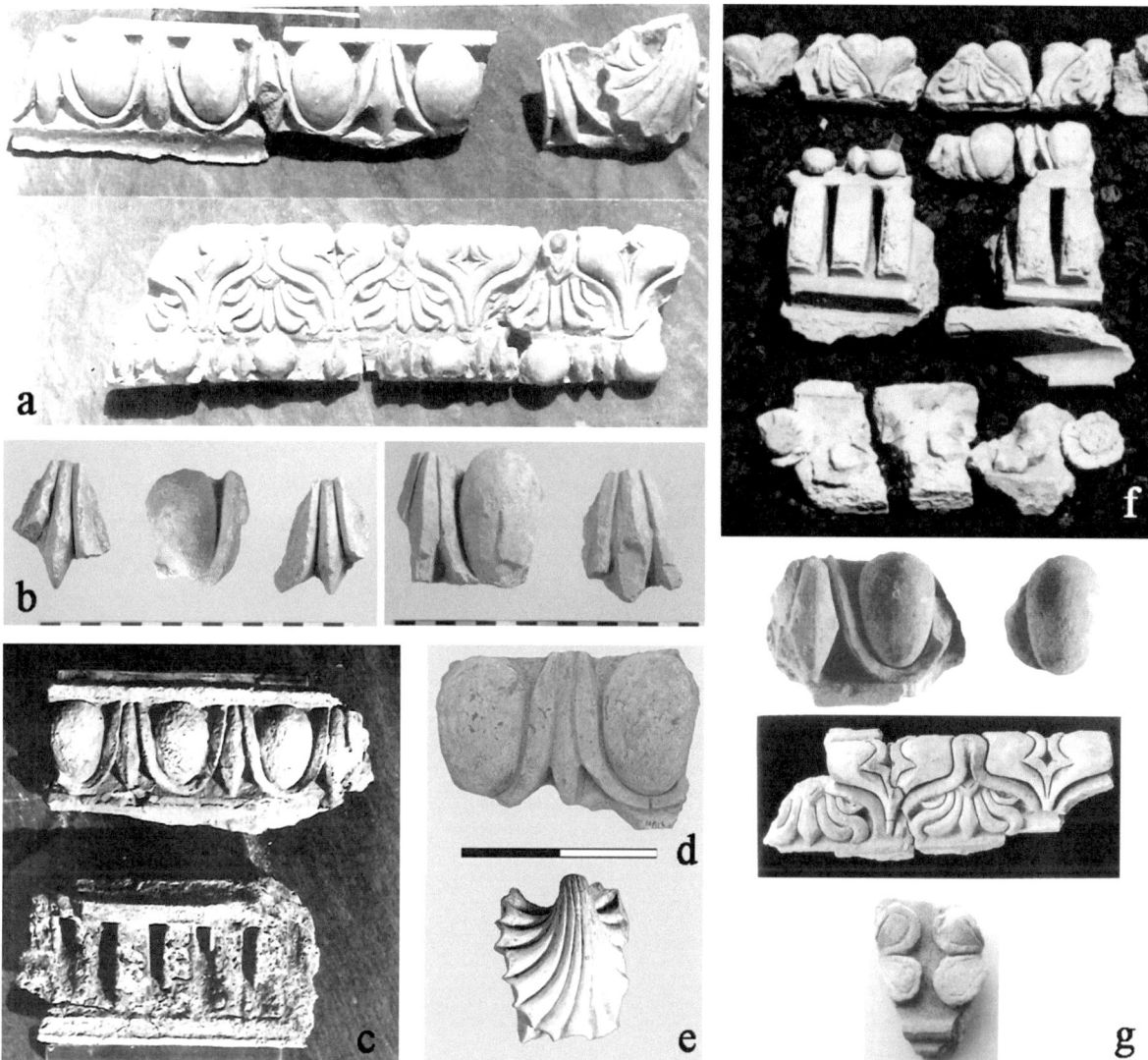

to Lady Astarte of Malta" that emphasises the divinity's regional connotation.[23] The presence of an altar of Hellenistic cultural origin is of particular importance in the sanctuary of Astarte, and in all likelihood should be understood together with the transformation of the ground altar – which was converted into a more "Greek" type through the addition of lateral shoulder-pieces (Fig. 7b).[24]

The few stucco items found during excavations are also worthy of note. However, the famous comments of Diodorus Siculus regarding the skill of Maltese craftsmen – "artisans skilled in every manner of craft" – and the quality of the houses – "the dwellings on the island are worthy of note, being ambitiously constructed with cornices and finished in stucco with unusual workmanship"[25] – are not backed by

Figure 9. Stucco fragments: a – Carthage, Chapelle Carton; b) Pantelleria, S. Teresa; c) Carthage, Museum; d) Malta, Tas-Silġ, North area; e) Malta, Tas-Silġ, South area; f) Carthage, Byrsa, Quartier Hannibal; g) Carthage, Quartier Magon. a – Ferchiou 1989, Fig. 62; Pl. LXXXIX,a; b – Müller 2015, Abb. 4-5; c – Ferchiou 1989, Pl. Pl. XCII,b; d – Ciasca 1966, tav. 26, 1; e – Cardona 2015, Fig. 6:8, a, reworked; f – Ferchiou 1991, Abb. 16; g – Laidlaw 1997, Taf. 134 a, 135 b, f.

23 On the basis of comparison with similar formulas documented in Carthage and Cagliari, it has been proposed that Astarte 'NN was the protector goddess of the entire island of Malta (see Amadasi Guzzo 1993, 210; Amadasi Guzzo 2016, 396-397).

24 The ground altar and the votive objects were obliterated by the late Republican rebuild, while the table altar remained in use until the Byzantine era. An in-depth study of the selection, obliteration and preservation of cult facilities conducted at the beginning of the 1st century BCE may be found in Bonzano 2017b. There is a discussion of the rituals practised in the sanctuary in this period in Bonzano 2021, 197-199.

25 Diod. V, 12, 1-4.

finds from the sanctuary, which offer few examples of a practice that must have been more widespread. A fragment of Ionic *kyma* (Fig. 9d; Ciasca 1966, 39, n. 5, tav. 26,1) and a piece of pilaster may be related to the internal decoration of a building known as Rooms 38-43 – perhaps a *sacellum* or place of worship, or indeed a reception suite (Fig. 4.8; Semeraro 2012, 116). *Kymatia* that are stylistically very similar have been found in Carthage, in the German excavations of the *domus* near the Baths of Antoninus (Laidlaw 1997, n. 17b, Fig. 16, 221, 226, Pl. 134c) and the French excavations on Byrsa Hill (Figs. 9c, f; Laidlaw 1997, Fig. 21a), and in the *Quartier Magon* (Fig. 9g) as well as in the *chapelle Carton* at Salammbô (Fig. 9a; Ferchiou 1989, Cat. XVIII.I.G.2, 334-335, Fig. 62, Pl. LXXXIX,A; Laidlaw 1997, Fig. 21b, Pl. 137a.). Very similar stuccoes come from the excavations at Utica. They belong to the wall of a building of unknown function, of which N. Ferchiou has proposed a reconstruction (see Ferchiou 1995, 68-70, Figs. 27-28). The stucco fragments unearthed during excavations on the acropolis of Santa Teresa on the island of Cossyra / Pantelleria have similar characteristics (Fig. 9b).

The use of such decoration in the Tas-Silġ sanctuary is also attested by a stucco palmette (Fig. 9e) that is stylistically similar to the corner element present in the *chapelle Carton* frieze, which terminates an Ionic *kymation*.[26]

The *hellénisation de Carthage* and the Punic world: An overview

The architectural finds just discussed raise a question that has arisen repeatedly during studies of these matters, in part due to the disproportionate quantity of Greek sources, *i.e.* the presumed "Hellenisation" of Carthage and the Punic world.[27] However, only archaeological and epigraphic evidence may be used to evaluate the ways and means in which Greek culture penetrated Carthage (Bonnet 2006, 366). It is of course necessary to define what is meant by the term "Hellenisation": if it indicates the adoption of Greek language, customs and cults, then such a phenomenon never occurred in the Punic world; on the other hand, the presence of artefacts does not necessarily imply the permanent habitation of those associated with them, but may have been due to the city's long-standing role as a commercial hub. The arrival of Greek features cannot be considered as adaptation to a "higher" cultural model, but rather as a choice to adopt certain forms of artistic and cultural expression as a means of modifying them, and not as simply an objective. Furthermore, it is necessary to clarify what is meant by the term "Greek": in the case of Carthage and the Punic world, where Sicily was an important mediator, the "Greekness" with which Carthage came into contact was of western origin, both politically and culturally (Bonnet 2006, 367-369).

Traditionally, the (alleged) Hellenisation of Carthage is often linked to the introduction of the cult of Demeter and Kore, witnessed by Diodorus for the year 396 BCE, which served to repay Himilco's act of impiety in desecrating the suburban temple of these two divinities in Syracuse (Diod. XIV, 77, 4-5; Xella 1969). The introduction of the cult took place with great public ceremony: The goddesses' statues were brought into the city, Greek-type sacrifices were made and the city's

---

26 Found during excavations conducted in the Southern Area by the University of Malta among dumped material (Bonanno 2005, 285; Cardona 2015, 322, Fig. 6:8, a).

27 A workshop held in 2005 (published in 2006 as *L'hellénisation en Méditerranée occidentale au temps des guerres puniques [260-180 av. J.C.]* in *Pallas*, 70), was dedicated to Hellenisation dynamics in the western Mediterranean at the time of the Punic Wars. The subject was developed above all by French-speaking scholars, starting with Gsell 1920; for a *status quaestionis* see also Fantar 1988.

most prominent Greeks were involved in conducting the related daily tasks.[28] Recent scholarship has seen as less important the allochthonous aspect without local modification, evaluating the event within a broader framework of acquisition of Greek cultural elements (see Garbati 2003; Peri 2003). It would perhaps be more correct to speak of the cult's conscious public appropriation, without this implying syncretic dynamics or the implementation of a genuine religious reform in the aftermath of Himilco's defeat and suicide. Thus a political interpretation sees the adoption of the cult – borrowed from Sicily and practised in the Greek way – as an instrument aimed at reaffirming a sort of territorial and cultural unity: *"l'hellénisation ne serait donc nullement un processus acculturatif venu d'en haut, imposant aux Carthaginois une culture supérieure, mais plutôt un choix sélectif opéré par les Carthaginois eux-mêmes afin d'enrichir et d'enraciner leur propre domination"*; the conceptual category of Hellenisation should therefore be abandoned in favour of an approach aimed at understanding *transferts culturels* (see Bonnet 2006, 376).[29]

This reflects all the more reason that the signs of Greek cultural penetration identified elsewhere in the Punic world should be evaluated with similar caution, such as the tophets of Mozia, and later Lilibeo, where steles reproducing Greek architectural forms are attested, together with the adoption of Greek vessel forms in depositions, and the use in the sanctuary's structures of architectural features of similar origin (see Orsingher 2013, 695). In Carthage, the steles in the tophet dating to the first half of the 4th century BCE show the introduction of Greek elements that point to the city's role as an intermediary between Greek culture and the Alexandrian East.[30] An analogous situation is seen in the tophets of Sulcis, Sousse and Monte Sirai. However, in the tophet of Tharros – a trading centre involved in the importation of luxury goods and the imitation of Greek styles – these indicators found in other sanctuaries are absent, suggesting that "... the Hellenisation of the Punic world produced only secondary changes in Tophets, which reflect the already visible transformations in buildings from architectural traditions of Greek origin or the diffusion of new food habits, testified by the presence of innovative ceramic forms for ritual use from the late 5th century BCE. There are no signs of deeper changes, involving ceremonies and cults" (Orsingher 2013, 695-696).

The adoption of Greek elements in Punic culture was pervasive, as also shown by the residential area that grew on the acropolis of Selinunte between the late 4th and mid-3rd century BCE. Here, the adoption of Greek habits is not indicated by the district's organisation or the house plans, but rather by the forms of the stone and stucco architectural decorations. Doors and windows are surrounded by cornices with dentils and astragals, while the stucco decorations display Ionic and Lesbian *kymatia* (see Helas 2011, 168-169), in line with a trend also found, as we have seen, in Carthage and Malta. Although Greek architectural styles seem to be used for

---

28 Diod. XIV, 63-77. This did not imply adherence to the eschatological and mystical ideology due to a "lack of spirituality" of the Punic religion or the decline of the traditional pantheon (see Peri 2003, 147-153; Bonnet 2006, 375-376, with bibliography).

29 An interesting example regards the evocation of Athena by Agathocles in 310: When preparing for a battle on African soil, the king had many owls released. Flying round the battlefield, these evoked the presence of the divinity who supported the Greeks and guaranteed the victory of "Hellenism" over Punic barbarism (Diod. XX, 8, 3-4). According to Corinne Bonnet: *"... la présence d'Athéna semble relever d'une certaine koiné cultuelle qui se nourrit de passerelles, d'interprétations, d'équivalence"* (Bianco and Bonnet 2016, 157). Athena – according to the tradition of Philo of Byblos the daughter of the Phoenician Cronos – was sent to Athenian soil by her father only later; the scholar observes that, rather than suggesting the concept of "syncretism", this striking reversal of perspective orients us towards the *"bricolage identitaire que l'hellénisme ... a largement favorisé"* (*ibid.* 173-175).

30 Lancel 1992, Fig. 180, 182, 211; for the pillar in Fig. 182 see also Ferchiou 1989, 454, Pl. CXI d, with a late 4th – early 3rd century BCE date. The refined acanthus leaves that decorate the echinus of the anta capital resembles forms attested both in the Peloponnese (Tegea, Epidaurus) and eastern areas (*Didymaion*).

purposes of self-representation, as their presence on the facade of the courtyard of a house on the main road might suggest[31], nevertheless the adoption of Greek moulding decorations does not mean that the inhabitants were Greek, nor that the owners of the houses wanted to live "Greek-style" lives, since housing culture and religious practices do not show a similar process of Hellenic penetration (see Helas 2011, 171-173, with bibliography).

At the end of the 4th century, Carthage had reached a level of cultural refinement such that Agathocles was surprised to see the countryside full of houses "constructed in luxurious fashion and covered with stucco" in a landscape of "gardens and plantations of every kind".[32] Archaeological data confirm that in Carthaginian homes from the 4th century onwards, the internal stuccoes incorporated Greek-style ornamental motifs that resemble the First Style decorations in the houses of Pompeii (see Ferchiou 1991; Laidlaw 1997; Mancini 2010, 59-60), while some details show features typical for Carthage (see Lappi 2018). These elements are juxtaposed with Egyptian-type mouldings, but belong to a distinctively Punic style of building techniques, measures, and water management employing typical "bathtub" cisterns.[33] Furthermore, the data from settlements in north-western Sicily suggest that the Lesbian *kyma* motif attested at the end of the 2nd century BCE in this area of Sicily is of Punic origin. It closely resembles examples from Carthage dated between the late 3rd to the first half of the 2nd century BCE (Campagna 2011b, 216-217).

Regarding Hellenic influences in Punic Sardinia, although the steles – especially at Sulcis – differ from those of Carthage for the presence of Greek architectural motifs, monumental architecture on the other hand seems to have resisted the incorporation of these motifs, except for some cases and limited to decorative details. The motivation does not lie in the "greater or lesser permeability of Punic-Sardinian craft culture to inspirations of Greek origin", but rather in the conscious selection of the architectural languages available according to the meaning attributed to them.[34] Study of the religious areas – in particular the Nora sanctuaries of Coltellazzo and Sa Punta 'e su Coloru – has shown that the architectural models employed are influenced, albeit in different ways, by practices widespread in the eastern Phoenician zone, constituting an "ideological" reference to the community's roots (see Oggiano 2005; Bondì 2016, 590-591). On the other hand, the steles seem to have been chosen by individual clients, who were more inclined to adopt stylistic elements in common use at the time, as also attested by certain decorative details in monumental complexes such as the half-column structure of the base of the Temple with Doric Columns in Tharros (see above).

---

31 Werner 2011; the facade contains a door surrounded by a dentilled frame, between two windows flanked by columns surmounted by Ionic capitals and crowned by a tympanum.

32 Diod. XX, 8, 3-4: "The intervening country through which it was necessary for them to march was divided into gardens and plantations of every kind, since many streams of water were led in small channels and irrigated every part. There were also country houses one after another, constructed in luxurious fashion and covered with stucco, which gave evidence of the wealth of the people who possessed them. The farm buildings were filled with everything that was needful for enjoyment, seeing that the inhabitants in a long period of peace had stored up an abundant variety of products. Part of the land was planted with vines, and part yielded olives and was also planted thickly with other varieties of fruit-bearing trees. On each side herds of cattle and flocks of sheep pastured on the plain, and the neighbouring meadows were filled with grazing horses. In general there was a manifold prosperity in the region, since the leading Carthaginians had laid out there their private estates and with their wealth had beautified them for their enjoyment".

33 Laidlaw 1997; Tang 2005, 98-99; for examples of Punic houses with floors in cocciopesto with *tesserae* and bathtub cisterns cf. 99-106. On the use of stucco mouldings in the internal decoration of religious buildings, see the section on composite architecture above.

34 Bondì 2016, 585-586. Analysis of the motifs present on the Sulcis steles indicates – in accordance with a hypothesis previously formulated by Moscati – not only that the craftsmen who made them were itinerant, but that they had direct knowledge of Greek workshops or models (*ibid.*, 588-589).

Defensive architecture also seems to have undergone a process of "Hellenisation of Punic defensive architecture", as demonstrated by the progressive assimilation of Greek-style *opus quadratum* and the adoption of frequent square towers in the town wall.[35]

Conclusions: Cultural identity and composite architectures

In the light of the foregoing, the (Late)-Punic-(Hellenistic) phase of the Tas-Silġ sanctuary fits well with the lively western Mediterranean Punic-influenced cultural milieu, while retaining specifically religious features in its conservation of part of the Late Neolithic structures.

The composite architecture that we have seen reflects a double input: on one hand the sea brought a flux of people, ideas and cultural models that helped to define its cultural identity; on the other, a strong and recognisable identity was created and established, rooted in a strong tradition. Current knowledge is insufficient to determine whether (and if so, what) particular semiotics were attributed to the individual groups of architectural motifs: Was it a repertoire from which individual clients chose freely, or were specific values or meanings associated with the various areas of cultural origin?

This question is difficult to answer, above all due to uncertainties regarding the reconstruction of the architectural complexes involved, especially with respect to Carthage.

While taking into account the fragmentary nature of the evidence available, the western Mediterranean basin in this period seems to exhibit a fully "Hellenistic" spirit. A characteristic traditionally attributed to early Hellenistic architecture is the tendency to experiment and develop original solutions even within a shared repertoire[36], in this case through the adoption of a "mixed" architecture typified by the "syncrétisme égypto-grec" evoked by Lancel with regard to Carthage (Lancel 1992, 337).; The concepts of *identity* and *hybridisation* in Hellenistic architecture have been developed for the East (see Kouremenos *et al.* 2011), but not the West.

Within the eparchy there existed a number of manifestations of "Punic-ness", sharing a common cultural base (see Bondì 2014, 67). This seems an appropriate perspective for the situation in Malta, which for the period in question showed a marked propensity to accept allochthonous forms and interpret them according to local taste. It also seems true for the other centres in the Carthaginian eparchy that adopted architectural forms in which individual decorative elements and architectural typologies (part of a shared heritage) were used in apparently unconstrained ways, though they were distinctive of each place. This trend was subsequently developed in Numidian architecture, in which decorative features such as Aeolian capitals, cornices with Egyptian mouldings and Greek architectural features were used consistently and with few variations. It is no coincidence that the term "Hellenistic" has been repeatedly used for these buildings.

As mentioned above, it is not possible to establish the extent to which in the 4th and 3rd centuries BCE what happened in Carthage was emulated elsewhere in an expression of "Punic" identity. The fact remains that some models could have arrived without the mediation of Carthage, as perhaps happened for the Aeolian capitals attested in Malta. In addition, even if the use of Greek-type decorative styles,

---

35 De Vincenzo 2016, 161 with regard to Erice. Further examples of the "degree of Hellenisation seen in the Punic fortifications" consist of the *proteichismata* attested from the end of the 4th century BCE in Lilybaeum, in line with the Syracuse Agathoclean mode.

36 On the distinctive characteristics of Hellenistic architecture see Lauter 1999, 261-275.

techniques and architectural models was widespread, this did not affect the varied and distinctive identities of the individual centres.[37]

The impression is of a world open to trade, vivacious and "Hellenistic", characterised by the circulation of stylistic models that were conveyed by the sea and trading routes, and therefore widely differentiated. Malta's central position with regard to Mediterranean routes is also evident in the fact that decorative styles are combined and reworked to produce original solutions, which in turn express a cultural and religious identity. Both hybridisation and identity are evident in Tas-Silġ: The dedication to "Lady Astarte of Malta" is engraved in the Phoenician language on the *kymation* of a Greek-style altar. There are many aspects that we still do not understand – from the Phoenician deity's relationship with the remains of the megalithic temples, to ritual practices, and how the divine *persona* of this particular Astarte was perceived by visitors who disembarked in the port of Marsaxlokk below – but the attention and fame generated in Roman times by this *fanum Iunonis antiquum* (Cic. *In Verrem*, II, 4,103) reflect the importance of this place of worship that looks out "naturally" over the sea.

Acknowledgements

The Università Cattolica del Sacro Cuore of Milan contributed to the funding of this research project and its publication.

References

Acquaro, E., 1991a. Tharros tra Fenicia e Cartagine. *Atti II congresso internazionale studi fenici e punici*, 547-558.

Acquaro, E., ed., 1991b. *Atti del II congresso internazionale di studi fenici e punici* [Roma, 9-14 novembre 1987]. Collezione di Studi Fenici, 30. Rome: Consiglio nazionale delle ricerch.

Amadasi Guzzo, M.G., 1993. Divinità fenicie a Tas-Silġ, Malta, I dati epigrafici. *Journal of Mediterranean Studies*, III (2), 205-214.

Amadasi Guzzo, M.G., 2016. Arredi cultuali iscritti a Tas-Silġ. I frequentatori del santuario. *In*: S. Lusuardi Siena, C. Perassi, F. Sacchi and M. Sannazaro, eds. *Archeologia classica e post-classica tra Italia e Mediterraneo. Scritti in ricordo di Maria Pia Rossignani*. Contributi di Archeologia, 8. Città di Castello 2016, 393-402.

Annan, B., 2013 *«Parce qu'il a entendu sa voix, qu'il le bénisse»*: représentations d'orants et d'officiants dans les sanctuaires hellénistiques d'Oumm el-ʿAmed [Liban]. *Histoire de l'Art*, 73, 43-56.

Aounallah, S. and Mastino, A., eds. 2018. *Carthage: Maîtresse de la Méditerranée, Capitale de l'Afrique [IXe siècle avant J.-C. – XIIIe siècle]*. Tunis: Agence de Mise en Valeur du Patrimoine et de Promotion Culturelle (AMVPPC).

Aubet, M.E., 2009. *Tiro y las colonias fenicias de occidente*. Barcelona: Edicions bellaterra.

Bechtold, B., 2018. La distribuzione della produzione anforica di Poseidonia/Paestum [V-I sec. a.C.] nell'area di influenza punica [Sicilia, Tunisia, Malta]: una revisione dei dati editi e prospettive di ricerca. *FACEM* [online], version 06 December 2018. Available from: http://www.facem.at/project-papers.php [Accessed 17 July 2020].

---

37   Similar reflections have been made regarding the Oumm el-ʿAmed sanctuary in Lebanon, where the architecture and decorations reflect both a clearly Phoenician tradition together with several lines of contemporary development widespread in the Hellenistic world, such as the adoption of Greek elements (Nitschke 2011; Annan 2013).

Bessi, B., 2009. La stratigrafia e i materiali delle fasi ellenistiche e proto-romane – Catalogo [Parte I, Il mausoleo punico-ellenistico di Sabratha]. *Quaderni di Archeologia della Libia*, 20, 11-92.

Bianco, M. and Bonnet, C., 2016. Sur les traces d'Athéna chez les Phéniciens. *Pallas*, 100, 155-179.

Bonanno, A., 2005. *Malta Phoenician, Punic, and Roman*. Malta: Midsea Books Ltd.

Bonanno, A. and Vella, N.C., eds., 2015. *Tas-Silġ, Marsaxlokk* [Malta] *I: Archaeological Excavations Conducted by the University of Malta, 1996-2005*. Ancient Near Eastern Studies supplement 48. Leuven: Peeters uitgeverij.

Bondì, S.F., 2014. Phoenicity, punicities. *In*: J. Crawley Quinn and N.C. Vella, eds. *The Punic Mediterranean. Identities and Identification from Phoenician Settlement to Roman Rule*. Cambridge: Cambridge University Press, 58-68.

Bondì, S.F., 2016. Influssi greci nella Sardegna di età punica, tra architettura e rilievo lapideo. *In*: J. Bonetto, M.S. Busana, R. Ghiotto, M. Salvadori and P. Zanovello, eds. *I mille volti del passato. Scritti in onore di Francesca Ghedini*. Rome: Edizioni Quasar, 583-592.

Bondì, S.F., Botto, M., Garbati, G. and Oggiano, I., 2009. *Fenici e Cartaginesi. Una civiltà mediterranea*. Rome: Istituto Poligrafico dello Stato.

Bonnet, C., 2006. Identité et altérité religieuse. A propos de l'hellénisation de Carthage. *Pallas*, 2006, 365-379.

Bonzano, F., 2004-2005. Appendice. L'altare ellenistico del santuario: proposta di identificazione e ipotesi ricostruttiva. *Scienze dell'Antichità*, XII, 2004-2005, 365-369.

Bonzano, F., 2017a. *Fanum Iunonis melitense. L'area centrale del santuario di Tas-Silġ a Malta in età tardo-repubblicana*. Malta: Scavi e ricerche della Missione Archeologica Italiana, 2 Bari.

Bonzano, F., 2017b. Note di biografia culturale di un luogo di culto: selezione, conservazione e costruzione della memoria storica nel santuario di Tas-Silg a Malta. *Mare Internum*, 9, 99-112.

Bonzano, F., 2021. The Maltese Islands between Isolation and Interconnections: An Architectural Perspective. *In*: L. Dierksmeier, F. Schön, A. Kouremenos, A. Condit and V. Palmowski, eds. *European Islands Between Isolated and Interconnected Life Worlds: Interdisciplinary Long-Term Perspectives*. Tübingen: University of Tübingen Press, 185-206.

Bruno, B., 2004. *L'arcipelago maltese in età romana e bizantina. Attività economiche e scambi al centro del Mediterraneo*. Bari: Edipuglia.

Cagiano de Azevedo, M. ed., 1972. *Missione Archeologica Italiana a Malta. Rapporto preliminare della campagna di scavo 1969*. Rome: Pontificia Università Gregoriana.

Cagiano de Azevedo, M. ed., 1973. *Missione Archeologica Italiana a Malta. Rapporto preliminare della campagna di scavo 1970*. Rome: Pontificia Università Gregoriana.

Cagiano de Azevedo, M., 1973. La campagna 1970. *In*: M. Cagiano de Azevedo, ed. *Missione Archeologica Italiana a Malta. Rapporto preliminare della campagna di scavo 1970*. Rome: Pontificia Università Gregoriana, 97-100.

Campagna, L., 2011a. Exploring social and cultural changes in provincia Sicilia. Reflections on the study of urban landscapes. *In*: F. Colivicchi, ed. *Local cultures of South Italy and Sicily in the late republican period: between Hellenism and Rome*. Journal of Roman Archaeology Suppl. 83, Portsmouth, RI: Journal of Roman Archaeology, 161-184.

Campagna, L., 2011b. Sistemi decorative parietali ellenistici in Sicilia: le cornici in stucco. *In*: G.F. La Torre and M. Torelli, eds. *Pittura ellenistica in Italia e in Sicilia. Linguaggi e tradizioni*. Atti del convegno di studi, Messina 24-25 settembre 2009. Rome: Giorgio Bretschneider Editore, 187-225.

Canfora, L., 1987. *Ellenismo*. Rome and Bari: Laterza.

Caprino, C., 1972. Lo scavo dell'area Sud. *In*: M. Cagiano de Azevedo, ed. *Missione Archeologica Italiana a Malta. Rapporto preliminare della campagna di scavo 1969*. Rome: Pontificia Università Gregoriana, 31-46.

Caprino, C., 1973. Lo scavo dell'area Sud. *In*: M. Cagiano de Azevedo, ed. *Missione Archeologica Italiana a Malta. Rapporto preliminare della campagna di scavo 1970*. Rome: Pontificia Università Gregoriana, 43-57.

Cardona, D., 2015. The worked stone. *In*: A. Bonanno and N.C. Vella, eds. *Tas-Silġ, Marsaxlokk* [Malta] *I: Archaeological Excavations Conducted by the University of Malta, 1996-2005*. Ancient Near Eastern Studies supplement 48. Leuven: Peeters uitgeverij, 299-350.

Cassia, M., 2008. L'arcipelago maltese sotto il dominio romano. *In*: A. Bonanno and P. Militello, eds. *Malta in the Hybleans, the Hybleans in Malta. Malta negli Iblei, gli Iblei a Malta [Proceedings of the Conference Catania 30 September, Sliema 10 November 2006]*. KASA 2. Palermo: Officina di studi medievali, 133-194.

Ciasca, A., 1966. Lo scavo. *In*: M. Cagiano de Azevedo, ed. *Missione Archeologica Italiana a Malta. Rapporto preliminare della campagna di scavo 1965*. Roma, 25-45.

Ciasca, A., 1969. Lo scavo. *In*: M. Cagiano de Azevedo, ed. *Missione Archeologica Italiana a Malta. Rapporto preliminare della campagna di scavo 1968*. Rome: Pontificia Università Gregoriana, 29-46.

Ciasca, A., 1972. Lo scavo dell'area Nord. *In*: M. Cagiano de Azevedo, ed. *Missione Archeologica Italiana a Malta. Rapporto preliminare della campagna di scavo 1969*. Rome: Pontificia Università Gregoriana, 19-24.

Ciasca, A., 1976-1977. Il tempio fenicio di Tas-Silġ. Una proposta di ricostruzione. *Kokalos*, XXII – XXIII, 162-172.

Ciasca, A., 1991. Documenti di architettura fenicia a Malta. *In*: E. Acquaro, ed. *Atti del II congresso internazionale di studi fenici e punici [Roma, 9-14 novembre 1987]*. Collezione di Studi Fenici, 30. Rome: Consiglio nazionale delle ricerche, 755-758.

Ciasca, A., 1993. Some considerations regarding the sacrifical precincts at Tas-Silġ. *Journal of Mediterranean Studies*, 3 (2), 225-244.

Coarelli, F. and Thébert, Y., 1988. Architecture funéraire et pouvoir: réflexions sur l'hellénisme numide. *Mélanges de l'école française de Rome. Antiquité*, 100 (2), 761-818.

Crawley Quinn, J., 2013. *Monumental power: 'Numydian Royal Architecture' in context. In*: J.R.W. Prag and J. Crawley Quinn, eds. *The Hellenistic West. Rethinking the Ancient Mediterranean*. Cambridge: Cambridge University Press, 179-215.

Crawley Quinn, J. and Vella, N.C., 2014a. *Introduction. In*: J. Crawley Quinn and N.C. Vella, eds. *The Punic Mediterranean. Identities and Identification from Phoenician Settlement to Roman Rule*. Cambridge: Cambridge University Press, 1-8.

Crawley Quinn, J. and Vella, N.C., eds., 2014b. *The Punic Mediterranean. Identities and Identification from Phoenician Settlement to Roman Rule*. Cambridge: Cambridge University Press.

D'Andrea, B., 2017. Recensione al volume K. Melliti, Carthage: histoire d'une métropole méditerranéenne, Paris 2016. *CaSteR*, 2, 1-5. Available from: http://ojs.unica.it/index.php/caster/article/view/3026 [Accessed 22 October 2017].

Del Vais, C. Guirguis, M. and Stiglitz, A., eds., 2019. *Il tempo dei Fenici. Incontri in Sardegna dall'VIII al III sec. a.C.* Nuoro: Ilisso.

De Vincenzo, S., 2016. *Modelli mediterranei ed elaborazioni locali. Le mura di Erice nel quadro delle fortificazioni del Mediterraneo occidentale alla luce delle indagini stratigrafiche*, Analysis Archaeologica. An International Journal of Western Mediterranean Archaeology. Monographs Series 2. Rome: Edizioni Quasar.

Dench, E., 2003. Italy and Sicily in the Hellenistic Age. *In*: A. Erskine, ed. *A Companion to the Hellenistic World*. Oxford: Blackwell, 294-310.

Di Vita, A., 1968. Influences grecques et tradition orientale dans l'art punique de Tripolitaine. *Mélanges de l'Ecole Française de Rome. Antiquité*, LXXX, 7-84.

Di Vita, A., 1976. Il mausoleo punico-ellenistico B di Sabratha. *Mitteilungen des deutschen archaeologischen Instituts. Römische Abteilung*, 83, 273-285.

Di Vita, A., 1983. Architettura e società nelle città di Tripolitania fra Massinissa e Augusto: qualche nota. *In*: Ecole française de Rome, ed. *Architecture et société de l'archaïsme grec à la fin de la République romaine [Actes du colloque international, Rome 2-4 décembre 1980]*. Collection École Française de Rome, 66. Rome: Publications de l'École française de Rome, 355-376.

Di Vita, A., 2010. I mausolei punici di Sabratha e l'impianto urbano della città ellenistica: prodotti di un sincretismo culturale. *Bollettino di archeologia ondine*, 1-6. Available from: https://bollettinodiarcheologiaonline.beniculturali.it/wp-content/uploads/2019/01/1_DiVITA.pdf [Accessed 17 July 2020]

Dunand, M. and Saliby, N., 1985. *Le temple d'Amrith dans la Pérée d'Aradus*. Paris: Paul Geuthner.

Ensoli, S., 2016. Alessandria e Cartagine: interazioni artistiche e culturali tra Egitto ellenistico e Maghreb ellenizzato. *In*: L. Vaccaro, ed. *Africa / Ifrīqiya. Il Maghreb nella storia religiosa di Cristianesimo e Islam*. Storia religiosa Euro-Mediterranea 5. Azzate: Libreria Editrice Vaticana, 45-75.

Erskin, A., 2013. The view from the East. *In*: J.R.W. Prag and J. Crawley Quinn, eds. *The Hellenistic West. Rethinking the Ancient Mediterranean*. Cambridge: Cambridge University Press, 14-34.

Fantar, M.H., 1988. *À propos de la présence des Grecs à Carthage. Antiquités africaines*, 34, 11-19.

Fariselli, A.C. and Secci, R., eds. 2018. *Cartagine fuori da Cartagine: mobilità nordafricana nel Mediterraneo centro-occidentale fra VIII e II sec. a.C. Atti del Congresso Internazionale [Ravenna, 30 novembre – 1 dicembre 2017]*. Lugano: Agorà & Co.

Fentress, E., 2013. Strangers in the city: élite communication in the Hellenistic central Mediterranean. *In*: J.R.W. Prag and J. Crawley Quinn, eds. *The Hellenistic West. Rethinking the Ancient Mediterranean*. Cambridge: Cambridge University Press, 157-178.

Ferchiou, N., 1989. *L'évolution du décor architectonique en Afrique proconsulaire des derniers temps de Carthage aux Antonins. L'hellénisme africain, son déclin, ses mutations et le triomphe de l'art romano-africain*. Gap: Imprimerie Louis-Jean.

Ferchiou, N., 1991. Stucs puniques hellénistiques de Carthage. *Kölner Jahrbuch für Vor- und Frühgeschichte*, 24 (4. Internationales Kolloquium zur römischen Wandmalerei [Köln, 20.-23. September 1989]), 19-26.

Ferchiou, N., 1995. Stucs puniques hellénistiques d'Utique. *Antiquités africaines*, 31, 53-79.

Floris, S., 2014-2015. Architettura templare a Tharros – I. Il "Tempio monumentale" o "delle semicolonne doriche" fra tarda punicità e romanizzazione. *Byrsa*, 25-26 / 27-28, 39-79.

Garbati, G., 2003. *Sul culto di Demetra nella Sardegna punica. In*: G. Regalzi, ed. *Mutuare, interpretare, tradurre: storie di culture a confronto [Atti del II incontro «Orientalisti», Roma, 11-13 dicembre 2002]*. Rome: Universitá degli studi "La Sapienza", 127-143.

Gilkes O. and Vella N.C., 2001. The Lure of the Antique: Nationalism, Politics and Archaeology in British Malta [1880-1964]. *Papers of the British School at Rome*, 69, 353-384.

Griesbach, J., 2010. Le statue onorarie nel santuario di Apollo a Delo: mutamenti del concetto di autorappresentazione in età ellenistica. *Bollettino di Archeologia online* [online], I/ C/C8/2. Available from: http://www.bollettinodiarcheologiaonline.beniculturali.it/documenti/generale/2_GRIESBACH.pdf [Accessed 03 July 2017]

Griesbach, J., 2013. Zur topographie hellenistischer 'Ehrenstatuen' auf Delos. *In*: M. Galli, ed. *Roman Power and Greek Sanctuaries. Forms of Interaction and Communication*. Tripodes, 14. Athens: Scuola Archeologica Italiana di Atene, 83-124.

Gsell, S., 1920. *Histoire ancienne de l'Afrique du Nord IV*. Paris: Librairie Hachette.

Guirguis, M., ed. 2017a. *La Sardegna fenicia e punica. Storia e materiali*. Nuoro: Poliedro.

Guirguis, M. ed., 2017b. *From the Mediterranean to the Atlantic: people, goods and ideas between East and West, 8th International congress of Phoenician and Punic Studies [Carbonia, Sant'Antioco 21th – 26th October 2013].* Folia Phoenicia I. Pisa and Rome: Fabrizio Serra Editore.

Helas, S., ed., 2011. *Selinus II. Die punische Stadt auf der Akropolis.* Deutsches Archäologisches Institut Rom, Sonderschriften 15. Wiesbaden: Verlag Dr. Ludwig Reichert.

Kouremenos, A., Chandrasekaran, S. and Rossi, R., eds., 2011. *From Pella to Gandhara. Hybridisation and Identity in the Art and Architecture of the Hellenistic East.* BAR Internatinal Series 2221. Oxford: British Archaeological Reports Oxford Ltd.

Laidlaw, A., 1997. Report on Punic Plaster. *In*: F. Rakob, ed. *Karthago II. Die deutschen Ausgrabungen in Karthago.* Mainz a.R.: Philipp von Zabern Verlag, 215-228.

Lancel, S., 1992. *Carthage.* Paris: Fayard.

Laporte, J.-P., 2012. Massinissa et Ptolémée VIII Évergète II. Ou: "de la gastronomie à la politique internationale". *In*: S. Guédon, ed. *Entre Afrique et Égypte: relations et échanges entre les espaces au sud de la Méditerranée à l'époque romaine.* Scripta antiqua 49. Bordeaux: Ausonius, 213-219.

Lappi, T., 2018. Spätpunische Wanddekorationen Cathagos und ihre überregionalen Vergleiche. *In*: Y. Dubois and U. Niffeler, eds. *Pictores per provincias II – Status quaestionis [Actes du 13e Colloque de l'AIPMA, Lausanne 12-16 septembre 2016].* Basel: Archäologie Schweiz, 257-267.

Lauter, H., 1999. *L'architettura dell'ellenismo* [original Ed. Darmstadt 1986]. Milano.

Lézine, A., 1961. *Architecture punique. Recueil de documents.* Tunis: Publications de l'Université de Tunis.

Mancini, L., 2010. L'architettura templare di Cartagine alla luce delle fonti letterarie e delle testimonianze materiali. *Byrsa*, 17-18, 39-72.

Marcone, A., 2013. Concezioni di ellenismo tra '800 e '900. Droysen, Tarn, Rostovtzeff. *In*: G. Zecchini, ed. *L'ellenismo come categoria storica e come categoria ideale.* Temi metafisici e problemi del pensiero antico 130. Milano: Vita e Pensiero – Pubblicazioni dell'Università Cattolica del Sacro Cuore, 217-232.

Marconi, C., 2014. The Mozia Charioteer: A Revision. *In*: A. Avramidou and D. Demetriou, eds. *Approaching the Ancient Artifact. Representation, Narrative, and Function. A Festschrift in Honor of H. Alan Shapiro.* Berlin: De Gruyter, 435-447.

Melliti, K., 2016. *Carthage. Histoire d'une métropole méditerranéenne.* Paris: Perrin.

Mertens, D., 2006. *Città e monumenti dei Greci d'Occidente: dalla colonizzazione alla crisi di fine V secolo a.C.* Rome: ⌈L'Erma di Bretschneider.

Nitschke, J., 2011. 'Hybrid' Art, Hellenism and the Study of Acculturation in the Hellenistic East: The Case of Umm el-'Amed in Phoenicia. *In*: A. Kouremenos, S. Chandrasekaran and R. Rossi, eds. *From Pella to Gandhara. Hybridisation and Identity in the Art and Architecture of the Hellenistic East.* BAR Internatinal Series 2221. Oxford: British Archaeological Reports Oxford Ltd., 85-104.

Oggiano, I., 2005. Lo spazio sacro a Nora. *In*: A. Spanò Giammellaro, ed. *Atti del V congresso internazionale di studi fenici e punici, [Marsala-Palermo, 2-8 ottobre 2000].* Palermo: University of Palermo, 1029-1044.

Olcese, G., 2015. Produzione e circolazione mediterranea delle ceramiche della Campania nel III secolo a.C. Alcuni dati della ricerca archeologica e archeometrica. *In*: A. Siciliano and C. Mannino, eds. *La Magna Grecia da Pirro ad Annibale [Atti del cinquantaduesimo convegno di studi sulla Magna Grecia, Taranto 27-30 settembre 2012].* Taranto: Istituto per la Storia e l'Archeologia della Magna Grecia, 159-210.

Orsingher, A., 2013. The Hellenisation of the Punic World: a View from the Tophet. *In*: L. Bombardieri, A. D'Agostino, G. Guarducci, V. Orsi and S. Valentini, eds. *SOMA 2012. Identity and Connectivity [Proceedings of the 16th Symposium on Mediterranean Archaeology, Florence, Italy, 1-3 March 2012]. Vol. II.* BAR International Series, 2581. Oxford: British Archaeological Reports Oxford Ltd., 693-698.

Peri, C., 2003. Demetra e Core nella religione punica. *In*: G. Regalzi, ed. *Mutuare, interpretare, tradurre: storie di culture a confronto [Atti del II incontro «Orientalisti», Roma, 11-13 dicembre 2002].* Rome: Universitá degli studi "La Sapienza", 145-154.

Pesce, G., 1961. Il tempio punico monumentale di Tharros. *Monumenti Antichi*, 45, coll. 333-440.

Portale, E.C., 2015. Un confronto. La Sicilia nel III secolo. *In*: A. Siciliano and C. Mannino, eds. *La Magna Grecia da Pirro ad Annibale [Atti del cinquantaduesimo convegno di studi sulla Magna Grecia, Taranto 27-30 settembre 2012].* Taranto: Istituto per la Storia e l'Archeologia della Magna Grecia, 699-736.

Portale, E.C., 2017. Siracusa e la Sicilia nel III sec. a.C.: problemi conoscitivi e proposte di lettura dei fenomeni urbanistici e architettonici. *In*: L.M. Caliò and J. Des Courtils, eds. *L'architettura greca in Occidente nel III secolo a.C.* Thiasos monografie 8. Rome: Edizioni Quasar, 133-177.

Prados Martínez, F., 2008. *Arquitectura púnica. Los monumentos funerarios.* Anejos de archivio español de arqueología XLIV. Madrid: Consejo Superior de Investigaciones Científicas, CSIC.

Prag, J.R.W. and Crawley Quinn, J., 2013a. Introduction. *In*: J.R.W. Prag and J. Crawley Quinn, eds. *The Hellenistic West. Rethinking the Ancient Mediterranean.* Cambridge: Cambridge University Press, 1-13.

Prag, J.R.W. and Crawley Quinn, J. eds., 2013b. *The Hellenistic West. Rethinking the Ancient Mediterranean.* Cambridge: Cambridge University Press.

Purcell, N., 2014. The Ancient Mediterranean. *In*: P. Horden and S. Kinoshita, eds. *A Companion to Mediterranean History.* Oxford: Wiley Blackwell, 59-76.

Rakob, F., 1991. Ein punisches Heiligtum in Karthago und sein römischer Nachfolgbau. *Mitteilungen des Deutschen Archäologischen Instituts. Römische Abteilung*, XCVIII, 33-80.

Rakob, F., 1996. Dorische Architektur in Karthago. *In*: E. Acquaro, ed. *Alle soglie della classicità. Il Mediterraneo tra tradizione e innovazione. Studi in onore di Sabatino Moscati.* Pisa and Rome: Istituti Editoriali e Poligrafic, 925-934.

Regalzi, G., ed., 2003. *Mutuare, interpretare, tradurre: storie di culture a confronto [Atti del II incontro «Orientalisti», Roma, 11-13 dicembre 2002].* Rome: Universitá degli studi "La Sapienza".

Rossignani, M.P., Cazzella, A., Semeraro, G., Recchia, G. and Bonzano, F., eds., in press. *The sanctuary of Tas-Silġ in Malta: from neolithic place of worship to heathen sanctuary, to Christian church. Old and new excavations of the Italian archaeological Mission [1963-2012].* Malta. Scavi e ricerche della Missione Archeologica Italiana 1. Bari: Edipuglia.

Russo, A., Guarnieri, F., Xella, P. and Zamora López, J.A., eds., 2019. *Carthago. Il mito immortale, catalogo della mostra [Roma, 27 settembre 2019 – 12 aprile 2020].* Milano: Electa.

Sagona, C., 2002. *The Archaeology of Punic Malta.* Ancient Near Eastern Studies supplement 9. Leuven: Peeters.

Sagona, C., 2015. *The Archaeology of Malta. From the Neolithic through the Roman Period.* Cambridge: Cambridge University Press.

Semeraro, G., 2012. Il santuario di Tas-Silġ in età storica. Contributo alla storia delle pratiche rituali e dell'organizzazione spaziale: l'area settentrionale. *Scienze dell'antichità*, 18, 107-118.

Tang, B., 2005. *Delos, Carthage, Ampurias. The Housing of Three Mediterranean Trading Centres.* Analecta Romana Instituti Danici, Supplementum XXXVI. Rome: L´Erma di Bretschneider.

Van Dommelen, P. and López Bertran, M., 2013. Hellenism as subaltern practice: rural cults in the Punic world. *In*: J.R.W. Prag and J. Crawley Quinn, eds. *The Hellenistic West. Rethinking the Ancient Mediterranean.* Cambridge: Cambridge University Press, 273-299.

Vidal Gonzáles, P., 1996. *La Isla de Malta en Época Fenicia y Púnica*. BAR International Series, 653. Oxford: British Archaeological Reports Oxford Ltd.,

Wallace-Hadrill, A., 2013. Hellenistic Pompeii: between Oscan, Greek, Roman and Punic. *In*: J.R.W. Prag and J. Crawley Quinn, eds. *The Hellenistic West. Rethinking the Ancient Mediterranean*. Cambridge: Cambridge University Press, 35-43.

Werner, A., 2011. Die Hoffassade eines Hauses an der Hauptstraße. *In*: S. Helas, ed. *Selinus II. Die punische Stadt auf der Akropolis*. Deutsches Archäologisches Institut Rom, Sonderschriften 15. Wiesbaden: Reichert Verlag, 198-204.

Wilson, R.J.A., 2013. Hellenistic Sicily, c. 270-100 BCE. *In*: J.R.W. Prag and J. Crawley Quinn, eds. *The Hellenistic West. Rethinking the Ancient Mediterranean*. Cambridge: Cambridge University Press, 79-119.

Xella, P., 1969. Sull'introduzione del culto di Demetra e Kore a Cartagine. *Studi e Materiali di Storia delle Religioni*, 40, 215-228.

Becoming a man ashore: The role of the sea in Sappho's Brothers Song[1]

Laura C. Schmidt

Abstract

Sappho's Brothers Song is currently one of the most commonly-discussed ancient texts. In the last seven years, philologists have proposed various interpretations which partly draw on Sappho's transmitted biography (hence the title Brothers Song), partly on the song's context in Greek literature. Much prominence is given to the suggested parallels with Odysseus' wanderings: Sappho's older brother Charaxus becomes an alternative Odysseus, her younger brother Larichus a second Telemachus, she herself another waiting Penelope and the Brothers Song becomes a lyric remake of the Odyssey itself. The differences between the two works are significant and should not be dismissed too fast. As I show, a comparison of Charaxus with Telemachus reveals a new perspective on the song. For both Charaxus and Telemachus, seafaring constitutes a kind of rite-de-passage which symbolises their coming of age. Their coping with the sea shapes the perception of their identity by their fellow-citizens. In opposition to them, Larichus has to cope with a metaphorical sea to gain the same recognition and become a substitute for the absent Charaxus. This substitution is preferred by the speaker of the song, as Larichus' seafaring ashore is within her reach and thus open to her influence. Importantly, his coming of age is still expressed in the maritime language and mindset of Charaxus' journey.

Sappho, Brothers Song, seafaring, coming of age

---

1   I would like to thank Prof. Lutz Käppel, Hauke Schneider and Ioanna Pateraki for listening to and commenting on my ideas and Dr. Kleoniki Rizou and Anja Rutter for their advice and criticism on my first drafts. I also thank my parents for their perspective and advice on ethical questions regarding the papyri with the newest Sappho fragments. I owe special thanks to Pantazis Sarafis for patiently listening to and discussing with me all my considerations during the preparation of this paper at literally any moment.

Introduction

Sappho's so-called "Brothers Song" is one of two songs published by Dirk Obbink in 2014 unknown until then. It is transmitted on a piece of papyrus, the faked and probably illegal provenance of which is currently object of a scandal.[2] Before starting to set my own interpretation of the song out, I will make a few notes about the song's title and its implications for its understanding. The song is called *Brothers Song* or *Brothers Poem* due to the overlap of two male names (Charaxus and Larichus) found in it with two men mentioned in ancient sources as two of Sappho's three brothers. When Obbink published the song in the *ZPE* (2014, 32), he began his article with a reference to Herodotus' account on a brother of Sappho called Charaxus (Herodotus 1,135). Many scholars follow a biographical reading of the song, introducing details delivered in such external sources into the interpretation of the song.[3] Given the evident gap between the depiction in external sources and the depiction in the *Brothers Song*, this biographical reading has also found critics.[4] Some of Sappho's already-known songs supposedly deal with the story of Charaxus – albeit without containing the names of Sappho or her brothers – as they include motifs of absence at sea, hope for return and notions of (past) mistakes of the absent

---

2   The scandal reached the broad public since at least the article "A scandal in Oxford: the curious case of the stolen gospel" written by Charlotte Higgins and published in *The Guardian* on the 9th January 2020 (https://www.theguardian.com/news/2020/jan/09/a-scandal-in-oxford-the-curious-case-of-the-stolen-gospel). The article concerns not only the authenticity and provenance of the gospel referred to in the title, but also of the so-called *P. Sapph. Obbink*, containing the *Brothers Song*. Most classical scholars regard the *text* as authentic Sapphic, but this positive evaluation relies mostly on the physical examinations of the papyrus and its ink recorded by Obbink 2014 and 2016 and on the overlap with *POxy.* 2289 fr. 5. The claimed provenance has been doubted (*e.g.* Mazza 2014 and 2015) as has been – rarely – also the text (cf. the considerations of Nongbri 2021). In 2020, Sampson displays evidence that suggests that the claimed provenance is faked and in fact illegal. Nevertheless, he concludes that the text is authentic. In March 2021, the editors of the most recent volume on the new fragments (Bierl and Lardinois 2016) have marked Obbink's chapter on provenance, authenticity and text of the fragments as retracted. In writing this contribution I am relying on the conclusions of papyrologists on the papyrus' authenticity and I agree with the philologists on Sappho's authorship of the song. I condemn the illegal acquisition of ancient papyri and the display of faked provenance which must be prevented by scholars as well as publishers of new texts. I am nevertheless convinced that a *condemnatio memoriae* of the already published song is impossible – since the text is now inscribed into the minds of all its readers – and of no avail for the following necessary investigations on the provenance of the papyrus and the necessary judicial consequences. For this reason, I decided not to hold back my considerations on this song although I distance myself from the way how the text seems to have been made accessible at first hand to its anonymous owner and scholarship.

3   Cf. *e.g.* Papadimitropoulos 2016, p. 6 n. 5: "I think that, in all probability, the scenario implied is factual [...]" Details from biographical testimonies appear to add clarity to the song, *e.g.* Charaxus' liaison with a woman called Rhodopis/Doricha explains his absence, his stay at Egypt and his engagement in trade, the father's death explains the origin of the collective's problems. On Egypt, see Martin 2016, 118f., Bowie 2016, 155, Bierl 2016, 310, 318, Caciagli 2016, 443, Nagy 2016, 449, 452. Most extensive on the question of Charaxus' journey to Naucratis in Egypt and his trading activities there is Raaflaub 2016, 127-141, but he considers important (133) that Egypt and Naucratis (as well as the *hetaera* connected with Charaxus and these places) are not mentioned in the song. The death of the father (Ov. *Her.* 15,61-62) has been – partly tacitly – accepted as essential for the song's content by several scholars, *e.g.* Bettenworth 2014, 18, Obbink 2015, 3, Bierl 2016, 331, Benelli 2017, 91. Bierl 2016 prefers a fictional reading, but nevertheless regards the testimonies as helpful in the interpretation because they would rely on Sappho's songs. This approach can be observed also in other fictional readings, cf. *e.g.* Lardinois 2016, esp. 169-173, and Stehle 2016, esp. 266f.

4   Cf. *e.g.* Gribble 2016, esp. 29-41 and 45, Bär 2016, 10-15, Neri 2015, 58 n. 30 (esp. on Ov. *Her.* 15,61-62). Gribble discusses the previous literature on Charaxus' love story and its (in-)dependence on Sappho's poetry.

man.[5] Other fragments have been adduced in comparison to these "Brothers Songs" as well, because they also deal with the sea, wishes for good travel or return and similar and could, thus, be about Charaxus.[6] Finally, some scholars search for the thematic similarities with other songs of Sappho, notably her love songs.[7] It should be maintained that these overlaps are not essential enough to allow the reader to deduce from one fragment information for the interpretation of another song: while the songs are surely dealing with common matters, the exact relationship between them – *e.g.* in terms of chronology and perspective – cannot be reconstructed from the often very fragmentary pieces.

The *Brothers Song* is a rare example of a nearly complete text of Sappho. Comparison with other songs – not only of Sappho, but also of other poets – lead to the impression that rather than an autobiographical testimony, this song is an example of a lyric sub-genre.[8] In a literary approach, some scholars examine possible points of intertextuality with Homer's *Odyssey*, Hesiod's *Opera et Dies* and the myth of Castor and Pollux, the Dioscuri.[9] Ambiguities in the song such as actual family bonds or the reason for Charaxus' absence – important as they are for a biographical reading – do not affect the literary reading, as will become clear. In what follows, I will present a literary approach that concentrates on the *Brothers Song* exclusively. The comparisons with the *Odyssey* are intriguing, but I will show that a focus on the *Telemachy* will bring forth Sappho's innovation in this song without rendering her song a lyric version of (part of) the *Odyssey*. I will stick to the song's title as *Brothers Song* (*BS* in abbreviation) out of convenience for the reader.

The text of the *Brothers Song* is available in various versions that differ only in some minor points. The most obvious difference is the change of line numbering between Obbink's first and his last version (2014, 2016): traces of two lines preceding the text preserved on the *Papyrus Sappho Obbink* are printed in Obbink's recent edition, numbered as the two final lines of a preceding stanza. These stem from an older papyrus (*Papyrus Oxyrhynchus* 2289 fragment 5). The overlap of the papyri

---

5   Sa. 5 mentions a "brother" and a "sister", Sa. 15 has striking similarities with it. On their connection cf. Bär 2016, esp 17f., noting that Sa. 5,6 (χάραν γένεσθαι) "can be interpreted as an etymological pun on the name of Charaxus as 'bearer of joy' (< χάρα and ἄγειν)", the same also Gribble 2016, 57, Lardinois 2016, 171, Burris *et al.* 2014, 24. The name of Doricha (but not Rhodopis, the name given by Hdt. 2.135) has been tentatively restored in Sa. 5,13 (completely in the lacuna), 7,1 (either Δωρί]χας or]κας) and 15,11 (Δ]ωρίχα). On the recent reading of the name in Sa. 5, cf. West 2014, 6 (favouring) and Gribble 2016, 57-59 (against).

6   Sa. 3, 7, 9, 17 and 20 are considered most often. Cf. *e.g.* Obbink 2014, 35 (Sa. 5, 15, 20, *BS*), Liberman 2014, 1-2 with nn. 5 and 6 (Sa. 5, 7, 15, *BS*, cautiously 3, very cautiously 16, against 17), Ferrari 2014 (Sa. 5, 15, *BS*, against 20), Rayor and Lardinois 2014, 162f. (Sa. 5, 7, 9, 15, *BS*), Lardinois 2014, 185-187 and 191, and again 2016, 171-173 (Sa. 5, 15, *BS*, cautiously also 3, 7, 9 and 20), Neri 2015, 67-71 with n. 107 (Sa. 5, 9, 17, *BS*), Gribble 2016, 38 n. 28 and 40 n. 34 (Sa. 20, *BS*, sceptic on 15), Mueller 2016, 28 and 40-43 (Sa. 5, 15, 17, *BS*), Raaflaub 2016, 130f. (Sa. 3, 5, 7, 9, 15, *BS*), Bierl 2016, 323f. (Sa. 3, 5, 7, 9, 15, 17, 20, *BS*, but cf. also the next note), Caciagli 2016, esp. 434-437 (Sa. 5, 15, 17, *BS*), Benelli 2017, 56, 66, 99 (Sa. 3, 5, 9, 15, 17, 20, *BS*). A connection between Sa. 5, 7 and 15 had already been proposed before the *BS*, *e.g.* by Dale 2011, 67- 71, Bagordo 2009, 63, on basis of Doricha's name and the tradition about Sappho's brother. If "[...] these songs were composed independently of one another or were part of a cycle of songs that told a story from beginning to end [...]" (Rayor and Lardinois 2014, 162f.), is answered differently by the scholars.

7   See Bierl 2016, esp. 305f., Nagy 2016.

8   Cf. Gribble 2016, 40 n. 34: "Alcaeus, too, had a 'brothers' song (frag. 350), addressed to his brother Antimenidas, on the occasion of his return after serving as a mercenary abroad" and Mueller 2016, 42 (on Sa. 5, *BS*, and by implication also on Sa. 15 and 17): "[...] the similarity of theme – a brother returning unharmed – and the deictic adverb [*i.e.* τυίδε] suggest that prayers directed at a safe return constitute a sort of a mini-genre of their own within Sappho's corpus."

9   For Hes. *Op.*, see Lardinois 2014, 192f. (comparing also Archil.), and Martin 2016, 118f. with n. 20 (for the iambic potential of Hes. *Op.* and Sa. *BS*). For a comparison with paraenetic poetry as Hes. *Op.*, but also Thgn., Semon., Mimnermus, Archil., cf. already Dale 2011, 67-71, although based in many parts on external sources (esp. Hdt. 2,135, Ov. *Her.* 15 *etc.*) that cannot be supported with Sappho's poetry. For the Dioscuri, see Kurke 2016, 252-262, and below.

is based only on few letters and is not beyond doubt.[10] Following the (probable) hypothesis that some lines have preceded, I will give the traces of *Papyrus Oxyrhinchus* 2289 fragment 5 as representative of these lost lines and as a reminder of the fragmentary state of the song, but I will not engage in the discussion on the content of these lines. I give the text in the shape and with the line numbering of Obbink's latest edition (2016, 25f.) with a few changes marked in the footnotes.[11]

Text and translation

[1-5 lines]
[]

[. . . .]λα[
[. . .]σέμα[4
ἀλλ' ἄϊ θρύλησθα Χάραξον ἔλθην
νᾶϊ σὺν πλέαι,[12] τὰ μὲν, οἴομαι,[13] Ζεῦς
οἶδε σύμπαντές τε θέοι· σὲ δ' οὐ χρῆ
ταῦτα νόησθαι,[14]   8

ἀλλὰ καὶ πέμπην ἔμε καὶ κέλεσθαι
πόλλα λίσσεσθαι βασίληαν Ἥραν
ἐξίκεσθαι τυίδε σάαν ἄγοντα
νᾶα Χάραξον   12

κἄμμ' ἐπεύρην ἀρτέμεας. τὰ δ' ἄλλα
πάντα δαιμόνεσσον ἐπιτρόπωμεν·
εὔδιαι γὰρ ἐκ μεγάλαν ἀήταν
αἶψα πέλονται.   16

τῶν κε βόλληται βασίλευς Ὀλύμπω
δαίμον' ἐκ πόνων ἐπ' ἄρηον[15] ἤδη
περτρόπην, κῆνοι μάκαρες πέλονται
καὶ πολύολβοι·   20

κἄμμες, αἴ κε ϝὰν κεφάλαν ἀέρρη
Λάριχος καὶ δή ποτ' ἄνηρ γένηται,
καὶ μάλ' ἐκ πόλλαν βαρυθυμίαν κεν
αἶψα λύθειμεν. ⊗   24

---

10   Against the theory of a lost stanza, cf. Bär 2016, 27-31: the lines *POxy.* 2289 fr. 5,1-2 could also belong to the end of a preceding song; for another alternative, cf. Benelli 2017, 89-91. I cannot find persuasive Bär's hypothesis of a song starting with ἀλλά, being put into an alphabetical sequence starting with Ο-Π, even though following relatively close, but not directly after, another "Brothers Song" (Sa. 5).

11   I omit underdots marking incomplete letters most of which are confirmed by the context or comparisons.

12   On πλέαι (ms.) instead of πλήαι (Obbink), cf. Benelli 2017, 97f., Liberman 2014, 4: the supposed Lesbian form with η is not transmitted anywhere and this might be an intended Homeric form.

13   I follow Ferrari 2014, 1f., in marking this as a parenthesis.

14   On νόησθαι (Obbink) instead of νοεῖσθαι (ms., Liberman 2014, 4), cf. Benelli 2017, 99: in contrast to πλέαι, the Lesbian form νόησθαι is transmitted on a papyrus of Alc. 48,16.

15   Obbink's ἐπάρωγον is the correction by a second hand in the ms. from the original ἐπάρηγον'. On the emendation ἐπ' ἄρηον (West 2014, 9; ἐπ' ἄρηον' Libermann 2014, 8f.; ἐπ' ἀρη{γ}ον Benelli 2017, 87), cf. West, Ferrari 2014, 2f., and the extensive and persuasive discussion of Benelli, pp. 101-104. Favouring Obbink's text: Bierl 2016, 313f., Neri 2015, 63-66, Lardinois 2016, 177. I follow the argumentation of West that otherwise the syntax is too strained.

...
But you are always babbling that Charaxus set out[16]
with a full ship, something, I think, Zeus knows
together with all the gods: but you should not
think this,   8

but send me and command me
with earnest prayer to beseech[17] queen Hera
that Charaxus may arrive here, bringing
the safe ship   12

and finding us safe and sound. Everything else
let us entrust to the gods:
for fair weather out of great gales
quickly arises.   16

those, whose fate[18] the king of Olympus
wants from troubles for the better
to turn, those become blessed
and very fortunate.   20

also we, if Larichus lifts up his head
and even at some time becomes a man,
then indeed from much depression
we might quickly be released.   24

---

16   Most scholars translate both ἔλθην and l. 7 ἐξίκεσθαι as "arrive", cf. *e.g.* Obbink 2014, 2015, 2016,
      Lardinois 2016, 174f., Kurke 2016, 239 n. 5, Stehle 2016, 272-274, Benelli 2017, 88. Obbink 2015, 3,
      refers to a note of Mark Griffith that ἤλθεν could have the meaning "'went', 'departed'" here (cf.
      LSJ s.v. ἔρχομαι 1. "*start, set out*"). This meaning is accepted *e.g.* by Ferrari 2014, 2-3, Martin 2016,
      120f. with n. 27. No point of arrival or departure is marked in this line and four arguments have
      been developed for the understanding. 1) the grammatical use of an aorist infinitive after a verb
      of speech appear to favour a non-temporal use of the aorist (so a future meaning, cf. *e.g.* Kurke,
      relying on Donald Mastronarde). There is no consensus on the applicability of this rule on Sap-
      pho: the evidence is mostly younger and the comparisons are regarded as insignificant *e.g.* by
      Ferrari. 2) Lardinois claims: "Forms of the verb ἔρχομαι elsewhere in Sappho and Alcaeus always
      seem to have the meaning of 'to come' (*e.g.* Sappho fr. 1.5, 8, 25)". This argumentation relies on
      very scarce evidence and excludes the possibility that this could be the very first case. 4) The
      following statement (τὰ μὲν … Ζεῦς / οἶδε σύμπαντές τε θέοι) has been adduced as argument both
      in favour of "come" (esp. Lardinois) and of "set out" (esp. Ferrari, Martin). I agree with Martin (p.
      121 n. 27): "It is more plausible that the narrator refers to the gods' knowledge of facts (the setting
      out of a ship, *e.g.*) about which the addressee allegedly chatters, rather than about the addressee's
      desire for Charaxos to come (as Obbink's version would seem to suggest)."

17   The *LSJ* records the repetitive use πολύ and πολλά (s.v. πολύς III. a) and most translations and
      interpretations rely on this, cf. esp. Papadimitropoulos 2016, further Rayor and Lardinois 2014,
      160 and 162-164, Obbink 2014, 39, and 2016, 32, Gribble 2016, 42, Bowie 2016, 157-160, Lardi-
      nois 2016, 175, Kurke 2016, 242, Rayor 2016, 399f., Nagy 2016, 459, West 2014, 8. Benelli 2017,
      87ff., reads πόλλα as direct object of λίσσεσθαι and the following infinitives as final clauses (cf.
      Neri 2015, 55). The adverb πολλά marks also the intensity of prayers (also recorded in the *LSJ*
      a.l. "so of earnest commands and entreaties" with the example: πολλὰ λισσομένη, Hom. *Il.* 5,358;
      Benelli (p. 99) adds Hom. *Il.* 21,367-71, where the beseeched goddess is Hera as well). A few scho-
      lars include the meaning suggested here, partly despite using the former meaning elsewhere: *e.g.*
      Lardinois 2014, 188, Neri 2015, 61, Bär 2016, 54 with n. 89, and explicitly Bierl 2016, 333.

18   Following West 2014, 9, I prefer to understand δαίμον' here as "fate", not as a (minor) divinity
      sent by Zeus. Another early instance where δαίμων refers to the personal fortune of men is Pind.
      Pyth. 5,122f. (Διός τοι νόος μέγας κυβερνᾶ / δαίμον' ἀνδρῶν φίλων – "Zeus' great mind steers the
      fortune of the men dear to him [Arcesilas]"). This text has been considered as relevant for Sa. *BS*
      in respect to the two brothers as Dioscuri by Kurke 2016, 252-254, with n. 43 drawing attention to
      the maritime meaning of κυβερνᾶ. However, Kurke (258-260) prefers reading δαίμων as a direct
      reference to the Dioscuri and thus as (minor) divinity.

In its extant form, the song presents four figures: an unnamed first-person speaker, an unnamed addressee and two named male figures, Charaxus and Larichus. The speaker expresses disagreement about the addressee's behaviour in the face of Charaxus' absence and demands a prayer to Hera. Obviously both speaker and addressee are concerned by Charaxus' absence at sea and his return, but in a different way. At this point, the speaker starts speaking collectively in the first-person plural. After a gnomic statement about human dependence on Zeus and the gods, the speaker draws attention to Larichus as a solution for the apparently problematic situation of the collective. The identity of the speaker, the addressee and the collective as well as the relationships between all figures remain unspecified. The sea plays an important role not only for the absence and hoped/prayed for return of Charaxus, but also in the gnomic statement which applies to all humankind and, thus, also to the speaker, the addressee and Larichus.

Among the literary approaches, comparisons with the *Odyssey* are most popular. With the *Odyssey*, the *Brothers Song* shares the constellation of figures and the basic narration: one or more figures "at home" wait for (and depend on) the (belated) return of a male person, and a younger male figure is discussed as possible succession for the absent male. With the focus on Charaxus, the *Brothers Song* then could be called a *nostos* ("homecoming") song in the tradition of the *Odyssey*.[19] The speaker (Sappho) would correspond to Penelope, Charaxus to Odysseus and Larichus to Telemachus.[20] Of course, the family bonds do not match, if the traditional view on Sappho's family is accepted. Yet, according to Bär this only intensifies the bonds between the two works (2016, 24).

I agree with Bär that the comparison with the Odyssey can fruitfully further our understanding of Sappho's song, especially when concentrating on the disagreements of the two works – even though this will lead to a rejection of an intended intertextuality in my case.[21] As I will show, this disagreement concerns mostly the role of Telemachus/Larichus. However, in order to fully appreciate this difference, I will first offer an overview of the comparisons. I will start with the basic situation at home, since its interpretation influences the understanding of the figures, secondly, I will turn to the figure of Charaxus-Odysseus, thirdly, to the identity of the speaker, the addressee and the collective "we", then to Larichus-Telemachus. Finally, I will show how a shift of focus from the Odyssey to the Telemachy helps us understand some peculiarities of the song and its underlying social ideas.

The situation "at home"

The song closes with the hope for change of the situation for the collective "we" which is described as βαρυθυμία, "depression". Other lines have also been

---

19   Bierl 2016, 315, observes that the *nostos* motif is visible already on verbal level, in the repetition of ἐκ and ἐξ- compounds (ll. 11, 15, 22, 27). Further, he (316), considers the etymological connection between *nostos* (return) and *noos* (mind), and (332) the effects of this etymology for νόησθαι (l. 8): "'you are forbidden (οὐ χρῆ) to think these things (ταῦτα νόησθαι)' (7-8): meaning, '[...] beware, you've interfered in the sphere of the gods; you do not have the power and legitimacy to think or to use *noos* to activate Charaxos in these terms': rather the gods must bring *noos* for *nostos*, and change his mind to make him return."

20   Different points of connection between Sa. *BS* and Hom. *Od.* are discussed *e.g.* by Nünlist 2014, Prauscello in Ferrari 2014, 3 n. 6, Neri 2015, 59, Sironi 2015, Kurke 2016, 249-251, Bierl 2016, 326, but the intertextuality is focused on esp. by Bär 2016, esp. 23-27, Mueller 2016. Mueller considers the *BS* as mainly influenced by the return of Nestor (Hom. *Od.* 3,168-175), agreeing nevertheless with the comparisons of Sappho with Penelope, Charaxus with Odysseus and Larichus with Telemachus.

21   Cf. Gribble 2016, 59-64, on waiting women and absent men also in the succeeding Greek literature. Accordingly, Gribble considers the place of Sappho in this tradition more generally and not some specific and intended allusion of Sappho to older literature.

adduced to specify the nature of this "depression", especially: the full and the safe ship (lines 6 and 11), the adjectives ἀρτέμεας (line 13), μάκαρες and πολύολβοι (lines 19-20), and the activity of Larichus (lines 21-22). That these lines all concern the same problem, has been questioned: Mueller supposes that besides Charaxus' absence, Larichus is "a different source of family unrest" (2016, 27 and 38f.). However, if Larichus' activity and Charaxus' return did not belong to the same problem of the collective, the proposal of the last stanza would appear to be very disconnected from the controversy of the opening stanzas despite being connected by verbal echoes throughout the song.[22] For this reason, I assume that the lines refer all to one and the same problematic situation. Depending on the emphasis given on one single or a selection of these expressions, various explanations have been proposed and often some of these are imagined together.[23] The most prominent include:[24]

1. economic problems
2. social problems
3. political problems.

Of these, economy is the reason most often regarded as the one or at least main reason for the collective's problematic situation. Defenders of this theory mostly emphasise the full ship and sometimes the adjectives μάκαρες and πολύολβοι.[25] Nünlist (2014) was the first to draw the attention to the speaker's substitution of the addressee's "full ship" by a prayer for a "safe ship". He deduces from this substitution a difference of interest between the speaker and the addressee in the economy and safety of Charaxus' journey.[26] Liberman thinks about specific economic activities also for Larichus (2014, 3), but else, the activity of Larichus is rarely supposed to have (purely) economic implications.

Readers of the *Brothers Song* struggle with the expression of Larichus "lifting his head". An economic, social or political implication can only be inherent, if the term bears not the same meaning as the preceding "becoming a man". In that case, lines 21-22 would point to a fixed point in the future, to Larichus' birthday so to

---

22 On verbal repetitions linking the storms, the gnomic notice about Zeus and the last stanza: cf. *e.g.* Mueller 2016, 38f., (ἐκ in Sa. *BS*,15, 18 and 23, juxtaposing the storms with the troubles of l. 18 and the collective's heavy-heartedness); Bierl 2016, 313-315, (πέλονται in ll. 16 and 19, αἶψα in ll. 16 and 24 and ἐκ in ll. 15, 18 and 23); Lardinois 2016, 177, (ll. 15-16, 18-19 and 23-24). Bierl further notices that the repetition of ἐκ enforces the emphasis on the prefix ἐξ- in l. 11.

23 Cf. Bettenworth 2014, 18 (social and economic threat), Ferrari 2014, 3f. (social and economic uncertainty), Rayor and Lardinois 2014, ad Sa. *BS*,13 (economic and other problems), Lardinois 2016, 176f. (political as well as economic problems), Nagy 2016, 452 (fear of "disgraceful loss of wealth and prestige").

24 Other proposals include – partly together with those stated above: βαρυθυμία as the speaker's and addressee's disability to dance (Kurke 2016, n. 32, relying on a private communication with Melissa Mueller) or as consequence of Charaxus' possible death (Sironi 2015, 115), as the fear for "Charaxos' life, his welfare, his return, the reunion with his family and friends, and, last but not least, the political existence of the *hetaireia*" (Bierl 2016, 310f., 316-218 with n. 28); Larichus "lifting his head" as recovery from illness, literary growing taller or figuratively standing up (Lardinois 2014, 190f., Rayor and Lardinois 2014, 164), as marriage (Rayor and Lardinois 2014, 164); cf. Obbink 2014, 35, giving a summary on the varying meaning of ἄνηρ in the oeuvre of Sappho and Alcaeus.

25 See *e.g.* See Obbink 2014, 35, again 45; West 2014, 9; Liberman 2014, 6-7.

26 Cf. also Ferrari 2014, 3, Liberman 2014, 6-7, Neri 2015, 55 n. 10, Lardinois 2016, 175, Bierl 2016, 333f. Against the differentiation: Nagy 2016, 473, Raaflaub 2016, 139 n. 43. The scholars disagree whether the "safe ship" also includes an interest in cargo (esp. Liberman, Neri) or not (esp. Nünlist 2014). Gribble 2016, 46, understands ναῖ σὺν πλέαι as "'with the company intact'." Bierl understands the correction as a shift from secular to religious interest in form of the demanded prayer, where "wealth has no relevance". According to him, the dialogue contains an intended misunderstanding between speaker and addressee with regard to the two adjectives μάκαρες and πολύολβοι as either religious (the speaker's perspective: "blissed, initiated and happy, though perhaps only as dead and immortalized heroes") or economic (the addressee's perspective: "happy and very rich").

speak. I regard this chronological understanding as unlikely: according to Denniston (1991, 248), the particle combination καὶ δή corresponds in Homer (it is not extant in the fragments of Sappho and Alcaeus) to the later used καὶ δὴ καί and "introduces something similar in kind to what has preceded, but stronger in degree, and marks a kind of climax",[27] δή ποτ' (line 22) can denote either the passing of time or impatience,[27] but the change of the situation is said to happen "quickly" (line 24 αἶψα), signifying a sudden change rather than a predictable date in the remote future.[28]

Accordingly, most scholars claim that "becoming a man" and "lifting the head" signalise a change in the social or political status – so our second or third possibility – due to Larichus' coming of age: he should become a fully respected man, a member of the aristocracy. Some scholars suggest that Larichus was formerly in a state of humiliation and shame. This is most often explained biographically.[29] The exact kind of Larichus' activity remains unexpressed: the song signalises solely a lack of it. Our second and third category have also been argued for from other perspectives. According to Lardinois, Kurke and Gribble, the storms could hint at a political level of (part of) the problems.[30] More precisely, Kurke compares Odysseus' wish for civic harmony (*Odyssey* 13,46) the "ship of state" in songs by Pindar and Alcaeus (Kurke 2016, 241-242, 251, 254) all directing at a political meaning. Bowie accepts that the exact nature of the situation is unknown but suggests that it is social (2016, 161).

Other songs of Sappho have also been adduced to specify the kind of problems faced by the collective.[31] I mention these comparisons despite the ambiguities in the song's relation and their differences in the solutions hoped for,[32] because Gribble suggests in the case of Sappho fragment 5 that the nature of the situation was intentionally left to imagination to make the song more suitable for "any (Mytilenean) woman". For this reason, Gribble (2016, 57-59) excludes the name Doricha from the song, which had been restored by West (2014, 6). Other songs of Sappho – like the *Brothers Song* – make use of names and these names do not necessarily exclude the applicability to other persons, but everybody could depend on a Charaxus at sea or a youngster Larichus.[33] Therefore, this applicability is a sound explanation for the lack of details despite the inclusion of names.

The different terms referred to above appear to indicate a complex situation of the collective that includes economic as well as political or social components and

---

27 See Lardinois 2014, 191, translating (180f.) "in time". Cf. *LSJ*, s.v. δήποτε, *"at some time, once upon a time."*

28 *Pace* Papadimitropoulos 2016, 5, claiming that the current situation and the solution of the family's problems are "separated by a considerable temporal hiatus".

29 See *e.g.* Ferrari 2014, 4. Reasons given for the humiliation include the father's death, the elder brother's absence, the superior status of the surrounding men. Ferrari compares Andromache's fantasy about Astyanax' future after his father's death: he will constantly "bow" his head (Hom. *Il.* 22,491). For the suppressing environment, cf. Bierl 2016, 314f., considering erotic suppressions, and Liberman 2014, 7f., 11, Obbink 2014, 35. In contrast, Stehle 2016, 273f., claims that Larichus' activity at the *prytaneum* is pleasant and that Sappho tries to awake him (against his will) from this state. In contrast to humiliation, Benelli 2017, 105f., compares Latin expressions like *caput tollere, extollere, efferre* with the meaning "sich auszeichnen": Larichus should gain future honours.

30 See Lardinois 2014, 189f., and 2016, 176f. (considering also economic problems), Kurke 2016, 254, and Gribble, 51f. Liberman 2014, 6-7, recognises possible danger for the collective, but supposes economic reasons. Kurke compares songs of Alc. and Pind. on the Dioscuri and the "ship of state", suggesting that the sea signalises similar political associations here. Gribble compares Alc. in this regard.

31 For comparisons of Sa. *BS* with esp. Sa. 5 and 15, see *e.g.* Ferrari 2014, 5f., and West 2014, 5, Bär 2016, 17f., 39 with n. 38, 53, Gribble 2016, 56-59, Nagy 2016, 450f. Noteworthy is the explicit inclusion of social categories in Sa. 5 (ll. 6-8 friends and enemies, l. 14 citizens) and the lack of any economic problems (*pace* Bär). Ferrari, 9, links a censure of the citizens (5,14 ἐπαγ[ορί]αι πολίταν) to the humiliated status of Larichus in the *BS*. West, 5-7, explains the line differently. Note that Gribble compares also Sa. 5 to Hom. *Od.*, but also to the myth of Orestes.

32 Cf. Ferrari 2014, 9; neither Larichus nor a collective is visible in Sa. 5, 15.

33 Songs with personal names, but without a definite identification include *e.g.* Sa. 1 (Sappho), 16 (Anactoria).

is perceived differently by the speaker and the addressee. The first stanza with its "full ship" depicts the addressee's interest in economic well-being. The interest of the speaker is more complex: the (physical) well-being of both Charaxus and the collective seem to play a role as well as the hope for – material or immaterial – fortune, which can include social as well as political dimensions.[34]

The situation can be compared to the situation at Ithaca in the *Odyssey*: Odysseus' absence affects the situation at Ithaca, it affects Penelope – pressed by her suitors -, the property and household of the family – eaten up, controlled and seduced by the suitors – and Telemachus – not respected and nearly killed by the suitors. The threat at Ithaca is mostly social due to Telemachus' and Penelope's inferiority in front of the suitors, but it has also economic implications. Many scholars suggest that the problem in the *Brothers Song* is induced or intensified by Charaxus' mere absence.[35] The underlying idea is that the collective, understood as family, lacks a male adult leader: Charaxus is absent, Larichus is not (yet) an adult.[36] This depends on the identification of the collective and the addressee to which I shall return later. There are, then, some loose parallels between the problematic situation at home in the *Odyssey* and the *Brothers Song*.

Charaxus as Odysseus?

Most important for the comparisons of the *Brothers Song* with the *Odyssey* are Charaxus and his "model" Odysseus: both men are absent and in danger of not returning home, they might bring goods home and their people at home are in danger.[37] Odysseus starts his journey for the Trojan war and gets his cargo during his wanderings from several sources: by looting, raiding and as gifts.[38] Charaxus' reason for travel is not stated in the song: most scholars suspect trading, but other possibilities as a military office, an expedition (like Telemachus') or anything else are possible as well and the kind of cargo – merchandise, spoil or gifts – depends on this.[39] While Odysseus loses his whole cargo, fleet and crew and gains new cargo,

---

34 According to Rayor and Lardinois 2014, ad Sa. *BS*,13, πολύολβοι can refer "to material as well as spiritual wellbeing." Cf. Bierl 2016, 317f., on μάκαρες and πολύολβοι: "in the Brothers Song both adjectives simply mean 'fortunate' (μάκαρες, 19) and 'very rich' (πολύολβοι, 20), in a secular and material sense. But for initiates their meaning blossoms to 'happy' and 'much blissed', typical markers of said initiates, who have gained a deeper knowledge, and of those who are immortalized as heroes upon death."

35 See *e.g.* Stehle 2016, 272, Bettenworth 2014, 18, Ferrari 2014, 4, Gribble 2016, 46, Papadimitropoulos 2016, 7 n. 10. Often his biographically recorded encounter with a courtesan is adduced, *e.g.* by Liberman 2014, 6-7, Obbink 2014, 45 (as one possibility), Papadimitropoulos, 3f.

36 Biographically, three other figures are attested: a father, a third brother and Sappho's husband. The latter is neglected in interpretations of Sa. *BS*, the father is regarded as death following two lines of Ovid (Ov. *Her.* 15,61-62). On the problem of Eurygius *cf.* Neri 2015, 58 n. 33 (only for the case that he was the addressee). Cf. Ferrari 2014, 12, on testimonies about Eurygius, esp. Sa. 213A h (= *POxy*. 2506 fr. 48 col. III) l. 40f., but without consequences for Sa. *BS*.

37 Sironi 2015, 114 n. 16., adds that both men are delayed by women: Doricha/Rhodopis matches esp. with Calypso. The *cause* for Charaxus' delay appears to be irrelevant in Sa. *BS*. Similarly, Odysseus' stay with Calypso is *one* of *several* causes for his delay: it has in itself no relevance for the situation at Ithaca or Telemachus' voyage.

38 Cf. *e.g.* Hom. *Od.* 5,37-40 (Zeus promises gifts to Odysseus that would surpass his spoil from Troy), 9, 39-42 (raiding the Cicones), 4,464f. (stealing sheep from Polyphemus), 13,10-15 (gifts by the Phaeacians).

39 Gribble 2016, 46, considers as possible reasons for Charaxus' absence: trade, military expedition, exile. Neri 2015, 67, notes "la perdurante assenza del fratello maggiore (volontaria, e come tale disdicevole, o forzosa)". Cf. Mueller 2016, 30-32, preferring trade. Prauscello in Ferrari 2014, 3 n. 6, considers it as difference between Hom. *Od.* and Sa. *BS* that Odysseus' cargo consists of gifts, not of merchandise. The trading theory relies mostly on biographical testimonies, cf. *e.g.* Ferrari 2014, 1, with some notes on Naucratis, the supposed market place of Charaxus. Raaflaub 2016, esp. 127-141, considers further the historical background.

the prayer for Charaxus' return includes his safety and the safety of his ship (and possibly his crew), but not necessarily- from the speaker's perspective – the cargo.[40]

The danger for those at home is based on the use of the rare adjective ἀρτέμεας "safe and sound" (line 13; Homer *Odyssey* 13,42-43): like Charaxus, Odysseus also hopes to find his people "safe and sound".[41] The two scenes have not only the use of the adjective in common: both times, the speaker wants to be sent,[42] cargo/convoy and safe return are separately expressed,[43] and it is acknowledged that the success is granted by the gods.[44] Noteworthy is the difference of focus: on the returning man (Odysseus) in the *Odyssey* and on the person at home (speaker) in the *Brothers Song*.[45] Only Bär considers the possibility that the parallel use of the adjective ἀρτέμεας was no intended allusion: in this case, Bär assumes, the hope for the safety of the collective would be "surprising, perhaps even slightly inappropriate" as the prayer was meant to be for Charaxus (2016, 41 note 58). However, the shift from Charaxus towards the collective introduces a shift of focus in the message of the song: from Charaxus' state at sea to the collective's state here, from hope for Charaxus' return to hope for an amendment for the collective. The addressee's hope for the *full* ship shows already that the situation at home is the real reason for the displayed unease.

Sappho's speaker, addressee and the collective in the Odyssey

Differences from the *Odyssey* are even more obvious in the case of the speaker, the addressee and, relevantly, in the relationships between the figures. The identity of the dialogue partners and their gender are not marked in the song. The identity of Sappho as speaker – the historical person or her *persona* – is accepted nearly without discussion in scholarship: a lyric 'I' is speaking also in other songs of Sappho and only in a few of them the identification as 'Sappho' is explicit. Nevertheless, this identity is standardly accepted because no differentiation between the named and the unnamed speaker is discernible.[46]

The identification of the unnamed addressee is more difficult. Several proposals have been made including specific figures or groups to which the addressee could belong.[47] Of these, four have been or could be compared with the Odyssey: the

---

40   The difference appears less harsh against Hom. *Od.* 13,42-43: there the opposition between cargo (taken for sure) and safe return (hoped for) could be identified with the position of the addressee (positive about cargo) and the speaker (uncertainty about safety). This puts much weight on the recognition of many details based on only a single word, ἀρτέμεας, on which see the main text. Loss of cargo could be a matter of Sa. 20,9-13, with "wind" (ἀήταις) and "shipload" (τὰ φόρτια) close together. That Odysseus fails to bring his crew safe back home is noted by Obbink 2014, 42, who compares Hom. *Od.* 3,61 and 9,173.

41   For the parallel cf. esp. Nünlist 2014, Sironi 2015, 114, Kurke 2016, 249-251, Bär 2016, 24f.

42   *Pace* Lidov 2016, 57-59, and Bowie 2016, 157-160. Lidov supposes a third party being sent *by* the speaker in Sa. *BS*,9-10; Bowie emends ἔμε to ἔμα ("send my stuff"). See Lardinois 2016, 175, for problems of the identity of Lidov's third party and the relation of the addressee to the sending activity of the speaker and the word order of Bowie's emendation.

43   This is noticed by Prauscello in Ferrari 2014, 3 n. 6.

44   Cf. Kurke 2016, 250f. This is true only if the Homer's relative τά (*Od.* 13,41-42: πομπὴ καὶ φίλα δῶρα, τά μοι θεοί οὐρανίωνες / ὄλβια ποιήσειαν – "conveyance and pleasant gifts; may the gods of heaven / bless them for me") is understood as applying to both δῶρα and πομπή and if the wishes of 44-46 (ὑμεῖς δ' – "but you", spoken to the Phaeacians) are indirectly also understood for Odysseus himself.

45   Cf. Kurke 2016, 250f.

46   The missing (gender) identity and the recognition as "Sappho" with the help of other Sapphic songs is discussed or noticed *e.g.* by Neri 2015, 55, Bär 2016, esp. 10-15, Gribble 2016, 43, Benelli 2017, 91.

47   Cf. Obbink 2014, 41f. Lists of the so-far proposed identifications are included by Neri 2015, 58-59, and Papadimitropoulos 2016, 6 n. 3.

speaker's nurse,[48] a self-address of the speaker identified both with Penelope and with Odysseus' nurse Eurycleia,[49] Sappho's mother,[50] and Larichus.[51] Different text restorations of the song's first lines could support the identification with the mother, the nurse or Larichus.[52] All three readings have (papyrological) difficulties.[53] The decision for one or another of these options is based mostly on preliminary interpretative decisions or extratextual considerations: for example, the identification of the addressee as nurse relies on the identification of the *Odyssey* as reference text for the *Brothers Song*.[54] For the plot of the *Odyssey*, neither the nurse nor Odysseus' mother nor indeed any other figure play a crucial role in comparison with the figures of Odysseus, Penelope and Telemachus. In one of the passages considered by Bär, Sironi and Bettenworth as key scenes for the identification of the addressee as Odyssean nurse, Penelope reveals a significant lack of faith in Telemachus (4,722-734) – a lack that she shares with Euryclea (2,361-370). Here, Euryclea may appear apt for the identification with the addressee who does not consider Larichus as a solution, but is only reminded of him by the speaker. However, this reveals the incongruity between Penelope and the speaker: Penelope has no faith in Telemachus, while the speaker relies on Larichus.

In line 13 of the *Brothers Song*, the speaker introduces a first-person plural "we" and so far, I have called this plural the "collective". This unspecified group is strongly

---

48   See Bettenworth 2014, Sironi 2015.

49   Bär 2016, 17-23, compares the third-person reference to a sister (Sa. 5) and Odysseus' address to his heart (Hom. *Od.* 20,18).

50   The mother is the most prominent option so far, see *e.g.* West 2014, 7-9 (comparing Sa. 9 and 98 for Sappho's mother), Ferrari 2014, 4, Lardinois 2014, 191, Rayor and Lardinois 2014, 162 (as one possibility), Obbink 2014, 41f., and 2015, 2, Neri 2015, 56 and 60, Papadimitropoulos 2016, 3, Bierl 2016, 309, Kurke 2016, 239f., 244f. (accepting also the possibility of other female figures, esp. 245 n. 26, 251 n. 38), Benelli 2017, 91. A connection with Hom. *Od.* has not yet been considered for the mother, but cf. Odysseus' dialogue with his dead mother Anticlea (11,152-225): here, interest in the state at Ithaca (Odysseus: 170-179, Anticlea: 181-203) prevails over Odysseus' fate at sea (Anticlea: 160-161, Odysseus: 166-169) and this prevalence could be compared to the shift in the Brothers Song from Charaxus' fate at sea to the state "here".

51   See Stehle 2016, 268-271, Rayor 2016, 399, and independently Rudolf Wachter in a private email to Bär 2016, 37 n. 25. As addressee, Larichus has not been considered in comparison with Hom. *Od.*

52   West 2014, 8f., proposes to read *POxy.* 2289 fr. 5,2 as]σέ, μᾶ[τερ for the mother, Bettenworth 2014]σέ, μα[ῖα for the nurse, Neri 2015, 54-56, Stehle 2016, 268f. and Bierl 2016, 309 and 315, propose for the preceding line (]Λα[ριχ-) for Larichus, so far the only suggestion there, but only Stehle takes Larichus as addressee.

53   West 2014, 9, the first making any suggestions on the letters of *POxy.* 2289 fr. 5 in the context of Sa. *BS*, includes an estimation of the space before the readable syllables. With regard to Sa. *BS*,4, West states: "the space before it seems impossibly narrow to accommodate two syllables, and if there was only one, the alpha has to be short" – impossible for both μᾶ[τερ and μα[ῖα. Cf. Neri 2015, 56 with n. 18, for possible short two-syllable words for the beginning. Caciagli 2016, 436 n. 56, observes that a stroke identified as part of the α is more likely part of the preceding μ, so the α is uncertain. In the next line, λ stands almost exactly above the μ, leaving, according to West's estimation, space for two to three syllables. If Larichus was written in this line, it must have been two and, if it was the vocative form Λάριχε, it must have been followed by a consonant lengthening the short -ε or by a long vowel. Against Larichus, Neri 2015, 58 n. 32, notes that the addressee (2nd person) would then in the finale stanza be included both in 3rd person (as Larichus) and in the 1st person plural (as "we"). Bär's 2016, 17-23, bifurcation of the speaker draws upon Sa. 5 which is not comparable to the differentiation of the duties of the two persons in *BS*,7-10. This is incomparable in Greek literature, as observed also by Bär. Against the nurse esp. Caciagli 2016, 435 n. 54, Neri 2015, 58 n. 36. Bär 2016, 41f. with n. 54, shows the power of Eurycleia over the hopeful Penelope – a power better comparable to the admonishing speaker than the hopeful addressee. Regarding the mother: Bettenworth 2014, Bär 2016, 15-17, and Nünlist 2014, Bierl 2016, 328f.

54   Sironi 2015, esp. 113, supposes that μαῖα could be an intended allusion to Homer, who uses – in contrast to the lyric poets – this word regularly for Eurycleia. Bär 2016, 16f., notices this use as well and emphasises its appearance esp. in Hom. *Od.* 23, considered by Bettenworth 2014 as most relevant for the identification as nurse. Bettenworth, Sironi and Bär compare several scenes from Hom. *Od.* with Sa. *BS*.

connected to the men's, especially to Larichus' behaviour and is obviously depending from them. It has been variously identified by the scholars: besides the speaker it may include the addressee, Larichus and unnamed others.[55] Kurke proposes the inclusion of the addressee only.[56] Often the collective is understood as the family of the speaker (to which the addressee may or may not belong).[57] Others suppose that the group must comprise women only, either the family, Sappho's circle or some other group.[58] Only rarely do scholars highlight the ambiguity of the collective's identity.[59]

I support Kurke's reading: she emphasises that the speaker and the addressee are united in the plural form.[60] This is especially important given their obvious disagreement in the first extant lines of the song. The disagreement between the speaker and the addressee in the first stanzas has been observed by several scholars and it comprises three points: the addressee's vain presumptions (line 5) should be replaced by a command and a prayer (lines 9-10), the "full ship" (line 6) is replaced by a "safe ship" (lines 11-12) and the assumed departure (line 5) by a prayed for arrival (lines 11-12).[61] The speaker's reproach concerns, thus, the style, form and content of the addressee's statement, especially the false focus (on the departure) and interest (economic *vs.* safety).[62]

The speaker's following proposal to "entrust (everything else) to the gods" has been described by some scholars as conventional.[63] It has nevertheless a function in the song: it picks up all of those aspects that were hoped for by the addressee and dismissed by the speaker. By the entrustment to the gods, the speaker shows to the addressee that these hopes must not be in vain – the gods *can* bring good weather – and at the same time the speaker can draw the attention to that what they can actually *do* and this enables the union with the addressee.

In this union of speaker and addressee, a group becomes visible which is affected by the absence of Charaxus and can be affected by the activity of Larichus, a group that is united by a shared threat and a shared hope. In the *Odyssey*, there is a much more accurately identified group of persons endangered by the events at Ithaca:

---

55 Mueller 2016, 35, and Bierl 2016, 314, include either the song's external audience or the singer Sappho and her chorus in the song's "we". Mueller takes the external audience as the "people from all of Lesbos" present during the song's performance at the sanctuary at Mesa. Bierl (327) considers all other mentioned identifications as possible as well.

56 See Kurke 2016, 248, but cf. also Martin 2016, 212, Lardinois 2016, 176, Bierl 2016, 327, Gribble 2016, 46. Bierl and Gribble consider also other possibilities.

57 See *e.g.* West 2014, 8, Bowie 2016, 161, Bierl 2016, 327. Bierl allows the family to be the "clan" in a wider sense.

58 Cf. *e.g.* Ferrari 2014, 2, Neri 2015, 59, Bierl 2016, 327, Gribble 2016, esp. 43 and 50. Ferrari translates Sa. *BS*,9 with female forms "e trovi noi sane e salve", although he later (p. 3) paraphrases "e trovando sani e salvi". Gribble supposes the group could be a circle (Sappho's?) of young women or a politically linked group, but he considers also a restriction to the (female) addressee and the speaker.

59 See Caciagli 2016, 435, with regard to the inclusion of the addressee and the gender of the group.

60 See Kurke 2016, 248, cf. also similarly, but with less emphasis, Martin 2016, 121.

61 My translation "Charaxus already set out with a full ship" is – for the economically interested addressee – similarly reassuring as the alternative "he will come with a full ship". The present translation more pointedly marks the difference between the thoughts of the addressee and the suggestion of the speaker; cf. Obbink 2015, 3 "taken in this sense, ἔλθην would also contrast in a more balanced way with ἐξίκεσθαι in 11." In the substitution of the departure by the arrival, also the dangers of the sea become visible: between the "setting out" with a full ship and the "arriving safe" with a ship (full or not, but safe) lies a huge sea and a long time, whether or not he started with a full ship is unimportant, his arrival and safety are important.

62 For the disagreement, cf. Mueller 2016, 32, Kurke 2016, 240f., and Rayor 2016, 399f. Mueller (36f.) contributes the inclusion of τυίδε in the speaker's intended prayer to the stylistic differences required in prayers. Rayor 2016, 399f., supposes that the disagreement between the speaker and the addressee is still perceptible in Sa. *BS*,20: πολύολβοι replaces νᾶϊ σὺν πλήαι: "full of good fortune rather than full of cargo."

63 Cf. *e.g.* Obbink 2014 a.l., West 2014, 8. Supposing that the song would be complete, this would be the centre of the song and – according to Bär 2016, 24 – a marked allusion to the fulfilment of Odysseus' return by the gods, especially by Zeus and Athens.

besides Penelope and Telemachus, also the faithful members of the household and certain friends of the family. In the *Brothers Song*, any decision for one identification of the addressee or the speaker and a comparison with an Odyssean figure can only be regarded as paradigmatic.[64] For the speaker, the identification with Penelope appeared to be self-evident, although the difficult position of the addressee reveals incongruity also for the speaker's comparison with Penelope as the model lacks faith in her son, which is the specific characteristic of the Sapphic speaker. As I will show, the case of Larichus and Telemachus will be even more difficult.

Larichus as Telemachus?

One argument for the identification of Larichus with Telemachus is the "coming of age" of both figures. As son of Odysseus and Penelope, Telemachus is evidently much younger than both his parents and, being a boy when Odysseus leaves for Troy (*Odyssey* 4,112), he is about twenty at the start of his search for his father and his final reunion with him at Ithaca. The estimations of the speaker's age and the relative age of the figures of the *Brothers Song* are based nearly solely on external, much younger texts. [65] The *Brothers Song* presents Larichus as not yet an adult (line 22). Gribble suggests that this line and other intratextual signs point to a relatively young age of not only Larichus, but also Charaxus and the speaker, and to an unmarried status of the latter: "A woman deeply concerned about the fate of a brother and praying for his safety is likely to be an unmarried woman, one not under the protection of a husband."[66]

Martin suggests that the last stanza of the Brothers Song – with the impatient δή ποτ' in line 22 – presents an "insulting swipe" against Larichus who is – more in terms of behaviour than in terms of age – not yet a man.[67] Although I agree with Martin, I suppose that the swipe is rather light and does not diminish the hope put onto Larichus. The addressee's focus on Charaxus indicates that his person appears more natural for the solution of the collective's state; this would be understandable, if Charaxus' were older than Larichus. However, Charaxus might be at the threshold of adulthood as well, but preferred by the addressee due to his behaviour or activity

---

64   Cf. Mueller 2016, 31f., considering the identity of the addressee as indefinable beyond the characterisation as "woman of similar social rank", cautiously preferring the mother (or possibly a sister-in-law).

65   The same: Bär 2016, 35 n. 11. For more certain opinions on the age, cf. *e.g.* Obbink 2015, 3, (the speaker is "in her early to late teens", Larichus was "around 12 years"), West 2014, 9 (the speaker is "possibly still in her late teens"). Ferrari 2014, 1, estimates the place of this song in the transmitted chronology of Sappho. Bierl 2016, 306f., considers the effect of the sibling's supposed age difference for their relationship in terms of the "typical" sister-brother relationship. The age difference is deduced mostly from *POxy.* 1800 fr. 1,1-35, where Charaxus is called the oldest of her three brothers (ἀδελφοὺς δ'] ἔσχε τρεῖς, [Ἐρ]ίγ[υιον καὶ Λά]ριχον, πρεσβύ[τατον δ[ὲ Χάρ] αξον) and Larichus – according to an emendation – young (τὸν δὲ Λάριχον <νέον> ὄντα). Sappho's relative age in comparison to Larichus or even Charaxus is not mentioned, nor that of Eurygius (*Pace* Caciagli 2016, 436, taking Eurygius as middle brother). Athen. 10.425a, Eust. *Il.* 1205.17ff., schol. T *Il.* 20.234 = Sa. 203 V (cf. Sa. 252 V) depict Larichus as a wine-pourer at the Prytanaeum of Mytilene, an activity considered as apt before adulthood. Ferrari 2014, 1, and Liberman 2014, 2-3, suppose that Sa. *BS* supports this impression of Larichus' minor age in comparison to Sappho, cf. also Stehle 2016, 267.

66   See Gribble 2016, 50. He takes the speaker to be older than both Larichus and the addressee because of the exhortation of the former and the consolation of the latter. Alternatively, he explains: "the status as consoler comes perhaps partly from her position as poet". The same might be true for the exhortation.

67   See Martin 2016, 121. He accepts Larichus' young age on the basis of the identification with Odysseus' "laggard twenty-something slacker son" Telemachus, not as confirmation of it. For a possible critique on Larichus, cf. also Bierl 2016, 321f., and Bowie 2016, 163, who suggests that wine-pouring (Sa. 252 V) was in fact shameful; the opposite is claimed by Gribble 2016, 39 n. 30: Larichus would gain honour as cup-bearer.

or because he was *slightly* older. The two men's exchangeability proposed by the speaker could signify a similar social status and a similar age.[68] Accordingly, I suppose that the speaker is a young female adult – able and accepted to openly speak about the collective's problems, but depending on others – while both Charaxus and Larichus are young men at the threshold of adulthood.

As I have shown above, the last stanza implies a change in the behaviour of Larichus. Bär suggests that it is a change of moral behaviour that "also encompasses a sense of 'daring to speak up' and thus of 'beginning to have a say in society, perhaps even with the connotation of being enraged and raising one's voice." Bär compares Larichus to Telemachus who raises his voice against the suitors so that they become silent (Odyssey 2,35-83): at this moment Telemachus would suddenly become a man in front of the suitors – and similarly also Larichus would suddenly (αἶψα) become a man and thus would be able to replace Charaxus.[69] The suitor's silence lasts only four lines (2,80-83), but then they reproach Telemachus (84-128). His helplessness against them is often expressed: he complains that he cannot change their behaviour (299-373), he cannot prepare a ship on his own (177-295, 382-392), only with Athena's help can he leave the suitors (398-405), and this situation is described by Telemachus to Nestor (3,201-209), by Peisistratos to Menelaos (4,155-167), and by Telemachus to Menelaus (315-331).

The social understanding of the change in behaviour depends on the understanding of the social constellation of the imagined society, as Larichus' relation to other persons is not described. Kurke observes that Larichus' "lifted head" is opposed on a lexical level to the collective's βαρυθυμία, their heavy-heartedness, in line 23. According to Kurke, the two terms could represent opposite movements: a dragging down stopped eventually by the lifting up of Larichus. Metaphorically, Larichus rescues the collective from their death by drowning.[70] This is especially interesting as this interpretation integrates Larichus and the collective into the nautical sphere of the first part of the song.[71]

Larichus is characterised as a young man at the threshold of adulthood. His passing into maturity – his coming of age – appears to be not so much a matter of time: it is no event in the far future, but it rather depends on his activity and behaviour. Apparently, Charaxus and Larichus share several characteristics: they appear to be both relatively young and they represent the hope for a change for the collective, although the ability to accomplish this change is distrusted in both cases, both times the sea is included at least metaphorically to express this hope. Charaxus differs from Larichus possibly not so much in age as in his activity: being at sea, he is already active.

Telemachus' coming of age is a crucial point in the Odyssey not only for Telemachus himself, but also for the women around him: Penelope accuses Telemachus for misbehaving as an adult despite his already mature appearance (18,217-219), while Eurycleia expresses her hope that Telemachus may finally take up his duties as an adult (19,22-23).[72] For Telemachus the process is difficult to accomplish: he is socially inferior and in order to become recognised as equal, he must give proof of his worth – and he obviously manages this first by leaving the island in search for news about his father,

---

68   The closeness in age assimilates the two even more to Castor and Pollux, the parallel discussed by Kurke 2016.

69   See Bär 2016, 25f. and 41f. n. 62. Cf. Neri 2015, 66 with several textual parallels in n. 98.

70   See Kurke 2016, 255. She reports Richard Neer's idea that the βαρυθυμία could denote the heaviness of the limbs. The sea metaphor is especially important for Kurke's comparison of the two men with the Dioscuri. Cf. also Obbink 2014, 45, for the lifting of the head as saving of one's (own) life, outside the sea metaphor.

71   Bierl 2016, 316-317, discerns nautical and economic metaphors throughout the song. He compares nautical metaphors by other poets both erotic and political contexts (Hom. *Od.* and Alc.), but the most important level of the song is for him erotic because of the song's "strictly female perspective".

72   Hom. *Od.* 19,22-23 has been compared also by Sironi 2015, 115.

that is the "Telemachy", and then by killing the suitors together with Odysseus and by punishing the disloyal servants.[73] In the *Brothers Song*, Larichus' social inferiority due to age and his difficulties in changing his behaviour and position are comparable to the *Odyssey*,[74] but he crucially differs from Telemachus by staying at his home island.

The Brothers Song through the lens of the Telemachy

I started my examination of the *Brothers Song* and its comparison with the *Odyssey* with Bär's remark on the intensifying function of the Homeric background even by divergence from its original structures. In the detailed examination of the texts, ambiguities rather than certain similarities between the two texts became visible. This cannot be attributed only to the shortness of Sappho's song or its fragmentary state, but the ambiguity must be understood as a characteristic of it which possibly enabled the reperformance at different occasions and by different singers. The motifs – sea and sea voyage, absence, distance, staying behind and waiting – are natural elements in a maritime environment such as Lesbos and are no proof of the song being a lyric "remake" of the *Odyssey*.

The *Odyssey* is nevertheless an important text for the understanding of the *Brothers Song* and its context in early Greek literature. Listeners and readers of the *Brothers Song* were surely familiar with the *Odyssey* and its setting, as they were also with other stories like that of the Dioscuri Castor and Pollux. While comparisons so far focused on the pairs Charaxus-Odysseus and Larichus-Telemachus, I would like to suggest a comparison also of the pair Charaxus-Telemachus to make visible some innovative ideas of the *Brothers Song*. In the *Odyssey*, the role of the "young man staying behind" (Telemachus) is prominently discussed and his problem famously solved. His role – and the role of the sea and travelling for his growing up – is focused on in this volume by Hauke Schneider. Without repeating his arguments, I will give a brief account of what is relevant for the comparison with Sappho.

Charaxus as Telemachus?

Charaxus shares with Telemachus some characteristics that he does not share with Odysseus. The identification of Charaxus with Odysseus and Larichus with Telemachus relies on the former's absence and the latter's presence. These identifications presuppose a strict differentiation of the two brothers, mostly in terms of age, which cannot be supported by the song itself. The two male figures share several similarities, including their age. The meaning of their names might tentatively be added to the similarities mentioned above. Charaxus' name is standardly deduced from χαρά and

---

73 See Schneider in this volume. In contrast to Penelope and Eurycleia, Odysseus (in disguise) emphasises his son's maturity already before the punishments (Hom. *Od.* 19,85-88); on these lines cf. also Sironi 2015, 115.

74 Martin 2016, 122-123 with n. 30, compares Hom. *Il.* 10,29-31 and 10,77-85 for the lifting of one's head: in both instances the phrases "describe two heroes who are roused and ready to find solutions to the troubles that beset the Achaeans." Martin also considers parallels for "being a man" – *e.g.* addressed by Agamemnon to his troops in order to encourage them for fight (*Il.* 5,528, 6,112, 8,174, 11,287, 15,487, 561) or by Nestor to the troops in order to remember one's family (15,661). Especially the later appears most relevant to Martin as it deals with a man remembering his kin: Larichus should do so, too.

ἄγειν, meaning "bearer of joy".[75] Larichus' name is most often deduced from λαρός. Mauerhofer suggests to Bär that it has the meaning "sweetie", because Larichus would be the sweet baby of the family, while Bierl compares the meaning "pleasant" to "happiness" (χαρά) in the name of Charaxus: "λαρός with a long α means 'pleasant', – 'joyous', Charaxos, thus finding its substitute in 'pleasant', Larichos [...]"[76]

The substitution of the two men is an important point for the speaker and enforces their similarities. Bierl suggests that both brothers go through a rite of passage. In the case of Larichus, this is for Bierl the cup-bearing at the *prytaneum* attested in external sources.[77] Charaxus' rite of passage can be compared to Telemachus': both are young man, both go out on a sea voyage, connected with both men is the hope for the family's relief, both are confronted with the danger of not returning home. Nevertheless, Charaxus' voyage is no remake of the Telemachy – as it is no remake of the Odyssey, but it can be compared in terms of behaviour, as a rite of passage.

Larichus as Charaxus

If Larichus is the alternative for Charaxus and may substitute him, what is the difference between them? One significant difference between the two brothers is clearly depicted in the song: while Charaxus is absent with his ship, Larichus is apparently "here", namely ashore. When the speaker demands from Larichus to become a man, he is obviously asked to do so where he is, ashore, in contrast to both Telemachus and Charaxus, who are at sea. In the figure of Larichus, an alternative model arises: while both Charaxus and Telemachus are struggling at sea, their respective communities anxiously waiting for them, fearing their death, but hoping for their return that will – thanks to the *timê* (together possibly with other goods) they gain for their travel – change the current situation, Larichus is supposed to bring this change without going to sea. This difference between the two men, Larichus and Charaxus, could explain also the addressee's consideration only of Charaxus as solution: Larichus is not at sea and thus not expected to return and bring a change.

The song presents in its first extant lines the man Charaxus: he is at sea, his return is hoped for as is his cargo, but he is in danger of not returning home. The song does not specify what kind(s) of danger must be considered except for the statement "fair weather out of great gales quickly arises." It can easily be imagined that "great gales" are endangering Charaxus at sea while good weather would enable his return home. Interestingly, the comment on bad or fair weather appears to apply not only to Charaxus. The following stanza is in fact the same statement in a gnomic form: bad weather turns to good weather and Zeus turns fate from bad to good. That the gods are involved in the change of weather is indicated by lines 13-14.

---

75 See *e.g.* Bär 2016, 17f., 26f., Bierl 2016, 319 n. 37, Gribble 2016, 57, Lardinois 2016, 171, Burris *et al.* 2014, 24, with Sa. 5,6, Poseidippus 17,3 *GP* and Ov. *Her.* 15,117. Bierl supposes a possible mystic connotation in this χαρά. In Sa. *BS*,11-12, Charaxus brings no joy, but his safe ship (σάαν ἄγοντα νᾶα Χάραξον) – an intended alternation of the pun? Alternative etymologies cannot be supported by such puns, but draw also on the motifs of the Charaxus-story: Wachter (2014 in a private communication with Bär) deduces Χάραξος as "sea-plougher" from χαράσσω ("to scratch"), Dale 2011 either from the passive form χαράσσομαι ("to be angry or exasperated", referring to *LJS* s.v. χαράσσω II. 1. Pass.) or from χάραξ "used of a vine-prop". The active χαράσσω appears twice in passive for the furrowed sea or its waves in the *Anth. Pal.* (10,2,1-2; 10,14,2), both times it is furrowed by fret (φρίξ).

76 Mauerhofer 2014 in private communication with Bär 2016, 26f. Bierl 2016, 321. Wachter (2014 in private communication with Bär 2016, 26f.) explains Λάριχος as "babbler" from λῆρος, referring to his silly baby talk. For the suffix cf. von Wilamowitz-Moellendorf 1913, 23 n. 1, comparing τέττιχος from τέττα, φρύνιχος from φρῦνος *etc.* He suggested λάρος (with a short α), "kleine Möwe", but in Sa. *BS*,22 the α must be long.

77 See Bierl 2016, 307, 320f. Bierl emphasises the importance of sexuality for both young men. He does not accept Larichus as a "real alternative" for Charaxus because both brothers are victims of love and desire, just like Sappho.

When Sappho, then, returns to the personal level, she has prepared the listeners of her song to identify Larichus as the origin of this change and thus as substitute for Charaxus. This implies that the claim about weather applies – on a metaphorical level now – also to Larichus: the stanzas are connected by the use of the adverb αἶψα in lines 24 and 15-16 in exactly the same position. The parallel strongly suggests that Larichus *is* this "fair weather" against the "great storms" depressing the collective.[78]

How to become a man?

Larichus is presented by the speaker as the more reliable option: he is at hand and simply has to "lift his head" so that the problems of the group will be solved. Nevertheless, he is not considered by the addressee as solution at first hand and he is not said to already have done or to surely do his part in near future. What is, then, the "problem" of "becoming a man"? Drawing also on proposals of other scholars, three answers are possible. The change depends on:

1. the passing of time (*i.e.* Larichus must reach a certain age)
2. the gods, especially Zeus
3. Larichus himself.

The first explanation is favoured by Papadimitropoulos and goes without assuming social changes of Larichus' behaviour. Although chronological dimensions are emphasised throughout the song (lines 16 and 24 αἶψα, line 18 ἤδη), these do not describe a (long) process but suddenness – with line 22, δή ποτ', as an exception which indicates rather the speaker's impatience than patience for a process that necessarily takes time. Further, Sappho's phrasing is not chronological, but conditional (line 21: αἴ κε, "if").

The difference between the second and third option could be considered as a matter of religious faith: an action by Larichus could be interpreted as an (unperceived) intervention of a god. However, the song seems to emphasise the importance of human agency and, thus, the third rather than the second option. Of course, divine agency, divine knowledge and the entrustment to the gods are central motifs throughout the song (lines 6-7, 10-11, 13-14, 17-20). The last two stanzas are connected with each other by their parallel structure: the condition of the last stanza – if Larichus grows up – seems to reflect upon the general condition of good fortune of the preceding stanza – Zeus' will. Sappho assimilates here the actions of Larichus – turning his head upwards – and Zeus – turning the fate towards the better. The effect is that Larichus is easily identified with Zeus' action.[79] Nonetheless Larichus' action does not depend on Zeus' activity. The conditional phrase marks Larichus as sole agent and the previously discussed fields in which Larichus should become energetic to "become a man" – be they political, social or economic – present fields of human agency rather than divine.

---

78 Cf. Neri 2015, 66f.: "[...] la perdurante assenza del fratello maggiore [...] impone al minore di "sollevare la testa" e "diventare uomo", "in fretta" (e αἶψα potrebbe allora comunicare tale urgenza)". Cf. also Kurke 2016, 255f. On the parallel in Sa. *BS*,16 and 24, cf. Papadimitropoulos 2016, 5. In contrast, Liberman 2014, 8, calls αἶψα here a stop-gap, as also ἤδη (l. 18), and considers Sa. *BS* prosaic and unembellished, a "hasty composition".

79 Based on the ancient correction of Sa. *BS*,18, ἐπάρωγον "as a helper", scholars identify Larichus as *daimon* sent by Zeus, cf. *e.g.* Lardinois 2014, 190, Gribble 2016, 44f. with n. 42. Gribble compares the divine appearance of Odysseus in Hom. *Il.* and suggests a divine intervention as solution for Sa. *BS*.

Will there be a happy ending?

In any case, the precondition for a change of the situation of the collective is the success of either Charaxus or Larichus. Several scholars suggest that Sappho transmits a feeling of confidence in one of the solutions.[80] The speaker obviously prefers Larichus as a solution to Charaxus. The outcome – positive or negative – for the collective depends on our understanding of the last conditional construction. Most scholars take the conditional phrase as possibility (likely or unlikely to happen), but the main clause as certain consequence, that is: "if Larichus should become a man (which may or may not happen), we will be free."[81] A few scholars take the *apodosis* as a possible but uncertain outcome: "if Larichus …, we might…"[82] Larichus' activity, then, does not depend on Zeus intervention, but it is the precondition for Zeus' – possible but uncertain – intervention.

I suggest that this understanding also agrees better with the sea storm metaphor prevalent in the *Brothers Song* and with the substitution of Charaxus by Larichus. The picture of the sea storm applies to Charaxus, Larichus and the collective of this song on different levels. This becomes visible in the verbal repetitions that can be found throughout the song.[83] First, it applies on a literal level to Charaxus for whom good weather will save his life endangered by sea storms. Secondly, the same good weather could save – via Charaxus – also the collective, as is hoped for by the addressee. The addressee sees in Charaxus the (metaphorical) "good weather" that will save them. As the speaker shows, the precondition for Charaxus as "good weather" is the safety of Charaxus provided by the literal good weather. However, this literal good weather – as emphasised by the shift from the "full ship" to the "safe ship" – does not necessarily lead to Charaxus as "good weather", it is only one necessary precondition that provides a possibility, no certainty. This certainty would probably also depend on the safe ship and this is why it is hoped for by the addressee. Thirdly, also Larichus seems to be confronted with a difficult situation which he has to overcome ("lifting his head") – another metaphorical storm. Fourthly, the speaker suggests that Larichus' accomplishment presents another possible (metaphorical) "good weather" for the collective.

This reading has consequences for the outcome of the song: it remains uncertain. The speaker substitutes a hope for a change that leaves only prayer and passivity to the persons hoping – as Charaxus is out of reach – by another, more reliable hope that depends on the activity of a person present – Larichus. In contrast to Charaxus, whose return depends on his own skills as well as on outer circumstances, Larichus could obviously overcome his state by himself and thus presents a more reliable "good weather". This change is paralleled by a shift from a model of social recognition via display of nautical skills and success (Charaxus/Telemachus) to a model of social recognition via behaviour in front of the group.

Nevertheless, this new model is expressed in a language that is obviously rooted in the nautical context of its alternative, the nautical context of the island and the

---

80   For the faith in Charaxus' return, esp. thanks to the comparison with Hom. *Od.* as example for a
     successful return, see Bär 2016.
81   Cf. *e.g.* Ferrari 2014, 2, Obbink 2016, 33, Lardinois 2016, 180f., Kurke 2016, 255, Stehle 2016, 268,
     Bierl 2016, 309. On the grammatical construction see Bierl 2016, 309 and 314.
82   Cf. *e.g.* Martin 2016, 121, Rayor 2016, 399.
83   Bierl 2016, esp. 308f., offers a presentation of the Greek text, a parallel English summary and
     an English translation where different colours present different motifs of the songs and the
     repetition of colours shows the repetitions of motifs and vocabulary. Such repetitions have been
     used also by other scholars in order to identify Charaxus and/or Larichus with storms and good
     weather, *e.g.* Papadimitropoulos 2016, 7 n. 10, Gribble 2016, 43f., Mueller 2016, 38f. Papadimitro-
     poulos and Gribble see in Larichus the good weather and in Charaxus the storm for the collective.
     Mueller considers literal storms faced by Charaxus and metaphorical storms created by Larichus'
     immaturity and faced by the collective.

nautical imagination of the speaker and the listeners of the song. Both brothers are simultaneously confronted with storms and the hope for good weather (literal or metaphorical) and provide the possibility, in case of their success against the storm in the first place, to become themselves "good weather" for the storms endangering the collective. Sappho presents a group that should place its hopes for "good weather" in a figure who will hopefully accomplish his "sailings" and surpass the social storms of his environment.

References

Bagordo, A., 2009. *Sappho. Gedichte.* Sammlung Tusculum. Düsseldorf: Artemis & Winter.

Bär, S., 2016. "Ceci n'est pas un fragment": Identity, Intertextuality and Fictionality in Sappho's "Brothers Poem". *SO*, 90 (1), 8-54.

Benelli, L., 2017. *Sapphostudien zu ausgewählten Fragmenten. 2. Vol.* Paderborn: Ferdinand Schöningh.

Bettenworth, A., 2014. Sapphos Amme: Ein Beitrag zum neuen Sapphofragment (Brothers Poem). *ZPE*, 191, 15-19.

Bierl, A., 2016. 'All You Need Is Love': Some Thoughts on the Structure, Texture, and Meaning of the Brothers Song as well as on Its Relation to the Kypris Song (P. Sapph. Obbink). *In*: A. Bierl and A. Lardinois, eds. *The Newest Sappho: P. Sapph. Obbink and P. GC inv. 105, Frs. 1-4.* Studies in Archaic and Classical Greek Song 2. Leiden and Boston: Brill, 302-336.

Bowie, E., 2016. How Did Sappho's Songs Get into the Male Sympotic Repertoire? *In*: A. Bierl and A. Lardinois, eds. *The Newest Sappho: P. Sapph. Obbink and P. GC inv. 105, Frs. 1-4.* Studies in Archaic and Classical Greek Song 2. Leiden and Boston: Brill, 148-164.

Burris, S., Fish, J. and Obbink, D., 2014. New Fragments of Book 1 of Sappho. *ZPE*, 189, 1-28.

Caciagli, S., 2016. Sappho Fragment 17: Wishing Charaxos a Safe Trip? *In*: A. Bierl and A. Lardinois, eds. *The Newest Sappho: P. Sapph. Obbink and P. GC inv. 105, Frs. 1-4.* Studies in Archaic and Classical Greek Song 2. Leiden and Boston: Brill, 424-448.

Dale, A., 2011. Sapphica. *HSPh*, 106, 47-74.

Denniston, J.D., 1991. *The Greek Particles.* Reprint of 2nd Ed (1950). London: Oxford University Press.

Ferrari, F., 2014. Saffo e i suoi fratelli e altri brani del primo libro. *ZPE*, 192, 1-19.

Gribble, D., 2016. Getting Ready to Pray: Sappho's New 'Brothers' Song. *G&R*, 63 (1), 29-68.

Kurke, L., 2016. Gendered Spheres and Mythic Models in Sappho's Brothers Poem. *In*: A. Bierl and A. Lardinois, eds. *The Newest Sappho: P. Sapph. Obbink and P. GC inv. 105, Frs. 1-4.* Studies in Archaic and Classical Greek Song 2. Leiden and Boston: Brill, 238-265.

Lardinois, A., 2014. Sappho en haar broers: en nieuw lied van Sappho. *Lampas*, 47 (3), 179-201.

Lardinois, A., 2016. Sappho's Brothers Song and the Fictionality of Early Greek Lyric Poetry. *In*: A. Bierl and A. Lardinois, eds. *The Newest Sappho: P. Sapph. Obbink and P. GC inv. 105, Frs. 1-4.* Studies in Archaic and Classical Greek Song 2. Leiden and Boston: Brill, 167-187.

Liberman, G., 2014. *Réflexions sur un nouveau poème de Sappho relatif à sa détresse et à ses frères Charaxos et Larichos. Paper delivered at F.I.E.C. Bordeaux, August 2014. Translated from the French by Paul Ellis.* Available from: http://www.papyrology. ox.ac.uk/Fragments/Liberman.FIEC.Bordeaux.2014.pdf [Accessed July 6, 2021]

Lidov, J., 2016. Songs for Sailors and Lovers. *In*: A. Bierl and A. Lardinois, eds. *The Newest Sappho: P. Sapph. Obbink and P. GC inv. 105, Frs. 1-4.* Studies in Archaic and Classical Greek Song 2. Leiden and Boston: Brill, 55-109.

Martin, R.P., 2016. Sappho, Iambist: Abusing the Brother. *In*: A. Bierl and A. Lardinois, eds. *The Newest Sappho: P. Sapph. Obbink and P. GC inv. 105, Frs. 1-4.* Studies in Archaic and Classical Greek Song 2. Leiden and Boston: Brill, 110-126.

Mazza, R., 17 April 2014. Papyri, Private Collectors and Academics: Why the Wife of Jesus and Sappho Matter." *In*: R. Mazza ed. Weblog *Faces & Voices: People, Artefacts, Ancient History* [online]. Available from: https://facesandvoices. wordpress.com/2014/04/17/papyri-private-collectors-and-academics-why-the-wife-of-jesus-and-sappho-matter [Accessed 6 July 2021].

Mazza, R., 15 January 2015. The New Sappho Fragments Acquisition History: What We Have Learnt so Far. *In*: R. Mazza ed. Weblog *Faces & Voices: People, Artefacts, Ancient History* [online]. Available from: https://facesandvoices.wordpress. com/2015/01/15/the-new-sappho-fragments-acquisition-history-what-we-have-learnt-so-far/ [Accessed 6 July 2021]

Mueller, M., 2016. Re-Centering Epic Nostos: Gender and Genre in Sappho's Brothers Poem. *Arethusa*, 49, 25-46.

Nagy, G., 2016. A Poetics of Sisterly Affect in the Brothers Song and in Other Songs of Sappho. *In*: A. Bierl and A. Lardinois, eds. *The Newest Sappho: P. Sapph. Obbink and P. GC inv. 105, Frs. 1-4.* Studies in Archaic and Classical Greek Song 2. Leiden and Boston: Brill, 449-492.

Neri, C., 2015. Il 'Brothers Poem' e l'edizione alessandrina (in margine a P. Sapph. Obbink). *Eikasmos*, 26, 53-76.

Nongbri, B., 3 March 2021. The Retraction of Dirk Obbink's Sappho Chapter and the Question of Authenticity. *In*: B. Nongbri ed. weblog *Variant Readings. Thoughts on History, Religion, Archaeology, Papyrology, etc. by Brent Nongbri* [online]. Available from: https://brentnongbri.com/2021/03/30/the-retraction-of-dirk-obbinks-sappho-chapter-and-the-question-of-authenticity/ [Accessed 6 July 2021]

Nünlist, R., 2014. Das Schiff soll unversehrt sein, nicht voll! Zu Sapphos neuem Lied über die Brüder. *ZPE*, 191, 13-14.

Obbink, D., 2014. Two New Poems by Sappho. *ZPE*, 189, 32-49.

Obbink, D., 2015. Interim Notes on 'Two New Poems of Sappho'. *ZPE*, 194, 1-8.

Obbink, D., 2016. The Newest Sappho: Text, Apparatus Criticus, and Translation. *In*: A. Bierl and A. Lardinois, eds. *The Newest Sappho: P. Sapph. Obbink and P. GC inv. 105, Frs. 1-4.* Studies in Archaic and Classical Greek Song 2. Leiden and Boston: Brill, 13-33.

Papadimitropoulos, L., 2016. Sappho's "Brothers Poem": An Interpretation. *SO*, 90 (1), 2-7.

Raaflaub, K.A., 2016. The Newest Sappho and Archaic Greek-Near Eastern Interactions. *In*: A. Bierl and A. Lardinois, eds. *The Newest Sappho: P. Sapph. Obbink and P. GC inv. 105, Frs. 1-4.* Studies in Archaic and Classical Greek Song 2. Leiden and Boston: Brill, 127-147.

Rayor, D.J. 2016. Reimagining the Fragments of Sappho through Translation. *In*: A. Bierl and A. Lardinois, eds. *The Newest Sappho: P. Sapph. Obbink and P. GC inv. 105, Frs. 1-4.* Studies in Archaic and Classical Greek Song 2. Leiden and Boston: Brill, 127-147.

Rayor, D.J. and Lardinois, A., 2014. *Sappho: A New Translation of the Complete Works.* Cambridge: Cambridge University Press.

Sironi, F., 2015. La nutrice di Saffo in P. Oxy. 2289 e i paralleli Omerici nel 'Carme dei fratelli'. *Acme*, 68 (2), 111-118.

West, M.L., 2014. Nine Poems of Sappho. *ZPE*, 191, 1-12.

Wilamowitz-Moellendorf, U. von., 1913. *Sappho und Simonides. Untersuchungen über die griechischen Lyriker.* Berlin: Weidmannsche Buchhandlung.

STPAS: Scales of Transformation in Prehistoric and Archaic Societies

The book series 'Scales of Transformation in Prehistoric and Archaic Societies' (STPAS) is an international scientific series that covers major results deriving from or being associated with the research conducted in the Collaborative Research Centre 'Scales of Transformation: Human-Environmental Interaction in Prehistoric and Archaic Societies' (CRC 1266). Primarily located at Kiel University, Germany, the CRC 1266 is a large interdisciplinary project investigating multiple aspects of socio-environmental transformations in ancient societies between 15,000 and 1 BCE across Europe.

Volume 1
Das Jungneolithikum in Schleswig-Holstein
Sebastian Schultrich | 2018
ISBN: 9789088907425
Format: 210x280mm | 506 pp. | Language: German | 43 illus. (bw) | 103 illus. (fc)
Keywords: Late Neolithic, Single Grave Culture, Corded Ware Culture, transformation, solid stone axe, battle axe, fragments of axes | Jungneolithikum, Einzelgrabkultur, Schnurkeramische Kultur, Transformation, Felsgesteinäxte, Streitäxte, Axtfragmente

Volume 2
Embracing Bell Beaker
Adopting new ideas and objects across Europe during the later 3rd millennium BC
(c. 2600-2000 BC)
Jos Kleijne | 2019
ISBN: 9789088907555
Format: 210x280mm | 300 pp. | Language: English | 91 illus. (fc)
Keywords: archaeology; Late Neolithic; Bell Beaker phenomenon; settlement archaeology; innovation; network analysis; mobility; prehistoric potter

Volume 3
Habitus?
The Social Dimension of Technology and Transformation
Edited by Sławomir Kadrow & Johannes Müller | 2019
ISBN: 9789088907838
Format: 210x280mm | 232 pp. | Language: English | 15 illus. (bw) | 65 illus. (fc)
Keywords: European prehistory; archaeology; habitus; technology; transformation; social dimension; ethnoarchaeology

Volume 4
How's Life?
Living Conditions in the 2nd and 1st Millennia BCE
Edited by Marta Dal Corso, Wiebke Kirleis, Jutta Kneisel, Nicole Taylor, Magdalena
Wieckowska-Lüth, Marco Zanon | 2019
ISBN: 9789088908019
Format: 210x280mm | 220 pp. | Language: English | 29 illus. (bw) | 43 illus. (fc)
Keywords: Bronze Age, domestic archaeology, household archaeology, daily life,
routine activities, diet, waste, violence, health, natural resources, food production

Volume 5
Megalithic monuments and social structures
Comparative studies on recent and Funnel Beaker societies
Maria Wunderlich | 2019
ISBN: 9789088907869
Format: 210x280mm | 382 pp. | Language: English | 114 illus. (bw) | 246 illus. (fc)
Keywords: Megalithic graves, monumentality, Funnel Beaker Complex, ethnoar-
chaeology, Sumba, Nagaland, social organisation, cooperation

Volume 6
Gender Transformations in Prehistoric and Archaic Societies
Edited by Julia Katharina Koch & Wiebke Kirleis | 2019
ISBN: 9789088908217
Format: 210x280mm | 502 pp. | Language: English | 114 illus. (bw) | 58 illus. (fc)
Keywords: academic fieldwork; gender archaeology; social archaeology; environ-
mental archaeology; history of archaeology; Mesolithic; Neolithic; Bronze Age; Iron
Age; Europe; South-west Asia; Central Asia

Volume 7
Maidanets'ke
Development and decline of a Trypillia mega-site in Central Ukraine
René Ohlrau | 2020
ISBN: 9789088908484
Format: 210x280mm | 326 pp. | Language: English | 141 illus. (bw) | 93 illus. (fc)
Keywords: settlement archaeology; prehistoric archaeology; early urbanism;
geophysical survey; paleodemography; Trypillia; mega-site

Volume 8
Detecting and explaining technological innovation in prehistory
Edited by Michela Spataro & Martin Furholt | 2020
ISBN: 9789088908248
Format: 210x280mm | 248 pp. | Language: English | 22 illus. (bw) | 37 illus. (fc)
Keywords: archaeology; prehistory; technology; innovation; invention; tradition;
chaîne opératoire; knowledge acquisition; knowledge transfer; Neolithic; Bronze
Age; Iron Age; ethnography; ceramic; metal; bone

Volume 9
Archaeology in the Žitava Valley I
The LBK and Želiezovce settlement site of Vráble
Edited by Martin Furholt, Ivan Cheben, Johannes Müller, Alena Bistáková,
Maria Wunderlich & Nils Müller-Scheeßel | 2020
ISBN: 9789088908972

Format: 210x280 | 546 pp. | Language: English | 50 illus. (bw) | 157 illus. (fc)
Keywords: European Early Neolithic; LBK, settlement patterns; social organization; social conflict; village and neighbourhood structures; burial rites; enclosure; excavation report

Volume 10
Hellenistic Architecture and Human Action
A Case of Reciprocal Influence
Edited by Annette Haug & Asja Müller | 2020
ISBN: 9789088909092
Format: 210x280mm | 208 pp. | Language: English | 38 illus. (bw) | 29 illus. (fc)
Keywords: Classical archaeology; Hellenistic architecture; agency; perception

Volume 11
Interdisciplinary analysis of the cemetery Kudachurt 14
Evaluating indicators of social inequality, demography, oral health and diet during the Bronze Age key period 2200-1650 BCE in the Northern Caucasus
Katharina Fuchs | 2020
ISBN: 9789088909030
Format: 210x280mm | 406 pp. | Language: English | 25 illus. (bw) | 137 illus. (fc)
Keywords: North Caucasian archaeology; Bronze Age; burial practice; social inequality; human remains; palaeopathology; oral health; C and N stable isotopes

Volume 12
Tripolye Typo-chronology
Mega and Smaller Sites in the Sinyukha River Basin
Liudmyla Shatilo| 2021
ISBN: 9789088909511
Format: 210x280mm | 422 pp. | Language: English | 100 illus. (bw) | 90 illus. (fc)
Keywords: Prehistoric archaeology; Tripolye; chronology; mega-sites; Sinyukha River Basin; pottery; carbon dating; typochronology; Eastern Europe

Volume 13
Vom Kollektiv zum Individuum
Transformationsprozesse am Übergang vom 4. zum 3. Jahrtausend v. Chr. in der Deutschen Mittelgebirgszone
Clara Drummer| 2022
ISBN: 9789464270129
Format: 210x280mm | 343 pp. | Language: German | 53 illus. (bw) | 95 illus. (fc)
Keywords: Neolithic; Germany; Lower Mountain Range; migrations; identities; social transformations; Corded Ware; Bell Beaker; funerary archaeology; ancient DNA

Volume 14
Millet and What Else?
The Wider Context of the Adoption of Millet Cultivation in Europe
Edited by Wiebke Kirleis, Marta Dal Corso & Dragana Filipović | 2022
ISBN: 9789464270150
Format: 210x280mm | 328 pp. | Scales of Transformation 14 | Series: Scales of Transformation | Language: English | 61 illus. (bw) | 13 illus. (fc) | Keywords: archaeology; millet; Europe prehistory; Bronze Age; archaeobotany; zooarchaeology; miliacin; prehistoric agriculture

Volume 15
The Life and Journey of Neolithic Copper Objects
Transformations of the Neuenkirchen Hoard, North-East Germany (3800 BCE)
Henry Skorna | 2022
ISBN: 9789464270303
Format: 210x280mm | 198 pp. | Scales of Transformation 15 | Series: Scales of Transformation | Language: English | 50 illus. (bw) | 37 illus. (fc) | Keywords: neolithic; copper; metallurgy; hoard; isotopes; archaeometry; dagger; transformation

Volume 16.1
Unter Hügeln (Band 1)
Bronzezeitliche Transformationsprozesse in Schleswig-Holstein am Beispiel des Fundplatzes von Mang de Bargen (Bornhöved, Kr. Segeberg)
Stefanie Schaefer-Di Maida | 2023
ISBN: 9789464280487
Format: 210x280mm | 540 pp. | Scales of Transformation 16.1 | Series: Scales of Transformation | Language: German | 9 illus. (bw) | 164 illus. (fc) | Keywords: bronze age; northern Germany; funerary archaeology; chronology; burial rites; barrows; urnfields; radiocarbon dating; anthropology; palynology; archaeobotany

Volume 16.2
Unter Hügeln (Band 2)
Bronzezeitliche Transformationsprozesse in Schleswig-Holstein am Beispiel des Fundplatzes von Mang de Bargen (Bornhöved, Kr. Segeberg)
Stefanie Schaefer-Di Maida | 2023
ISBN: 9789464280517
Format: 210x280mm | 446 pp. | Scales of Transformation 16.2 | Series: Scales of Transformation | Language: German | 9 illus. (bw) | 164 illus. (fc) | Keywords: bronze age; northern Germany; funerary archaeology; chronology; burial rites; barrows; urnfields; radiocarbon dating; anthropology; palynology; archaeobotany

Volume 17
Separation, Hybridisation, and Networks
Globular Amphora sedentary pastoralists ca. 3200-2700 BCE
Johannes Müller | 2023
ISBN: 9789464270488
Format: 210x280mm | ca 396 pp. | Scales of Transformation 17 | Series: Scales of Transformation | Language: German | 38 illus. (bw) | 244 illus. (fc) | Keywords: prehistoric archaeology; pottery studies; ceramics; neolithic; globular amphorae; separation; hybridisation; connectivity; transformation

Volume 18
Mediterranean Connections
How the sea links people and transforms identities
Edited by Laura C. Schmidt, Anja Rutter, Lutz Käppel & Oliver Nakoinz | 2023
ISBN: 9789464270693
Format: 210x280mm | ca. 236 pp. | Scales of Transformation 18 | Series: Scales of Transformation | Language: English | 21 illus. (bw) | 20 illus. (fc) | Keywords: Mediterranean; transformation; connectivity; networks; seafaring; Classics; archaeology